9501066

✓
8/01

P9-BZZ-226
0 1021 0072695 3

ON LINE

MILITARY HISTORY
Wolfe at Quebec
The Destruction of Lord Raglan: A Tragedy of the Crimean War
Corunna
The Battle of Arnhem
Agincourt
Redcoats and Rebels: The War for America, 1770–1781
Cavaliers and Roundheads: The English at War, 1642–1649

HISTORY
King Mob: Lord George Gordon and the Riots of 1780
The Roots of Evil: A Social History of Crime and Punishment
The Court at Windsor: A Domestic History
The Grand Tour
London: The Biography of a City
The Dragon Wakes: China and the West, 1793–1911
The Rise and Fall of the House of Medici
The Great Mutiny: India 1857
The French Revolution
Rome: The Biography of a City
The English: A Social History 1066–1945
Venice: The Biography of a City
Florence: The Biography of a City

BIOGRAPHIES
Benito Mussolini: The Rise and Fall of Il Duce
Garibaldi and His Enemies: The Clash of Arms
and Personalities in the Making of Italy
The Making of Charles Dickens
Charles I
The Personal History of Samuel Johnson
George IV: Prince of Wales, 1762–1811
George IV: Regent and King, 1811–1830
Edward VII: A Portrait
Queen Victoria in Her Letters and Journals
The Virgin Queen: Elizabeth I, Genius of the Golden Age

NELSON

A PERSONAL HISTORY

* * *

Christopher Hibbert

Addison-Wesley Publishing Company

Reading, Massachusetts   Menlo Park, California   New York
Don Mills, Ontario   Wokingham, England   Amsterdam   Bonn
Sydney   Singapore   Tokyo   Madrid   San Juan
Paris   Seoul   Milan   Mexico City   Taipei

Library of Congress Cataloging-in-Publication Data

Hibbert, Christopher, 1924–
    Nelson : a personal history / Christopher Hibbert, — 1st ed.
      p. cm.
    Includes bibliographical references and index.
    ISBN 0-201-62457-5
    1. Nelson, Horatio Nelson, Viscount, 1758–1805. 2. Great
Britain—History, Naval—18th century. 3. Great Britain—
History, Naval—19th century. 4. Great Britain. Royal Navy—
Biography. 5. Admirals—Great Britain—Biography.   I. Title.
DA87.1.N4H53   1994
940.2'7'092—dc20
[B]   94-39545
                                              CIP

First published in England by Viking

1 2 3 4 5 6 7 8 9-MA-9897969594
First printing, November 1994

For Tony and Elizabeth
with love

Contents

List of Illustrations

BLACK AND WHITE

Illustration Acknowledgements

The author and publishers are grateful to the following for permission to reproduce the illustrations in this book.

COLOUR

National Maritime Museum, London: 1, 2, 3, 4, 7, 8, 9, 10, 11, 16, 17, 18, 22, 25, 27, 30, 31, 32, 33; Rafael Valls Gallery, London/ Bridgeman Art Library: 5; Portsmouth City Art Gallery/Bridgeman Art Library: 6; Manchester City Art Gallery: 12; The Hamilton Collection at Lennoxlove: 14; The Trustees of the Royal Naval Museum, Portsmouth: 13; The Welsh Industrial and Maritime Museum, Cardiff: 15; The Nelson Museum, Monmouth: 19, 35; Christopher Gibbs, London: 20; Christie's, London/Bridgeman Art Library: 23; Philip Mould, Historical Portraits Ltd, London/Bridgeman Art Library: 21; The National Portrait Gallery, London: 24; The Royal Collection © 1993 Her Majesty The Queen: 26; Christie's, London/e. t. Archive: 28; British Museum/e. t. Archive: 29; The Dean and Chapter of Westminster: 34

BLACK AND WHITE

The National Maritime Museum, London: 1, 3, 4, 5, 6, 7, 10a, 10b, 13, 18, 19, 20, 21, 23, 24, 25, 26, 27, 29, 30, 33; The National Maritime Museum, London/Bridgeman Art Library: 2; The Morden College, Corporation of London/Bridgeman Art Library:

Author's Note

This book is based to a large extent on the letters and other writings of Nelson and Lady Hamilton and on the letters, diaries and reminiscences of Nelson's family, friends and contemporaries. Much of this material is available in Sir Harris Nicolas's seven volumes of *Dispatches and Letters of Lord Nelson*, in the collections edited by Alfred Morrison and George Naish, and in the early biographies of James Harrison, Clarke and M'Arthur, and Thomas Pettigrew. But, since both Nelson and Emma Hamilton were prodigious correspondents and their liaison gave rise to such widespread interest and speculation, there is unpublished material still to be found and I am most grateful to those who have helped me in my search for it. I am particularly indebted to Dr Roger Morris, of the National Maritime Museum, Greenwich, to Andrew Helme, Curator of the Monmouth Museum, to Colin White, Head Curator of the Royal Naval Museum, Portsmouth, to Ben Burgess and the Trustees of the Ben Burgess Nelson Memorabilia Collection, and to Oliver Everett, Librarian, Windsor Castle, and Lady de Bellaigue, Registrar, the Royal Archives. I am also much indebted to Libby Joy who worked for me and transcribed letters in the British Library.

For the use of the Bonsor Papers I have to thank Sir Nicholas Bonsor; and, for other unpublished letters in their collections, Mrs Wilma Laws and Professor Charles Marsden. F. C. Jolly, Administrator, Holkham Estate Office, has kindly answered questions about the Coke Papers.

I have also to acknowledge the help of county archivists in tracing Nelson's movements and activities when he was ashore in

England and Wales, especially A. M. Wherry, County Archivist, Hereford and Worcester County Record Office; Mrs M. M. Rowe, County Archivist, and Paul Brough, Senior Assistant Archivist, Devon Record Office; R. J. Chamberlaine-Brothers, Archivist, Warwickshire County Record Office; Miss K. Haslem, Searchroom Supervisor, Gloucestershire County Record Office; John Davies, Senior Archivist, Dyfed County Record Office; Anthony Hopkins, County Archivist, Gwent County Records Office; Miss Jean Kennedy, County Archivist, Norfolk County Record Office; Michael Phelps, Archivist, County Archive Services, Swansea; Miss M. Lock, Archives Assistant, Hampshire Record Office; and Dr D. B. Robinson, County Archivist, Surrey Record Office.

I also am most grateful to the Earl Nelson; Sir Geoffrey Bellaigue, Director of the Royal Collection; the Viscount Bridport for information about the Bronte estate in Sicily; Mrs Anna Tribe, great-granddaughter of Horatia Nelson's eldest son; Michael Nash of Marine Books, Hoylake, Wirral, Honorary Chairman of the 1805 Club; Clive Wilkinson, Archivist of the Nelson Society; Dr N. A. M. Rodger, author of *The Wooden World*; Flora Fraser, author of *Beloved Emma: The Life of Emma Lady Hamilton*; Dr Conrad Swan, Garter Principal King of Arms; Stanley Martin, former Assistant Marshal of the Diplomatic Corps; Professor M. R. D. Foot; Philip Russell of the National Museums and Galleries on Merseyside; Mrs J. S. Dormer and David Taylor of the Maritime Information Centre, Greenwich; John Sunderland, Witt Librarian, the Courtauld Institute of Art; Miss Akua Anin of the Director's Office, Iveagh Bequest, Kenwood; M. T. Harrington of the Newspaper Library, Colindale; Richard Walker for information about Nelson's portraits and other pictures; C. D. Brown, Headmaster, and Dr Paul Cattermole, Archivist, of Norwich School; R. J. H. Hill, Senior Librarian, Hereford City Library; Mrs Richards of the Local Studies Department, Gloucester Library.

For their help in a variety of ways I am also much indebted to Richard Hough; John Berney; Joy Woolley; Jean Clissold; Alison Riley; Margaret Lewendon; Rosemary Foster; Diana Cook; John Guest; Ursula Hibbert; Hamish Francis; Eleo Gordon and Peter Carson of Viking; Bruce Hunter of David Higham Associates;

Esther Sidwell who copy-edited the book; Josine Meìjer who helped me choose the illustrations; and, lastly, my wife for making the comprehensive index.

Above all I am grateful to Tom Pocock who has most generously lent me all the papers he assembled for his own biography of Nelson as well as all the material he has collected since. He has also read the book in typescript and given me much valuable advice for its improvement.

CHRISTOPHER HIBBERT

THE NELSON FAMILY

William Nelson ═══ Mary Shene

Rev. Edmund Nelson ═══ Mary Bland   Rev.

Rev. Edmund Nelson (1722 –

Maurice · Rev. William ═══ (1) Sarah Yonge   HORATIO ═══ Frances Nisbet
(1753 – 1801) (1757 – 1835) (2) Hilare   VISCOUNT NELSON (née Woolward)
          1st EARL   Barlow   (1758 – 1805)

Horatio   Charlotte ═══ 2nd Baron Bridport
(d. 1808)   (d. 1873)   (d. 1868)
                              │
                           issue

                    Horatio ═══ Lady Mary Jane
                    (1823 – 1913)   Diana Agar
                    3rd EARL   (d. 1904)

            Thomas Horatio
            (1857 – 1947)
            4th EARL

                    Albert Francis
                    Joseph Horatio
                    (1890 – 1957)
                    6th EARL

Robert Walpole (1676 – 1745)
1st EARL OF ORFORD

Sir Charles Turner ═ Mary Walpole

Maurice Suckling ═ Mary Turner

1802) ═ Catherine Suckling (d.1767)

Edmund   Suckling   Susannah ═ Thomas Bolton   Anne   Catherine ═ George
(1763–86)   (1764–99)   (d.1813)   (d.1834)   (d.1784)   (d.1842)   Matcham
                                                                            (d.1833)

                          Thomas ═ Frances
                        (1785 1835) Elizabeth Eyre
                          2nd EARL   George
                  (changed surname to Nelson)   (1789–1877)

Edward Agar Horatio ═ Geraldine Cave
     (1860–1951)   (d.1936)
       5th EARL

Henry Edward   George Joseph   John Marie ═ Kathleen Mary Burr
Joseph Horatio   Horatio   Joseph Horatio
(1894–1972)   (1905–81)   (d.1970)
  7th EARL   8th EARL

                          Peter John Horatio ═ Maureen Diana Kilkenny
                              (b.1941)
                              9th EARL
                                  Simon John Horatio
                                     (b.1971)

I

Burnham Thorpe

I only took them because every other boy was afraid.

Soon after the death of the rector's wife, her brother, Captain
Maurice Suckling, arrived at Burnham Thorpe parsonage house to
see what he could do for the children. There were eight of them,
the youngest only ten months old; and their father, the Rev.
Edmund Nelson, disturbed by the thought that it had fallen to his
'Lott to take upon [himself] the care and affection of double
parent', was clearly in need of support and guidance.[1] He was an
affectionate though strict parent, insisting upon the most decorous
behaviour, particularly at mealtimes when the backs of those
children old enough to sit at table must not touch the backs of
their chairs, and even forbidding the use of spectacles, as Queen
Charlotte did at court.[2] Yet he did not strike his parishioners as a
man of forceful character and was himself aware that he lacked the
confidence ever to become a pillar of the Church, being 'tremulous
over trifles and easily put in "a Fuss"'.[3] Tall, and grey-haired at
forty-six, he had never been robust: he had been spared the rigours
of a public school by his father, an old Etonian who had also been
a parson, as, indeed, had his father-in-law, Dr Maurice Suckling,
prebendary of Westminster.

The Nelson family had been settled in Norfolk for generations;
yet, while of good stock, they could not, as Edmund Nelson –
whose mother's father had been a Cambridge baker – sadly
conceded, boast of the grand connections of his late wife. For she, a
capable, outspoken woman, remembered alike for her high regard
for the Royal Navy and her hatred for the French, was pleased to
observe that her grandmother had been the sister of King George
II's great minister, Sir Robert Walpole, who had been created

Earl of Orford and lived in splendid style at Houghton Hall, twenty miles or so from Burnham Thorpe.* Indeed, when the third Earl of Orford died in 1791, Edmund Nelson saw to it that his household went into mourning, writing in his large, childlike hand to a daughter who had left home, 'You may with great propriety do the same. If any ask why? you may say that the late Lord's grandfather, Sir R. Walpole, and your great-grandmother, were sister and brother. So stands the consanguinity.'[4]

The Nelsons were, however, never invited to Houghton Hall; and, although they were sometimes asked to stay with their cousins, the Walpoles of Wolterton Hall, these occasional invitations came as acts of condescending kindness to poor relations.

The first Lord Walpole of Wolterton was the first Earl of Orford's younger brother, a forthright man of slovenly appearance who spoke with a pronounced Norfolk accent and, through his brother's influence, became a successful diplomat. His son, the second baron, who married a daughter of the Duke of Devonshire, was less successful but more gracious. From neither, however, did the Nelson children receive much help of a practical kind.

For this they looked to their mother's brothers, their uncles William and Maurice Suckling. William, who held a profitable though none-too-demanding post as a commissioner in the Excise Office, lived in Kentish Town, then 'a most agreeable rural retreat ... absolutely out of the influence of the London smoak' with several good taverns 'much resorted to, especially in summer time, by the inhabitants of London'.[5] Here he had a comfortable house with several portraits of grand if rather distant relations hanging on its walls, a black butler who went by the name of Price, and a garden extending to five acres.

But although Uncle William Suckling managed to obtain an appointment as a clerk in his office for the eldest of the Nelson boys, it was upon William's brother, Uncle Maurice, that their father rested his main hopes for his children's progress in the world. For Maurice Suckling was a good-natured, generous man, a captain in the Royal Navy, who had much distinguished himself

* See the family tree

in the Caribbean in the recent war against the French and had, in consequence, become a hero in the Nelson family. He had inherited money from his affluent father, the prebendary of Westminster; had added to his wealth by the prize-money awarded to sailors on the capture of enemy ships; and had married his cousin, Mary, daughter of Lord Walpole of Wolterton, who had brought him a handsome dowry. They lived at Woodton Hall and were on friendly terms with other Norfolk families, to most of which they were distantly or closely related, among them the Wodehouses of Kimberley, the Durrants of Scottow Hall, the Townshends of Raynham, the Bullens of Blickling – with one of whose sixteenth-century daughters King Henry VIII had been so passionately in love – and the Jermyns of Deepden, a family from whom, in the seventeenth century, there had sprung that indulged courtier, Henry Jermyn, Earl of St Albans, who, thanks to the generosity of King Charles II, was able to develop the land between St James's Square and Pall Mall, where so many of the streets still bear the names of his family and friends.

When Captain Suckling came to Burnham Thorpe to see what he could do for his brother-in-law after his sister's death, there were five nephews and three nieces whose future he had to consider. It was clear that they did not live in much comfort. The parsonage house had originally been little more than a largish cottage until an addition had been built on at right angles and roofed with the same red tiles as the older part.* It was a pleasant enough place with a well-stocked garden, to which roses added bright colours in their season, surrounded by some thirty acres of glebe land on which the rector grew corn and turnips, beans and peas with inconsiderable success. But in the winter when the high winds blew and the sky suddenly darkened and gulls, flying inland from the

---

* Burnham Thorpe Parsonage as Nelson knew it is no more. The present rectory was built at the beginning of the nineteenth century. A painting of the old Parsonage by Francis Pocock is in the National Maritime Museum, Greenwich. The church of All Saints survived and has been restored. A painting of it by M. E. Cotman can also be seen in the National Maritime Museum. The church contains the font at which Nelson was baptized and a lectern and rood beam made from wood from the flagship in which he died.

nearby sea, fluttered down on the frozen lawn, the exposed house
was dreadfully cold. In those days it seemed a long walk to the
parish church of All Saints, half a mile or so distant. It was an
even longer walk to the two other churches in the rector's care, those
at Burnham Ulph and Burnham Sutton, but these were so dilapidated that services were most infrequently held in either of them.

Although much cast down by the death of his wife, and feeling
'insipid, Whimsicall and very unfitt for society', as he put it
himself, the rector did not preside over a miserable household.[6] It
was conducted as strictly as it had ever been; the family rose early,
sat down to dinner at four o'clock in the afternoon and went to
bed at nine; meals were adequate rather than appetizing. But the
children were content; and so, as they afterwards testified, were the
servants, the girls who came up from the village, and 'Will indoors'
and 'Peter without', and Tom Stocking, and Nurse Blackett, who
later became Mrs High, wife of the landlord of the Old Ship,
Brancaster Bay.[7]

Captain Suckling, who had no children of his own, took stock of
the rector's. First there were the three daughters: the eldest,
Susannah, was to be apprenticed to a milliner at Bath and then,
having come into a substantial legacy from her uncle, was to
marry a merchant who was, as her father was careful to point out,
not only in 'a prosperous way of trade in corn, malt, coals etc' but
also a gentleman of worthy birth, his grandfather having been
rector of Hollesley.[8] As Mrs Thomas Bolton of Wells-next-the-Sea,
Susannah was to be comfortably placed, cheerful, forthright and
generous. The middle sister, Anne, was also to be sent from home
to be apprenticed, for a premium of £100, at a Capital Lace
warehouse in London where she was to be seduced and, having
borne a child whose father abandoned her, to return home in
disgrace at the age of twenty, and, not long afterwards, to die at
Bath, having caught a chill 'occasioned by coming out of the
ballroom immediately after dancing'.[9] The youngest sister,
Catherine – Kate, Katty or Kitty as the others called her – still a
baby, was to grow into an attractive, vivacious girl for whom her
brothers were always to feel much affection.

*

Most of her brothers were to be neither so successful nor so content as Kate. The eldest, the conscientious, kindly and rather dull Maurice, unable to live on his pay in the Navy Office, was soon to get into debt. William, a selfish and at that time timid boy, was to go without enthusiasm into the Church. Edmund was to entertain thoughts of becoming a lawyer but, after leaving school, was to drift into an appointment as accounts clerk in his brother-in-law Thomas Bolton's business; while the youngest boy, Suckling, was to be considered for no higher calling than that of draper: apprenticed to a shopkeeper in Beccles, Suffolk, he was to use a legacy to buy a village shop at North Elmham near Burnham Thorpe, a business he was to neglect for the more entertaining pastimes of greyhound racing and drinking in the local inn. With hopes of rescuing him from such an unprofitable and demeaning life, a place was to be obtained for him at Christ's College, Cambridge. Thereafter, he would no doubt, as his father gloomily commented, 'pass amongst a Crowd of undistinguished preachers, and gain some respect in the village of his Residence from his quiet disposition, his liking to a little conviviality and his passion for Grey-hounds and Coursing'.[10] With the help of extra tuition, Suckling Nelson eventually contrived to pass his exams. He was ordained and became curate at Burnham Norton two miles or so north of Burnham Thorpe. His duties there were performed indifferently, and his death at an early age was not widely regretted.

Whether or not Captain Maurice Suckling recognized the seeds of failure or insignificance in the two eldest and two youngest boys at Burnham Thorpe parsonage house, he evidently regarded the middle son in a different light.

This was Horatio or, as he preferred to be known then – and signed himself – Horace, to the displeasure of his father, who once crossed out the offending signature in a register and substituted the Latin version of the name. Horatio was, after all, as the rector pointed out, the name of their revered kinsman the first Lord Walpole of Wolterton, as well as of the second Lord Walpole, who was the boy's godfather. It had also been the name of the boy's elder brother who had died in infancy, and of Sir Robert Walpole's fourth son, the writer and connoisseur, though he, like Master Nelson, preferred Horace, 'an English name for an Englishman'.[11]

In any event the boy eventually reconciled himself to the name he was given at his baptism, which took place on 9 October 1758, ten days after his birth. He was nine years old when his mother died, a slight, pale, eager-looking boy, then a pupil at the Royal Grammar School, Norwich, an ancient school inside the cathedral close, where he was a boarder, thankful to be able to leave the school on half holidays for the firesides of his great-aunt, Mrs Henley, and of a cousin, Mrs Berney, whose husband's family had lived in Norfolk for generations. After his uncle's visit to Burnham Thorpe, the boy was removed from the school at Norwich and sent to a smaller school nearer home, the recently established Sir William Paston's School at North Walsham, a private academy at that time presided over by a robust Welsh parson, John Price Jones, whose Greek and Latin lessons were interrupted by bursts of flogging said to be as severe as those inflicted by Richard Busby, Head Master of Westminster School and 'notorious for his Spartan discipline'.[12]

From the accounts of Horatio Nelson's childhood that have come down to us and from reports by family, servants and friends, no doubt embellished in the telling, it seems that he was well able to withstand the rigours of Mr Jones's discipline, which apparently did not deter him from stealing the martinet's pears, maintaining that he 'only took them because every other boy was afraid'.[13] It is also said – and has been retold in almost every biography of Nelson – that the boy, lost on a bird-nesting exhibition and cut off from home by a fast-flowing river, was scolded when he eventually found his way back to Burnham Thorpe by his grandmother who said, 'I wonder that fear did not drive you home.' 'Fear,' the boy replied. 'I never saw fear. What is it? It never came near me.'[14] Just as commonly related is the story of the time when he and his brother William, having set out for Burnham Market to catch the coach to take them to school at North Walsham at the beginning of the winter term, returned home to say that they were unable to get through the deep snow-drifts. Their father told them to try again and not to return home until they were quite sure there was no way of reaching the school. Once more they set off, but had not gone far when William decided the road was impassable and they must turn back. The younger Horatio disagreed. 'Remember, brother,' he said to William in words which sound more pious in modern ears than they would have done in those of the readers of the Rev. James Stanier Clarke, the Prince of Wales's librarian and chaplain at Carlton House, who recorded them soon after Nelson's death, 'Remember, brother, it was left to our honour.'[15]

It was while on holiday from Sir William Paston's School that the two brothers read in the *Norfolk Chronicle* that their uncle, Captain Maurice Suckling of Woodton Hall, who had long been on half pay, had been appointed to the command of the sixty-four-gun ship of the line, the *Raisonnable*, which had been captured from the French twelve years before and was now to set sail again from Chatham.

Horatio Nelson had long had thoughts of becoming a sea officer.* In later years he well remembered how as a boy he had ridden to the coast at Burnham Overy Staithe or Wells-next-the-Sea to watch the coasters warping their way up the creek or passing down with the tide, how he had learned to recognize the sails and rigging, the masts and cut of the jibs of the vessels that sailed in and out of the harbours, the luggers and hoys, the brigantines and wherries, the galliots and billanders; and he would remember, too, the smell of the sea and of the boats, the smell of

---

* Although his family had no strong naval tradition (Maurice Suckling's father was a clergyman), the profession of sea officer was a likely choice for a boy of Nelson's background. Unlike the army, whose officers largely came from a higher social standing, the navy drew most of its officers from middle-class families. Professor Michael Lewis studied the origins of 1,800 officers who served in the navy between 1793 and 1815. Of these, 216 were the sons of peers or baronets, 494 the sons of landed gentry; 71 came from business or commercial backgrounds; 120 were of working-class origin (18 of these had been pressed into the service). Well over half the total, 899, were the sons of professional men, a large proportion of their fathers – the highest proportion after naval officers – being clergymen. Many of them came from Norfolk, a county which provided more officers than all but six other coastal counties (Lewis, *A Social History*, 31, 36, 62; Marshall (1825); William O'Byrne, *A Naval Biographical Dictionary* (1842)). (Details of sources, where not given in full, will be found in the Bibliography, pages 444–53.)

fish and tar and wet rope carried by the wind across the sand dunes and salt marshes.

'Do write to my father at Bath,' he said to his elder brother, William, 'and tell him I should like to go to sea with my uncle Maurice.'[16]

Captain Suckling agreed to take the boy aboard, and wrote to the father to tell him so, adding a cheerfully facetious warning: 'What has poor Horace done, who is so weak, that he, above all the rest, should be sent to rough it out at sea. But let him come and the first time we go into action a cannon-ball may knock off his head and provide for him at once.'[17]

2

Chatham, the Arctic and the West Indies

He felt as easy when I was on deck as any officer in the ship.

The boy certainly looked as though he would find it difficult to 'rough it out at sea'. Twelve years old, he seemed even younger, and, although there were numerous midshipmen and captains' servants of his age, there were few who appeared as vulnerable as Horatio Nelson.* His father thought it as well to travel with him to London and to see him from there on to the coach for Chatham. When he arrived at Chatham on a cold day early in January 1771 he made his way with his baggage down the cobbled streets to the dockyard where the first seamen he approached knew nothing of the *Raisonnable* or of Captain Suckling. At length he discovered where the ship lay, but had no idea how to get out to her; and he was wondering what on earth to do when an officer, pitying the small and lonely figure, took him in hand, led him off for a meal and afterwards found a boat to ferry him across the Medway to Captain Suckling's ship.[1]

He climbed aboard but Captain Suckling was not there, and no one seemed to be expecting him. For want of anything better to do, the boy paced up and down the deck in the cold wind, as much at a loss as he had been on the river bank, sharing the

---

* It was more usual for boys intending to become officers to be entered in a ship's books as 'captain's servants' or 'able seamen', but Suckling entered Nelson as 'midshipman' so that his seniority would date from the day the entry was made – 1 January 1771. Not all midshipmen were boys. Indeed, those who persistently failed in their examination for lieutenant might remain midshipmen for years. One of these men who had joined the service in 1755 was not promoted lieutenant until 1790 at the age of fifty-seven (Lavery, 90).

experience of an earlier newcomer to the 'wooden world' in which 'all seemed strange': 'I could not think what world I was in, whether among spirits or devils ... different language and strange expressions of tongue ... I thought myself in a dream, never properly awake.' Until the next day little notice was taken of the new boy aboard the *Raisonnable*; and it was not for several days that Captain Suckling was piped aboard and summoned the boy from the cramped, dark midshipmen's berth on the orlop deck to his light and spacious cabin above.

By then the boy had learned something of a midshipman's life and a midshipman's duties, and had begun to apprehend the various skills he would be expected to master – the ability to go aloft with the topmen, to practise sail drill, fire drill and gun drill, to supervise the hoisting in of the longboat, the hauling of the hempen cables and the weighing of the anchor, which was so immensely heavy that the strength of as many men as could push the capstan bars was needed to lift it from the seabed. He had been made aware that the passage of time at sea was marked by the changing of the watch, each watch lasting four hours, except for the two dogwatches of two hours each between four o'clock in the afternoon and eight in the evening. Every half-hour was measured out by a sand-glass, and when the glass turned a bell was rung; at eight bells the watch changed. 'Lack of sleep was a constant hardship of the sea life for everyone in watches.'[2]

As seaman after seaman stepped aboard, some of them not to step ashore again for months or even years, it became ever clearer that life in a ship in port did indeed constitute a 'little world' of its own, as it was described by another young sailor, who was 'surprised at the number of people, men, women and children'. 'There were shops and stalls of every kind of goods, and people crying their different commodities about the ship as in a town.'[3] There were topmen clambering about on the yards, carpenters hammering, sailmakers stitching, armourers at work on the guns, some boys swabbing the decks and others – some as young as six years old – known as 'powder monkeys', learning how to bring up powder from the stores for the gun crews when the time for fighting came, while men who had no immediate duties to perform were dancing and drinking and smoking their pipes, playing backgammon and cards, dangling fishing lines over the sides, talking to their wives and women.

On the lower deck, where the muzzles of the guns had been run out of the ports to make more room in the confined space between the bulkheads, men were sitting on their sea chests, which would be stored away when the ship set sail. Their hammocks, slung close together from the beams of the deckhead, were rolled up by day and stowed in netting troughs above the tables where the men ate their meals in messes of six. The food, notoriously disgusting as it often had been in earlier years and still was on long voyages, had improved somewhat of late, though there were well-authenticated stories still of biscuits crawling with weevils, meat so tough that men used it for carving instead of wood, and rancid butter given to the boatswain for greasing the rigging. An eleven-year-old boy, who was to die three years later having fallen out of the rigging of his ship, told his parents:

Indeed we live on beef which has been ten or eleven years in corn and on biscuit which quite makes your throat cold in eating it thanks to the maggots which are very cold when you eat them, like calves-foot jelly or blomonge ... We drink water of the colour of the bark of a pear-tree with plenty of little maggots and weavils in it and wine which is exactly like bullock's blood and sawdust mixed together ... Indeed, I do not like this life very much ... I hope I shall not learn to swear, and by God's assistance I hope I shall not.[4]

Bread came in the shape of loaves in port as well as in a kind of biscuit; beef and pork were pickled in casks; cheese and butter also came in casks. The Victualling Board were supposed to supply peas as a staple vegetable, raisins as a common fruit. Oatmeal was to be issued as well as oil and vinegar and as much as a gallon of beer a day. Fresh meat was supplied by all manner of animals brought aboard, cattle and sheep, pigs, goats, hens and geese, a cargo which necessarily exacerbated the frowstiness of the atmosphere on the lower deck, particularly at sea when the gun ports were kept closed and hundreds of unwashed men in damp clothes sat at their tables in the dim light filtering through the gratings, eating the food brought to them from the great cauldrons on the iron stove.[5]

When Captain Suckling came aboard the *Raisonnable*, Midshipman Nelson had grown accustomed to the smells of the lower deck, the stench of sweat and tallow, tar and boiling salt meat. He had helped to pack the ship's provisions and the huge casks of beer in storerooms; he had also helped to get the ship's guns aboard, and had, with the rest of the ship's officers and men, witnessed a sailor being tied to an upturned grating and flogged by a boatswain's mate for theft and another seaman being given twelve lashes from a cat-o'-nine-tails for brawling.*

When the *Raisonnable* was ready to sail and her crew thus disciplined, the danger of war with Spain, for which she had been recommissioned, had passed and the ship was kept at anchor. Captain Suckling was transferred to a guardship which lay off the sandbank known as the Nore to protect the estuaries of the Thames and the Medway, while his nephew – for whom the humdrum life aboard such a vessel was considered no fit training – was sent to sea aboard a merchantman belonging to the old

---

* The Admiralty's Regulations and Instructions of 1806 laid down twelve lashes as the maximum punishment a captain could impose on his own authority. But this number seems quite often to have been exceeded throughout Nelson's service. One officer at least recorded twelve lashes in his official log and the actual number given in a private journal. Courts martial tended to authorize far severer punishments than most captains. Sentences of several hundred lashes by courts martial were not unknown. Two of the *Victory*'s crew were given thirty-six lashes for drunkenness two days before Trafalgar. When a large number of lashes with a cat-o'-nine-tails were inflicted, the victim was sometimes provided with a leather belt to protect his kidneys. For theft, an instrument known as a 'thieves' cat', which had larger and harder knots, was used. The worst offenders were sentenced to death or to being flogged round the fleet which some considered as terrible as death. 'It was a dreadful sight,' wrote a witness of this punishment; 'the unfortunate [was] rowed from ship to ship, getting an equal number of lashes at the side of each vessel from a fresh man ... He was rowed back to the *Surprise*, his back swelled like a pillow, black and blue; some sheets of thick blue paper were steeped in vinegar and laid to his back. Before he seemed insensible, now his shrieks rent the air.' (Baynham, 31–2; Rodger, *The Wooden World*, 218–20; Lavery, 216–17.)

merchant firm of Hibbert, Purrier and Horton. In this West Indiaman, Horatio Nelson twice crossed the Atlantic, dreadfully seasick at first; and, on his return to Captain Suckling, he was considered to have gained sufficient experience of seamanship to be appointed to command the longboat of his uncle's ship, which was used to ferry goods, men and dispatches to and from Sheerness, Gravesend, Woolwich, Greenwich, Deptford and the Pool of London. Thus it was, as he later put it himself, that 'by degrees' he became 'a good pilot for vessels of that description ... and confident of myself amongst rocks and sands'.[6]

Soon his experience was to be still further widened when two ships, built for shore bombardment and known as bomb-ketches, were fitted out for an expedition in Arctic waters; and Midshipman Nelson sought permission to sail aboard one of them, the *Carcass*. The leader of the expedition, the twenty-nine-year-old Captain the Hon. Constantine Phipps, eldest son of the first Lord Mulgrave, had orders to try to find 'a passage by, or near, the North Pole' to India; and his two bomb-ketches, the *Carcass* and the *Racehorse* – both with specially thickened hulls and buttressed bows to withstand the pressure of ice – were well supplied with ample stores of thick clothes, good cured beef and pork, and plenty of mustard and pepper, strong beer, double stocks of both wine and spirits, and even bricks with which to build shelters in the frozen waste should the ships be lost.

No fault was afterwards found in the planning of the expedition, which set sail at the beginning of June 1773; but with the seas to their north completely blocked, and ice of incalculable depth closing in behind them, the two ships were trapped and in danger of being crunched and splintered within a month of their departure from Spitzbergen. In the middle of August, however, so a man aboard the *Carcass* recorded in his journal, the wind began to blow and the ice to part 'in an astonishing manner, rending and cracking with a tremendous noise surpassing that of the loudest thunder. At this very instant, the whole continent of ice ... moved together in various directions, splitting and dividing into vast bodies and forming hills and plains of various figures and dimensions. The sails were now all spread so that the ships might have the full

advantage of the breeze' which allowed them to escape to the
south and to reach Spitzbergen again in safety.[7]

The expedition could not but be accounted a failure. Yet
Midshipman Nelson was not sorry to have been part of it and ever
afterwards remembered the terrible beauty of those frozen seas, the
extraordinary shapes of the vast blocks of ice, the ships drifting
through thick fog, keeping in touch with each other by the tapping
of drums, the constant daylight of the North Atlantic, walruses
flapping their clumsy bodies off ice floes, and whales spouting
water high into the air and driving through the waves with a
splash of shiny black tail. One night, when the light was obscured
by a heavy mist, Nelson and another midshipman crept from
the ship, determined to shoot a bear for its skin. 'Between three
and four in the morning,' wrote Captain Skeffington Lutwige, in
command of the *Carcass*,

the mist somewhat dispersed and the hunters were discovered at a
considerable distance, attacking a large bear. The signal was instantly
made for their return; but it was in vain that Nelson's companion urged
him to obey it. He was at this time divided by a chasm in the ice from his
shaggy antagonist, which probably saved his life; for the musket flashed
in the pan and their ammunition was expended. 'Never mind,' exclaimed
Horatio, 'do but let me get a blow at this devil with the butt end of my
musket and we shall have him.'

A blank shot fired from one of the *Carcass*'s guns alarmed the
bear, which turned away over the ice. Midshipman Nelson
returned to a severe reproof from Captain Lutwige, who, in his
own words, 'reprimanded him rather severely for such rashness,
and for conduct so unworthy of the situation he occupied, and
desired to know what motive he could have for hunting a bear.
Pouting his lip, as he was wont to do when agitated, [the midship-
man] replied, 'Sir, I wished to kill the bear, that I might carry its
skin to my father.'*[8]

Soon after the *Carcass* had docked at Deptford, Nelson, by now

* Richard Westall's painting of Nelson's attack on the bear is in the National
Maritime Museum.

fifteen years old, heard that his uncle, Captain Suckling, had made arrangements for him to sail in a frigate, the twenty-gun *Seahorse*, to India. He was away for two and a half years, all the time improving his knowledge of navigation and signalling, of hydrographical charts and the ways and wiles of seamen. He saw Madras and Bombay, Calcutta and Ceylon; he sailed across the Arabian Sea to Basra at the head of the Persian Gulf. He was in action for the first time when the *Seahorse* came across a ship flying the flag of Haidar Ali, the Muslim ruler of Mysore. Sitting at a gaming table one day with some amiable Indian merchants, he won, so he claimed, £300 and was so startled by the thought that he might have lost this enormous sum, which would today be worth about £60,000, that he resolved never to gamble again. It was at this time that he became firm friends with a midshipman of his own age, the son of an Irish baker in the Strand, Thomas Troubridge, who had himself a 'slight touch of the brogue' and had joined the *Seahorse* a few days before Nelson.[9] It was also while Nelson was in eastern waters that he suffered his first attack of malaria and grew so ill that he had to be hoisted aboard the *Dolphin* to be carried home, miserable and wasted and dreadfully seasick, tossed about in the squalls and storms of the Indian Ocean. It was feared for a time that he might die, as the *Dolphin*'s young boatswain did; and he might well, indeed, have perished had the ship not spent a month lying off the southern coast of Africa at Simonstown to repair the damage caused by the rough passage from Bombay, to caulk the decks and take aboard fresh supplies. He recovered slowly, but, utterly worn out by fever, sleeplessness and racking vomiting, he fell into a deep despair, almost, so he confessed, wishing himself overboard. 'I felt impressed with a feeling that I should never rise in my profession,' he wrote years later. 'My mind was staggered with a view of the difficulties I had to surmount and the little interest [influence] I possessed. I could discover no means of reaching the object of my ambition.' But then, as the *Dolphin* sailed on again, up the west coast of Africa, towards the equator and beyond to the cooler northern seas, Nelson experienced a sudden transformation of feeling such as that which overwhelmed St Paul on the road to Damascus. He

said that he had a vision of a 'radiant orb'. 'A sudden glow of patriotism was kindled within me,' he recalled, 'and presented my King
and Country as my patron. "Well then," I exclaimed, "I will be a
hero and, confiding in Providence, I will brave every danger."'
Thereafter he was rarely to doubt that he was a man of destiny.[10]

This belief seemed to be confirmed when, upon the *Dolphin*'s
return to England, he was informed that his uncle had been
unexpectedly appointed Comptroller of the Navy, and that,
through his influence, he was to be promoted acting lieutenant,
and to be sent aboard a ship of the line. Moreover, now that
France was openly supporting the American rebels in their
demands for independence from the British Crown and a new war
was in sight, there would be opportunities enough not only for
further promotion but also for prize-money and fame in battle.

In April 1777 the eighteen-year-old Horatio Nelson, eager and
confident, taking his former captains' references with him,
presented himself at the Admiralty for the interview which was to
determine his suitability for a promotion to which he was too
young to be officially entitled. He was shown into a room where
several senior officers sat behind a table. Among them was his
uncle, the Comptroller; but Captain Suckling looked at him as
though he had never seen him before in his life.

The young man standing before the examiners had not grown
much in the past year or so.* His face, bearing signs of his recent

---

* Nelson's height is a matter of some dispute. One naval historian has expressed
the opinion that he was 'less than five feet tall' (Dudley Pope, *The Great Gamble:
Nelson at Copenhagen*). Another believed he was 5 ft 5 in (Bennett, *Nelson the
Commander*). This is the height of the effigy in Westminster Abbey, which is
believed to be life-size. Lieutenant-Commander C. P. Addis, a former commanding
officer of HMS *Victory* and former editor of the *Nelson Dispatch*, the journal of the
Nelson Society, stated categorically: 'Nelson was 5ft 2in tall. This has been
deduced from the several full-length contemporary portraits of him. An officer
when he joined a ship was measured for the cot in which he slept and in which, if
he died at sea, he was committed to the grave' (*Nelson Dispatch*, vol. 1, part 7, July
1983, 110–11). Oliver Warner concluded that Nelson was 5 ft 4 in. 'There is
evidence of his surviving uniform clothes for one thing,' Warner wrote, 'and for
another a mark in the old Admiralty Board Room known to some as "Nelson's
Spot"' (*Spectator*, 17 June 1972). Colin White, Head Curator of the Royal Naval

illness, was pale, the features strongly marked, the mouth wide and sensitive; the eyes, beneath thick brows, were deeply set. When he spoke his voice was slightly high-pitched and nasal, and marked by what was later to be described as a 'strong Norfolk dialect'.[11] At first he 'appeared somewhat alarmed'; but when the questions asked held no difficulty for a sailor who, though so young in appearance, had already had six years' experience, his confidence returned. It was not considered necessary to prolong the interview, and the officers soon indicated that they had heard enough. The Comptroller then asked leave to present his nephew to the other members of the Board, one of whom expressed surprise that they had not been informed of the relationship before. 'No, I did not wish the younker to be favoured,' Suckling said. 'I felt convinced he would pass a good examination, and you see, gentlemen, I have not been disappointed.'[12]

A day or two later Lieutenant Nelson wrote in his small, neat hand to tell his brother William the good news, without mentioning the part that their uncle had played: he had been ordered to 'a fine Frigate', the *Lowestoffe*, which was being fitted out at Sheerness for the Jamaica station. He had 'been left in [the] world to fend' for himself but hoped he would do his duty 'so as to bring credit to [himself] and friends'. He remained, with a flourish, 'Your affectionate Brother, Horatio Nelson'.[13]

His first duty was, however, not likely to bring him much credit. This was to command a press-gang to seize men to make up the *Lowestoffe*'s crew. Seamen could be legally impressed, even those

---

Museum, Portsmouth, having examined, among other things, Nelson's undress uniform coat, concludes he was considerably taller, perhaps 5 ft 6 in (*Nelson Dispatch*, vol. 4, part 5, 7 Jan. 1991, 93). He was certainly not as puny as he has sometimes been presented. On his joining the navy one of his superior officers even described him as being rather stout with a fresh, florid complexion. In later years his waist measurement, again according to his uniform coats and waistcoats, seems to have been about 32 in (*Nelson Dispatch*, vol. 4, part 8, Oct. 1992, 157; vol. 4, part 10, April 1993, 197). James Bagley, a marine who fought at Trafalgar, wrote: 'He is a man about five feet seven'; and Benjamin Silliman, the American geologist and chemist, who also saw him in 1805, described him as being 'of about middle height or rather more'.

who were already employed; so could watermen; so, in fact, could any man who looked strong enough and could not bribe or, with the help of influential friends, argue himself out of service or pay a deputy to go to sea in his place. Should not enough men be found by pressing, recourse would be had to criminals being sentenced to a term aboard ship instead of to prison. The officer in command of the press-gang was not required to lead it in person into the dockland ale houses where suitable seamen were most likely to be found; and Lieutenant Nelson established himself at an inn where, so posters informed the passers-by, volunteers for service in his majesty's frigate, the *Lowestoffe*, would be well received. While on this duty, Nelson one night suddenly began to feel ill and very cold. Feverish and shivering, with all the symptons of a recurrence of malaria, he collapsed on the floor in delirium. A hefty midshipman lifted him up and carried him aboard the *Lowestoffe*, where the ship's captain was called to look at him.

This was William Locker, the second son of John Locker, who was clerk of the Leathersellers' Company and a scholar described by Samuel Johnson as 'a gentleman eminent for curiosity and literature'. Captain Locker had been to Merchant Taylors' School like his father and had entered the navy as a captain's servant at the age of fifteen. He had served with distinction in the Seven Years' War against the French and had been wounded in the leg when leaping from his ship, the *Experiment*, to board an enemy privateer off Alicante. Now forty-six years old, a bluff, brave and cheerful officer, who was to occupy his time in later life by collecting a large amount of material for a naval history, he still walked with a pronounced limp and was forthright in his belief that the decisive action which had led to his injury was the best way to deal with the enemy. 'Always lay a Frenchman close,' was his advice to young officers, 'and you will beat him.' Nelson was to conceive a lasting admiration for him. 'I have been your scholar,' he was to tell him. 'It is you who taught me to board a Frenchman by your conduct when in the *Experiment* . . . and my only merit in my profession is being a good scholar. Our friendship will never end but with my life.'[14]

Unwilling to lose the services of his young lieutenant, Captain

Locker decided to keep him aboard, ill though he seemed; and so Nelson set sail with the *Lowestoffe*, leaving behind a half-finished portrait in the studio of the Italian-born artist, John Francis Rigaud, who had settled in England some years before and had been elected an Associate of the Royal Academy in 1772.*

As Locker had hoped, Nelson soon recovered; and by November he was well enough to ·display a characteristic zeal when the *Lowestoffe* overtook an American merchantman in heavy seas. In such circumstances it was expected of the first lieutenant that he should board the prize; but evidently the *Lowestoffe*'s first lieutenant baulked at such a difficult duty in so rough a sea and Captain Locker, impatient of the delay and fearful of losing both prize and the almost waterlogged boat which had been brought alongside to take the first lieutenant across to it, called out, 'Have I no officer in this ship who can board the prize?' Responding to this exasperated plea, the master, the *Lowestoffe*'s senior warrant officer, ran to the gangway and would have jumped into the swaying boat had not Nelson, crying out, 'It's my turn now,' forestalled him, leapt over the side and with great skill successfully performed the dangerous operation.

'This little incident has often occurred to my mind,' he was afterwards to write with more than a hint of self-congratulation. 'I know it is in my disposition that difficulties and dangers do but increase my desire of attempting them.'[15]

By the time of this 'little incident', the young lieutenant and his seasoned captain had become good friends, enjoying long talks together during the Atlantic crossing; and when, on their arrival in Jamaica, Locker had been carried ashore, prostrate with malaria, Nelson had warmly affirmed this friendship and had added, on a note rather less comforting than he intended, 'should anything

---

* Rigaud completed this portrait of Nelson three years later, changing the uniform to that of a post-captain and painting in as background the castle of San Juan where Nelson had achieved distinction in the meantime. One of several portraits of naval officers painted by Rigaud for Locker, it was bought by the Nelson family in the late nineteenth century for £70. It is now in the National Maritime Museum.

happen to you, (which I sincerely pray God, may not) you may be assured that nothing shall be wanting on my part for the taking care of your effects and delivery safe to Mrs Locker . . . the most amiable of women . . . such of them as may be thought proper not to be disposed of'.[16]

Upon his recovery Captain Locker appeared to go out of his way to show his confidence in his favourite lieutenant, giving him the command of a captured schooner and complimenting him in the manner of the captain of a convoy with which Nelson had earlier sailed as an acting lieutenant, Captain Mark Robinson, who had expressed the opinion – as Nelson himself was proud to relate – that 'he felt as easy when I was on deck [in charge of a watch] as any officer in the ship'.[17]

Nor was it only Captain Robinson and Captain Locker who were impressed by Nelson's abilities. War had now broken out with France, for so long an abettor of the American rebels, and a senior officer had been appointed to the command at Port Royal, Jamaica. This was Rear-Admiral Sir Peter Parker, the son of an admiral and the father and grandfather of boys who were to become admirals. An impulsive and cantankerous officer, still smarting from his catastrophic repulse by the American rebels at Charleston, Parker was as eager as any of his fellow officers to profit in any way he could from showing favour to the nephew of the influential Comptroller of the Navy. He lost no time in having him transferred to his flagship, the *Bristol*, where he was soon promoted first lieutenant, and then given command of the brig, the *Badger*, with the rank of commander. Concerned for his own welfare and future, as he undoubtedly was, Parker was not entirely prompted by selfish motives. There could be no doubt that Horatio Nelson was a highly competent young officer; and, if he did entertain a good opinion of his own talents, this evidently did not prevent his getting on well with his fellow officers as, for instance, with Cuthbert Collingwood, who took his place in the *Lowestoffe* and had every reason to resent him. For Collingwood, a man of exceptional ability, had been at sea as a volunteer at the age of eleven when Nelson, eight years his junior, had not yet even started school. The son of an impoverished family without influence, Collingwood was still a lieutenant, a rank to which he had recently been promoted after brave service at Bunker Hill, the first full-scale battle of the American War.

Nelson's rise, in contrast, seemed unremitting and in no way impeded by the death of his influential uncle on 14 July 1778, a death he much lamented, adding in a sententious letter to his other uncle, William, 'I trust I shall prove myself, by my actions, worthy of supplying that place in the service of my country which my dear uncle left me . . . I feel myself to my country his heir. I feel . . . had I been near him when he was removed, he would have said, "My boy, I leave you to my country; serve her well, and she'll never desert you, but will ultimately reward you." '[18]

After only a short time with the *Badger*, Nelson was appointed post-captain, which meant in effect that his future promotion would be by seniority; and, after Spain had joined France as another of England's enemies, he had been sent as commander of the vital shore battery of Fort Charles, 'the most important post in the whole Island', whose hundred heavy guns helped to protect the anchorage of Kingston. Here Nelson was introduced to the pleasures of Jamaican social life, to dinner at Admiral's Pen, Sir Peter Parker's house in Kingston – where the formidable Lady Parker presided imperiously over her large table – and to parties at the handsome houses of rich sugar planters and ship owners, the sight of whose numerous black slaves, hovering in their well-pressed uniforms at every door, did not disconcert him. 'I was bred in the good old school,' he was later to explain when defending the 'just rights' of the planters.[19]

It was an anxious time, though; the French admiral, the Comte d'Estaing, had evaded British ships in American waters and was said to be approaching the West Indies with as many as a hundred ships and 25,000 soldiers. Admiral Parker's fleet would thus be far outnumbered, as would the men under Nelson's command, most of them ill-trained militia. 'I leave you to judge what stand we shall make,' Nelson wrote to Captain Locker, who had returned to England on sick-leave. 'I think you must not be surprised to hear of my learning to speak French.'[20]

The Comte d'Estaing's fleet changed course, however.

Summoned to help the American rebels, his ships sailed for
Georgia; and by the beginning of September, Nelson was at sea
again in command of a frigate, and was soon sailing along the
Mosquito Shore, the coasts of Nicaragua and Costa Rica, provinces
of New Spain.

Sir John Dalling, the Governor in Jamaica, and Lord George
Germain, Secretary of State for the American Colonies in London,
both had their eyes on these provinces, which lay between the
Caribbean Sea and the Pacific Ocean on the narrow strip of land
which divides the South American continent from the North; for it
occurred to the British high command that an attack on Spanish
garrisons there would result not only in pinning down Spanish
troops but might also result in the establishment of British forces
in a position of strategic importance where, by way of the Rio San
Juan, Lake Nicaragua and a short canal, a navigable waterway
might be opened up between the Atlantic and Pacific Oceans.

Plans were accordingly made for an invasion of the Mosquito
Shore, an advance up the San Juan river and an assault upon the
Spanish fort which guarded the approach to Granada, Nicaragua's
largest town.

Captain John Polson, of the 60th Foot, the King's American
Regiment, promoted lieutenant-colonel for the enterprise, was to
command the land forces, men from his own regiment and from
another newly raised regiment, the Liverpool Blues, reinforced by
released convicts, freed slaves and drifters enlisted from the taverns
and shacks of the Jamaican waterfront, a ragged assembly later to
be described by the Lieutenant-Governor of Jamaica as 'half
clothed and half-drunk'. 'They seemed to possess the true
complexion of buccaneers,' he added, 'and it would be ill-bred to
suppose their principles were not in harmony with their faces. A
hundred of them . . . seemed so volatile and frolicsome, I thought
it good policy to order ten guineas for them to be drunk in grog on
board their transports and embarked them with three cheers to the
great satisfaction of the town of Kingston.'[21]

Colonel Polson was extremely thankful to have at least a few
regular troops. He was also relieved to hear that the expedition's
chief medical officer was to be Benjamin Moseley, the highly

regarded and widely experienced surgeon-general in Jamaica and an authority on tropical diseases as well as on voodoo and hydrophobia, even though Moseley was to leave a deputy, Dr Thomas Dancer, to accompany the expedition once all the necessary arrangements for its health had been made. Polson could take further comfort from the appointment of an efficient Irish officer from the 50th Foot, Captain Edward Despard, as his chief engineer. But Polson was not at all sure what to make of the young naval officer, Captain Nelson, who was to escort the convoy of troopships and smaller craft to the mouth of the San Juan river. 'A light-haired boy,' Polson commented, 'came to me in a little frigate, of whom I at first made little account.'[22]

3
The Mosquito Shore

I . . . was a principal cause of our success.

Nelson was feeling ill again. Dr Moseley, no skilful diagnostician despite his knowledge of yellow fever and dysentery, assured him with characteristic self-confidence that he was suffering from gout in the chest; but, whether or not the complaint was a recurrence of malaria, the general belief among Jamaica's medical fraternity was that the patient would have to go home soon if his health did not improve. It was not likely to be improved by such duties as one of the first he had to perform aboard the *Hinchinbrooke*, which set sail for the Mosquito Shore on 3 February 1780 – the reading of the burial service of a sergeant of the 79th who had died of malaria. Nor was the health of the troops improved by their being so tightly packed together in the troopships during the crossing of the Caribbean to the Nicaraguan coast. Indeed, by the time the convoy reached Cape Gracias a Dios at the mouth of the river which divides Nicaragua from Honduras, it was decided that the men must be brought ashore even though the camp-site chosen was infested by mosquitoes.

The leader of the expedition had been encouraged by reports of the healthiness and pleasant prospect of this part of Central America, which was said to be 'open and dry . . . and abounding with necessities of every kind'. The reality was very different, just as the expedition itself was to be far less smoothly conducted than had been expected in Kingston.

There were disasters from the beginning. The greatest difficulty was experienced in getting the small craft carrying soldiers and supplies into the mouth of the fast-flowing San Juan river. Overloaded boats capsized in the brown water; others collided, throwing stores and men overboard. Captain Nelson, whose duties had officially ended with the arrival of the convoy at the river's mouth, soon realized that the expeditionary force would never get on its way without experienced guidance, still less could the canoes and dories, the pitpans and *pangas* be safely negotiated past the shoals and cataracts ahead. Well aware that he might make his name if the expedition were to be successful, and that it might also make him rich, Nelson offered to remain with Colonel Polson and give him the benefit of his advice. 'I want words to express the obligation I owe that gentleman,' Polson wrote afterwards, deeply grateful to the 'light-haired boy' of whom he had formerly made such 'little account'.[1]

With Nelson's help, the loading of the boats was reorganized and the expedition began its passage up river led by Indian guides and scouts. At first all went well. The boats were paddled vigorously against the stream between banks of high grass and the dark leaves of overhanging trees, in which monkeys threw themselves with astonishing agility from branch to branch and the feathers of parrots, egrets and cormorants could be seen in the flickering sunlight. Below them turtles lay motionless on the rocks, large tails of alligators occasionally flicked spray from the surface of the water.[2]

But the going was lamentably slow; and from time to time a boat stuck fast on a shoal or a sandbank and sailors had to jump overboard to push it off. By the time darkness fell the leading boats had covered less than seven miles, and others lay stranded behind them, overloaded and immovable. After a cold night on shore, with mosquitoes buzzing around their ears, their sleep disturbed by the strange, inexplicable noises of the jungle, the men, suffering from severe headaches caused by the reflected glare of the sun, spent the next day lightening the loads of the grounded boats and relieving them of bulky pieces of artillery and heavy sacks of stores. Even so, on the following two days, progress was as slow as on the first: boats continued to go aground; the convoy became increasingly extended; and, as the grass of the savannahs gave way to ever-darker jungle and the sky was blocked from view by the thick foliage of the trees of the rain forest, the voyage upstream in the humid, murky, greenish air became an ordeal that the men would never forget. Once the pilots, coming to a break in the river, chose the wrong course and led the expedition for almost three miles up a backwater before they realized their mistake.

Nelson decided to lead the expedition himself and thereafter the going was easier. Over the next three days he and Despard, frequently together in the first canoe and sharing a tent for the night, took the boats almost thirty more miles towards the fortress of San Juan. The nights, though, were still a torment, with mosquitoes and other insects buzzing through the cold, damp air, leeches clinging to exposed flesh, and snakes slithering through the undergrowth or lying in coils beneath the soldiers' hammocks. A soldier was bitten in the eye by a snake into which he stumbled as it hung from the branch of a tree. He died soon afterwards and his body had begun to putrefy before he could be buried.[3]

About seventy miles upstream scouts reported having come across a Spanish battery on an island guarding the approaches to the fortress. An attack on this island was swiftly planned: one assault party was to slip silently up river past the island to threaten it from the rear; a second party was to give covering fire from the bank of the river; a third was to be paddled across the stream and to make a frontal assault upon the battery at dawn. This frontal assault was to be led by Captain Nelson. It was hoped that the Spaniards would be taken by surprise; but, as usual, the British sailors had trouble with their unwieldy craft, several of which went aground, and by the time the attack got under way, the Spanish sentries, alerted by the splash of oars and paddles, were ready to resist it. As they opened fire with both musket and cannon, Nelson leapt from his pinnace, sword in hand, sinking to his knees in thick mud that sucked off both his shoes. With Despard by his side, he dashed towards the battery and the enemy fled; when confronted by the fire of the British who had paddled round behind them, the Spaniards obediently surrendered.

A decisive small victory had been won at a cost of only two wounded soldiers; yet the steep white walls of the castle of San Juan, El Castillo de la Immaculada Concepción, still towered above the river. Nelson urged an immediate attack. However,

Colonel Polson, recently informed that reinforcements were on their way, decided to proceed more warily; and when his boat rounded the bend in the river and he saw how formidable the castle appeared, its ramparts and bastions covered by heavy guns, he was confirmed in his belief that an immediate assault might end in disaster. He decided to send a party of fifty men to occupy the higher ground beyond the castle and then proceed to besiege it in the manner laid down in military manuals.

He came near to disaster, all the same. The party sent to take the high ground behind the castle found it impossible to hack their way through the almost impenetrable jungle, the deep ravines and treacherous swamps. They withdrew to the river, carrying a soldier mangled by a jaguar. The expected reinforcements failed to arrive; so did the scaling ladders. So also did new stocks of ammunition; and the guns, which had been skilfully laid by Despard and Nelson, were compelled to fall silent, having merely splintered the castle's flagstaff.

When the troops bringing fresh ammunition at last arrived, they dolefully reported that most of it had been lost overboard from capsized boats. In desperation Colonel Polson ordered the engineers to dig their way beneath the castle walls and bring them down with a mine; but, after long hours of exhausting work, they came upon a face of solid rock.

Then, in the middle of April, lightning flashed, thunder roared, the sky darkened and the rain poured down in torrents, flattening the tents, soaking the men, almost blinding them by the force of the deluge. Already many were ill, having drunk water poisoned by the fruit of a manchineel tree which had fallen or been thrown into an apparently clear pool.

Nelson was among the sick, suffering from dysentery, a recurrence of fever, the effects of drinking the poisoned water and from pains in his chest.[4] Indeed, when dispatches arrived from the coast informing him that he had been appointed to the command of the frigate *Janus*, and was to return at once to Jamaica, there was concern that he might be too ill to move. Yet, since it was thought that he was just as likely to die in his sodden tent by the waters of the San Juan river as he was on the journey to the coast, he was helped to a canoe and sent on his way downstream back to the Mosquito Shore. Here his emaciated appearance and yellow skin shocked Cuthbert Collingwood, who had taken over the *Hinchinbrooke*, just as they were later in Jamaica to shock another of his friends, the fat, red-faced Hon. William Cornwallis, captain of the *Lion*, son of the 1st Earl Cornwallis and brother of the general fighting the American rebels.

Cornwallis, the popular 'Billy Blue', 'Coachee' and 'Mr Whip' as he was also variously known, saw him carried ashore and insisted that he be taken, not to the local hospital, where so many patients died, but to a woman who would nurse him with expert care. This was 'Cuba' Cornwallis, a jolly, lovable Jamaican whom Cornwallis had released from slavery and employed as his house-keeper before she established herself as a lodging-house keeper. Her methods of treatment, passed on to her through generations of black women skilled in herbal remedies and well-tested cures, were unconventional but usually effective; and under her ministrations Nelson began to get better and was taken to convalesce at the Parkers' house above Kingston, Admiral's Mountain on Cooper's Hill. Here Lady Parker and her housekeeper nursed him at-tentively; but when they left for the admiral's house on the coast, Nelson was handed over to the negligent ministrations of their staff and wished that he had been left to recover at 'Cuba' Cornwallis's. 'Oh! Mr Ross!' he complained to a friend of Locker, a sugar planter who had entertained them both at his house. 'What would I give to be at Port Royal. Lady P. not here, and the servants letting me lay as if a log, and [taking] no notice.'[5]

The Governor came to see him; and, although Nelson left him in no doubt that, had an immediate assault been made on the castle of San Juan as he had recommended, it would probably have then fallen into British hands, he was careful not to blame Polson for the long delay in capturing it, as the colonel evidently feared he might. In any event, at the beginning of June, news reached Jamaica that the castle – which, having no well, could not rely for long on an inadequate cistern – had had to surrender. Pleasure at this news, however, soon turned to deep disappointment when Colonel Stephen Kemble of the 10th Foot, who had been appointed to succeed Polson, arrived at the castle with reinforcements to find 'the troops under Colonel Polson's command in a most deplorable state' and 'everything in the greatest confusion'. Almost all the soldiers were ill and, since the medical supplies had been left behind on the coast as being an unnecessary encumbrance, there was no way of treating them. Colonel Kemble's reinforcements soon fell ill, too; and, short of rations as well as medicines, he felt obliged to retreat to the coast, with further devastating loss of life.

'I lament exceedingly the dreadful havoc Death has made among the troops,' Lord George Germain wrote severely to Governor Dalling, 'especially as from the entire failure of the Expedition no public benefit has been derived from the loss of so many brave men.'[6]

On his way home aboard the *Lion* – whose captain, Cornwallis, cared for him so tenderly that he gave him credit for saving his life – Nelson comforted himself with the thought that he, for one, had come through the disaster without blame. Indeed, Commander James Clarke, whom the Governor sent to Nicaragua to consider the possibility of another expedition, thought that, had Nelson's plans been approved, such severe loss of life would never have been suffered. Certainly, Nelson himself considered so, and wrote in self-congratulatory vein of his part in the enterprise: 'Major Polson, who commanded the soldiers, will tell you of my exertions: how I quitted my Ship and carried troops in boats one hundred miles up a river . . . It will then be told how I boarded (if I may be allowed the expression) an out-post of the Enemy, situated on an island in the river; that I made batteries, and afterwards fought them, and was a principal cause of our success.'[7]

'I return to England hope revives within me,' he told Hercules Ross in one of his sparsely punctuated letters. 'I shall recover and my dream of glory be fulfilled. Nelson will yet be an Admiral. It is the climate that has destroyed my health and crushed my spirit. Home and dear friends will restore me.'[8]

4

The North American Station

The West Indies is the station for honour.

Nelson arrived at Portsmouth at the beginning of December 1780 still so frail that he was advised to take a course of the baths and waters at Bath before even considering a return to duty. His father – who by now regularly escaped from what he called the 'wind and storm and rattling hail' of Norfolk – was already there, staying at the house of an apothecary at 2 Pierrepont Street near the Pump Room; and Nelson, too, took a room in the house where, for a time, he felt feebler than ever, worrying so much that poor health would deny him the fame he sought that on occasions he seemed a confirmed hypochondriac. 'I have been so ill since I have been here,' he told William Locker, 'that I was obliged to be carried to and from bed with the most excruciating tortures ... I am physicked three times a day, drink the waters three times and baths every other night, besides not drinking wine which I think the worst [torture] of all.'[1] Three weeks later his fingers' ends were still 'as if half dead', and he had not yet recovered the use of his left arm, which alarmed him by suddenly going white and numb and then swelling agonizingly. However, his doctors assured him that it would eventually 'all go off' and that it would not be long before he was employed again. In the meantime, he said, he would drink Locker's health in 'a drought of [his] physician's cordial'.[2]

The next month he was well enough to go to the theatre, where he saw the young and heavily pregnant Mrs Siddons at the Orchard Street Theatre in one of her last performances before her departure to Drury Lane;[3] and in April 1781 he took the London coach to stay with his uncle in Kentish Town.

*

In the first week of May 1781, Nelson went to the Admiralty for an interview with Lord Sandwich, who had been at the head of the Navy's affairs since 1771. An ugly, dissipated and charming man of fashion, Sandwich was known to employ the immense patronage at his disposal for personal and political motives. Yet he was clever, versatile and as hard-working as any eighteenth-century minister was expected to be. For all his faults – and his reputation as the man who was supposed to have invented the sandwich so that he could eat without leaving the gambling table – he was a conscientious First Lord of the Admiralty, prepared to advance the talented as well as the rich and influential. His manner towards Nelson was brisk though not unfriendly. He told him that no ship was at present available, but that he would bear his application in mind. In the meantime he advised him to concentrate upon regaining his strength. Certainly Nelson was in need of such advice: since returning to London he had been feeling ill again and his left arm was still giving him much pain. His left leg, too, was now troubling him, as painful on occasions as the arm. He had consulted Robert Adair, Surgeon-General to the King, only to be told, as the doctors in Bath had also assured him, that the malady would cure itself in time: he must be patient. He returned to his uncle William's house in Kentish Town, and then decided to try the Norfolk air on a visit to his family at Burnham Thorpe.

His brothers, he found, were doing as little as ever to enhance the family's name: the youngest was still apprenticed to the Beccles linen draper; Edmund still plodding away at his brother-in-law's counting house in Ostend; William had decided that a curate's life was not a congenial one and was looking for a more rewarding career.

Their eldest sister, Susannah, was now well established as Mrs Bolton at Wells-next-the-Sea, where her husband, in an increasingly satisfactory way of business, was often to be seen at meetings of the Wells Club at the Three Tuns. She seemed contented enough in that limited society; but Horatio hoped that their youngest sister, Kate, a spirited, pretty girl, would do better for herself. 'Although I am very fond of Mrs Bolton,' he confessed, 'yet I own I should not like to see Kate fixed in a Wells' society.'[4]

Family affairs being as they were, Horatio was deeply thankful
to receive a letter informing him that a ship, the frigate *Albemarle*,
had been found for him at last. He left for London almost immediately, leaving his brother William more frustrated than ever
by the progress of his own unsatisfactory career. For William had
made up his mind to become, with his brother's help, a naval
chaplain, and Horatio had strongly advised him against it: he
would find the pay inadequate; he might well be sent aboard a
ship whose officers, from whose company he could not escape,
would make his voyages with them miserable; naval chaplains
were generally far from being the most respectable of their calling.
William persisted, while Horatio continued to urge him to abandon
the plan. 'The more I see of chaplains of men-of-war, the more I
dread seeing my brother in such a disagreeable situation of life,' he
told him.[5] Besides, it was a dangerous life as well as a most
uncomfortable one. In the end, however, Horatio gave way to his
brother's pestering and agreed to take him aboard his own ship
'for a few months', provided he returned to Burnham Thorpe in
the winter 'to keep our father and sister [Kate] company in that
lonesome place'. Further letters followed, and one in particular
Horatio found exasperating. 'You ask,' he replied, 'by what interest
did I get a ship? I answer, having served with credit was my
recommendation to the First Lord of the Admiralty . . . Come
when you please, I shall be ready to receive you. Bring your
canonicals and sermons. Do not bring any Burnham servants.'[6] So
William did go to sea as a naval chaplain; but he liked the life no
better than his brother had predicted and, pleading illness, he soon
returned to England.

Nelson had found the *Albemarle*, a captured French merchantman, formerly *La Ménagère*, in dock at Woolwich having her
underwater timbers sheathed with copper plate. Captain Locker,
whom Nelson had taken with him to look the ship over, did not
much like what he saw; but Nelson, anxious to get to sea again,
would have none of Locker's criticisms. He was 'perfectly satisfied
with her as a 28-gun frigate' and was later to express equal
satisfaction with the ship's company, not a man of which he
'would wish to change', though some of these he had impressed

himself with ruthless efficiency and were by no means willing hands. They were seamen returning to the London docks aboard four merchant ships. Nelson had chased these Indiamen and, when they ignored his signals, he had had a blank charge fired at them. In their eagerness to escape, the merchant ships sped on under full press of canvas; but when the master of the leading ship saw the *Albemarle*'s gun ports open and the guns run out, and when broadsides of nine- and eighteen-pounder shots were fired in earnest, his ship and the three behind all hove to. The unfortunate seamen taken off them, so near to reaching home, were bundled aboard the *Albemarle* and two other ships under Nelson's command. They were soon sailing across the North Sea to escort a convoy home from the Baltic.

In early November they reached the Danish fortress of Helsingør where Nelson – angered that his ship was greeted by a visit from a lone midshipman instead of the salutes from guns he had expected – made his feelings very clear to the boy who reported them to the Danish admiral. When his own guns fired a salute, those in Kronborg Castle accordingly returned the compliment.

Nelson was still unwell; and several months later, after escorting another convoy across the Atlantic with bullion valued at £100,000, he and many members of the crew, having been without fresh meat and vegetables for weeks on end, came down with scurvy. Their gums became spongy, their limbs ached; they were overcome by depression and lassitude; their breath smelt foul.

The men in Nelson's ships suffering from this painful complaint were taken to hospital in Quebec, where Nelson himself, having ordered fresh provisions from the town, began to feel the benefit of the bracing autumnal air. 'Health,' he wrote to his father, 'that greatest of blessings, is what I never truly enjoyed until I saw *Fair Canada*. The change it has wrought, I am convinced, is truly wonderful. I most sincerely wish, dear Father, I could compliment you in the same way.'[7]

Well again at last, and stimulated by the cheerful social life of Quebec which his hero, James Wolfe, had captured from the French twenty-odd years before, Nelson fell in love for the first time. The girl was Mary Simpson, the pretty, demure daughter of

Colonel Saunders Simpson, the Provost-Marshal of the garrison. She was sixteen years old; Nelson was now twenty-four. She evidently found him attractive and his attentions flattering, but she had to admit that he was rather 'stern of aspect'; and she was not as responsive to his advances as he would have liked. He himself was 'violently attached' to her, he confided to Alexander Davison, a rich merchant of Scottish descent whom he had met in Quebec; and he was resolved to marry the girl. Davison advised caution. But Nelson was 'determined to press his suit'; and, when he received orders to escort a convoy to New York, he told Davison he found it 'utterly impossible to leave [Quebec] without waiting on her whose society [had] so much added to its charms and laying [himself] and [his] fortunes at her feet'.

'Your utter ruin, situated as you are at present, must inevitably follow,' Davison replied, recording the conversation as he remembered it.

'Then let it follow, for I am resolved to do it.'

'And I also positively declare that you shall not.'[8]

According to Davison, Nelson at length saw reason, gave way obediently, returned to his ship – whose sails were frozen to the yards – and sailed as ordered to New York to report to Rear-Admiral the Hon. Robert Digby, commander of the North American Station, a younger brother of the first Earl Digby.

'You are come on a fine station for making prize-money,' Digby told him complacently on his arrival.

'Yes, sir,' Nelson replied in that occasionally sanctimonious manner which some of his fellow officers found so irritating. 'But the West Indies is the station for honour.'[9]

Yet while complaining to naval officers on the North American station that money seemed to be the 'great object' out there, and that 'nothing else [was] attended to', Nelson did not forgo opportunities to make money himself and was naturally much disappointed when, having chased and boarded a French merchantman worth, with its cargo, some £20,000, Rear-Admiral Lord Hood, the highly respected and forthright commander of a squadron on its way to the West Indies, ruled that, as the ship had been taken within sight of the rest of the squadron, the prize-money would have to be shared with the Admiral himself and the captains of all the other ships.*

In hopes of gaining permission to take the *Albemarle* to the West Indies under Lord Hood's command, Nelson applied for an interview with the admiral. For this interview he donned his full-laced uniform; and when he came aboard the admiral's flagship his appearance struck a young midshipman as decidedly peculiar. This midshipman was King George's third son, Prince William, shortly to be created Duke of Clarence and, upon the death of his eldest brother, to be crowned King William IV.

Captain Nelson appeared to be the 'merest boy of a captain I ever beheld', recorded Prince William who was himself but seventeen.

And his dress was worthy of attention . . . his lank, unpowdered hair was tied in a stiff Hessian tail of an extraordinary length; the old-fashioned flaps on his waistcoat added to the general appearance of quaintness of his figure . . . I had never seen anything like it before, nor could imagine who he was, nor what he came about. My doubts were, however, removed when Lord Hood introduced me to him. There was something irresistibly pleasing in his address and conversation; and an enthusiasm when speaking on professional subjects that showed he was no common being.[10]

Prince William was an odd boy. Truculent, boorish and obstinate, sometimes a bully and often a buffoon, he had been sent to sea at the age of thirteen in the hope that the Royal Navy would save him from falling under the influence of his dissolute brothers; and it had to be conceded that, for all his faults, he was not an incompetent seaman, though scarcely deserving the high praise which, in reports to his father, his seniors thought it as well to bestow upon him.

* Lord Hood's ruling did not affect Nelson's admiration for him. Some years later Nelson was to say that he considered Hood 'the first officer in our Service . . . the greatest sea officer I ever knew' (Clarke and M'Arthur, i, 191), 'the best officer, take him altogether that England has to boast of' (Mahan, ii, 175). Collingwood did not agree with this verdict. In his opinion, 'Lord H's ambition [was] far exceeding his abilities' (Collingwood, ed. Hughes, 43).

Nelson himself, a man with a high opinion verging upon reverence for royalty, also spoke most highly of him. He was to know him as a martinet – 'a disciplinarian and a strong one', with a firm belief in the efficacy of the lash – as having an insatiable appetite for coarse and scatological jokes, which he did not hesitate to repeat in mixed company, and for making long, boring and often quite irrelevant speeches at every opportunity. Nelson was also to learn that the Prince was a notorious womanizer, picking up girls in every port, frequenting brothels, contracting venereal diseases, making reckless proposals of marriage to the most unsuitable of ladies. Yet he immediately decided, upon being granted 'the honour of an introduction to him', that unless he was 'much mistaken', he would make 'a good sailor . . . an ornament to our Service . . . We shall be proud of him.'[11] With the best 'temper and good sense, he cannot fail of being pleasing to everyone'. He was 'superior to near two thirds of the List'. 'In every respect, both as a Man and a Prince,' Nelson concluded, 'I love him.'[12]

Nelson was, of course, acutely aware how useful the friendship of the King's son might be to him. Not long before he had complained, 'My interest at home is next to nothing, the name of Nelson being little known; it may be different one of these days.' Now, having made a good impression upon Lord Hood, who had been a close friend of his uncle, Maurice Suckling, as well as upon Prince William, Nelson could report to William Locker that he had at last found the influential support he had been seeking ever since Captain Suckling's death. Lord Hood treated him as though he were his son. 'He will,' Nelson was confident, 'give me anything I can ask of him; nor is my situation with Prince William less flattering.'[13]

The opportunity to deepen this friendship was presented to Nelson when, to Prince William's annoyance, a ceasefire was arranged in Paris between the American Congress and the British Government. As a consequence of this ceasefire, Prince William was ordered to make an official goodwill visit to Havana, the most important link in the chain between Spain and her possessions in the Caribbean and the Americas. He was to sail in a convoy escorted by the *Albemarle* and Captain Nelson was to be his aide-de-camp. In this capacity Nelson was afterwards said to have performed a valuable service; for the Prince, in his highly susceptible way, fell in love with one of the daughters of the Spanish admiral commanding in Cuba and it was evidently 'a question whether his Royal Highness would have seen England again, had it not been for Captain Nelson, who plainly saw the danger that impended over his royal friend and urged his immediate departure'.[14]

5

France and the Leeward Islands

O what a transition from happy England!

The Prince and Captain Nelson – with forty gallons of rum for
Captain Locker – arrived home in England within a few hours of
each other on 26 June 1783; and soon afterwards Lord Hood took
Nelson to a levee at St James's Palace where the King – who had
learned of his wayward son's friendship with this promising and
evidently respectable young officer – was sufficiently interested in
cementing it to invite the captain to Windsor Castle. Here Nelson
was to say goodbye to the Prince, who would soon be going to
Hanover for lessons in German and French and in the hope that a
supervised sojourn there would do more for his manners and
bearing than life in a rough and rowdy midshipmen's mess had
done.

Prince William suggested that a smattering of French would not
do Nelson's future career any harm, either; and Nelson himself
could not but agree: a man with a command of French was 'an
ornament to society'; besides, were war with France to break out
again, the language would certainly be useful, particularly in
talking to captains of captured prizes. So, having found a travelling
companion in Captain James Macnamara, whom he had known
in America, and having obtained six months' leave from the
Secretary to the Admiralty, he set out on the Dover Road. 'I have
closed the war without a fortune,' he wrote in characteristic vein to
Hercules Ross, the Scottish sugar planter, before his departure.
'But I trust and, from the attention that has been paid to me,
believe there is not a speck on my character. True honour, I hope,
predominates in my mind far above riches.'[1]

This was to become a familiar refrain. Nelson, as he was to

assure correspondents in letter after letter, was a man of honour to whom duty was a sacred trust; had he been less honourable, he might have become a very rich man. 'I defy any insinuations against my honour,' he once told the Commissioners of the Victualling Board. 'Nelson is as far from doing a scandalous or mean action as the heavens are above the earth.' 'One of my greatest Boasts,' he wrote in another letter, 'is that no man can ever say I have told a lie.'[2]

Nelson and Macnamara landed at Calais, after a pleasant crossing of less than four hours, and made their way to an inn kept by a Monsieur Grandsire, 'whose mother', so Nelson told Captain Locker, 'kept it when Hogarth wrote his "Gate of Calais"'. From Calais they had at first intended going straight to St Omer, but this, Nelson was warned, was 'a dirty, nasty town'; so they decided to make instead for Boulogne. They might have travelled by a public coach which could carry up to thirty passengers, but as Arthur Young, the well-travelled agriculturist discovered, the diligence was a 'detestable' conveyance, 'overcrowded and badly sprung', whose French passengers so stunned him with their rowdy singing of French airs that he would 'almost as soon have rode the journey blindfold on an ass'.[3]

Nelson and Macnamara therefore chose to travel by a hired post-chaise, which arrived at their inn in the care of a postillion wearing the immense boots, 'as big as oyster barrels', peculiar to his calling. French postillions were generally considered the plague of the post routes, 'lazy, lounging, greedy, impertinent rascals', as Tobias Smollett described them, in dirty sheepskin coats and greasy night-caps. 'If you chide them for lingering, they will continue to delay you the longer,' Smollett added. 'If you chastise them with sword, cane, cudgel or horse-whip, they will either disappear entirely and leave you without resources, or they will find means to take vengeance by overturning your carriage.'[4]

Nelson found the unsprung French carriages and the ill-paved French roads quite as exhausting as did Smollett and other English travellers. 'We set off *en poste*, they called it,' he told his father. 'We did not get on more than four miles an hour. Such *carriages*, such

horses, such *drivers*, and such *boots*, you would have been ready to
burst with laughing at the ridiculous figure they made together.
The roads were paved with stones; therefore by the time we had
travelled fifteen miles, we were pretty well shook up, and heartily
tired.'[5]

As for the inn where – cutting short their bumpy journey to
Boulogne – they decided to stay in Marquise, this was truly appalling. '"Inn" they called it,' Nelson complained in a letter to
Captain Locker. 'I should have called it a pig-stye. We were
shown into a room with two straw beds, and, with great difficulty,
they mustered up clean sheets, and gave us two pigeons for supper,
upon a dirty cloth and wooden-handled knives. *O what a transition
from happy England!* But we laughed at the repast and went to bed
with the determination that nothing should ruffle our tempers.'[6]

Boulogne was a far less distressing place than Marquise; but it
was crowded with English people who looked rather undesirable in
Nelson's eyes and who, so he considered, might well have been
drawn to the place by the high quality and cheapness of the wine
which he himself was served at breakfast.

In St Omer also there were large numbers of English visitors
whom Nelson thought it as well to avoid, in particular two 'noble
Captains' whose names he knew to be Shepard and Ball and whose
uniforms, 'great coxcombs' as they were, were decorated with 'fine
epaulettes', a new and unofficial fashion of which – always con-
temptuous of sartorial innovation – he strongly disapproved, though
his own uniform was later to be adorned in the same way.*[7] St
Omer itself, however, far from being the 'dirty, nasty' place of
which Nelson had been warned, was a most pleasant town, with
fine houses, well-paved, well-lit streets and welcoming shops, a
delightful improvement upon the dark and dismal villages through

---

* Nelson considered these captains 'a little cheap for putting on part of a
Frenchman's uniform', but many naval officers did wear epaulettes when on
leave. New regulations of 1795 permitted them for officers above the rank of
lieutenant, one on the left shoulder for a commander, one on the right for a
captain of less than three years' seniority, and one on each shoulder for higher
ranks. Rear-admirals were entitled to wear one star on their epaulettes, vice-
admirals two and admirals three (Lavery, 104).

which he had passed. Having taken lodgings with a Madame La Mourie, Nelson set out to buy a copy of Chambaud's *Grammar of the French Tongue* and wrote purposefully on the title-page, 'Horatio Nelson began to learn the French language on the first of November, 1783.'[8]

However, he did not get on with his studies very well. There were two La Mourie daughters, one of whom served their guests breakfast, the other dinner, but neither could speak English, nor evinced interest in learning it; so, while Nelson was as yet incapable of addressing them in their own language, the card games they all played – after dinner had been sent in by the keeper of a nearby eating-house – were accompanied by smiles and gestures rather than words.

This proving extremely tedious, Nelson soon took to spending his evenings in the company of the family of an English clergyman named Andrews, a man with a large number of dependants including a son in the Navy, two daughters about twenty years old and various other persons whose relationship to Mr Andrews was unclear. It was the girls who interested Nelson; and with one, who sang so prettily after dinner, he fancied himself in love. 'My heart is quite secured against the French beauties,' he wrote to his brother William. 'I almost wish I could say as much for an English young lady, the daughter of a clergyman with whom I am just going to dine and spend the day. She has such accomplishments that, had I a million of money, I am sure I should at this moment make her an offer of marriage: my income at present is by far too small to think of marriage, and she has no fortune.'[9]

Nevertheless, with marriage in mind, he wrote a begging letter to his Uncle William Suckling, who was informed, without preamble, that there arrived a time in the life of a man who had friends that 'either they place him in a situation that makes his application for anything farther totally unnecessary, or give him help in a pecuniary way, if they can afford it, and he deserves it. That critical moment in my life has now arrived,' he continued in this laboured and importunate manner.

. . . Either I am to be happy or miserable: it depends solely on you . . .

There is a lady I have seen of a good family and connexions, but with a small fortune – 1,000l,* I understand. The whole of my income does not exceed 130l. per annum. Now I must come to the point – will you, if I should marry, allow me 100l. a year until my income is increased to that sum either by employment or any other way? A very few years will, I hope, turn something up, if my friends will but exert themselves. If you will not give me the above sum annually, to make me happy for life, will you exert yourself either with Lord North [until recently Prime Minister] or with Mr Jenkinson [Charles Jenkinson, later 1st Earl of Liverpool, a friend of North supposed to have great influence at court], to get me a Guardship, or some appointment in a Public Office, where the attendance of the principal is not necessary, and of which they must have a number to dispose of . . .

If nothing is done for me, I know not what I have to trust to. Life is not worth living without happiness; and I care not where I may linger out a miserable existence.

I am prepared to hear your refusal and have fixed my resolution if that should happen; but in every situation I shall be a well-wisher to you and to all your family, and pray that they nor you may never know the pangs which at this instant tear my heart.

God bless you, and assure yourself that I am your most affectionate and dutiful nephew,

Horatio Nelson.[10]

Suckling made a note on the back of the letter to the effect that he would agree to help. But it seems that Miss Andrews was not as anxious to become Mrs Nelson as her suitor was to make her so; and by the time he heard of his uncle's decision, Nelson had decided he would never be a linguist and had gone back to London, where he found all his friends and acquaintances caught up in the excitement of politics and of the forthcoming election.

He considered the possibility of standing for Parliament himself,

---

* Because of the fluctuating rate of inflation and other reasons it is not really practicable to translate eighteenth-century sums into modern equivalents. Multiplying the figures given in the book by about sixty should give a rough guide.

though he had no firmly held political convictions and had no reputation either as an administrator or as an orator. He greatly admired the high-minded, patriotic and unsociable William Pitt, an exceptionally gifted politician only a few months older than himself, 'the greatest Minister this country ever had, and the honestest man'.[11] He also entertained a high opinion of Henry Addington, a sincere Tory, who was to succeed Pitt as Prime Minister in 1801.[12] Yet on the other hand he was hopeful that some good might come from his connections with the leading Whig families of East Anglia, remote though these were. At the same time he had very low opinion of Charles James Fox and those other Whiggish, Francophile friends of the Prince of Wales, 'a turbulent faction, striving to ruin this country'.[13] It was said that, on learning that the father of one of his midshipmen had decidedly Whiggish views, he had called the boy into his cabin as soon as he came aboard the ship and had 'immediately addressed him in the most impressive manner, to the following effect: "There are three things, young gentleman, which you are constantly to bear in mind: first you must always implicitly obey orders, without attempting to form any opinion of your own respecting their propriety; secondly, you must consider every man as your enemy who speaks ill of your King; and, thirdly, you must hate a Frenchman as you do the devil."'*[14]

Nelson's political views were much influenced by Admiral Hood, Fox's rival and soon to be returned at the head of the poll for

---

* Hatred of the French was a persistent theme in Nelson's letters: '*Down, down* with the French villains . . . Excuse my warmth; but my blood boils at the name of a Frenchman . . . You may safely rely that I never trust a Frenchman . . . I hate the French most damnably . . . I hate them all – Royalists and Republicans . . . Down, down with the French is my constant prayer . . . "Down, down with the French" ought to be placed in the Council-room of every country in the world.' When peace terms were agreed with the French in 1801 and the carriage of the French ambassador was dragged through the streets of London by a cheering crowd, Nelson was enraged. 'Can you cure madness?' he asked his doctor, 'for I am mad to hear that our damned scoundrels dragged a Frenchman's carriage. I am ashamed for our country . . . I hope never more to be dragged myself by such a degenerate people.'

Westminster,* at whose house in Wimpole Street he was more than once a dinner guest, as he was at the rooms in Lincoln's Inn where Alexander Davison, having made a fortune, later to be immensely augmented as a none-too-scrupulous government contractor, was then living in appropriate comfort. Yet, while other young officers with less influential friends found seats, Nelson did not; and by the end of January 1784 he had given up hopes of getting one. 'As to your having enlisted under the banner of the Walpoles,' he wrote to his brother William, now rector of Brandon Parva, Norfolk, 'you might as well have enlisted under those of my grandmother. They are altogether the merest set of *cyphers* that ever existed ... Mr Pitt, depend upon it, will stand against all opposition: an honest man must always in time get the better of a *villain*; but I have done with politics, let who will get in, I shall be left out.'[15]

Years later Nelson received a proposal to enter Parliament as a member for Ipswich. Despite all that he had said in the past, he replied that he could do so only in support of the Whigs and the Duke of Portland, who was then serving as Home Secretary in Pitt's government. Nothing, however, came of this proposal.

Having 'done with politics', Nelson thought of going up to Burnham Thorpe where his sister Kate, now the only daughter there since the death of Anne the year before, was in need of company. But, 'pulled down most astonishingly', he went instead to Bath, where his father was taking his annual cure, and while there learned that decisions as to his future had been taken out of his hands: he had been appointed to the command of the twenty-eight-gun frigate, the *Boreas*.

His first duties with this ship were scarcely to his taste. He was to act as a kind of chaperon to Lady Hughes, wife of Rear-

* The Westminster election was a fiercely fought contest, Hood, backed by the government, winning 6,694 votes, Fox 6,233. On the second day of the campaign a gang of Hood's sailors intimidated a group of Fox's supporters until driven off by a gang of Irish sedan chairmen (Loren Reid, *Charles James Fox: A Man for the People*, London, 1969, 200).

Admiral Sir Richard Hughes, who was crossing the Atlantic to join her husband, commander-in-chief at the Leeward Islands, an officer who had contrived to amass so much money in his profession that he was able to bequeath his stepson the princely fortune of £40,000 a year.[16] Lady Hughes seemed a tiresome, garrulous woman, with what Nelson called 'an eternal clack'. She was a great-niece of Sir Hans Sloane, the physician and Lord of the Manor of Chelsea, and the mother of an apparently equally tiresome, perky and plain daughter, who was also to sail in the *Boreas* with the ill-concealed intention of finding a husband either on board or in the West Indies. As well as these two women, Nelson was to take with him some thirty midshipmen, mostly bound for other ships in West Indian waters, including George Andrews, brother of the clergyman's daughter whom he had been so set upon marrying in St Omer. The ship was, indeed, 'full of young Midshipmen' and 'pretty well filled with *lumber*'.[17]

The voyage got off to a forebodingly bad start. 'On Monday April 12th [1784] we sailed at daylight,' Nelson recorded in an account which revealed his exasperation and ill temper.

The damned pilot – it makes me swear to think of it – ran the Ship aground, where she lay with so little water that people could walk around her till next high water. That night and part of the next day, we lay below the Nore with a hard gale of wind and snow ... Wednesday I got into a quarrel with a Dutch Indiaman ... the Dutchman made a complaint against me; but the Admiralty, fortunately, have approved my conduct in the business, a thing they are not very guilty of where there is a likelihood of a *scrape*.[18]

This quarrel was a foretaste of worse experiences to come. There was the inescapable presence of Lady Hughes, whose husband had once commanded the *Boreas*; there was the equally inescapable presence of Miss Hughes, whom no officer in the ship, least of all himself, seemed to fancy; there was the purser's attractive wife, to whom both the ship's lieutenants, as well as her surgeon, were making improper advances. There was the necessity of playing the usual games upon crossing the equator, when those on board had to be summoned before King Neptune's court and ceremoniously ducked; and there was also the need to deliver a lecture to officers and men about the precautions which they must take to maintain their health in a tropical climate. There was, worst of all, the duty upon landing in the Leeward Islands of having to serve as senior captain and second-in-command under Sir Richard Hughes.

The son of the first baronet, a man who had done well for himself as Commissioner for the Navy at Portsmouth, Sir Richard was a pleasant, easy-going man, who seemed more like an amiable country doctor than a senior naval officer. He had lost an eye, but this was the result not of a war wound, but of an accident with a table-knife during an attempt to squash a cockroach. Nelson decided immediately that he could neither respect nor like the man. 'The Admiral and all about him are great ninnies,' he wrote. 'I do not like him, he bows and scrapes too much for me.' He was an 'excellent fiddler'. Indeed he spent so much time tuning his violin that his squadron was 'cursedly out of tune'. 'He lives in a boarding-house at Barbadoes, not much in the style of a British admiral,' Nelson added. 'He has not that opinion of his own sense that he ought to have. He does not give himself that weight that I think an English admiral ought to do.'[19]

Certainly Nelson, for his own part, had no doubt as to what might or might not be permitted to an English captain; and, upon receiving an invitation to join Sir Richard and Lady Hughes at a dinner to be given by the Governor of the Leeward Islands, General Sir Thomas Shirley, he took it upon himself to bring a midshipman with him. 'Your Excellency must excuse me for bringing one of my midshipmen,' he announced. 'I make it a rule to introduce them to all the good company I can as they have few to look up to beside myself during the time they are at sea.'[20]

By this time Nelson had come to the conclusion that Lady Hughes at least was not so intolerable after all; nor was her daughter, Rosie, once it had been established beyond doubt that he was not to be considered as a possible suitor. But his relationship with her father grew from bad to worse. Sir Richard, in Nelson's opinion, had allowed discipline on the station to become disgracefully lax. He himself had had the unpleasant duty of witnessing a sailor being flogged round the fleet soon after the *Boreas* had docked, as a deterrent to seamen tempted by cheap rum or black girls to misbehave or desert. It distressed him to see other senior officers tolerant of ill discipline. Ships were not saluted properly; and, when his own was not granted the usual courtesies, he did not attempt to hide his severe displeasure. There was also trouble when Nelson noticed that the Commissioner of the Navy at English Harbour, Antigua, was flying the broad pennant of a commodore to which, as an officer in a civil appointment on half pay, he was not entitled. Nelson called the captain of the ship, who was junior to himself, aboard the *Boreas*, and made a memorandum of their conversation:

QUESTION – 'Have you any order from Sir Richard Hughes to wear a Broad Pennant?'

ANSWER – 'No.'

QUESTION – 'For what reason do you then wear it in the presence of a Senior Officer?'

ANSWER – 'I hoisted it by order of Commissioner Moutray.'

QUESTION – 'Have you seen by what authority Commissioner Moutray was empowered to give you orders?'

ANSWER – 'No.'

QUESTION – 'Sir, you have acted wrongly, to obey any man you do not know is authorized to command you.'

ANSWER – 'I feel I have acted wrong; but being a young Captain did not think proper to interfere in this matter as there were you and other older Officers upon this Station.'[21]

Nelson then wrote to protest to the Commissioner himself (who did not insist on his right to the pennant) and dispatched two letters of remonstrance to Sir Richard (who had authorized the Commissioner to hoist it). Until the Commissioner was properly appointed he would not 'obey any order' he received from him, Nelson announced. 'I know of no superior officers beside the Lords Commissioners of the Admiralty, and my seniors on the post list.'[22]

Not content with these letters of protest, Nelson wrote also to the Secretary to the Admiralty in London. Although it had to be admitted at the Admiralty that the man was quite right – and commissioners of the navy were thereafter always required to be serving officers on full pay – Nelson's appealing to the Admiralty over the head of his superiors earned him a strong rebuke. Captain Nelson 'ought to have submitted his doubts to the Commander-in-Chief on the station', he was told, 'instead of having taken upon himself to controll the exercise of the functions of his Appointment'.[23]

There was worse trouble soon to come. Sir Richard, badgered by West Indian merchants, planters and officials of the Custom House, had been prevailed upon to waive the enforcement of the Navigation Acts which, originally designed to protect English shipping and increase revenues from colonial trade, had proved largely unworkable even before the American War of Independence. But Nelson refused to accept the view that the trade, much of it in the hands of Americans – once subjects of the King of England, now foreigners – could not reasonably be stopped and might just as well be tolerated. He condemned Sir Richard as 'the dupe of some artful people', insisted that the Commander-in-Chief had no right to waive laws which had not yet been repealed by Parliament. He contended that the laws were 'in the interests of Great Britain' and consequently must be enforced whatever the difficulties. 'The residents of these islands are Americans by connexion and interest and are inimical to Great Britain,' he declared. 'They are as great rebels as ever were in America.'[24] On St Kitts they had gone so far as to fly Irish flags on St Patrick's Day, a disgraceful celebration by 'these *vagabonds*', which had induced him to refuse an invitation from the President of the island.[25]

In company with his friend Cuthbert Collingwood, who had come out to the West Indies as captain of the *Mediator*, Nelson went to see the Commander-in-Chief. Admiral Hughes, anxious as usual to avoid any unpleasantness, hummed and hawed, agreed to look into the problem posed by American merchantmen, admitted that he was not at all sure what the Navigation Acts were all about. Nelson said that he thought this 'very odd' since 'every captain of a man-of-war was furnished with the Statutes of the Admiralty in which was the Navigation Act'. Eventually, under pressure, Sir Richard agreed that perhaps the law ought to be enforced; but then, his violin playing disturbed by angry representations from injured merchants, he changed his mind, and decreed that the 'residents of the various islands' should be allowed to 'decide the various cases' for themselves. He was, Nelson told Locker, 'led by the advice of the Islanders to admit the Yankees to a Trade; at least to wink at it'.[26]

Nelson would not accept this. He protested to Sir Richard; he protested on several occasions to the Admiralty; he protested to the government, assuring the Secretary of State that, although his name was 'probably unknown' to him, his 'character as a man' would, he trusted, 'bear the strictest investigation'.[27] He even protested to the King in a memorial which explained that the need for such an unconventional approach to his majesty was prompted by the fear that the point of principle he was maintaining might lead to his ruin.[28] He went to see the Governor, Sir Thomas Shirley, who patiently explained the difficulties. For example, he was told, American ships would put in at a port, swearing 'as the sea-phrase is "through a nine-inch plank" that their vessel leaked, or had [lost] a mast. Then the Customs grant a permit to land a part of their cargo to pay expenses, under which permits they land innumerable cargoes.'[29] Nelson was not impressed by these excuses and his importunity drove Sir Thomas to remark crossly that old generals such as himself 'were not in the habit of taking advice from young gentlemen'.[30]

'I have the honour, sir,' Captain Nelson riposted, 'of being as old as the Prime Minister of England, and think myself capable of commanding one of His Majesty's ships as that Minister is of governing the State.'[31]

Determined to show that he at least would do his duty by his country, and borne up, as he later self-righteously put it, by 'conscious rectitude', he took every opportunity he could to enforce the law; and on a cruise to St Kitts and Nevis he first of all forced several American merchant ships to turn back from their intended ports of call, then seized four others which disobeyed his orders to depart from Nevis roads. This was too much for the people of the island, whose livelihood was threatened. They collected money so that the owners of the ships could sue Nelson for assault and wrongful arrest, obliging him to stay on board the *Boreas* for almost two months for fear that he would be carried off to prison should he step ashore. A fellow officer, in expressing sympathy for Nelson in this plight, used the word 'pity', at which Nelson flared up and exclaimed, 'Pity, did you say? I shall live, Sir, to be envied! And to that point I shall always direct my course.'[32]

When news of Nelson's impending trial reached London it was decided there that the costs of his defence would have to be met by the Treasury. The ship that conveyed this welcome information also brought an unexpected letter congratulating Rear-Admiral Sir Richard Hughes and the officers under his command on their valuable service in enforcing compliance with the Navigation Acts, a letter which greatly annoyed Nelson, who felt, with justice, that the congratulations, if to be offered at all, were due to himself alone.[33]

By now Nelson had made himself *persona non grata* in almost every merchant's house in the Leeward Islands, even more so when his seizure of the American merchantmen was upheld in court. 'You will believe I am not very popular with the people,' he wrote to William Locker. 'They have never visited me, and I have not set foot in any house since I have been on the Station, and all for doing my duty by being *true to the interest of Great Britain*.'[34] Nor were his fellow officers, apart from Cuthbert Collingwood and Collingwood's younger brother, Wilfred, much comfort to him. They were, in general, 'a sad set' of 'geese' who accepted the impossibility of enforcing the Navigation Acts. Even Charles Sandys, of whom he had been fond in the past, was no sort of companion now, having taken to the bottle, going through 'a regular course of claret every day', and having fallen in love with a young woman in Antigua who repulsed his advances.[35] 'Were it not for Mrs Moutray, who is *very very* good to me,' he wrote, 'I should almost hang myself at this infernal hole.'[36]

6

The Island of Nevis

*I can't express what I feel for her and your good heart I am sure will
sympathize with mine.*

Mary Moutray was the young wife of the elderly Commissioner
with whom Nelson had crossed swords over the hoisting of the ill-
authorized pennant. She was pretty, amusing and *simpatica*; and
both Cuthbert Collingwood and Nelson were soon in love with
her. She seemed to prefer Collingwood, who, reserved and diffident,
pedantic, even dour on first acquaintance, was a most attractive
companion to those whom he grew to know well. She allowed him
into her boudoir at Antigua where he helped her curl her hair; and
he stood beside her to turn over the sheets of music when she
played the piano. He became, in fact, as she put it herself, like 'a
beloved brother in our house'. Tall and strong, his long hair tied
behind the coat of his uniform in a queue, he was at this time far
more prepossessing than his friend. For Nelson, pale and thin, had
had to have his hair shaved off because his scalp itched unbearably
when in a malarial sweat. His head was consequently covered by
an incongruous and ill-fitting yellow wig.[1] Yet, while she mocked
the wig, Mrs Moutray welcomed its wearer as warmly as she did
Collingwood to her house on Antigua, where Nelson later decided
he had spent some of his 'happiest days in this world'. He dreaded
the day of Mrs Moutray's departure home with her ailing husband.
He knew he would miss her 'greviously'. She was 'quite a delight'
and made 'many an hour cheerful that without her would be dead
weight'. Her equal he had never seen 'in any country or in any
situation'; she was such a 'sweet, amiable friend', a '*treasure* of a
woman'. What an example of a female she was 'to take pattern'
from.[2] He took leave of her when the time came 'with a heavy
heart'; and after she had gone he climbed up the hill to look at the

house which she had graced and which looked so melancholy now that she had left it. Even 'the trees drooped their heads,' he told his brother William, 'and the tamarind tree died: – all was melancholy; the road is covered with thistles; let them grow. I shall never pull one of them up. By this time I hope she is safe in Old England. Heaven's choicest blessings go with her.'[3]

By then Nelson had made the acquaintance of another family whose hospitality was to prove a source of comfort to him after dear Mrs Moutray's departure. This was the household of John Richardson Herbert, President of the Council of the Island of Nevis, a very rich, very demanding and, according to Nelson, 'very proud' man, who lived in splendid style in a large colonnaded white house on the island, attended by numerous black slaves. His wife was dead; he had quarrelled with his only daughter over her choice of a husband; and so his house, Montpelier, was kept for him by a young widowed niece, Frances Nisbet, whom he treated and expected to behave as his own child. Various other nieces and the daughters of cousins were to be seen at Montpelier from time to time, most of them in search of husbands. At least one of these was delivered to the house by Captain Nelson, who admitted that such duties were confidently entrusted to him by parents and guardians, he 'being an old-fashioned fellow'.[4]

Another of these nieces reported to Mrs Nisbet, who was visiting friends in St Kitts at the time, the arrival at Montpelier of 'the little Captain of the *Boreas* of whom so much has been said':

He came up just before dinner much heated and was very silent yet seemed, according to the old adage, to think the more. He declined drinking any wine; but after dinner, when the President, as usual, gave the following toasts, 'the King', 'the Queen and Royal Family', and 'Lord Hood', this strange man regularly filled his glass, and observed that those were always bumper toasts with him; which having drank, he uniformly passed the bottle, and relapsed into his former taciturnity.

It was impossible, during this visit, for any of us to make out his real character; there was such a reserve and sternness in his behaviour, with occasional sallies, though very transient, of a superior mind. Being placed by him, I endeavoured to rouse his attention by showing him all the civilities in my power; but I drew out little more than 'Yes' and 'No'.

If you, Fanny, had been there, we think you would have made something of him; for you have been in the habit of attending to these odd sort of people.[5]

On a subsequent visit to Montpelier, Captain Nelson arrived so early in the morning that the only member of the family up and about was Mrs Nisbet's five-year-old son Josiah; and when Mr Herbert came downstairs to greet his guest he found him – 'this great little man of whom everyone is so afraid' – in the dining-room playing with the little boy under the table.[6] Upon meeting the boy's mother, he was thanked so charmingly that he was at once reminded of the former Commissioner's wife. 'Her manners are Mrs Moutray's,' he decided, and he could not have bestowed higher praise. Later he told Mrs Nisbet herself how strongly she resembled Mrs Moutray. 'A more amiable woman can hardly exist,' he said with tactless enthusiasm. 'I wish you knew her; your minds and manners are so congenial that you must have pleasure in the acquaintance.'[7]

Frances Nisbet, upon whom this unwelcome comparison was pressed, was then twenty-seven. Her father had been a judge on the island; her husband, the family's doctor, formerly an apothecary in Coventry, had suffered so severely from the tropical illnesses he had been called upon to treat that he had retired with his wife to England, where he had died. The widow returned to Nevis with her baby son to seek the protection of her uncle, who, although 'a man who must have his own way in everything', as Nelson discovered, had a kind and generous heart.

She acted the part of Mr Herbert's hostess with grace; she dressed elegantly; she spoke French well; she was a skilful needle-woman, a competent pianist and, while she could not be described as pretty, she had a pleasant expression and a skin so fair and so carefully protected from the West Indian sun that it looked as though she had never left England. Her 'Mental accomplishments' Nelson described as 'superior to most people of either sex'.[8] That she was not a very practical woman, he either did not notice or chose to ignore. It was not long before he decided he was in love again. He declared his high regard for Mrs Nisbet, spoke to her uncle, then wrote to her, misspelling her name:

My dear Mrs Nisbit,

To say how anxious I have been, and am, to receive a line from Mr Herbert, would be far beyond the descriptive powers of my pen. Most fervently do I hope his answer will be of such a tendency as to convey real pleasure, not only to myself, but also to you. For most sincerely do I love you, and I think that my affection is not only founded upon the principles of reason but also upon the basis of mutual attachment. Indeed, My charming Fanny, did [I] possess a Million, my greatest pride and pleasure would be to share it with you; and as to living in a Cottage with you, I should esteem it superior to living in a palace with any other I have yet met with.

My age is enough to make me seriously reflect upon what I have offered, and commonsense tells me what a Good choice I have made. The more I weigh you in my mind, the more reason I find to admire both your head and heart . . .

My temper you know as well as myself, for by longer acquaintance you will find I possess not the Art of concealing it. My situation and family I have not endeavoured to concial.*

Don't think me rude by this entering into a correspondence with you. [9]

To this letter he received no answer, so he wrote again: 'Do I ask too much when I venture to hope for a line? Otherwise I may suppose my letters may be looked on as troublesome.' Nor did he receive a very satisfactory reply from Mr Herbert; and when he did eventually hear from him, the letter was polite but did not

* Nelson's spelling was never very reliable, the manuscript of his letters often differing very considerably from the doctored versions as published. Indeed, as Captain Mahan remarked, 'being so young when [he first went to sea], he, in common with many of the most successful seamen of that day, got scanty schooling; nor did he, as some others did, by after application, remedy the eccentricities of style, and even of grammar, which are apt to result from such early neglect. His letters, vigorous and direct as they are, present neither the polished diction of Collingwood, nor the usual even correctness of St Vincent and Saumarez, but are, on the contrary, constantly disfigured by awkward expressions and bad English' (Mahan, i, 7).

contain any reference to the financial provisions which he hoped her uncle would make for his niece.

He knew him to be rich. To be sure his expenses 'must be great as his house [was] open to all strangers and he [entertained] most hospitably'. But his income was clearly 'immense'. 'Many estates in the island are mortgaged to him,' Nelson understood. 'The stock of Negroes upon his own estate and cattle are valued at 60,000l. sterling and he sends to England (average for 7 years) 500 casks of sugar . . . and as he says and told me at first, that he looked upon his niece as his child, I can have no reason to suppose that he will not provide handsomely for her.'[10]

Still, nothing definite had been said as yet; and when Nelson did manage to bring him to the point in rather a strained interview, Mr Herbert remained vague and noncommittal. Yes, his niece would be well provided for upon his death: she would have £20,000 or, if his estranged daughter died before him, even more, the major part of his property; but no, he could not do much for her in his lifetime, his expenses being so heavy. Perhaps he might be able to afford £200 or £300 a year. In any case, he could not really spare his niece until he retired and that would not be for about eighteen months.[11]

So it seemed that Nelson would have to provide money himself. 'I want some prize-money,' he told Collingwood; but, since this was hard to come by in peacetime, he approached his own uncle as he had done when he wanted to marry Miss Andrews, providing some unreliable information about his intended bride, whom he described as being five years younger than she really was:

I open for business which perhaps you will smile at, in the first instance, and say 'This Horatio is for ever in love.' . . . I have told [Mr Herbert] I am as poor as Job; but he tells me he likes me, and I am descended from a good family, which his Pride likes . . . Who can I apply to but you? . . . My future happiness, I give you my honour, is now in your power: if you cannot afford to give me anything for ever, you will, I am sure, trust to me, that if I can ever afford it, I will return it to some part of your family. I think Herbert will be brought to give her two or three hundred a year during his life; and if you will either *give me* . . . either one hundred a year, for a few years, or a thousand pounds, how happy you will make a couple who will pray for you for ever. Don't disappoint me or my heart will break.[12]

While enduring the long wait for a reply to this letter, Nelson returned to his duties; and found himself temporary commander of the Leeward Islands station after the return home of Sir Richard Hughes in the wake of his wife – to whom her husband had been unfaithful after her departure – and of his daughter, who had at last found a husband in the person of a Major John Browne of the 67th Regiment.

From Barbados, Dominica and Antigua, and the other places to which his duties took him, Nelson wrote a series of letters to Fanny Nisbet, telling her of his difficulties in finding her a hat she wanted for riding, of his success in obtaining a grey parrot, though not the red bird she had asked for, of the fearful row the piano tuner made while her instrument was being transported to St Kitts, complaining of loneliness, 'mosquitoes and melancholies', of a fever that rendered him almost delirious, assuring her of his high regard for her, of his doing his best for her sake to improve his strength by drinking beef tea and a pint of goat's milk every morning, his desire to return to her as soon as he could:

My greatest wish is to be united to you; and the foundation of all conjugal happiness, real love and esteem, is, I trust, what I possess in the strongest degree towards you . . . I daily thank God, who ordained that I should be attached to you. He has, I firmly believe, intended it as a blessing to me . . . It must be real affection that brings us together, not interest or compulsion, which makes so many unhappy.[13]

'Had I taken your advice and not seized any Americans, I should now have been with you,' he wrote in one rather self-righteous letter. 'But I should have neglected my duty, which I think your regard for me is too great for you to have wished me to have done. Duty is the great business of a Sea-officer. All private considerations must give way to it, however painful it is.'[14]

In another letter, which she must have been rather put out to receive, she was informed of Nelson's distress at hearing of the death of dear Mrs Moutray's husband and of the Admiralty's refusal of a pension for her: 'I can't express what I feel for her and your good heart I am sure will sympathize with mine. What is so truly affecting as a virtuous woman in distress? But if partaking in grief is an alleviation of the sufferings of that all-amiable woman, she has many sharers. When you know her, you must love her.'[15]

Another tactless letter followed when Prince William returned to the West Indies in command of the frigate *Pegasus*. 'His Royal Highness often tells me he believes I am married,' Nelson wrote, 'for he never saw a lover so easy, or say so little of the object he has regard for. When I tell him I certainly am not, he says, "Then he is sure I must have a great esteem for you, and that it is (vulgarly), I do not much like the use of that word, called love". He is right: my love is founded on esteem.'[16]

Nelson went on to recount the Prince's free and easy ways with the young ladies of Dominica and the mortification of the older ones because of his refusal to dance with them. Although he had 'not more than twice or thrice' been to bed himself before morning, he was 'reconciled to the business of attending upon his Royal Highness' because he 'really loved to honour the Prince'. Honour him as he did as a member of the royal family, however, Nelson could not deny that the young man, however reluctant he was to admit it, was often a fearful nuisance. There was, for instance, the affair of Isaac Schomberg, who, as an efficient and sensible if rather opinionated and self-important officer, had been placed aboard the *Pegasus* as first lieutenant with a view to ensuring that the unpredictable royal captain had at his side a reliable officer twelve years older than himself.

Schomberg, distantly related to the Graf von Schönberg, a German soldier of fortune who had settled in England a century or so before, was obviously not an admirer of Prince William, as Nelson professed to be; and certainly his opinion of the Prince was shared by the officers and crew of the *Pegasus*. Drinking too much, suffering from various unpleasant ailments, including gonorrhoea, worried about money and pursued by admonitory letters from his parents, Prince William was not at his best in command of the

Pegasus. He bothered the crew with endless petty orders, most of them unnecessary, some absurd, as, for instance: 'As it is the too frequent practice on board his Majesty's ships to make use of that horrid expression *Bugger*, so disgraceful to a British seaman, if any person shall be heard using this expression they may be assured they will be severely punished.' Severe punishments were undoubtedly inflicted. A sailor and a marine, for example, were flogged for hanging up their wet clothes to dry between decks.[17]

When Lieutenant Schomberg suggested that this punishment was unduly severe, he was curtly told not to give his 'sentiments unasked'; and when the first lieutenant later authorized the dispatch of a boat ashore without the captain's permission he was again reprimanded. Nettled beyond measure by this, Schomberg wrote to Captain Nelson demanding a court martial.

Unable to arrange a court martial because he did not have enough captains available, Nelson ordered Schomberg's arrest and issued an order forbidding officers to ask for court martials 'on a frivolous pretence'.[18] He might have had some sympathy for Schomberg, but he did not show it. To Captain Locker he wrote, 'His Royal Highness keeps up strict discipline in his Ship and, without paying him any compliment, she is one of the first ordered frigates I have seen. He has had more plague with his Officers than enough: his first Lieutenant will no doubt be broke. I have put him under Arrest.'[19]

Upon later consideration of the matter, Nelson decided that, perhaps, the Prince was equally to blame, and he wrote him a letter in which his anxiety not to give offence to a man whose patronage he was determined not to lose led him into the most extravagant unctuousness:

If to be truly great is to be truly good . . . it never was stronger verified in your Royal Highness in the instance of Mr Schomberg . . . Resentment I know your Royal Highness never had, or I am sure will ever bear any one: it is a passion incompatible with the character of a Man of Honour. Schomberg was too hasty certainly in writing his letter; but now you are parted, pardon me, my Prince, when I presume to recommend that Schomberg may stand in your Royal Favour. There only wants this to place your character in the highest point of view. None of us are without failings: Schomberg's was being rather too hasty; but that, put in competition with his being a good Officer, will not, I am bold to say, be taken in the scale against him . . . Princes seldom, very seldom, find a disinterested person to communicate their thoughts to. I do not pretend to be otherwise: but . . . I am interested only that your Royal Highness should be the greatest and best man this Country ever produced.[20]

The Prince, ignoring the compliments in the letter, responded huffily to the suggestion that he should forgive so disrespectful an officer. He never had done so, and never would do so – 'particularly Schomberg'. 'In my own ship I go on pretty well,' he ended his letter. 'I have had two court-martials, one on the master-at-arms, who was broke and received a hundred lashes, and the other on a seaman who received fifty lashes.'[21] He even ordered the flogging of a German artist, who had come aboard the *Pegasus* to paint tropical scenes and had given offence in some way; and he would have liked to order the flogging of various officers in his ship who showed their sympathy for Schomberg by visiting him in his cabin. One of them, Lieutenant William Hope, was sent home in disgrace without the certificate of service which he would have to produce before he was paid.[22]

Eventually, it was decided that Schomberg should be sent home, too, without a court martial, provided he apologized for his misconduct. The first lieutenant agreed to this; but the affair could not yet be forgotten.

Upon arriving home the miscreant was immediately appointed first lieutenant on Lord Hood's flagship, the *Barfleur*. Prince William was outraged, and wrote the Admiral a letter so impertinent that he might well have been considered to deserve a court martial himself:

I want words to express my feelings on this subject . . . There is nothing I feel so sensibly as an attack on my professional conduct, under which I now labour by your Lordship's support of Schomberg and Lord Howe's [First Lord of the Admiralty's] disapproving of my conduct about Mr Hope. Much as I love and honour the Navy, yet, my Lord, I shall beyond doubt resign if I have not a satisfactory explanation from both your noble Lordships.[23]

Nelson at least was on Prince William's side. 'He wrote Lord Hood what I cannot but approve,' he commented, expressing an opinion which induced the Prince to comment that, 'though a young man', Captain Nelson had a 'sound judgement'.

So the two men remained close; and when he heard that Nelson was intent upon marrying Mrs Nisbet, the Prince insisted upon being present, though when that might be he could not say. 'So much,' Nelson commented in a letter to his intended bride, 'for marrying a sailor!' However, he did want the Prince to be there. It would, indeed, be a 'mark of honour' to himself, Nelson told Mrs Nisbet, and as such he wished to receive it. 'Indeed, his Royal Highness's behaviour throughout has been that of a friend, instead of a person so elevated above me,' he continued. 'His Royal Highness has not yet been in a private house to visit, and is determined never to do it, except in this instance. You know I will ever strive to bear such a character, as may render it no discredit to any man ... to take notice of me. There is no action in my whole life, but what is honourable.'[24]

The marriage took place at John Herbert's house, Montpelier, on 11 March 1787, the best man being Lieutenant Digby Dent of the *Boreas*.[25] It was a pleasant occasion, carried off without mishap, the Prince making a jocular speech of, for once, not too unsuitable a length, congratulating his friend on having succeeded in carrying off 'the principal favourite of the island'.[26] Some other of Nelson's officers, however, were apprehensive about Nelson's choice. One was told that the bride was remarkable for two things only, her marvellous complexion and 'a remarkable absence of intellectual endowment'.[27] Another officer, Captain Thomas Pringle, with whom Nelson had sailed to America from Cork five years before, lamented, 'The Navy, Sir, [has now] lost one of its greatest ornaments ... It is a national loss that such an officer should marry. Had it not been for that circumstance, I foresaw Nelson would become the greatest man in the Service.'[28]

7
Norfolk

Not being a man of fortune is a crime which I cannot get over, and therefore none of the Great care about me.

The last of Nelson's days in command of the *Boreas* were so unpleasant and unrewarding that they might well have induced a less dedicated officer to settle down to married life on half pay without undue regret. First there was the problem posed by two merchants who produced detailed and damning evidence of the corrupt practices of certain government officials in the Leeward Islands. These officials approached Prince William with their complaints; he, in turn, handed the matter over to Nelson, who threw himself into the investigation of their claims with as much · assiduous industry as he had shown in his determination to implement the Navigation Acts. Convinced that the merchants' accusations of fraud within the customs service and naval department were well justified, Nelson bombarded government ministers and officials, from the Prime Minister downwards, with letters urging minute investigation of the charges, making himself as unpopular in Whitehall as he had been at the time of his relentless pursuit of American merchantmen. After many months of inconclusive correspondence, the Master General of the Ordnance wrote to Captain Nelson, 'With respect to yourself, I can only renew the assurances of my perfect conviction of the zeal for His Majesty's Service which has induced you to stir in this business.' For the immediate future, however, he was made to feel that such zeal was not necessarily a quality likely to endear him to the government in general and the Lords of the Admiralty in particular.[1]

Then there arose the case of an able seaman who had deserted Wilfred Collingwood's ship, the *Rattler*. Nelson, as president of the court, was obliged to condemn the man to death. Asked to grant a reprieve, he acceded to the request and took it upon himself to discharge the man from custody. Censured by the Admiralty for exceeding his responsibility, he defended his action, for which he was censured again, but not before he had displayed his determination to maintain discipline in his own ship by having three men flogged with a dozen lashes for drunkenness. Some weeks later Nelson – who had recently admitted to being 'very strict in his ship' and, as he got older, would 'probably become more so' – ordered eight other men to be flogged, three for 'using mutinous language' to their officers, five for 'disobedience and neglect of duty'. When the ship was at last paid off in November 1787 after a long delay occasioned by the threat of renewed war with France, the crew thankfully went their separate ways home, declining to offer to serve under their captain again as the whole company of the *Albemarle* had done at Portsmouth in 1783.[2]

Nelson was ill again on the voyage home, so ill, indeed, a midshipman recorded, that 'it was not expected he could live to reach England, and he had a puncheon of rum for his body in case he should die during the voyage'.[3]

He recovered his strength during the voyage; but on reaching England, so he reported, 'the rain and cold at first gave me a sore throat and its accompaniments: the hot weather has [since] given me a slow fever, not absolutely bad enough to keep my bed, yet enough to hinder me from doing anything; and I could not have wrote a letter for the world ... It is not kind in one's Native air to treat a poor wanderer as it has done me since my arrival.'[4]

His wife, too, had been ill. She had sailed to England with her uncle, John Herbert, in a comfortable West Indiaman; but she could not immediately join her husband, who had been ordered to the Nore to take aboard men pressed into the service, and was feeling in 'poor spirits'. 'The lot of a sailor's wife,' she decided, was hard indeed.[5]

By the end of the year, however, Nelson at least was feeling better and more cheerful, 'fit for any quarter of the Globe'. The threat of war had receded and he was able to turn his attention to disposing of the cargo he had brought back from the West Indies with him, writing quite shamelessly of his intention to smuggle goods into the country to avoid the high duties demanded by the Custom House, despite the rigour with which he had enforced the Navigation Acts on the far side of the Atlantic. 'Tamarinds and noyeau [noyau, a liqueur of brandy flavoured with fruit kernels] I must get smuggled, for duty on the former is so enormous that no person can afford the expense.'[6] He had brought home hogsheads of wine and casks of nuts, a sixty-gallon barrel of rum and box after box of dried and crystallized fruits. He sent generous presents of these to, among others, Captain Locker, who acknowledged them with the blunt comment that the wine, which included half a hogshead of Madeira, was not much good. Nelson replied that he was sorry for that: he had paid 'the best' price for it.[7]

Together at last, Nelson and his wife spent Christmas that year in the house which John Herbert had taken at 5 Cavendish Square. Soon after the Christmas holidays they took lodgings near by, on the other side of Oxford Street, first at 10 Great Marlborough Street, then at 6 Princes Street. They did not feel at home in either place. While Mrs Nelson was feeling unwell again, and complaining that the smoke of London was affecting her lungs, her husband was becoming aware that his zeal over the Navigation Acts, not to mention the fuss he had created over the accusations of fraud against the Customs in the West Indies, had led to his being regarded as undesirably officious by certain senior officers at the Admiralty. It seemed to him a token of their displeasure that not one of the temporary appointments he had made while in acting command of the Leeward Islands station had been confirmed.

His time in London was taken up not only with meetings in lawyers' offices over the litigation consequent upon his strict interpretation of the Navigation Acts but also with the case of the *Boreas*'s cooper, who had cut the throat of a prostitute in a Shadwell tavern. The defence had decided to enter a plea of insanity and had asked his former captain to speak on the man's behalf. Nelson readily agreed, and in doing so was as frank about himself as about the accused. 'That man,' he declared, 'appeared melancholy at times, but the quietest, soberest man that I ever saw in my life . . . When I heard of this affair I said, if it is true, he must be insane for I should as soon suspect myself, and sooner, because I know I am hasty; he is so quiet a man, and never committed a fault during the time I knew him . . . Seamen, I know perfectly, when they come home the landlords will furnish them with raw liquors. I saw myself thirty or forty from that ship that were as mad as if they were at Bedlam, and did not know what they did . . . [The accused] is not a drunkard by any means . . . At the island of Antigua, I think it was, he was struck with the sun, after which times he appeared melancholy. I myself have been struck in the brain, so that I was out of my senses.'

'Is he a man, from your knowledge of him, likely to commit a deliberate foul murder?' Nelson was asked.

'I should as soon suspect myself, because I am hasty, he is not.'

Largely as a result of this evidence, the man was declared guilty but insane, and spared the gallows.[8]

Satisfied as he had a right to feel for helping to save the cooper's life, Nelson could take no comfort from the progress of his own career. Twice he called at the Admiralty to see the First Lord in the hope of recouping the expenses he had incurred in investigating the accusations of fraud, and twice Lord Howe had been too busy to see him. He had to content himself with writing a plaintive letter in which he assured Lord Howe, 'My zeal for His Majesty's Service is as great as I once flattered myself your Lordship thought it.'[9] To Hercules Ross, the Scottish sugar planter whom he had met in Jamaica, he confided that, provided a man followed 'a uniform conduct of honour and integrity', he seldom failed in reaching 'the goal of Fame at last'. Posterity would do him justice, even though he had served 'an ungrateful Country'.[10]

Fanny Nelson felt unwanted also. Her uncle had not been as generous as she and her husband had hoped; he had agreed to make her an annual allowance of £100; but no capital sum was forthcoming and this £100 and the £100 a year which Nelson received from his own uncle – though the equivalent of about £12,000 in present-day terms – were not very satisfactory additions to Nelson's half pay of eight shillings a day. Mrs Nelson, therefore, considered ways in which she herself might add to their joint income; and, in hopes of improving their social as well as financial position, she asked her husband to approach his friend, Prince William, with whom he had recently celebrated the return to England of his ship, the *Pegasus*. Nelson accordingly addressed a letter to his royal highness:

There may be a thing, perhaps, within reach of your Royal Highness; therefore, trusting to your goodness, I shall mention it. The Princess Royal must very soon have a Household appointed her. I believe a word from your Royal Highness would obtain a promise of a situation in her Royal Highness's Establishment not unbecoming the wife of a Captain in the Navy; but I have only ventured to say this much and leave the issue to your better judgement.[11]

Nelson was no more successful in this application to Prince William than in his attempts to see Lord Howe.

By now he and his wife had left London. First they had gone to Bath, where Mrs Nelson took a course of the waters. From Bath they had gone on to stay with one of her aunts near Bristol, then to Exmouth in Devon, and, finally to Norfolk where Nelson's father had been extremely nervous about receiving them. He was sure Fanny would find the East Anglian weather insupportable after the balmy climate of Nevis and would be disconcerted to see 'rivers represented by a puddle, mountains by anthills, woods by bramble bushes'. She was probably a 'fine' lady who would want to bring her maid, and this maid would surely not get on with his own servants. 'To say the truth, I am not now anxious to see them,' he confided in his daughter Kate.

This for a day or two I should be glad of, but to introduce a stranger to an infirm and whimsical old man, who can neither eat nor drink, nor talk, nor see, is as well let alone ... I have requested [Horatio] not to think of bringing his lady and suite to Burnham till his other visits are at an end. Indeed, I am in no haste to see and receive a stranger; perhaps you may introduce her by and by. I believe she will form a valuable part of our family connections and certain it is that he has a claim to all my affection, having never transgressed. But every power of mine is in decay.[12]

His father evidently being so anxious about receiving his new daughter-in-law, Nelson decided to introduce her into the family circle by degrees. He took her first to visit his elder sister, Mrs Bolton, who had left Wells-next-the-Sea and was now living at Cranwich, near Hilborough; they then went to stay with Kate, now married to George Matcham, who, having made money in the service of the East India Company and having travelled widely in the East and the Levant, had settled down to the life of a country gentleman at Barton Hall. And then, in December 1788, the long-postponed visit to the parsonage at Burnham Thorpe was arranged.

The old parson got on with his daughter-in-law much better than he had expected. To be sure, she seemed sometimes rather fractious about her health and the coldness of the house in the bleak Norfolk winter, and about the lack of any social life, but she did not 'openly complain'. All the same, he wished he could find her some 'amusement', he told Kate, 'a little society and an instrument with which she could pass away an hour. Her musical powers I fancy are above the Common sort ... Her attention to me demands my esteem, and to her Good Husband she is all he can expect.'[13]

His guests had not planned a long visit: they had thought of going on to France, where Horatio intended to master French at a second attempt. But when it was suggested that they made their home at Burnham Thorpe until Horatio could find employment, Nelson agreed to stay in England, his 'Dear Little Island'.[14] It was a decision which Mrs Nelson came to regret. That winter was particularly severe; and the house, virtually cut off from the outside world – 'clothed with frosted robes', as the parson put it, 'powdered with snow, all trimmed in glittering icicles' – was so bitterly cold that the shivering bride took 'large doses of the bed' rather than endure the draughts that blew around her feet on the stone-flagged floors. 'She finds herself only comfortable when enclosed in moreen [stout material commonly used for curtains],' her father-in-law commented. 'Myself, more accustomed to the climate, give no heed to small inconveniences.' 'The severe season has affected both your brother and his lady,' the rector continued in a letter to Kate. 'They are moving just out of the bedchamber but both are brought to acknowledge that they never felt so cold a place.'[15]

When they could bring themselves to sit in the parlour of an evening she occupied herself with needlework, painting water-colours and playing games with her son, Josiah, home for the holidays from the boarding school at which he had been placed. Her husband studied his nautical charts, pored over his favourite books, including the accounts of the voyages and adventures of the buccaneer William Dampier, wrote letters to the Admiralty and glanced through the local newspapers, the *Norfolk News* and the *Norfolk Chronicle*, reading extracts to his father, whose eyes at the age of seventy-six could no longer make out the print but were not permitted the aid of spectacles, since failing sight was to be accepted as a punishment from on high.

From time to time Captain Nelson was called to London upon some tiresome legal business connected with the still-continuing action brought against him by the Americans whose ships he had seized; and one day, while he was out buying a pony at a local fair, there arrived at Burnham Thorpe two importunate men 'in appearance resembling Bow-Street officers'. They demanded to know whether or not Mrs Nelson was the wife of Captain Horatio Nelson, and handed her a document, which they told her to give to her husband, informing him that an action was being brought against him in the sum of £20,000.

When Nelson arrived home he was little troubled by the threat of legal action since the government had undertaken to support him; but he was infuriated by the insult offered to 'the lady of a Sea-Officer in His Majesty's Service'. 'This affront I did not deserve,' he wrote angrily to the Admiralty, sending their Lordships a copy of the document that had been pressed upon his wife.[16] In his anger, he declared that he would quit England altogether; he would enter the Russian service; he would even go to live in France, much as he hated 'their country and their manners'.[17]

Calmer when summer came, he threw himself into work on his father's glebe farm and in the garden. It had originally been George Matcham's idea that the parsonage garden should be improved by the creation of a small lake, the digging of a ha-ha and the planting of a rose garden, for which he promised to supply the bushes; and Matcham himself, 'Capability M' as his father-in-law called him, had begun the work with the help of one of his own servants. Now, the 'very energetic Captain' took up the work with a will, digging as though 'it were for the purpose of being wearied', suffering twinges of rheumatism in his shoulder, returning to the house with his dog, a pointer he had bought to save it from starvation, and then riding out on his pony to supervise the parson's farmland.[18]

The parson himself had moved out of the house to a small cottage in Burnham Ulph, one of the other parishes for which he was responsible. '*My town residence,*' as he called his new home in a letter to Kate, 'promises all that could be looked for. It is near my Chapell of Ease, warm and in the vicinity of what is usefull in food, clothing and physick, and most likely by and by, a little Social chatt may take place.'[19]

He left behind in the more remote parsonage at Burnham Thorpe not only his eldest son, and the captain, and his wife, but also his fourth son, Edmund, who had come home from the Boltons' counting-house in Ostend and was feared to be dying. Fanny Nelson did what she could for him; but he seemed to have lost interest in life and preferred to rely for such comfort as could be provided for him upon Dame Smith, the village nurse. Fanny herself was not well. She had trouble with her throat and with her chest; she suffered from rheumatism and bouts of nervous debility. Her father-in-law still worried about her. 'I wish [Burnham Thorpe] was a little better accommodated to Mrs N,' he wrote to Kate. '[She] is a woman who would sometimes choose a little variety.' As it was, 'her tryall was not a light one'.[20]

From time to time her husband took her out bird-nesting; but she was not really interested in English country pursuits. Nor, indeed, was her husband. He had once enjoyed coursing hares, but too often returned with a wet coat and consequently caught a cold; and he had never much taken to shooting.[21] Occasionally he organized a rough shoot for some of the male members of the family; but his brother-in-law, Tom Bolton, bagged most of the game, while his brother, the parson, William, threatened the birds and rabbits in his loud voice more often than he took aim at them. He himself, 'once shot a partridge', so it was said, 'but his habit of carrying his gun at full cock, as if he were going to board an enemy [ship], and firing as soon as a bird rose without bringing the piece to his shoulder, made him a dangerous companion'.*[22] 'It is not, therefore, extraordinary that his having once shot a partridge should be remembered by the family among the remarkable events of his life.'[23]

The weeks passed, the months, the years. In France the Bastille was stormed on 14 July 1789; in June 1791 King Louis XVI attempted to leave the country but was brought back to Paris a prisoner; and on 20 September 1792 at Valmy a well-trained Prussian army faltered, halted and turned aside, demoralized before the massed forces of the Revolution. 'On this day, at this place,' said Goethe, 'a new era opens in the history of the world.'

In Norfolk, Nelson went regularly down to Burnham Market and waited in the inn there for the *Norfolk Chronicle* to come in from Norwich; and 'he would ride over the low chalk hill to Burnham Overy Staithe and along the embankment which separated the creek from the meadows that had been reclaimed from the salt marshes; there, sheltered from the wind, he could read and think, while an occasional sail, passing to or from the sea, would sharpen his awareness of what he was missing'.[24]

The reports of discontent and political agitation in the country, particularly in Norfolk, distressed him deeply. Members of radical societies were going from alehouse to alehouse disseminating revolutionary ideas and 'advising the poor people to pay no taxes, etc.' He wrote to Prince William, now Duke of Clarence, to tell him about a clergyman, Joseph Priestley, a known supporter of the principles of the French Revolution, who had been propagating such ideas in Norfolk. He had asked a justice of the peace why, as the conduct of such a man as Priestley was known, he was not

---

* Nelson was, of course, an even more dangerous shooting companion after he had lost his right arm and had badly impaired his sight. He shot fairly often at Holkham but had little success (Holkham Game Book, 1793–8, Coke Papers, Holkham Hall).

arrested. And he had received the reply that 'no Justice would render himself unpopular at this time, by being singular: for that his life and property were gone, if the mob arose'.

Nelson added in his letter to the Duke that it was no wonder that the poor labourers should have been 'seduced by promises and hopes of better times', for they were 'really in want of everything to make life comfortable'. He set out an 'account of the earnings and expenses of a labourer in Norfolk with a wife and three children' which made pathetic reading and showed that their wages allowed for 'not quite twopence a day for each person; and to drink nothing but water, for beer our poor labourers never taste, unless they are tempted, which is too often the case, to go to the Alehouse'. Admittedly their wages had been raised recently, but had the 'Country Gentlemen' seen to it that this had been done earlier, the labourers would not have been so discontented, 'for a want of loyalty is not among their faults'.[25]

While concerning himself with the plight of labourers, Nelson wrote regularly to London to remind the Admiralty of his existence and of his eagerness to find employment. He sent a letter to his old friend, 'Billy Blue' Cornwallis, who had been promoted commodore and was rumoured to be taking a convoy to the East Indies. He told him that, although by now 'happily married' and 'set down in a country life', he was ready to serve at a moment's notice. He received no immediate reply, so, before the week was out, he wrote again: he was 'as happy in domestic life as a person can be'; but he was really anxious to serve under Cornwallis and 'for our Country'. Cornwallis could not help him: nothing would please him more than to have Nelson with him, but he had all the officers he needed already; if more ships came under his command 'nothing would give him greater pleasure than to have the happiness of seeing him in one of them'.[26]

Nelson had already written to Lord Hood on reading in the paper that a new Board of Admiralty had been appointed in Pitt's administration and that Admiral Hood was to be a Lord Commissioner under the Prime Minister's elder brother, the Earl of Chatham, who was to be First Lord of the Admiralty in succession to Lord Howe. He followed up his letter with a visit to London to seek an interview with Hood at the Admiralty. 'I saw Lord Hood this morning,' he reported to his wife. 'He made many enquiries after you and was very civil. He assured me that a ship in peacetime was not desirable; but that should any hostilities take place, I need not fear having a good ship.'[27]

Yet when hostilities did threaten, when it seemed probable that war would break out with Spain over disputed trading rights, and there were reports of ships being commissioned and officers recalled, Nelson, who had immediately taken a coach to London, was rebuffed, though it seemed to him that the 'whole Service' was being 'called forth'. He asked for an interview with the First Lord: Lord Chatham was too busy to see him. He called at No.12 Wimpole Street and asked to see Lord Hood: Lord Hood admitted him but bluntly told him something which was 'never to be effaced from [his] memory viz that the King was impressed with an unfavourable opinion' of Captain Nelson.[28]

Nelson could not but suppose that he was being blamed by the King for the ill behaviour and peccadilloes of his erstwhile charge, Prince William, just as he was blamed elsewhere for his excessively vigorous implementation of the Navigation Acts and his vexatious stirring of hornets' nests in government departments. Nelson was far too dedicated a royalist to blame the King himself. 'Neither at sea or on shore,' he declared, 'can my attachment to my King be shaken. That will never end but with my life.' Yet he was convinced that there must surely be a prejudice at court and at the Admiralty against him, though he could 'not in the least account for it'.[29]

He felt sure that, had he been a man of influence and fortune, the case might well have been different. 'Not being a man of fortune,' he complained to Captain Locker, 'is a crime which I cannot get over, and therefore none of the Great care about me.'[30]

'I am sensible I have no great interest to recommend me,' he wrote in yet another letter to the First Lord of the Admiralty, 'nor have I had conspicuous opportunities of distinguishing myself but ... I can say that I have ever been a zealous Officer.' The Duke of Clarence was also the recipient of numerous communications, in one of which Nelson regretted that he could not find words to express the mortification which he felt at his 'not being appointed to a Ship' and in another, evidently written merely to ensure that the duke would not forget him, he said how sorry he was to read in the newspapers – his only means of information in the 'retired situation' in which he was placed – that his royal highness had been prevented from attending the court at Windsor on the Prince of Wales's birthday.[31]

His own relations were of little help. His uncle, William Suckling, did admittedly write to Charles Jenkinson, now Lord Hawkesbury, and soon to be created Earl of Liverpool, on his behalf. But his godfather, Lord Walpole of Wolterton, a very boring man married to a very boring wife, the Duke of Devonshire's daughter was of no use at all. It had to be conceded that the Walpoles were hospitable: they had Captain Nelson and his wife to stay every year, much to the satisfaction of the Captain's father, who begged Kate to find her sister-in-law a 'handsome bonnet such as she may wear at Wolterton if need be, or what you yourself buy for dining, visits etc.' 'Send it down,' he wrote to her, 'and if any covering for the neck by way of a cloak is needful, add that also. Place them on my account.'[32] Lord Walpole, though, was a cipher; and, had he troubled himself on his godson's account, it was doubtful that much notice would have been taken of his recommendation. More notice would have been taken of the recommendation of his kinsman, George, third Earl of Orford, at whose death in 1791 Captain and Mrs Nelson donned mourning, though they had not once been asked to his nearby house. But Lord Orford had never taken much interest in the fortunes of so distant a relation.

Another Norfolk magnate had proved equally unhelpful. This was Thomas Coke of Holkham Hall, the immensely rich nephew of the Earl of Leicester and one day to be created Earl of Leicester himself. Nelson had been to Holkham to see Coke as a local magistrate, to get papers signed concerning his pay. He strongly disapproved of the man's Whig politics, his declared support for the American rebels in the recent war and his sympathetic attitude towards the French Revolution; but he would have readily accepted his patronage had it been offered him. It was not offered him. Coke was perfectly polite; but it was clear enough that he would not go out of his way to exercise his influence on his behalf.

Upon subsequently receiving an invitation to a Whig fête at Holkham Hall, Nelson, who had already declined an invitation to a ball, sent this curt reply in his wife's handwriting: 'Captain Nelson's compliments to Mr and Mrs Coke and is sorry it is not in his power to accept their invitation.'*[33]

He returned dispiritedly to his letter writing. 'If your Lordships should be pleased to appoint me to a *cockle-boat* I should be grateful,' ran one almost despairing letter to the Admiralty, which ended, 'I can hardly expect any answer.' Another letter, verging on self-pity, concluded, '. . . which has always been the way I have been treated'. He travelled up to London when he could, never seeking an interview with Lord Hood since that painful, unforgettable rebuff, but always leaving a card at his house in Wimpole Street. Every spring, too, he attended the royal levee. 'It must,' he believed, 'one day come to account.'

Then, one day in December 1792, there arrived at Burnham Thorpe a letter from the Secretary to the Admiralty which, while not immediately encouraging, gave grounds for hope that something might at last be done for him: 'Sir, I have received your letter of the 5th instant, expressing your readiness to serve, and I have read the same to my Lords Commissioners of the Admiralty.'[34]

* Relations between Nelson and the Cokes had evidently improved by 1791 when the Cokes paid a visit to Burnham Thorpe. Certainly by 1797 Nelson was accepting presents of game from Holkham Hall – on one occasion '6 partridges, 2 pheasants and 1 Hare' (Holkham Hall Game Book, 1793–8, Coke Papers, Holkham Hall).

8

The Mediterranean

*I am, now, only a captain; but I will, if I live, be at
the top of the tree.*

As soon as the Christmas holidays were over, Nelson set off for
London and on 7 January 1793 he could write to his wife:

Post nubila Phaebus: After clouds comes sunshine. The Admiralty so smile
upon me that really I am as much surprised as when they frowned. Lord
Chatham yesterday made many apologies for not having given me a Ship
before this time and said that, if I chose to take a Sixty-four to begin
with, I should be appointed to one as soon as she was ready; and,
whenever it was in his power, I should be removed into a Seventy-four
... Everything indicates War. One of our Ships, looking into Brest, has
been fired into: the shot is now at the Admiralty. You will send my father
this news, which I am sure will please him.[1]

Upon his return to Norfolk, Nelson learned of the execution of
King Louis XVI in Paris and that, according to the *Norfolk Chronicle*,
war seemed 'more certain than ever'. He also learned that he was to
be given command of the *Agamemnon*, said to be 'one of the finest
Sixty-fours in the service'. He enthusiastically set about recruiting a
crew, sending a lieutenant and four midshipmen to Norfolk's coastal
towns to enlist likely-looking volunteers. At the same time visitors
arrived at Burnham Thorpe, bringing boys anxious to go to sea with
Captain Nelson, including the sons of three Norfolk clergymen, one
of them William Bolton, son of the rector of Hollesby, his sister
Susannah's brother-in-law, another the delicate-looking William
Hoste, the twelve-year-old son of the Rev. Dixon Hoste, rector of
Godwick and Tittleshall, who had hopes that the boy might
eventually repair the family fortunes by winning prize-money.[2]

War was declared on 1 February; and that week, after giving a farewell party at the Plough Inn (now the Lord Nelson), Nelson left Burnham Thorpe for Chatham, taking with him a young man from the village to replace the servant, Frank Lepée, also a Norfolk man, who had been with him in the Americas and whom Nelson had had to dismiss for persistent drunkenness. This new servant, or 'wally-de-sham', as he chose to call himself, was Tom Allen, an illiterate, presumptuous and dogmatic youth, black-haired and stocky, who was to care for his master, in sickness and in health, in the manner of a managing nursemaid at once proud of her charge's attainments and impatient with his weaknesses, failings and disobedience. On occasions, Allen tried Nelson's patience sorely, and once, when the man had contrived to lose a case containing all his master's papers and £200, Nelson burst out angrily, 'What a beast he is! . . . He is such a notorious liar that he never says the truth – no, such is his delight in lying that even to do himself good he cannot resist the pleasure he has in telling a lie . . . He will one day ruin me by his ignorance, obstinacy and lies.'[3]

Nelson was frequently having to make excuses for the man's presumptuous behaviour. A midshipman, invited to dine at Nelson's table, recorded how the 'clumsy, ill-formed and vulgar' Allen had breezily asked one of his master's other guests, 'the captain of a dashing frigate, not noted for thinking small beer of himself', how a friend of his serving in the frigate was getting along.

The captain dropped his knife and fork, and raised his eye-glass with a stare of astonishment at honest Tom, who, nothing daunted, repeated the question. Lord Nelson's indignation now found vent in words.

'Quit the cabin, Thomas Allen! – I really must get rid of that impudent lubber. I have often threatened, but somehow he contrives to defeat my firm intentions, – he is faithful and attached, with great shrewdness mixed with his simplicity ... I mention these things, Captain Coffield, in palliation of his freedom, and shall be glad to take wine with you.'

The captain lowered his eye-glass, and raised his wine-glass, while he bowed to the sunny smile that oftimes irradiated the melancholy and rather homely visage of Lord Nelson.

Allen soon returned to the cabin not in the least abashed by his rebuke.[4]

Nelson also took with him in the *Agamemnon* his thirteen-year-old stepson, Josiah, much to the distress of the boy's mother, who could not contain her tears. 'Poor Mrs Nelson has, indeed, a severe trial,' commented her father-in-law.

She will be here and in the Parsonage a week or two, then makes a visit to [the Rev. William Nelson's Rectory at] Hilborough and looks out for a comfortable lodgings in Swaffham where she means to reside ... She will, I hope, bear up with a degree of cheerfullness at the separation from so Kind a Husband, and my own loss of the constant friendly and filiall regard I have experienced, I do feell.[5]

Her husband, in a very different mood from his wife's, climbed aboard the *Agamemnon*, happy and grateful beyond measure to be in command of a ship after over five years of seemingly interminable waiting. Contented as he was, he found Fanny's distress all the more exasperating, particularly so since she was showing herself to be inept as well as despondent. When they had been living together at Burnham Thorpe it had often been he rather than his wife who had attended to matters usually considered a woman's responsibility.

For instance, it was he who had dealt with the upholsterer when new loose covers were required for the sofa; it was he who wrote to complain when the cover of blue and white striped Manchester cotton which the upholsterer sent proved to be three inches too short and the wrong colour: 'Mrs Nelson requires a handsome, rich *blue* – but not dark.' Now Mrs Nelson herself was sending the wrong things, or not sending them at all, or not making sure they were properly packed. 'You forgot to send my things ...' he reproached her in one letter. 'I have got a keg of tongues, which I suppose you ordered, and also a trunk from Wells, Norfolk, and a hamper of three hams, a breast of bacon and a face, not very well packed, there being no straw between them, and the motion of the wagons here rubbed them very much. However, they will do.'[6]

He was impatient to set sail. But the *Agamemnon* was not ready yet; there were stores still to load. Seamen were still awaited; and, 'without a press', he had 'no idea' how the fleet could be manned.[7] The weeks passed; and it was not until after the middle of April

1. Horatio Nelson as an eighteen-year-old lieutenant. John Francis Rigaud began this portrait in 1777 and completed it three years later, portraying Nelson in post-captain's uniform with the fortress of San Juan, Nicaragua, in the background

2. The parsonage house at Burnham Thorpe, Norfolk, by Francis Pocock. Nelson lived here as a child. It has been suggested that he may be the small boy in the foreground waving a flag

3. The church of All Saints, Burnham Thorpe, where Nelson was baptized in 1758 by his father, the Rev. Edmund Nelson, rector of the parish. The painting (1840) is by M. E. Cotman, eldest son of John Sell Cotman

4. The Rev. Edmund Nelson (1722–1802) aged seventy-eight, by Sir William Beechey, who was persuaded to undertake the portrait by the rector's daughter-in-law, Fanny

5. A view of Greenwich in about 1760 by Thomas Priest, with the Royal Naval Hospital, designed by Wren and Hawksmoor, on the right

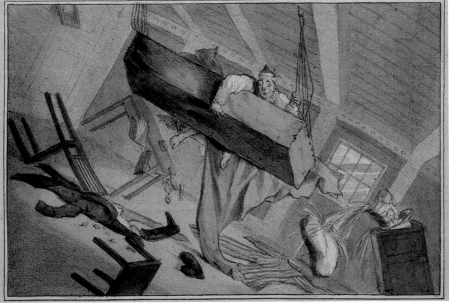

8. Robert Seymour's civilian passenger experiencing great difficulty in climbing into a cot of the standard type used by naval officers

6. (*opposite above*) Thomas Rowlandson's *Portsmouth Point* depicts the boisterous bustle outside the Ship Tavern. The crowds were so dense here when Nelson left England for Trafalgar that his barge was ordered to come to fetch him on the beach at Southsea

7. (*opposite*) Seamen carousing at their mess table on a gun deck by open ports

11. Frances Nisbet, the doctor's widow whom Nelson married on the West Indian island of Nevis in 1787

9. (*opposite above*) Richard Westall's painting of Midshipman Nelson's fight with the polar bear, whose skin he wanted to take home for his father

10. (*opposite*) Nicholas Pocock's painting of five of Nelson's ships, with sails loose for drying, at Spithead. From left to right they are: *Agamemnon, Vanguard, Elephant, Captain* and *Victory*

12. Angelica Kauffman's portrait of Ellis Cornelia Knight, the writer, whom Nelson met in Naples in 1793

13. A miniature of Lady Hamilton's mother, a blacksmith's widow, Mary Lyon, who preferred to be known as Mrs Cadogan

14. Sir William Hamilton, the connoisseur, collector and vulcanologist, who was British minister at the Neapolitan court from 1764 to 1800. A portrait by Charles Grignion, painted in about 1794

that the ship's sails were set and she left the Medway Estuary, Josiah Nisbet and his stepfather both seasick in a strong gale.

At two o'clock in the morning of 11 September 1793 the *Agamemnon* dropped anchor in the Bay of Naples. Nelson had been chosen to undertake an important mission to Ferdinand IV, the Bourbon King of Naples, whose realm, the largest in Italy, extended from the Papal States in the north to the southern coast of Sicily. He was to do all he could to ensure that the King and his managing wife, Maria Carolina, a sister of Queen Marie Antoinette of France and daughter of the Empress Maria Theresa, remained firm in their opposition to their common republican enemies in France and steadfast to the treaty between England and Naples which had been signed two months before.

The *Agamemnon* had not been long at anchor when a boat came alongside with a message to say that the King was on board his flagship and would like to see the English captain. Nelson climbed down into his barge and was rowed across to the royal ship. Smoke poured forth from Mount Vesuvius which, upon the *Agamemnon*'s arrival, had given an astonishingly splendid display of welcome, 'the lava spreading from the top', in the words of a delighted midshipman, 'and rolling down the mountain in great streaks of fire'.[8]

The city beneath this volcano, the most populous city on the continent of Europe after Paris, seemed more attractive at a distance than it did upon closer inspection. It swarmed with dirty life, with thousands of ragged fishermen and hawkers, porters and musicians, painted prostitutes and black-clothed clergy, with 'little brown children jumping about stark naked, the bigger ones dancing with castanets'. The poor lived cheek by jowl with the numerous nobility, whose grand and glittering apartments on the *piani nobili* of their *palazzi* were approached through narrow, squalid streets and by way of dark stairways from the often filthy lower floors. Children 'relieved themselves whenever they felt the urge' and 'even people in carriages often got out to mix with the pedestrians for the same purpose'.[9] Crowds of *lazzaroni* strolled through the streets, picking pockets when opportunity offered, poured into taverns from which they were thrown out into the streets, and walked down to the sea to take off what few clothes they wore and 'bathe themselves without ceremony', their behaviour tolerated because of their noisy loyalty to the King. They were, indeed, with the clergy, the Crown's principal allies in a state bent upon suppressing the aspirations of its intellectual and commercial classes.

Nelson discovered the King to be an ugly, ungainly man with an untrustworthy look in his protuberant eyes and a large, ill-shaped nose which was responsible for his nickname, *il Re Nasone*. Passionately devoted to hunting, or rather the slaughter of wild beasts, he also enjoyed fishing and, in shirt sleeves and apron, fried and sold the fish he caught in his own cook-shop, where he delighted in demonstrating his knowledge of the customs and language of the Neapolitan back streets. 'He rides and rows and hunts the wild boar [which he slaughtered from the safety of a sentry box],' reported Hester Piozzi, 'and catches fish in the bay and sells it . . . as dear as he can – but gives away the money . . . He dances with the girls, eats macaroni and helps himself to it with his fingers and rows against the watermen.'[10]

To Nelson he was friendly and welcoming. He said that he had already heard that the French port of Toulon – which the *Agamemnon* with Lord Hood's other ships had been sent to blockade – had been captured by the Spanish. Nelson hastened to correct him: Toulon, with over twenty French ships of the line, had surrendered to Lord Hood before the Spaniards had arrived. 'The King seemed surprised at this,' Nelson observed, 'but said he was glad to hear it.'

Encouraged by King Ferdinand's accommodating manner, Nelson now exceeded his instructions by telling him that the letters which he was to hand to the British envoy contained a request for the immediate dispatch of Neapolitan troops to Toulon to help the allied garrison of British, Spanish, Sardinian and French royalist troops defend it from the forces of the French republic. The King avoided comment on this request, contenting himself with some tactful remarks about the high regard in which the English were held in his country.

Having taken his leave of the King, Nelson went ashore and made his way to the Palazzo Sessa where Sir William Hamilton, the British envoy, had his large and amply furnished apartments.

Hamilton was then sixty-two years old, a man of distinguished appearance, tall, lean and sunburned, with 'a very aquiline' nose, in Sir Nathaniel Wraxall's description, and 'such an air of intelligence, blended with distinction in his countenance as powerfully attracted and conciliated all who approached him'.[11]

Collector, connoisseur and expert vulcanologist, he had made numerous and sometimes dangerous ascents of Vesuvius to observe at close quarters the phenomena of its eruptions. The son of Lord Archibald Hamilton and grandson of the third Duke of Hamilton, he had served for some years as an officer in the Third Foot Guards and for a shorter time was Member of Parliament for Midhurst. In 1758 he had married without enthusiasm an heiress through whom he obtained an estate in Wales worth £8,000 a year, a plain and pious young woman as devoted to her husband as he was unexpectedly to become to her. At the time of Nelson's arrival in Naples, Hamilton, by then a widower, had been British Envoy Extraordinary and Minister Plenipotentiary at court there for almost twenty years.

He had performed his duties conscientiously and with success. He had no distaste for the particularities of court life and had become a well-liked and respected figure at the royal palace, being a man 'of most elegant manners', a more than competent musician, and 'the best dancer at the Neapolitan court'. He was moreover a keen sportsman and a willing companion of the King on royal shooting and hunting expeditions, although his private opinion of King Ferdinand, a fundamentally idle man much given to fornication, was not a high one. 'His Majesty's habit of dissipation has taken such firm root [that there is] scarcely a possibility of his ever applying seriously to business,' Hamilton reported confidentially to the Foreign Secretary. 'The chase in winter and parties of sailing or fishing in summer call out His Majesty every day at Sun Rising and keep him out till it sets.' When the time came to attend in council with his ministers, 'he was more or less fatigued with the dissipations of the day'.[12]

The Queen always attended these meetings. It was she, in fact, who virtually ruled the kingdom in her husband's name. At the age of forty-five, having borne eighteen children, eight of whom had survived, she was not a prepossessing woman, despite her beautifully preserved white skin and the white hands of which she was so proud. Known to the people as '*Polpett Mbocca*', 'Mouthful of Rissole', because of the way she gabbled her words when she talked, she was far more intelligent, and more devious, than she seemed. She was also very devout: 'at times she stuck short prayers and pious ejaculations inside her stays, and occasionally swallowed them'.[13]

She did not interfere with her husband's amours except when it seemed that his women might threaten her influence over him. Then they were sent packing, like Sara Goudar, the Irish wife of an unscrupulous French card-sharper, who helped her husband run a casino at their villa at Posillipo and who – having been indiscreet enough to write a letter to the King in which she said she would await him 'in the same place at the same time with all the impatience of a cow who longs for the approach of a bull' – was ordered to leave Naples with her husband within three days.[14]

The Queen had a 'very good understanding', Hamilton reported, and was 'sensible that unless she applied to the business which the King avoids, the whole State would be in confusion'. She gave up 'the greatest part of her time daily in looking minutely into every paper & in preparing matters for the dispatch of business when she meets the King in council at night'. In this she was greatly helped by an English adviser, John Acton, who, while officially holding a quite minor ministerial post in the government, was undoubtedly its most influential member.

Acton, grandson of a prosperous London goldsmith and descendant of an ancient Shropshire family, had been born at Besançon in France where his father, who had been physician to Edward Gibbon's father, had established a medical practice and had married a Frenchwoman. He had joined the navy of the Grand Duke of Tuscany, the Queen of Naples's brother, and had so distinguished himself in that service that the Queen's then lover, Prince Caramanico, had suggested to her that she arrange for his transfer to the Neapolitan navy, which was at that time in much need of reorganization. 'By a succession of rapid steps,' in the words of a nineteenth-century biographer, 'he reached in a few years the highest pinnacle of power.'[15]

So it was naturally Acton whom Hamilton advised Nelson to approach immediately with the request for the dispatch of Neapolitan troops to Toulon. Nelson, impressed by the envoy's brisk manner, complimented him enthusiastically. 'Sir William,' he said, 'you are a man after my own heart; you do business in my own way!' And he could not forbear to add, 'I am, now, only a captain; but I will, if I live, be at the top of the tree.'[16]

Together the two men went to see Acton, who spoke English as indifferently as he spoke both French and Italian; but he was as accommodating as Hamilton: two thousand troops would be sent to Toulon within four days.

His mission satisfactorily accomplished, Nelson could now look forward to a few days' rest while the *Agamemnon* was being replenished with fresh provisions and water. During this time, he much enjoyed the company of Sir William Hamilton. He was also much taken with Hamilton's lovely young second wife.

9

The Palazzo Sessa

She is a young woman of amiable manners and who does honour to the
station in which she is raised.

The first Lady Hamilton had died in 1782, leaving her husband in
deep distress, 'quite unhinged,' so he told his sister, 'by the cruel
separation'.[1] He had returned to England the following year,
bringing his wife's embalmed body with him for burial; and in
August, while staying at Nerot's Hotel, King Street, Mayfair, he
met the young woman, the 'exquisite beauty', who was to become
his second wife.

Her name was Emma Lyon, though she preferred to be known
as Emma Hart. She was the daughter of a Cheshire blacksmith,
who had died some two months after her birth, and she was
brought up in her grandmother's house in Wales, where she
received such sketchy education as was considered appropriate for
a girl who was to go out to service as an under-nursemaid at the
age of twelve.

Emma soon left this employment for a similar post in London
found for her by her mother; and then she seems to have gone to
work as a maid in the household of Thomas Linley, the composer,
who bought David Garrick's share in Drury Lane theatre with
R. B. Sheridan and Richard Ford. By 1779, according to Henry
Angelo, the fashionable fencing-master, Emma Lyon had left the
Linley household and was living in Arlington Street at the house of
Mrs Kelly, a celebrated procuress and the 'abbess' of a brothel
later frequented by William Hickey and other such more or less
disreputable young men about town. Later, so it was rumoured,
she became the mistress of one of the Prince of Wales's most
intimate cronies, Captain John Willett Payne, and was perhaps to
be seen as an attendant in the Temple of Health and Hymen

where the Scottish charlatan James Graham gave his lectures on procreation and charged £50 a night for couples to enjoy the pleasures of his 'Grand Celestial State Bed' on which might be conceived perfect babies 'as even the barren must do when so powerfully agitated in the delights of love'.[2]

Whether or not Emma served as an attendant or chorister in Dr Graham's establishment, certain it is that by the time she was sixteen she had been established in a cottage near Uppark in Sussex by Sir Harry Fetherstonhaugh upon whose dining-room table she was said to dance naked and by whom – or possibly by Willett Payne – she had a child. It was at Uppark that she met the Hon. Charles Greville, second son of the Earl of Warwick and nephew of Sir William Hamilton.

Charles Greville was not a particularly attractive man in either appearance or character. Selfish, dissembling, calculating and excessively fastidious, he had spent much of his life up till now in endeavouring to support expensive tastes – a penchant for collecting antiquities and objects of virtu, and a passion for mineralogy – without having to do too much to pay for them. He had hopes of being officially recognized as his childless uncle's heir and, in the meantime, while supplementing a meagre income as an occasional art dealer, he had to marry a woman of fortune. With this end in view he borrowed an enormous sum of money to build himself a grand house in Portman Square which, he hoped, would entice a suitable bride. Having married her, he intended to sell the house and pay back the loan.

His offer of protection to Emma when Fetherstonhaugh tired of her was also largely prompted by financial considerations. Certainly he liked the idea of a settled sexual relationship with a beautiful young girl who could offer him some domestic comfort, unlike the prostitutes with whom he was in the habit of consorting, but he also had an idea of making money out of her by commissioning from George Romney a series of paintings which he could sell at a handsome profit. For her part, Emma, who may have become a prostitute herself as a means of livelihood after her break with Fetherstonhaugh, was desperately anxious that Greville should abide by his initially uncertain promise to care for her, particularly as support for both her mother and her baby daughter was to be included in the arrangement. 'I am almost distracktid,' she wrote to him in January 1782.

I have never hard from Sir H[arry] and he is not at Lechster now, I am sure . . . What shall I dow, good God what shall I dow, I have wrote 7 letters and no anser . . . I have not a farthing to bless my self with . . . For Gods sake . . . dear Grevell . . . write the minet you get this and only tell me what I ham to dow, derect some whay. I am allmos mad . . . What else am I but a girl in distres – in reall distres. O for God's sake tell me what is to become of me.[3]

The deal was struck; the arrangements made; Emma was established with her mother – who chose to be known as Mrs Cadogan – and two maids in a house in the Edgware Road; her baby daughter, referred to as Emma Carew, was sent to be looked after by her grandmother in Wales; and Greville, although demanding and highly critical of real or imagined faults on his occasional visits, settled down contentedly to his new existence with a young woman who was as accommodating as she was beautiful.

There were occasional quarrels when Emma did not live up to the high standards he set for her, when her need for admiration or attention irritated him. But he had no serious cause for complaint with the bargain he had made, apart from the girl's quick temper, for he conceded that she did everything she could to please him, to 'manege' herself, as she put it, '& try to be like Grevell'. So all went well enough until Greville found an heiress who, he thought, would make him a suitable wife, the Hon. Henrietta Willoughby, the eighteen-year-old daughter of a neighbour of his in Portman Square, the fifth Lord Middleton. Having settled in his mind to marry Miss Willoughby, Greville considered the problem of ridding himself of the encumbrance of Miss Hart. He turned for help to his uncle, Sir William Hamilton, who was asked to write a letter which would assure Lord Middleton that Greville was, indeed, his uncle's heir. Hamilton was also required to take over responsibility for Miss Hart on Greville's behalf.

Sir William wanted to help his nephew, of whom he was quite fond; but he was not at all sure that he wanted to become responsible for his nephew's mistress. Having met her, he decided that he liked her very much; indeed, after a time he could bring himself to say that he was much attracted to her, but there were obvious difficulties in having her come to live under his protection in Naples. 'There is a great difference between her being with you or me,' Sir William wrote after his return to Naples,

for she really loves you when she could only esteem and suffer me . . . I do assure you when I was in England, tho' her exquisite beauty had frequently its effects on me, it would never have come into my head to have proposed a freedom beyond an innocent kiss . . . I see so many difficulties in her coming here, should you be under the necessity of parting with her, that I can never advise it. Tho' a great city, Naples has every defect of a Province and nothing you do is secret. It would be fine fun for the young English Travellers to endeavour to cuckold the old Gentleman, their Ambassador, and whether they succeeded or not would surely give me uneasiness . . . I am not a match for so much youth and beauty.[4]

Besides, Emma's presence in the Palazzo Sessa might well cause unwelcome gossip and spoil his happy relationship with the King and Queen.

Greville persisted: Emma could be placed in 'a small retired house on the hill at Naples, very small'. She would not 'want to go about'. As to Englishmen, there was 'nothing to fear'. 'I am sure I would not let her go to you, if any risque of the usual coquetry of the sex being likely to give uneasiness . . . Let her learn music or drawing, or anything to keep her in order . . . I never saw any one so compleately led by good nature.' The girl had 'good natural sense and quick observation'. There was admittedly 'a degree of *nature* in her', yet she was 'no fool': she had 'natural gentility' and took 'easily any hint that [was] given with good humour'. Greville did not, of course, mention a fault that his kinsman, William Beckford, remarked upon, that she had 'the devil of a temper when set on edge'. As for Emma as a mistress, she was the only woman Greville had slept with without having ever had any of his 'senses offended, & a cleanlier, sweeter bedfellow [did] not exist'.[5]

So it was agreed that Emma and her mother should go to

Naples and that Emma's child, now nearly four years old, should remain in England in the care of a Mr and Mrs Blackburn of Market Street Lane, Manchester, where she would be brought up with the Blackburns' own two daughters. Emma, however, was not to be told that her exile would be permanent. She wrote to Sir William in a letter far better spelled than her usual communications, and clearly written under Greville's watchful eye.

Emboldened by your kindness to me when you was in England, I have a proposal to make that I flatter myself will not be disagreable to you. Greville (whom you know I love tenderly) is obliged to go for four or five months in the summer to places that I cannot with propriety attend him to . . . and as you was so good as to give me encouragement, I will speak my mind. In the first place, I should be glad if I was a little more improved than what I am, and as Greville is oblidged to be absent . . . he has out of kindness to me offer'd, if you are agreeable, for me to go to Naples for 6 or 8 months, and he will at the end of that time fetch me home and stay a while there when he comes, which I know you will be glad to see him . . . I could not bear the thought of staying at home by my self when I know if I come to see you (which will be the greatest pleasure on earth, Greville excepted) I shall be improving myself and making the time pass agreeable . . . I shall always keep my own room when you are better engaged or go out, and at other times I hope to have the pleasure of your company and conversation . . . I am, my dear Sir William, your oblidged humble servant, or affectionate Emma, which you like best.[6]

Despite the assurances given in this letter, Sir William did not look forward to Emma's arrival. He emphasized the temporary nature of the arrangement and his nephew's ultimate responsibility for a discarded mistress. However, he would 'hobble in and out' of the 'scrape' as decently as he could. When Emma did arrive, however, he was once again captivated by her beauty and good nature. Like his vases and paintings, she was a work of art. He kindly gave up all business for the first few days of her stay so that he could make her feel at home; and, as she reported to Greville, she could 'not move a hand or foot or a legg' without his complimenting her on its gracefulness. Yet, she added, she could never accept him as her lover. 'I have a great regard for him as the uncle & friend of you', she wrote, '& he loves me Greville. But he can never be anything nearer ... He never can be my lover ... Endead, I am sorry, I cannot make him happy. I can be civil, oblidging, & I do try to make myself as agreable as I can to him. But I belong to you.'[7]

As the months passed and Greville did not appear in Naples to fetch her home, she became almost frantic in her anxiety, protesting that she 'lived but on the hope of seeing' him, and that if he did not come she would return to him 'lett what will be the consequence'. 'I am sure to cry the moment I think of you,' she wrote despairingly.

I feil more & more unhappy at being seperatted from you ... To live without you is impossible. I love you to that degree that their is not a hardship upon earth ... I would not undergo ... my dear, dear Greville, if you do love me, for God sake and for my sake, try all you can to come hear as soon as possible ... I find life is insupportable without you. Oh! my heart is intirely broke. I dont know what to do ... To live without you is impossible ... Pray write to me and don't write in the stile of a friend but a lover. For I won't hear a word of freind. Sir William is ever freind. But we are lovers ...[8]

Yet Greville did not come; and Emma, receiving no reply to her beseeching letters, was forced in the end to realize that he had no intention of coming. Sir William still did all he could to make life as pleasant for her as he could. He had her painted in all manner of costumes and poses; he employed a singing master for her and a language master; he allowed her to accompany him to the opera and to 'walk in the Villa Reale every night' where she had 'generally two princes, two or 3 nobles, the English minister & the King with a crowd behind us'.[9]

Sir William did 'nothing all day' but look at her and sigh and point out her 'beauties' to his friends, particularly when, acting as what Horace Walpole called his 'Gallery of Statues', she performed her celebrated 'Attitudes'. An early performance of certain of these 'Attitudes' was given before Goethe, who was in Naples in 1787:

As a performance it's like nothing you ever saw before in your life . . .
She lets down her hair and, with a few shawls, gives so much variety to
her poses, gestures, expressions, etc. that the spectator can hardly believe
his eyes. He sees what thousands of artists would have liked to express
realized before him in movements and surprising transformations –
standing, kneeling, sitting, reclining, serious, sad, playful, ecstatic,
contrite, alluring, threatening, anxious, one pose follows another without
a break. She knows how to arrange the folds of her veil to match each
mood, and has a hundred ways of turning it into a headdress. The old
knight idolizes her and is enthusiastic about everything she does.[10]

Even when she had lost her perfect figure and become extremely
fat, Sir William delighted in her performances.

On one occasion [wrote a future visitor to Naples] being desirous to
astonish a gentleman who had just arrived and had not heard of her
attitudinal celebrity, she dropped from her chair on the carpet, when
sitting at table after dinner . . . Nothing could have been more classical
or imposing than this prostrate position. Sir William started up to open a
little of the curtain in order to admit the proper light, while the stranger
flew to the sideboard for water, with which he plentifully sprinkled the
fainting dame before he discovered it was a *scena*. 'You have spoiled, my
good friend,' said the Knight, 'one of the most perfect Attitudes that
Emma ever executed. How unlucky!'[11]

Fond of Sir William as she had become, Emma for long resisted
his polite advances and when Greville, in writing to her at last told
her to oblige him, she was 'all madness'. 'I will not answer you,'
she protested in indignant fury, 'for Oh if you knew what pain I
feel in reading those lines when you advise me to Whore, nothing
can express my rage . . . If I was with you, I wou'd murder you &
myself boath . . . It is not in your interest to disoblige me, for you
don't know the power I have hear, onely I will never be his
mistress. If you affront me, I will make him marry me.'[12]

Sir William had evidently begun to consider marriage himself.
It was not only that he doted on her, was 'in raptures' with her, as
she recorded with endearing satisfaction, that he spared her 'neither
expence nor pains in anything', he was quite obviously proud of

her accomplishments, of her singing, of her fluency in Italian, her accomplishments as a hostess. 'You can't think,' she wrote herself, 'how well I do the honours.'[13] Certainly the dinner parties over which she presided at the Palazzo Sessa were well attended. The guests, it had to be said, were at first mostly men. The Queen 'more than once expressed herself in a tone of great discontent,' so the Marchesa di Solari reported, 'that a man, honoured with an important mission, an English minister, should live publicly with a prostitute taken from the very streets of London'. Yet even the Queen treated Emma politely when she did meet her, while the King's admiration was undisguised; and, as time passed, whatever prejudices there had formerly been against Miss Hart, the balls at the *palazzo* were attended by what she termed 'good society'. 'Sir William will let you know on what a footing we are here,' she reported to Greville. 'I had near four hundred persons, all the foreign ministers & their wives, all the first ladies of fashion, Foreyners and neapolitans, our house was full in every room.'

Greville also heard from his uncle: 'Our dear Em. goes on now quite as I would wish, improves daily, & is universally beloved. She is wonderful, considering her youth and beauty, & I flatter myself that E. and her mother are happy to be with me, so that I see my every wish fulfilled.'

He had no hesitation in taking her with him when he went on one of his customary *villeggiature*, his visits to country villas; nor did he hesitate to indulge her when she expressed a longing for diamonds, laying out £500 on 'single stones of good water & tolerable size'.

'Sir William is very fond of me, and very kind to me,' she wrote to Charles Greville in her hurried scrawl.

The house is full of painters painting me. He as now got nine pictures of me, and 2 a painting ... There is another man modelling me in wax, and another in clay. All the artists is come from Rome to study from me ... Sir William is never a moment from me. He goes no where without me. He as no diners but what I can be of the party. No body comes without the are civil to me. We have always good company. I now live upstairs in the same apartments where he lives, and my old apartments is made the musick-rooms when I have my lesson in the morning . . . Sir William says he loves nothing but me.[14]

By then it was being reported that they were secretly married, and there was certainly no doubt that they had at last become lovers to the evident pleasure of them both. 'As to Sir W. I confess to you I doat on him,' she told Greville, 'nor I never can love any other person but him. This confession will please you I know.'[15]

No doubt this did please him; but when it became generally known that Sir William was going to England with his mistress to seek the King's permission to marry her, Greville – who feared that should they have a child he would no longer be his uncle's heir – was not pleased at all. Nor were the Hamilton family; and nor were many ladies in London society who strongly disapproved of a woman from such a background as hers being elevated in this way. It could not be denied that she was 'very handsome', as Lady Elizabeth Foster, the Duke of Devonshire's mistress, conceded; 'but her conversation, though perfectly good-natured and unaffected, was uninteresting, and her pronunciation very vulgar. In short, Lord Bristol's remark seems to me so just a one that I must end with it: "Take her as anything but Mrs Hart and she is a superb being – as herself she is always vulgar." '[16]

Yet most people, women as well as men, were eventually won over by the young woman's open, guileless charm. Even Horace Walpole, now the elderly and rather crotchety Earl of Orford, who had previously described her as 'Sir William's pantomime mistress', wrote warmly of her after having met her; and, although Queen Charlotte declined to receive her at court, the King made no objection to the marriage, which was celebrated on 6 September 1791 at St George's, Hanover Square.

Upon their return to Naples, the new Lady Hamilton, 'never so happy' in her life, was received with pleasure everywhere. 'All the Neapolitan Nobility,' so her husband said, 'have been to see her & show her every attention & the English Ladies, who are numerous here this year, are quite fond of her.' Lady Palmerston, who loved society as much as her husband did, thought that her voice was 'vulgar and she and Sir W. [were] rather too fond, but on the whole [Lady Hamilton was] a very extraordinary woman . . . and by her conduct [proved] how much she [merited] her great reverse of fortune'.[17]

Sir William certainly did not regret his marriage. 'As yet I have no reason to repent of a step which I took contrary to the approbation of the world,' he told Lady Mansfield. 'The marrying Emma was my own business. I knew what I was doing for as you know I had lived with her for five years before I married . . . Look round your circle of *prudent well assorted matches* in the great world and see how few turn out so well as our seemingly imprudent one.'[18]

As well as being a great comfort to her husband, who looked 'extremely ill', Lady Hamilton was also a great asset to him in his work, for she was now a favourite with the Queen, who showed her 'all sorts of kind and affectionate attentions' and who received in return, to assuage her insatiable curiosity, all the information and gossip which Lady Hamilton, as wife of the English minister, was able to impart.[19] By the time Captain Nelson arrived in Naples in September 1793, Queen Maria Carolina and Lady Hamilton were seen to be on terms of 'the closest intimacy', Lady Hamilton relishing the social opportunities which this intimacy gave her and the flattery bestowed upon her, the Queen finding the young woman extremely useful in communicating with the British minister without having to consult the King.

'I am got into politics,' Lady Hamilton told Charles Greville.

Send me some news political and private . . . I wish to have news for our dear much-loved Queen, whom I adore. Nor can I live without her, for she is to me a mother, friend and everything . . . She is the first woman in the world; and her heart is most excellent and strictly good and upright. But you'l say it is we are such friends, that I am partial, but ask everybody that knows her. She loves England . . . In the evenings I go to her and we are *tête-a-tête* 2 or 3 hours. Sometimes we sing. Yesterday the King and me sang duets 3 hours. But it was bad, as he sings like a *King*.[20]

Sir William and Lady Hamilton were both on excellent terms also with Captain Nelson. They had him to stay at the Palazzo Sessa;

and he entertained them to breakfast aboard the *Agamemnon*, together with several distinguished English tourists and members of the English colony, borrowing a large collection of cutlery and other tableware from the Palazzo Sessa for the occasion. 'Lady Hamilton has been wonderfully kind and good to Josiah [whom she took sightseeing],' Nelson told his wife. 'She is a young woman of amiable manners and who does honour to the station in which she is raised.'[21]

He was not, however, to get to know her very well as yet. On the day of the breakfast party, he was also, after the English had gone ashore, to have welcomed aboard the King, with whom he had already dined, sitting at his majesty's right hand, as he proudly recorded, 'before our Ambassador and all the Nobles present'.[22] But the King never came, for reports were received of a French corvette being sighted off the Sardinian coast; and there was 'nothing left for the honour of our Country but to sail', Nelson reported to his brother William, 'which . . . unfit as my Ship was . . . I did in two hours afterwards. It was necessary to show them what an English Man-of-War would do.'[23]

It was to be five years before Nelson saw Naples and Lady Hamilton again.

10

Corsica

I got a little hurt this morning: not much as you may judge from my writing.

On her passage to Sardinia, the *Agamemnon*, 'the finest ship' Nelson had ever sailed in, had her first 'little brush' with the enemy.[1] In the early hours of the morning, the ship's lookouts caught sight of a French convoy; and by dawn the *Agamemnon*'s guns were exchanging fire with one of the enemy frigates, the *Melpomène*. Both ships were badly damaged. Nelson called his officers to ask their opinion as to whether they considered the ship should be prepared for further immediate action. None of them did. The ship was undermanned, over a third of her crew having been left to help defend Toulon from the forces of the French Convention; and, although the *Melpomène* was a smaller ship than the *Agamemnon*, the combined strength of the enemy convoy was far greater than their own. So, as the *Melpomène* was towed away to Corsica, the *Agamemnon*, her carpenters and riggers having worked throughout the night, set sail for Tunis, the captain and ship's company both well satisfied as to how the *Agamemnon* had been handled in the brief, disappointing encounter. The crew, Nelson reported, had conducted themselves entirely to his satisfaction. As for their captain, one of his midshipmen wrote home, he was 'acknowledged one of the first characters in the Service, and is universally beloved by his men and officers'.[2]

At Tunis, Nelson's duty was to support Commodore Robert Linzee, Lord Hood's brother-in-law, in protesting to the Bey about his attitude towards revolutionary France, a squadron of whose ships was then lying under his protection in the harbour. This diplomatic mission was far from being as successful as Nelson's in Naples. The Bey was a wily man of Cretan descent who listened politely to the English officers' arguments and, when asked how he could 'give countenance and support to a government of assassins who had recently beheaded their monarch', blandly replied, through his interpreter, that, if historians were to be believed, surely something rather similar had happened in England towards the middle of the last century.

Nelson had no patience with the man, nor with Commodore Linzee's cautious method of dealing with him. Had he had his way, Nelson would, he said, have seized the French ships first, even though they were in a so-called neutral port, and talked to the Bey afterwards. The man had obviously been bought by the French and could just as well be bought by the English. He would swallow such principles as he had for £50,000, which was far less than the ships in his harbour were worth. 'The English,' he thought,

seldom get much by negotiation except the being laughed at, which we have been; and I don't like it ... [We] have never yet succeeded in a negotiation against the French, and we have not set the example at Tunis. Thank God, Lord Hood, whom Linzee sent to for orders how to act after having negotiated, has ordered me from under his command, and to command a Squadron of Frigates off Corsica ... I consider this command as a very high compliment – there being five older Captains in the Fleet ... Lord Hood is certainly the best officer I ever saw. Every order from him is so clear, it is impossible to misunderstand him.[3]

On his way to take up his new duties off Corsica, Nelson heard of another missed opportunity. The port of Toulon, battered by the guns of a young artillery officer whose name he later transcribed as 'Buona Parte', had fallen to the French and, although 15,000 of its threatened inhabitants had been taken aboard British ships, thousands more had been slaughtered in scenes of appalling cruelty for their real or supposed sympathies. At the same time Captain Sidney Smith, an officer fluent in French, six years younger than himself and equally desirous of fame, who had volunteered to burn such ships as could not be towed out of the dockyard, managed to destroy only nine, allowing twice that number to escape. It was not altogether Smith's fault, but since he was 'always panting for distinction', in the words of an army officer who knew him well, since he was 'extravagantly vain . . . and always talking of himself', he had made many enemies in his erratic and varied career and was just such a man as was likely to be blamed for the mistakes of others. Nelson had no doubt that the disaster at Toulon was his fault. 'Lord Hood mistook the man,' he commented: 'there is an old [saying], *Great talkers do the least, we see.*'[4]

When he arrived off Corsica, which it was hoped could be secured as a new British base with the help of the Corsican patriot, Pasquale Paoli, Nelson had further fault to find. The British commander there, Sir David Dundas, had supervised the British evacuation of Toulon and was in no mind to oversee another misadventure. His troops had captured the port of San Fiorenzo (St Florent) on the north-west coast of the island; but he was reluctant to mount assaults on its two main fortresses, those of Bastia and Calvi, until reinforcements arrived from Gibraltar. Nelson – whose task was to ensure that the French garrisons in these two places received neither reinforcements nor supplies – urged Lord Hood to authorize an attempt upon Bastia despite the caution of the army command, concealing from the Admiral the real strength of the enemy garrison, which he presented as being weaker than it was: 'Armies go so slow that Seamen think they never mean to go forward . . . We are few, but of the right sort . . . When was before the time that 2,000 British troops, as good as ever marched, were not thought equal to attack 8,000 French troops, allowing them to be in strong works? What would the immortal Wolfe have done?' Not to make the attempt would be a 'National disgrace'. 'A thousand men would, to a certainty, take Bastia; with 500 and *Agamemnon* I would attempt it.'[5]

Thus urged by Nelson, who had already made several raids on the coast, an attack upon Bastia was authorized. Two thousand troops were to be landed on a beach below the fortress under the command of Nelson and Lieutenant-Colonel William Villettes, the son of a diplomat of Huguenot descent. Despite the difficulties of dragging the heavy guns over the rocks and across the deep ravines with sledges and tackle, and building platforms and batteries in the thorny scrubland, the *maquis*, Nelson was confident of victory.

'The expedition,' he wrote home, 'is almost a child of my own, and I have no fears about the final issue. It will be a victory. Bastia will be ours ... My seamen are now what British seamen ought to be ... almost invincible: they really mind shot no more than peas.'[6]

It was dangerous work under heavy fire. Six of his ship's company, 'not the men to keep out of the way', were killed; Lieutenant George Andrews, the brother of the girl he had wanted to marry at St Omer, was wounded, and Nelson, never a man to shun danger himself, received a 'sharp cut' in the back on one day and was nearly killed on another when a shower of earth from a heavy shot knocked him over. His guns were taking their toll, however. A deserter reported that the cannon in Bastia had twice been put out of action. Also, thanks to Nelson's naval blockade, food in the town was almost exhausted; while British troops sent across the island from San Fiorenzo were approaching it through a pass from the landward side. On 23 May 1794 the garrison, alarmed by the prospect of falling into the hands of the merciless Corsican patriots, handed over the town gates to the British, whose troops marched in, a band blaring forth the National Anthem.

Bastia had been hard enough to take; Calvi was in an even stronger position. More lives were lost in besieging it; and Nelson, watching the bombardment at seven o'clock on the morning of 12 July, was again hit by a shower of earth and shattered rocks as a shell exploded on the sand-bagged ramparts. 'Was much bruised in the face and eyes by sand from the works struck by shot,' he recorded in his journal. And to Lord Hood he wrote, making light of the matter, 'I got a little hurt this morning: not much as you may judge from my writing.'[7] But as the days passed he was forced to the conclusion that the damage was more serious than he had at first supposed. With his right eye he could distinguish light from dark but could see nothing clearly; for all intents and purposes the sight was gone. However, he could comfort himself with the thought that he was 'within a hair's breadth' of not just losing an eye but his head; and, as for the eye, he wrote reassuringly to his wife, 'the pupil is nearly the size of the blue part, I don't know the name ... But the blemish is nothing, not to be perceived unless told ... So my *beauty* is saved ... And you must not think that my hurts confined me . . . no, nothing but the loss of a limb would have kept me from my duty.'[8]

Nelson had not only to contend with his eye, which grew worse as the weeks passed and was 'very painful at times'.[9] It was also insufferably hot and he, like his men, was suffering from what he called 'all the prevailing disorders'. The surgeons were busy in the camp treating cases of dysentery and malaria, heat exhaustion and typhoid fever. The thirteen-year-old Midshipman Hoste's life was despaired of; Lieutenant James Moutray, son of the much admired Mary Moutray, died. But, soon after Lord Hood had been informed that the siege would have to be lifted because of the shortage of fit men able to prosecute it, the garrison of Calvi, their ammunition exhausted, suddenly surrendered.

After the surrender of Bastia, Nelson had been distressed by the lack of public acknowledgement of his services. Lord Hood had barely mentioned his name in his report to the Admiralty.[10] Yet, 'the whole operations of the siege were carried on through Lord Hood's letters to me,' he told William Suckling in venting his grievance. 'I was the mover of it – I was the cause of its success.' He was anxious to impress this also upon his wife, who seemed never fully to appreciate the resolute manner in which he performed his duties:

I have acted for Lord Hood with a zeal which no one could exceed . . . I am sure you must feel the superior pleasure of knowing that my integrity and plainess of conduct are the cause of my being kept from you . . . If any accident should happen to me, I am sure my conduct will be such as will entitle you to the Royal favour: not that I have the least idea but that I shall return to you and full of honour. My name shall never be a disgrace to those who may belong to me.[11]

To his brother William, also, he stressed the value of his services:

I am now pointed out as having been this war *one hundred and twelve* times engaged against the French, and always successful to a certain degree. No officer in Europe can say as much . . . Mine is all *honour* . . . Opportunities have been frequently offered me, and I have never lost one of distinguishing myself, not only as a gallant man, but as having a head;

for, of the numerous plans I have laid, not one has failed, nor of opinions given, has one been in the event wrong.[12]

He wrote as much to the Duke of Clarence: 'It has pleased God this war not only to give me frequent opportunities of showing myself an officer worthy of trust, but also to prosper all my undertakings in the highest degree . . . My judgement being formed from common sense, I have never yet been mistaken.'[13]

His activities at Bastia having been so inadequately recognized, Nelson was resigned to his important role in the siege of Calvi being likewise dismissed. 'I am well aware my poor services will not be noticed,' he told his wife. 'I have no interest; but however services may be received, it is not right in an Officer to slacken his zeal for his Country.'[14]

His fears were realized; and he was more upset than ever. As he said, he did not know that anyone had done more at Calvi than he had himself.[15] 'One hundred and ten days I have been actually engaged, at sea and on shore, against the enemy; three actions against ships, two against Bastia in my ship; four boat actions and two villages taken and twelve sail of vessels burnt.' Even so, as he complained to his uncle:

My diligence is not mentioned . . . It is known that, for two months, I blockaded Bastia with a Squadron: only sixty sacks of flour got into the Town. At San Fiorenzo and Calvi, for two months before, nothing got in, and four French frigates could not get out and are now ours . . . Others . . . are handsomely mentioned. *Such things are.* I have got upon a subject near to my heart, which is full when I think of the treatment I have received. Every man who had a considerable share in the reduction has got some place or other – I, only I, am without reward. Nothing but my anxious endeavours to serve my country makes me bear up against it; but I sometimes am ready to give all up . . . But never mind, some day I'll have a *Gazette* of my own.[16]

In the meantime he was not only denied praise but also prize-money. 'I hope those who are to get so much money will make a proper use of it,' he told his wife.

Had I attended less than I have done to the service of my Country, I might have made some too: however, I trust my name will stand on record, when the money-makers will be forgot ... It is very true that I have ever served faithfully, and ever has it been my fate to be neglected; but that shall not make me inattentive to my duty. I have pride in doing my duty well, and a self approbation, which if it is not so lucrative, yet perhaps affords more pleasing sensations. I trust the time may come when I may be rewarded, though really I don't flatter myself it is near.[17]

There was further disappointment soon to come. The *Agamemnon*, in urgent need of repairs, put in to Leghorn; while Lord Hood, recalled to England, was temporarily superseded by Vice-Admiral William Hotham, the son of a baronet, an officer of undoubted courage but hesitant and unsure of himself in command, 'not intended by nature', in Nelson's opinion, 'for a Commander-in-chief'. As soon as his ship was seaworthy once more – and having in the meantime visited Genoa, the 'most magnificent' place he ever saw, where he was pleased to be received 'in some state, the Doge advancing to the middle of the room' to greet him[18] – Nelson joined Hotham off Toulon to attack the French fleet should it leave its moorings there. The weather was atrocious, the worst Nelson had known 'in any seas; it blew a perfect hurricane'. Moreover, he was feeling ill again 'with flux and fever'; and so were many of his ship's company.[19]

The blockade of Toulon was a long and dreary business. In the first week of March 1795, however, the French Admiral, Pierre Martin, received orders from the recently appointed Directory in Paris to sail out of Toulon as escort to a convoy of troops destined for an attack upon Corsica, now in the hands of the British. Martin was reluctant to obey: three quarters of his sailors had never been to sea before; many of his best officers had been arrested or executed in the days of the Terror; his ships, though more or less equal in number to the British, were not likely to be their match in gunnery or manoeuvrability.[20] But the Directory's instructions were categorical. So the French fleet left Toulon and was immediately in trouble.

Two ships collided and one of them, the eighty-four-gun *Ça Ira*, lost her fore and main topmasts. As she fell behind the others, Nelson, seizing his opportunity, took the *Agamemnon* racing after her. He closed to within a hundred yards of her stern, and watched with satisfaction as his gun crews, upon whose regular training he always set particular store, fired their broadsides. 'Scarcely a shot appeared to miss,' he wrote; and by one o'clock in the afternoon 'the *Ça Ira* was a perfect wreck, her sails hanging in tatters, mizzen topmast, mizzen topsail and cross-jack yards shot away'.[21]

By now Admiral Martin had turned to fight; but Hotham, unwilling to risk a full-scale encounter with the *Agamemnon* in danger of being cut off, hoisted the signal to break off the action. The next day the British fleet came upon the *Ça Ira* being towed away by the twenty-four-gun *Censeur*. After a sharp engagement both were taken and George Andrews was sent aboard to hoist English colours, while Nelson went to see Hotham to urge him to continue the chase and bring Admiral Martin to the battle he was obviously unwilling to fight. Both the captured ships had suffered heavy casualties, whereas – though 'all the sails were ribbons and all the ropes were ends' – only thirteen men had been wounded in the *Agamemnon*. The veteran commander of Nelson's division, Rear-Admiral Samuel Goodall, who had been promoted lieutenant two years before Nelson's birth, supported the captain's plea that a bold stroke might win 'such a day as ... the Annals of England never produced'. But Hotham was not a man for bold strokes. He had done what he had been asked to do; two French ships of the line had been captured; and the danger to Corsica had been for the moment averted. 'We have done very well.'[22]

Nelson was convinced that they had not done nearly well enough, that had he commanded the fleet, 'either the whole French Fleet would have graced my triumph, or I should have been in a confounded scrape'. 'My disposition cannot bear tame and slow measures,' he told his wife. 'I wish to be an Admiral and in command of the English Fleet; I should very soon either do much or be ruined.'[23] For the moment he could at least say, and did say, that all he had obtained he owed to himself. 'My character stands high with almost all Europe,' he continued in another letter.

Even the Austrians know my name perfectly ... I may venture to tell you, but as a secret, that I have a mistress given to me, no less a Personage than the Goddess Bellona [Roman goddess of war]. So say the French verses made on me and in them I am so covered with laurels that you would hardly find my sallow face. At one period I am 'the dear Nelson', 'the amiable Nelson', 'the fiery Nelson': however nonsensical these expressions are, they are better than censure, and we are all subject and open to flattery.[24]

There was another brief encounter with Admiral Pierre Martin's fleet in July; and once again it ended with Hotham's signal to retire. 'Thus ended our second meeting with these gentry,' Nelson told the Duke of Clarence. 'We had every prospect of taking every ship in the fleet.'[25]

Sir Hyde Parker, who came out as a temporary commander-in-chief when Hotham returned home, never to see active service again, was another indecisive officer, with whom Nelson was to cross swords later; but at the end of November 1796 a new commander was appointed in the Mediterranean. This was Admiral Sir John Jervis, then sixty-two years old, an officer of wide experience and forceful character, and a man, so Nelson said, after his own heart. The son of a barrister, who had given him £20 on his going out into the world and had thereafter refused him all assistance, he had joined the navy in the week of his fourteenth birthday and by the time he was twenty-four he was, in command of the *Porcupine*, a witness of James Wolfe's assault on the Heights of Abraham at Quebec. Nelson was delighted to welcome him as commander of the Mediterranean fleet. 'The moment I knew of your arrival,' he later told him, 'I felt perfectly at ease.' Jervis, in turn, seemed equally pleased to have Nelson under his command, treating him 'more like an associate than [an inferior] officer'.[26] Nelson was soon promoted commodore, which meant an increase in pay of ten shillings a day, and given to suppose that it would not be long before he was a rear-admiral.

Not all the officers in the fleet were as pleased as Nelson to hear of Jervis's appointment. There was an air of menace about him. With his powerful frame and stern features, he looked, as he could be, a formidable opponent. He had a reputation as a firm disciplinarian, and, as a man who knew him said, he was far from always 'preserving an unruffled command of his temper'. When roused 'a torrent of impetuous reproof in unmeasured language would violently rush from his unguarded lips'. 'He had, too, a certain grim humour in which he occasionally indulged at the expense of those who were powerless to retort. On the other hand, when an act of zeal, skill or gallantry merited his approval, it was given ungrudgingly . . . and in his private relations, though careful and economical, he was kindhearted and generous.'[27]

Nelson was to witness, and to endorse, his stern disciplinary methods. Four men in the fleet under his command were to be tried by court martial for mutiny in a ship, the *St George*, in which two homosexuals had already been hanged for their 'unnatural crime'. The mutineers were found guilty and were ordered to be hanged immediately. It happening to be a Sunday, Jervis's second-in-command, Vice-Admiral Charles Thompson, proposed a delay in the men's execution. For presuming to censure an execution on the sabbath, Thompson was sent home. Had it been Christmas Day, let alone a Sunday, Nelson assured Jervis's first captain, he would have hanged them himself.[28]

He had sympathy for the just grievances of the sailors: they were ill paid and, when discharged, 'shamefully treated'. He had no sympathy at all, however, with mutineers; and when reports came of a serious mutiny in May 1797 at the Nore, where sailors of the North Sea fleet had demanded improvements in their conditions, Nelson raised no objection to the severe punishments inflicted on the ringleaders. He fully recognized that some seamen had cause for complaint, he told William Hoste's father, but, as for the 'Nore scoundrels', he would have been happy to command a ship against them. 'At present we are all quiet in our Fleet,' he added, 'and if Government hang some of the Nore Delegates, we shall remain so.'[29]

Yet while approving hanging and flogging whenever considered necessary, Nelson, if possible, chose less violent methods of punishment, reasoning with disaffected crews and promising to investigate seemingly justified grievances. An American seaman, Jacob Nagle, serving in the *Blanche* in 1797, recorded in his journal an incident which well illustrates the trust which seamen reposed in 'our Nel'. A previous captain of the *Blanche*, Charles Sawyer, had been replaced when it became known that he had been summoning young sailors to his hammock late at night, telling them to put out the light and then taking hold of them 'about the privates'.[30] For a short time Captain D'Arcy Preston had been in command, before the appointment of Captain Henry Hotham, Admiral Hotham's nephew, whose reputation as a strict disciplinarian was well known, 'bearing the name of such a tarter by his own ships crew', in Jacob Nagle's words,

that our ship mutinized and entirely refused him.

He came on board [7 January 1797], had the officers armed on the quarter deck and all hands turned aft to hear his commission read at the capstain head. They all cried out, 'No, no, no.' He asked what they had to say against. One of the petty officers replyed that his ships company informed us that he was a dam'd tarter and we would not have him and went forward and turned the two forecastle guns aft with canester shot.

He then went in his boat on board [Commodore Nelson's ship] and returned with the com[modore's] first leutenant. When on b[oar]d he ordered all hands aft. He called all the petty officers out and pareded them in a line on the quarter deck. 'Now, my lads, if you resist taking Capt[ain] Hotham as your capt[ain], every third man shall be hung.' The crew flew in a body forward to the guns with match in hand, likewise crowbars, handspikes, and all kinds of weapons they could get holt of and left him, Capt[ain] Hothom, and the officers standing looking at us. They consulted for a moment and returned on b[oar]d Commodere Nelson['s ship].

In the space of half an hour the Commedore [himself] came on b[oar]d, call'd all hands aft, and enquired the reason of this disturbance. He was inform'd of Capt[ain] Hotham's caractor, which was the reason that we refused him.

'Lads,' said he, 'you have the greatest caracter on b[oar]d the *Blanch* of any frigates crew in the navy. You have taken two frigates supperiour to the frigate you are in, and now to rebel. If Capt[ain] Hotham ill treats you, give me a letter and I will support you.'

Amediately there was three chears given and Capt[ain] Hotham shed tears, and Nelson went on b[oar]d his ship.[31]

Cape St Vincent

I cannot, if I am in the field for glory, be kept out of sight.

Under Sir John Jervis's command, Nelson hoped that he might achieve the honours he had for long so keenly sought. For the moment, however, it was not himself but the Corsican officer, Napoleon Bonaparte, almost eleven years younger than himself, who was the talk of Europe. This man, who had come to prominence as commander of the artillery at the siege of Toulon, had now been appointed to the command of the army of Italy by the Directory, whose members were confident that he was brilliant enough to defeat the Piedmontese and Austrian armies and ruthless enough to replenish the Directory's empty coffers with treasures looted from the defeated enemies of revolutionary France. Their trust was not misplaced. Bonaparte's campaign in Italy was a triumph. By the end of April the Piedmontese had been obliged to agree to a separate peace; and in May French troops stormed the wooden bridge across the River Adda at Lodi and drove the Austrians from the far bank. A few days later Bonaparte entered Milan and occupied the palace from which the Austrian archduke had fled. He had now but to advance through the territories of the Venetian Republic to final victory over the Austrians. Spain was on the point of changing sides; Naples was wobbling; Leghorn had been taken, to deny the place to English shipping; the rest of Tuscany was about to be occupied; Genoa was so anxious not to offend the French that Nelson had cause to complain of his being 'very much surprised that, whenever he approaches any Town belonging to the Genoese government, they fire shot at him.'[1]

By now he had had to part company with the *Agamemnon*, which was in so sorry a state, a mere tub floating on the water, as her captain described her, that Jervis decided to send her home as escort to a convoy bound for England; and Nelson was ordered to transfer his commodore's broad pennant to the seventy-four-gun *Captain*. Aboard this ship Nelson did all that could be done to prevent supplies reaching the French army by sea. 'I cannot, if I am in the field for glory, be kept out of sight,' he assured his wife. 'Probably my services may be forgotten by the great by the time I get home; but my mind will not forget, nor cease to feel, a degree of consolation and of applause superior to undeserved rewards.'[2]

There was, however, no real glory for him to enjoy in the Mediterranean yet. At the end of September, he was given the task of supervising the evacuation of Bastia, then also that of Elba, on which he had but lately landed British troops. The government in London had decided that, with the French and Spanish fleets combined against them, they could no longer hold their own in the Mediterranean. Nelson was bitterly critical of this decision. 'At home they know not what this fleet is capable of performing,' he wrote. 'Much as I shall rejoice to see England, I lament our present orders in sackcloth and ashes, so dishonourable to the dignity of England, whose fleets are equal to meeting the World in arms. To say I am grieved & distressed but ill describes my feelings.'[3]

On his way home the English fleet was given just such an opportunity to show its worth as he had been looking for. Having sailed past Gibraltar and out into the Atlantic, he discerned through the thin patches of a drifting February fog the shapes of large ships also sailing in a westerly direction. His ship had been delayed in its progress because a sailor had fallen overboard and a jolly boat commanded by his first lieutenant, Thomas Hardy, had been lowered to pick the man up. The search – abandoned when the man was presumed drowned – had taken long enough for Hardy to be in danger of being captured by enemy craft sailing out of Algeciras. 'By God, I'll not lose Hardy,' Nelson had declared. 'Back that mizzentopsail.' This allowed the crew of the jolly boat, pulling furiously on their oars, to regain their ship, which had then drawn away fast from the Spanish ships, only to find herself in a new predicament.[4]

Nelson went to explain his problem to Sir Gilbert Elliot who, having been evacuated from Toulon, where he had been serving as civil commissioner, was now sailing home in the *Captain*. There was a difficult choice to be made, Nelson told Elliot: he must either try to find the rest of the British fleet and warn Admiral Jervis that the Spaniards were also in the Atlantic or, in case the Spanish ships were heading for the West Indies, to sail there to give warning of the enemy's approach. Elliot, aroused from a deep sleep, accepted the possibility of a long detour with weary imperturbability. 'We are only passengers,' he said, 'and must submit to circumstances.' He then went back to sleep.[5]

When he awoke he discovered that Nelson had, after all, decided not to make for the West Indies but to find the main British fleet, which, on the morning of 13 February 1797, was sighted off the Portuguese headland of St Vincent. The next day, St Valentine's Day, the Spanish fleet, whose signal guns had been heard booming throughout the night, was also sighted, making for Cadiz. At first the enemy ships were no more than vague shapes swirling in the mist; then they loomed larger. 'By my soul,' a signal lieutenant exclaimed, 'they are thumpers! They look like Beachy Head in a fog.'

Aboard the Admiral's flagship, the *Victory*, Sir Robert Calder, his first captain, was also looking through his glass at the approaching ships.

'There are eight sail-of-the-line, Sir John.'

'Very well, Sir.'

'There are twenty sail-of-the-line, Sir John.'

'Very well, Sir.'

'There are twenty-five sail-of-the-line . . . twenty-seven, Sir John.'

'Enough, Sir, no more of that, Sir,' exploded Jervis, who had but sixteen ships under command. 'The die is cast and if there are fifty sail I will go through them. England badly needs a victory at present.'[6]

Hearing these words, the Canadian Captain Ben Hallowell, whose own ship had been wrecked in a gale, was so overcome with excitement that he slapped the Commander-in-Chief on the back.

'That's right, Sir John, that's right. And by God, we shall give them a damned good licking.'[7]

The Spanish ships were sailing in two straggling groups, a gap of several miles between them. Jervis gave orders for his own ships to sail straight through the gap, then turn about and, in two divisions, engage the two groups separately. The seventy-four-gun *Culloden*, commanded by Thomas Troubridge, led the way, flying at them, in the words of Cuthbert Collingwood of the *Excellent*, the last ship in the line, 'as a hawk to his prey'. The manoeuvre was initially successful, but Nelson, whose ship was third from the rear of the British line, seeing that a large part of the Spanish fleet might escape unscathed, took the *Captain* out of the line, in accordance with what he understood to be Jervis's general plan but acting on his own initiative and offering himself to attack by seven Spanish ships, one of them the *Santísima Trinidad*, the largest warship in the world.[8]

Collingwood's *Excellent* and Troubridge's *Culloden* went to Nelson's help; so did the *Blenheim*. All were soon damaged by enemy broadsides; while the *Captain*, her rigging and wheel smashed, her sails in tatters, her fore-topmast broken, was incapable of further action. So Nelson gave the order for her to run alongside the nearest Spanish ship, the *San Nicolas*. As the two ships collided, Nelson shouted for a boarding party and, with a drawn sword, jumped himself on to the stern of the Spanish ship after a soldier of the 69th Regiment who was serving in the *Captain* as a marine. Other soldiers and seamen, including three midshipmen, scrambled after Nelson, clambering through the smoke across the bowsprit and springing, cutlasses in mouths, towards the rigging, or jumping from bulwark to bulwark, one soldier tumbling into the sea.

'I found the cabin doors fastened,' Nelson reported, 'and the Spanish officers fired their pistols at us through the windows, but, having broken open the doors, the soldiers fired.' On reaching the quarterdeck, Nelson found the Spanish ensign being hauled down by Edward Berry, formerly his first lieutenant, who had recently been promoted commander and was sailing in the *Captain* as a volunteer while awaiting another appointment.

Although the guns on the lower deck of the *San Nicolas* were still firing at the British ships, several Spanish officers handed Nelson their swords. As they were doing so there was an outburst of musket fire from the immense three-decker, the *San José*, whose rigging had become inextricably entangled with that of the *San Nicolas*. Seven of Nelson's boarding party were killed and several others wounded, together with about twenty Spaniards. Provoked by this, Nelson determined to bring into operation what he afterwards said was called in the Navy 'Nelson's Patent Bridge for Boarding First-Rates'. Ordering more men to be brought aboard the *San Nicolas*, although it was now on fire, he used that ship as a stepping-stone to take the *San José* as well.[9]

'I directed my brave fellows to board this first-rate,' his report continued; and he leaped aboard her himself, crying 'Westminster Abbey or Glorious Victory!' It was

done in a moment. When I got into her main-chains, a Spanish officer came upon the quarterdeck rail, without arms and said the ship had surrendered . . . It was not long before I was on the quarterdeck [where] the Spanish captain, with a bended knee, presented me with a sword and told me the Admiral was dying of his wounds below. I gave him my hand and desired him to call to his officers and ship's company that the ship had surrendered, which he did.

Nelson handed the sword, together with the swords of other officers, to one of his bargemen, 'who tucked these honourable trophies under his arm with all the *sang-froid* imaginable'.[10] 'I was surrounded by Captain Berry,' Nelson's report concluded, 'Lieutenant [Charles] Pierson (69th Regiment), John Sykes, John Thomson, Francis Cook, all old Agamemnons, and several brave men, Seamen and Soldiers. Thus fell these Ships. The *Victory* passing saluted us with three cheers, as did every Ship in the Fleet.'[11]

Having returned to the *Captain* to thank his second-in-command, the American Captain Miller, and to present him with one of the Spanish officers' swords, Nelson went on board the *Victory* at dusk. He looked a fright, he later told his family; his shirt and coat were both badly torn; he had lost his hat; his face, still unwashed, was streaked with gunpowder; his body was bruised; and he had been slightly wounded by a shell splinter. Jervis's uniform had no doubt been changed, as, during the battle, a marine had had his head blown off beside him as he stood on the poop, and the Admiral's face and chest had been so badly splashed with blood and brains, bits of bone and tissue, that an officer had rushed to his side, believing him to be badly wounded. He was not at all hurt, he assured him, calmly turning aside to ask a midshipman to fetch him an orange to rinse out his mouth.

'The Admiral received me on the quarterdeck,' Nelson recalled, 'and having embraced me, said he could not sufficiently thank me and used every kind expression which could not fail to make me happy.'[12]

Surely now, Nelson fervently hoped, his services would be duly recognized at home as they were in the fleet where, so he congratulated himself, stories about him were legion and he was becoming something of a legend. Collingwood agreed with him that he should be suitably honoured. 'My dear good Friend,' he wrote to him in answer to Nelson's letter of thanks for having supported him so well in the recent battle. 'You formed the plan of attack – we were only accessories to the Don's ruin . . . It added very much to the satisfaction which I felt in thumping the Spaniards that I released you a little.'[13]

Collingwood, like all the other captains of ships of the line engaged in the battle, was awarded a gold medal. Admiral Jervis was granted an annuity of £3,000, elected a Freeman of the City of London, and created Earl of St Vincent. Captain Calder, whose father had been Gentleman Usher to Queen Charlotte, was knighted. 'As for you, Commodore,' said Colonel Drinkwater, Sir Gilbert Elliot's aide, having heard Nelson's account of the battle, 'they will make you a baronet.' He was stopped from saying more by a hand on his arm and the warning, 'No. No. If they want to mark my services, it must not be in that manner.'

'Oh,' said I, interrupting him [Drinkwater's account continued]. 'You wish to be made a Knight of the Bath'; for I could not imagine that his ambition, at that time, led him to expect a Peerage. My supposition proved to be correct, for he instantly answered me, 'Yes; if my services have been of any value, let them be noticed in a way that the public may know me or them.'

I cannot distinctly remember which of these terms were used, but, from his manner, I could have no doubt of his meaning, that he wished to bear about his person some honourary distinction to attract the public eye ... What I had noticed in the above interview agreed perfectly with the opinion from all I observed during our subsequent acquaintance. The attainment of public honours, and an ambition to be distinguished above his fellows, were his master passions. His conduct was constantly actuated by these predominant feelings.[14]

To Sir Gilbert Elliot, who was now to sail home in the *Lively*, the ship entrusted with the Admiral's dispatches, Nelson wrote, 'If you can be instrumental in keeping back what I expect will happen, it will be an additional obligation.' He would be reluctant to accept a baronetcy: he could not afford to maintain a hereditary title; he was finding it difficult to make ends meet as it was. However, there were 'other Honours' which died with the possessor, and which he would be proud to accept if his efforts were 'thought worthy of the favour of the King'. As he had already intimated to Colonel Drinkwater, he had his eye on the Order of the Bath, which carried with it the right to wear a handsomely glittering star.[15]

When the Admiral's dispatches reached London and a *Gazette Extraordinary* was published on 3 March, however, it did not seem very probable that Nelson would be granted even a knighthood. No officer, apart from Calder, was mentioned by name, since 'the correct conduct of every Officer and man made it impossible to distinguish one more than the other'. In a private letter to Earl Spencer, who had succeeded Lord Chatham as First Lord of the Admiralty, the Admiral did say that Commodore Nelson, who 'was in the rear, on the starboard tack, took the lead on the larboard, and contributed very much to the fortune of the day'. But that was all. It was unfairly rumoured in the fleet that Calder, who disapproved of Nelson's independent action, had been responsible for the alteration of an original draft in which his services had been more fully and favourably noted.[16]

Nelson, as was his habit, took it upon himself to ensure that these services were made known to the world at large. He wrote a rather tendentious account of the action as fought and seen from his point of view and had it signed by Berry and Miller, who seemed to have suggested alterations so that they and others should receive some of the credit which, in the first draft, Nelson gave himself.[17] He sent the account to Captain Locker at Greenwich, authorizing him to send it to the newspapers, 'inserting the name of Commodore instead of "I"'.

When the account was duly published, Vice-Admiral William Parker, who had commanded the van in the battle, objected to some derogatory comments which were made upon the performance of his ship, the *Prince George*, whose broadsides, Parker contended, had seriously damaged the *San José* before Nelson boarded her. To Parker's objections Nelson replied: 'I must acknowledge receipt of your letter of 26 July and, after declaring that I know nothing of the *Prince George* after she was hailed [to stop firing] from the forecastle of the *San Nicolas* [which had surrendered], it is impossible I can enter into the subject of your letter.'[18]

Cadiz and Tenerife

Let me alone! I have got my legs left and one arm.

In England, Nelson's family anxiously awaited news. On 22 February 1797 a naval officer, looking through the newspapers in a coffee-house in Bath, read that Commodore Horatio Nelson had, in the course of seniority, been promoted rear-admiral of the Blue.* He rushed off to Bennett Street to tell Mrs Nelson and her father-in-law. Fanny had never seen anything 'elevate [the old rector] equal to this'. He sat down immediately to write a letter to his 'dear Rear-Admiral'. Then came news of the great victory which the country had so badly needed and which had, for the moment, lessened the fears of a foreign invasion. Mr Nelson had had to go back to his lodgings to hide his tears. 'The name and services of Nelson have sounded throughout the city of Bath, from the common ballad-singer to the public theatre,' he wrote later in a letter characteristic in both its orotund phrasing and affectionate tone. 'Joy sparkles in every eye, and desponding Britain draws back her sable veil, and smiles ... The height of glory to which your professional judgement, united with a proper degree of bravery, guarded by Providence, few sons, my dear Child, attain to, and fewer fathers live to see.'[1]

When he emerged from his lodgings, all sorts of people, many of whom he had never met, stopped him in the street to congratulate him on his son's great achievement. Bath and Bristol, as well as

---

* In the seventeenth century the fleet had been separated into three divisions, each carrying a different colour of ensign, the red taking precedence over white and blue. The system had long since been abandoned, but the titles of the ranks remained (Lavery, 99).

Norwich and London, had granted him their freedom. There was, indeed, great cause for celebration: Horatio Nelson was not only an admiral now, he had, as he had hoped, been created a Knight of the Order of the Bath.

So gratified was Nelson to have received the recognition and honours that he had for so long felt were his due that he even persuaded himself, as he told his wife, that his 'chains, medals and ribbons' were, 'with a contented mind', all now quite sufficient for him.[2] They were honours, so he assured his brother, that 'no fortune or connexion in England' could obtain. He would feel prouder of them than of all 'the titles in the King's power to bestow'.[3]

He would 'one day or other' come laughing home and he and his wife would settle down together in a cottage near Norwich or 'any other place' that Fanny liked better. He asked her to arrange for the purchase of 'fifty good large blankets with the letter N wove in the centre' for the 'next winter's gift' from his father to the poor of Burnham Thorpe;[4] and he began work on formulating his ideas for a coat of arms to be submitted to York Herald:

On one side [as supporters] a Sailor poorly habited, holding in his hand the Broad Pennant on a staff, and trampling on a Spanish flag; on the other side, the British lion tearing the Spanish flag, the remnants hanging down, and the flag in tatters . . . *Crest* – on a wreath of the colours, the stern of a Spanish Man-of-War, proper, inscribed, 'San Josef' . . . Motto – what my brother, William suggested, turned into English 'Faith and Works'.*[5]

He also sent Fanny a copy of a ballad written by 'an old sailor' which extolled his action on St Valentine's Day:

> This brave hero, Old England's boast
> Grappled two ships along,
> Forced them to strike on their own coast
> And lasting laurels won.

* In a postscript to a letter written to Sir Gilbert Elliot on 5 August 1796, Nelson had already claimed this motto as his own: 'It has ever pleased God to prosper all my undertakings and I feel confident of His blessing . . . I ever consider my motto, *Fides et opera* (Nicolas, ii, 234).

Long will this fact in history shine;
'Give me,' the fair sex say,
'A Nelson for my Valentine
On this auspicious day.'[6]

Also dispatched to Norfolk were 'five elegant drawings of the action', a copy of his 'Few Remarks relative to myself in the *Captain*, in which my pennant was flying on the most glorious Valentine's Day, 1797'. Appended to this was a note about 'Nelson's Patent Bridge for Boarding First-Rates'. In another letter came stories showing how well liked and respected he was in the fleet and a long and facetious recipe for 'Nelson's new art of cooking Spaniards'.[7] 'All do me that Justice I feel I deserve,' he wrote. 'You will receive pleasure from the share I had in making it a most Brilliant day, the most so of any that I know of in the annals of England.'[8]

He was clearly as anxious as ever to impress upon Fanny the brave and valuable services he had performed for his country, to emphasize the fame he had achieved, and to extract from her some words of pride and congratulation, some responses other than the expressions of anxiety as to his welfare which her letters so exasperatingly reiterated. 'The *Agamemnon* is as well known through Europe as one of Mr Harwood's [coasters] is at Overy,' he had told her when in command of this ship, 'one of the finest Sixty-Fours in the Service'; and, although it was 'all vanity' to himself, he added that a letter addressed to 'Horatio Nelson, Genoa' had found its way to him. The person who had written the letter, on being asked how he could have expected it to have reached its intended recipient with so brief an inscription, had replied at 'a large party, "Sir, there is but one Horatio Nelson in the world." I am known throughout Italy: not a Kingdom or state, where my name will be forgotten. This is my *Gazette*.'[9]

To such evidence of her husband's celebrity, Fanny Nelson made little reference in her replies. Her letters, instead, conveyed repeated intelligence of her anxieties in his long absence. 'I shall not be myself, till I hear from you again,' she wrote in one letter. 'Altogether, my dearest husband, my sufferings were great.' In other letters she told him that her anxiety was 'far beyond her powers of expression', that her 'mind and poor heart' were 'always on the rack'. In yet others she begged him never to board an enemy vessel again. 'You have done desperate actions enough ... You have been most wonderfully protected ... May I – indeed I do – beg that you never Board again. Leave it for Captains.' 'I sincerely hope, my dear husband,' she pleaded, 'that all these wonderful and desperate actions, such as boarding ships, you will leave to others. With the protection of a Supreme Being, you have acquired a character, or name, which all hands agree cannot be greater, therefore rest satisfied.'[10] Like 'an eager Schooll Girll reckoning the days when she shall be releived from her present anxiety', in her father-in-law's description,[11] Lady Nelson cannot have been other than dismayed and distressed to receive in reply to one of her letters a brief note written before an imminent engagement with an enemy fleet, 'My character and good name are in my own keeping. Life with disgrace is dreadful. A glorious death is to be envied.'[12]

'His poor wife is continually in a fret and worry about him,' his father commented. 'In such a state, the blessings of a marriage union are thus made a torment and most likely the health is destroyed, or the temper soured so as never to be recovered.' Nelson's own temper was certainly tried beyond measure by his wife's repeated injunctions not to risk his life, to take more care of his health, her frequent complaints that worry about him made her ill. Sometimes he replied comfortingly: 'I grieve to hear such a bad account of yourself. Cheer up, I shall return safe and sound ... All my joy is placed in you ... You are present to my imagination be where I will.' But, more often, he made no comment on 'her remonstrances', and occasionally wrote crossly, 'Why you should be uneasy about me so as to make yourself ill, I know not.' 'Why should you alarm yourself? I am well, your son is well, and we are as comfortable in every respect as the nature of our service will admit.' Yet the letters came as before. There were occasional passages that satisfied him. He was, for example, so he was told, 'universally the subject of conversation' in Bath; but then her letter continued with gossip about the people who were there taking the waters instead of the words of congratulation and praise he longed for.[13]

He had not been faithful to her – naval officers on long spells of duty abroad were scarcely expected to be faithful to their wives. In his biography of Nelson, James Harrison, who wrote on the authority of Lady Hamilton, conceded that, 'though by no means an unprincipled seducer of the wives and daughters of his friends', Nelson was 'always well known to maintain rather more partiality for the fair sex than is quite consistent with the highest degree of Christian purity. Such improper indulgences, with some slight addiction to that other vicious habit of British seamen, the occasional use of a few thoughtlessly profane expletives in speech, form the only dark specks ever yet discovered in the bright blaze of his moral character.'[14] At Leghorn, where he had a miniature of himself painted for her by a local artist, Nelson had met an opera singer, Adelaide Correglia, probably through John Udney, the British consul, who was frequently approached by naval officers for introductions of this sort. Signora Correglia was well known to be of easy virtue; and Nelson's unconcealed affair with the woman – to whom he sent money through an English merchant and Admiralty contractor in Leghorn[15] – was a cause of some surprise and censure among his fellow officers. 'Dined at Nelson's and his dolly,' recorded Captain Thomas Fremantle, who was not then married and by no means celibate himself. 'Called on old Udney, went to the opera with him. He introduced me to a very handsome Greek woman.' 'Dined with Nelson. Dolly aboard, who has a sort of abscess in her side,' Fremantle noted on later occasions. 'He makes himself ridiculous with that woman . . . Dined with Nelson and Dolly. Very bad dinner indeed.'*[16]

---

* It may well be that as well as serving as Nelson's mistress, Adelaide Correglia was acting as a spy. There is a hint of this in a letter which Nelson wrote to Sir Gilbert Elliot from Leghorn Roads on 3 August 1796: 'One *old* lady tells me all she hears, which is what we wish.' And in a letter to the woman herself, written in his rickety French, Nelson added a postscript which refers to some mission which she had undertaken for him: '*Ma chere Adelaide, Je suis partant en cette moment pour la Mere, une Vaisseau Neapolitan partir avec moi pour Livorne; Croire moi toujours*

While Nelson's affair with Adelaide Correglia, well enough known
amongst his fellow officers, never reached the ears of his wife, she
was not spared accounts of the risks he continued to take, despite
her protests. On 27 May 1797 she was told he had been ordered to
lie at anchor in his new flagship, the seventy-four-gun *Theseus*, off
Cadiz, where he would be 'in sight of the whole Spanish fleet . . .
barely out of shot of a Spanish Rear-Admiral';[17] and on 3 July
that year he was once more 'on service hand-to-hand with swords'
when, in an attack on Cadiz, his barge collided with that of the
Spanish commander, and the crews of the two boats leapt at each
other through the drifting smoke of the bombardment.

Nelson would have been killed, he said, but for the bravery of
his coxswain, a Lincolnshire man named John Sykes, who, so
another of the crew recorded, 'parried blows that must have been
fatal to Nelson . . . The Spaniards fought like devils and seemed
resolved to win from the Admiral the laurels of his former victory;
they appeared to know him and directed their particular attack
towards the officers.

'Twice Sykes saved him,' this sailor continued his account.
'When he saw a blow descending that would have severed the head
of Nelson . . . he interposed his own hand! We all saw it . . . and we
gave in revenge one cheer and one tremendous rally. Eighteen of
the Spaniards were killed and we boarded and carried [their
boat], there being not one man left on board who was not either
dead or wounded.'[18]

'Sykes, I cannot forget this,' Nelson told the coxswain, supporting
the badly wounded man in his arms, as their barge towed the
Spanish boat with its dead and bleeding cargo towards the *Theseus*.
Nor did he forget him, recalling the man's courage in a *Sketch of My
Life* which he later wrote for an early biographer. Nor yet did he
forget his own bravery: 'My personal courage was more conspicuous than at any other period of my life.'[19] To his wife, who so
persistently declared her wish to be spared reports of her husband's
reckless bravado, he wrote, 'My late Affair here will not, I believe,

---

Votre chere amie Horatio Nelson. Avez vous bien successe' (MS. in the Henry
E. Huntingdon Library, San Marino, California).

lower me in the opinion of the world. I have had flattery enough to make me vain, and success enough to make me confident.'[20] In his next brush with the Spaniards he was not to be so fortunate.

Less than a fortnight after this hand-to-hand fighting off Cadiz, Nelson received orders to 'proceed with the ships ... under [his] command ... with the utmost expedition to the Island of Tenerife and there make dispositions for taking possession of the town of Santa Cruz by a sudden and vigorous assault'.

A sudden attack was essential since, although Santa Cruz was believed to be garrisoned by an inconsiderable force of soldiers and inexperienced militia, its defences were known to be strong; and, once the castle and forts were fully manned, the place would not be taken easily. As it happened, however, there could be no question of a surprise attack; for, on the morning of the planned assault, an unusually strong inshore current swept the landing-craft down the coast, and, as alarm guns were fired in the town, Captain Troubridge, who had been entrusted with the task of landing a thousand men on shore at dawn, gave orders for the boats to be rowed back to the ships.

Determined not to be denied the opportunity of taking Santa Cruz – where a Spanish treasure-ship from the East Indies was reported to have arrived from Manila – Nelson gave orders for a second assault to be launched immediately upon the port. Although supported by a heavy bombardment from the fleet, this, too, was driven back. Yet, after a consultation with his captains, and encouraged by information brought by a deserter from the town who reported that the garrison were 'in the greatest alarm, all crying and trembling', Nelson decided upon yet another attempt upon the port, this time by night. From the beginning the army commanders had been advising caution; but Nelson dismissed their apprehension as pusillanimity.

'Soldiers have not the same boldness in undertaking a political measure that we have,' he wrote. 'We look to the benefit of our country and risk our own fame every day to serve her. A soldier obeys his orders and no more.'[21]

Nelson himself would command one of the six divisions into which the thousand or so sailors and marines were to be divided.

They were to land on the mole beneath the castle of San Cristóbal, charge the batteries defending the town, drive out the garrison and accept the Spaniards' surrender. To Betsey Fremantle it all sounded a simple operation with a foregone conclusion. The daughter of Richard Wynne, an eccentric Englishman living on the Continent, Betsey had married Thomas Fremantle in Naples at the age of eighteen six months before and was now living with him in the *Seahorse*. She had felt 'quite odd' at first to be parted from her family; but after a time she decided she could make no complaints. 'I am as happy in my situation as it is possible to be,' she wrote in her diary. 'Fremantle is all attention and kindness.' While 'old Nelson' (who at thirty-eight was not quite seven years older than her husband) was 'very civil and good natured' when he came to dinner, though he did 'not say much'. She had a 'comfortable little cabin' where she could do what she liked.[22]

After dining on the evening of 24 July aboard the *Seahorse* with Nelson and her husband and the other captains, Betsey watched them climb down into the boats, 'apprehending no danger for Fremantle'. She went to bed in the cabin on a lower deck which had been fitted up for her near the bunk of another woman, the sail-maker's wife, and was soon asleep. She was woken in the night by the sound of firing, but comforted herself with the thought that the deserter had said that 'nothing could be easier than to take the place': Tenerife would soon be in English hands and Fremantle would shortly be back with her. With the morning, however, came disillusionment. 'Great was our mistake,' she wrote in her journal. 'This proved to be a shocking unfortunate night.'[23]

The boats, flying Union flags on which the names of their ships had been painted in yellow, had been rowed towards the shore in a rough sea buffeted by a strong wind. The sentries of the garrison, far more alert than had been expected, soon saw the approaching craft and, as an officer in one of the boats recorded, 'the alarm now became general and they opened a cross-fire from all sides with cannon and musketry'. Most of the boats were swept past the mole in the strong current; many were dashed upon the shore; some were smashed upon the beach as the soldiers and marines, jumping for the land, came under a heavy fire 'from holes and corners'. 'Unfortunately many boats did not land owing to mistaken orders, darkness and confusion', and scores of the men in those that did, running ashore with cutlasses, pikes and swords, were brought down by sniper fire and salvoes of grapeshot. Fremantle was wounded; so were several other officers; Troubridge, taking cover in the convent of Santo Domingo, failed in two attempts to persuade the Spanish commander that the English invaders were strong enough to dictate terms of surrender.

Soon after sunrise, all hope lost, the invaders undertook to abandon their plans for further attacks on the Canary Islands on the understanding that they might return to their ships bearing their weapons.

'Our men drew up in solid files along the Plaza de la Pila with bands playing,' recorded a Spanish officer. 'The English, obeying orders, emptied their muskets by firing them into the sea, and, forming up afterwards . . . [marched] over the wall to their boats to cries of "*Viva la Republica! Viva la Libertad!*" . . . The mole was littered with dead bodies which were being removed so as not to offend the eye.'[24]

The British officers were invited to dinner by the Spanish commander but 'they hardly raised their eyes from the table'. Outside dead bodies were still being taken from the mole, and wounded British sailors were being ferried across to their ships from the town's hospital in Spanish boats. 'We behaved handsomely to them after our victory,' a Spaniard claimed; and it was true. For Nelson, who had lost many of his men and seven of his officers, it was a disaster.

Before dinner the night before he had changed into a clean uniform as surgeons always recommended since wounds were more likely to be infected by worn and dirty cloth. He had put on blue and white striped stockings in place of the usual plain white, and had buckled on a sword given to him by Captain Suckling, who had inherited it from his great-uncle and godfather, Captain Galfridus Walpole. Before climbing down into his boat, Nelson had sent for his stepson, Josiah Nisbet, now a lieutenant, and for that night officer of the watch. Nisbet had come into his cabin dressed to join the landing party. His stepfather had objected to his coming. 'Should we both fall, Josiah, what would become of your poor mother?' he protested. 'The care of the *Theseus* falls to you. Stay, therefore, and take charge of her.'[25]

'Sir,' Nisbet had replied, 'the ship must take care of herself. I will go with you tonight if never again.'

Nelson gave way and, when the young man had gone, he sat down to write to the Commander-in-Chief to inform him that the attack on Santa Cruz was about to take place and that tomorrow his head would 'probably be crowned with either laurel or cypress'. 'I have only to recommend Josiah Nisbet to you and my Country,' he added. 'The Duke of Clarence, should I fall in the service of my King and Country, will, I am confident, take a lively interest for my Son-in-Law [stepson] on his name being mentioned.' He made a will, leaving £500 to Josiah, £200 to his brother Maurice and the rest of his property to his wife, or to Josiah if she predeceased him.[26]

Not for the first or last time he had a premonition that he would be killed. Although he had earlier declared that he was convinced there was 'nothing which Englishmen are not equal to' and that he was 'confident in the bravery of those who would be employed', he afterwards described the enterprise as a 'forlorn hope' which his 'pride' and the 'honour of our country' demanded and from which he 'never expected to return'. He very nearly did not return.

No sooner had he jumped from the plunging barge on to the mole than he stumbled and collapsed backwards into the boat, his right arm pouring blood from a shattered elbow, dropping his sword which he picked up in his left hand, murmuring, 'I am a dead man!'[27] Nisbet, pushing his way to his side, placed his hat over the wound to hide the blood spurting from it and took off his black silk stock for use as a tourniquet while a sailor threw off his shirt and tore it apart for a sling. As the barge was pulled frantically back to the ships under the guns of the mole battery, Nelson asked to be lifted up so that he might 'look a little about him'. By the flashes of gunfire which momentarily lit up the surface of the stormy sea, he saw that a cutter had been hit below the water-line and all the men aboard had been cast into the sea.

He ordered the steersman of his barge to go back to pick up as many as could be rescued.

Half an hour passed before the barge reached the nearest ship; but this was the *Seahorse*, and Nelson refused to be carried aboard her, anxious not to frighten Betsey Fremantle. His life was in danger, he was urged: he must be got to a surgeon without delay; but he was adamant. 'Then I will die,' he said. 'I would rather suffer death than alarm Mrs Fremantle by her seeing me in this state, when I can give her no tidings whatever of her husband.'[28]

He was equally stubborn when at length the barge reached the *Theseus*. He refused to be helped aboard. 'Let me alone!' he snapped. 'I have got my legs left and one arm.' 'And he walked up the side of the ship, Lieutenant N[isbet] keeping so close that in case he had slipped he could have caught him.' Midshipman Hoste, who had not taken part in the assault, witnessed the Admiral's return 'with his right arm dangling by his side, while with the other he helped himself to [climb into the ship] and, with a spirit that astonished everyone, told the surgeon to get his instruments ready for that he knew he must lose his arm, and the sooner it was off the better'.[29] 'On getting on the quarter deck,' so his wife was told, 'the officers as usual saluted him by taking off their hats, which compliment Nelson returned with his left hand as if nothing had happened.'[30]

The surgeon was ready for him, his table and knives and saws prepared under the swaying lanterns of the cabin. Nelson had good cause to be grateful that he was not to be attended by the surgeon who would have operated upon him in the *Seahorse*, Mr Fleming, a 'clumsy fellow', responsible, so other surgeons considered, for Captain Fremantle's slow recovery. The *Theseus*'s surgeon was Thomas Eshelby; he performed the operation neatly and quickly, and his patient, held down firmly on the table, bore it without complaint. '1797. July 25,' the surgeon recorded in his log. 'Admiral Nelson. Compound fracture of the right arm by a musket ball passing through a little above the elbow, an artery divided: the arm was immediately amputated and opium was afterwards given.'[31]

Nelson might well have wished that opium had been given

beforehand, since the pain was intense, not from the sawing of the bone so much but from the cutting of the flesh with a cold knife. He afterwards laid down that surgeons must heat their knives before carrying out operations. However, the arm was soon off; and Nelson was asked what should be done with it: should it be embalmed and sent home to England for burial? 'Throw it into the hammock,' he ordered, 'with the brave fellow that was killed beside me.'[32]

Evidently the opium did not make Nelson drowsy for long; within half an hour of its administration he was giving orders to his flag-captain, again 'as if nothing had happened'. Soon afterwards he was busy dictating letters. To the Spanish commander, who had kindly agreed to the English fleet being provisioned from Tenerife, he sent his sincere thanks and a cask of English beer, together with a cheese. He also offered to take the Spaniards' dispatches to Cadiz, 'thus making himself the herald of his own defeat', and gratefully accepted two casks of Canary wine. To the Commander-in-Chief, Lord St Vincent, he reported, 'Although I am under the painful necessity of acquainting you that we have not been able to succeed in our attack, yet it is my duty to state that I believe more daring intrepidity was never shown than by the Captains, Officers and Men you did me the honour to place under my command.'[33]

In an accompanying and rambling letter, Nelson revealed the depths of his despondency. 'I am become a burthen to my friends and useless to my Country,' he wrote with his left hand in spidery writing which, little resembling the neat, sloping hand of his youth, was before long to become far more legible and distinctive than the hasty scribble of recent years.

When I leave your command I become dead to the World; I go hence, and am no more seen . . . I hope you will be able to give me a frigate, to convey the remains of my carcase to England . . . A left-handed Admiral will never again be considered as useful, therefore the sooner I get to a very humble cottage the better and make room for a better man to serve the state . . . You will excuse my scrawl, considering it is my first attempt.[34]

The deaths of so many of his men preyed upon his mind. The ships' flags and pennants were flying at half-mast in their memory;

and reports came in of the deaths of wounded sailors to add to the total of 153 killed, drowned or missing. Misled by reports of a demoralized, ill-trained garrison, and too ready to believe that he would succeed again as he had succeeded in the past, he had been foolhardy. He told a friend that he had 'reason to believe a full success would have crowned our endeavours' had he 'been with the first party himself'.[35] But, as it was, he had to face failure; and this realization, combined with the pain of his wound, made him extremely short-tempered. The surgeons who came to inspect the progress of his stump, and the surgeons' mates who hovered about him with their wet dressings, were grudgingly admitted and grumpily dismissed. Besides, his servant Tom Allen was irritatingly solicitous, rigging up a complicated contraption of pulley and cord by which Nelson could summon help whenever needed in the middle of the night.

The defeated Admiral was momentarily consoled when Lord St Vincent assured him that he was not to take the defeat at Santa Cruz too hard: 'Mortals cannot command success. You and your companions have certainly deserved it by the greatest degree of heroism and perseverance that was ever exhibited.' He was to sail home in the *Seahorse* with Thomas and Betsey Fremantle; and no doubt he would be feeling quite fit again by the time he reached England. St Vincent promised Nelson he would ask for him again as soon as he was ready; and he wrote to the First Lord of the Admiralty to say that he had 'very good ground of hope' that Admiral Nelson would be 'restored to the service of his King and Country'.[36]

Nelson was accordingly in better spirits when he came aboard the *Seahorse*: but Betsey Fremantle noted in her journal, 'I find it looks shocking to be without one arm.'[37] Nor was it only the empty sleeve pinned across his chest that had so much altered his appearance: his right eye, wounded at Calvi, was now fixed and dim and a milky blue in colour. His dry and frizzy hair was almost white, so nearly so indeed that he considered it needed no powder; and because he had lost so many teeth, his cheeks had sunk. When he smiled he kept his lips together, self-conscious about the missing teeth. He rarely laughed. He was thirty-eight years old.

*

Betsey Fremantle did not enjoy the voyage home. She had
described her husband on first meeting him as 'good-natured, kind
and amiable, gay and lively'. He was far from being so now. In
almost constant pain, he was 'very low spirited'. Quick-tempered
at the best of times, he was almost exhausted now and feeling
'wretched . . . very low indeed'.[38]

She herself was heavily pregnant and 'not well at all', though
the surgeon, Mr Eshelby, who had come over with Nelson from
the *Theseus*, did what he could for her, prescribing pills for her
morning sickness. She thought him a 'sensible young man' even
though 'highly stupid society at dinner', talking of 'nothing but
medicine, wounds and fever'. He was certainly a decided improvement on Fleming, who had been sent to another ship, having been
abused by other surgeons for not ensuring that Fremantle lived
high enough, 'not giving him Bark [quinine] and Port Wine'.
Eventually Fremantle was given bark but it did not agree with
him; and his arm remained 'so uncommonly painful', particularly
when he was lying in his cot and the wind was fresh. Nelson,
Betsey decided, was not much better. On 24 August she noted, 'A
foul wind makes the Admiral fret, he is a very bad patient.'[39] The
stump of his arm was not healing properly; and he could not sleep
at night because of the pain from the infection. As the *Seahorse*
approached the English shore he became increasingly concerned
about the reception he could expect.

13

Bath, London and Toulon

I believe firmly that it was the Almightys goodness, to check my consummate vanity.

On a sunny evening in the first week of September 1797, Fanny Nelson, her father-in-law and sister-in-law, Susannah Bolton, were sitting in the parlour of Fanny's lodgings in Bath when they heard the sound of a coach drawing up outside. Horatio Nelson had come home to his family. They had been expecting him for some time. A letter had arrived from the *Seahorse*: the writing had been unfamiliar and Fanny had dared not open it, believing that it would surely bring bad news. She handed it to the old clergyman, who had passed it to his daughter. Susannah had accordingly opened it, to discover that the writing was, after all, Horatio's. 'It was the chance of War,' Nelson had observed, explaining the use of his left hand, 'and I have great reason to be thankful, and I know it will add to your pleasure in finding that Josiah, under God's providence, was principally instrumental in saving my life . . . [I am] perfectly well and shall be with you perhaps as soon as this letter. I shall come to Bath the moment permission comes from the Admiralty for me to strike my Flag.'[1]

It was immediately obvious, though, when he arrived at Bath that he was far from perfectly well. His wound had not healed. The silk ligatures tied in a reef-knot around the arteries had not yet come away from the short and swollen stump; the wound was infected and still extremely painful. Unable to sleep without laudanum, he was looking tired and worn. 'I am beset with a physician, surgeon and apothecary,' he wrote a few days after his return, 'and, to say the truth am suffering much pain with some fever.'[2] 'His arm is by no means well,' Sir Gilbert Elliot reported.

The ligature has not come away, and they are afraid it has taken in the artery or even a sinew. They must wait till it rots off, which may be a great while. If they should attempt to cut it (it is two inches up the wound), and they should cut the artery, they would be obliged to amputate again higher up, which is not easy for the stump is very short already . . . He is impatient for the healing that he may go to sea again. He writes very tolerably with his left.[3]

At first Nelson's dressings were changed by a doctor; but thereafter, reluctant as she was to trust herself, Lady Nelson was expected by her husband to clean and dress the septic wound without professional help. She did so with evident trepidation and was thankful to get her husband away from Bath to London where the medical practitioners were more to be trusted with such patients than the physicians of Bath, skilled though they might be in dealing with rheumatism, arthritis and congestion of the liver.

In London, Nelson, with his father and his wife, her maid and his servant, Tom Allen, moved into lodgings at 141 Bond Street, which had been taken for them by his brother Maurice. Here a succession of visitors called upon the Admiral, not all of them welcome. One night a rowdy delegation of demonstrators banged on the door to demand why, unlike other houses in the street, lights had not been placed in the windows in celebration of Admiral Duncan's victory off Camperdown. The boisterous callers were informed that these were Admiral Nelson's lodgings; no one here had heard the news nor the sound of guns firing in celebration at the Tower; the Admiral, recovering from his recent wound, had gone to bed early as was his wont. The crowd moved off down the street, one of the leaders calling out, 'You'll hear no more from us tonight.'[4]

Nelson had had a tiring few days. He had consulted the physician to the Royal Hospital, Chelsea, Dr Benjamin Moseley, whom he had known in Jamaica; he had solicited the opinion of the surgeon, William Cruikshank, author of *The Anatomy of the Absorbing Vessels of the Human Body*, who had nervously attended Samuel Johnson in his last illness; and he had sought advice from Cruikshank's son-in-law, who had once been principal dresser to the renowned Dr William Hunter, President of the Medical Society, and from Thomas Keate, Surgeon-General to the Army, whose opinions were much valued by the Prince of Wales. But the general opinion was that nothing could be done; the septicaemia would have to run its course; and 'time and nature' would eventually heal the wound. In the meantime he could undertake as many social and professional engagements as he felt inclined.

There was, indeed, much business to be attended to. He had to go to Surgeons' Hall for an examination of his eye to qualify for a pension, declining to attend at six o'clock in the evening on the first or third Thursday in the month as dogmatically required, and insisting upon being attended to at a more convenient time in the morning or early afternoon. He thought it as well to go almost every morning to the Admiralty 'to keep in touch'; he went to the College of Arms to discuss various details in his coat of arms; he attended a ceremony at the Guildhall where he was granted the Freedom of the City of London; he also attended a service of thanksgiving for the naval victories of the war in St Paul's; he called upon the Duke of Clarence, who had asked to be one of the first to shake his hand when he came home and who had been assured in reply that 'not a scrap of that ardour with which [he] had hitherto served our King had been shot away'.[5]

Towards the end of September, at the first levee of the autumn season, he went to St James's Palace accompanied by his brother William and his former first lieutenant on the *Captain*, the handsome and impulsive Captain Edward Berry. The King, fully recovered from his first attack of porphyria, which had temporarily deranged him, was in cheerful mood. Peering at Nelson's empty sleeve, he observed in his bluff and tactless way, 'You have lost your right arm!'

'But not my right hand,' Nelson replied promptly, indicating his friend, 'as I have the honour of presenting Captain Berry.'

'Your country,' the King responded, according to Lord Eldon, 'has a claim for a bit more of you.'[6]

Nelson was then invested with the Most Honourable Order of the Bath, the star of which he was so proud to have displayed on the portraits of him painted thereafter.* The first of these portraits was painted by Lemuel Abbott at the suggestion of Captain Locker, who had commissioned the Rigaud portrait. Locker proposed that the sittings should take place not in Abbott's studio in Caroline Street, Bloomsbury, but at the house at Greenwich which Locker occupied as Lieutenant-Governor of Greenwich Hospital. Both painter and subject agreed to this proposal.

Lemuel Abbott, the son of a Leicestershire clergyman, was a frequent contributor to the exhibitions at the Royal Academy. He was renowned for getting a good likeness of his subjects and was, therefore, swamped by commissions, particularly from naval officers, many of which he had to decline or, having accepted, failed to fulfil, since he was 'of a penurious disposition', as his biographer put it, and declined to employ an assistant. His home life was unhappy, his wife being notorious for her eccentricities; and he himself was to die insane at the age of forty-two. His portrait of Nelson was generally considered to be the best likeness until the recent discovery of John Hoppner's more realistic oil sketch of 1800.†

---

* Awards of honours and knighthoods were always likely to cause as much disappointment and resentment as pleasure. Nelson's investiture much displeased Lady Calder, whose husband, Captain of the Fleet during the battle of St Vincent, had not been so honoured. 'Dined with Lady Calder,' Betsey Fremantle wrote in her journal on 25 October. 'The dear lady [who was to die insane] drank half a dozen glasses of wine after dinner which made her more talkative than ever . . . She talks of nothing but ships and sea service and of the red ribbon that was given to Admiral Nelson, instead of, very properly, bestowing it upon the great Sir Robert' (Fremantle, ii, 194–5).

† This sketch by Hoppner, a preparatory study for the formal portrait now in the Royal Collection, was discovered beneath a layer of overpaint in 1992. It was donated to the Boston Museum of Fine Art in 1922. The overpainted picture was sold by Christie's in New York in January 1992. It is now in the Royal Naval Museum, Portsmouth.

Lady Nelson was 'well satisfied', with Abbott's portrait. 'The likeness is great,' she told her husband. 'I really began to think he had no intention of letting me have my own property, which I am not a little attached to. Indeed, it is more than attachment, it is real affection. It is my company – my sincere friend, in your absence. Our good father was delighted with the likeness' (Nicolas, iii, 125).

Certainly Nelson himself was satisfied with the portrait, a distinct improvement upon a fanciful print which Locker had allowed a print seller named Shipster to engrave from Rigaud's portrait. It was also considered a far better likeness than the print which Lady Nelson authorized Robert Laurie to engrave from the miniature sent to her from Leghorn. Nelson did not begrudge Abbott's fee, which he could now well afford.

Money was, indeed, no longer a worry for him. He had accumulated considerable sums in prize-money and had received, or was due to receive, lesser sums from the parents of boys whom he had taken to sea as midshipmen. He could also count on a generous disability pension of £1,000 a year in addition to his pay as a rear-admiral. He had no longer to think in terms of the cottage, which he had mentioned several times in his letters to Fanny, but could now look out for a country house; and, without bothering to go to look at it, he decided to buy a property near Ipswich which Susannah Bolton's brother-in-law, Sam Bolton, had recommended as 'a gentleman's house'. This was a property – demolished in 1960 – called Roundwood, which the auctioneers described as 'a modern built messuage' with '2 genteel parlours . . . 3 vine vaults, 4 good bed chambers, 2 dressing rooms, and 2 servants' chambers'.[7] It was not a particularly imposing place, 'a plain and pleasant house with white stucco walls and a grey slate roof', as it was described at the beginning of this century; but its grounds extended to fifty acres, and it was not expensive.[8] Sam Bolton saw to it that it was bought at an auction held at the White Horse in Ipswich for £2,000. Nelson – who, so he told his brother William, had really 'desired Norfolk but it would not receive us'[9] – could but hope that when he went to sea again, Fanny would settle there in better health and spirits than she had done when living with her father-in-law at Burnham Thorpe or in lodgings at Bath.

He seemed unfailingly attentive towards her. When he was asked to dine at the house of the First Lord of the Admiralty, the austere and stately Lady Spencer was much surprised to receive a hint that Admiral Nelson would like to bring his wife with him. The Countess, the eldest daughter of the first Earl of Lucan, a woman renowned for her looks and intelligence as well as her rather intimidating manner, had already met Nelson in the drawing-room at the Admiralty and had been rather shocked at his appearance. 'A most uncouth creature I thought him,' she recorded. 'He had just returned from Tenerife, after having lost his arm. He looked so sickly it was painful to see him and his general appearance was that of an idiot; so much so that, when he spoke and his wonderful mind broke forth, it was a sort of surprise that riveted my whole attention.'[10]

She was, therefore, predisposed to raise no objections to his bringing his wife with him to dinner, even though this would upset her table arrangements and such occasions were, in any case, supposed to be formal and semi-official. She read Nelson's letter sympathetically:

Nelson said, that out of deference to my known determination, he had not begged to introduce Lady Nelson to me; yet if I would take notice of her, it would make him the happiest man alive.

He said he was convinced that I must like her. That she was beautiful, accomplished; but, above all, that her angelic tenderness towards him was beyond imagination. He told me that his wife had dressed his wounds and that her care alone had saved his life. In short, he pressed me to see her with an earnestness of which Nelson alone was capable.

In these circumstances I begged that he would bring her with him that day to dine. He did so, and his attentions to her were those of a lover. He handed her to dinner and sat by her, apologizing to me, by saying that he was so little with her that he would not voluntarily lose an instant of her society.[11]

Her attitude to him was equally attentive as she sat by his side, cutting up the food on his plate. Yet when, his wound having healed at last, Nelson left London to take up his next appointment, his irritation with her resurfaced upon his reaching Portsmouth, for he discovered that, once again, she had not only packed the wrong clothes, but had also forgotten to include various items, including a watch and some pieces of Portuguese gold which his father had given him and which he liked to keep about him as talismans. Weights had arrived but not the scales to go with them.

Tom Allen had been told always to lock inn doors before unpacking his master's boxes; and it had been impressed upon him that this was most essential on the road to Portsmouth, since there were so many valuable presents in the baggage. Tom had not been negligent, so presumably the missing items had not been stolen: Nelson could only presume they had not been sent. 'With great difficulty [he] found *one* pair of raw silk stockings'; but a day or two later his black stock and buckle had still not appeared, nor had Fanny remembered to send the keys to his dressing-stand. He could do without these things but it was 'a satisfaction to mention them'. Another day or two passed, then Nelson wrote again to complain that her list of linen bore little relation to what she had actually packed: the numbers of handkerchiefs, cravats, stocks and towels were all wrong. She replied with a kind of evasive airiness: she wished that it had been in her power to send his things 'more comfortably', but their 'going at different times and a change of servant in the midst of the last few days' had 'made all this confusion'; she felt sure the buckle and stock would turn up; so would the 'Portugal Pieces'; it was 'a sad thing to lose money'; anyway, she would leave the 'mortifying subject' for now; she 'rejoiced' to see him 'so exact'.[12]

Nelson had arrived in Portsmouth in March 1798 to board his flagship, the seventy-four-gun *Vanguard*, to be greeted by her captain, Edward Berry, who had been married a week before his appointment, to his cousin, a Norwich clergyman's daughter. Nelson opened his orders: he was to sail to Lisbon and from there to proceed to the dangerous waters of the Mediterranean, now firmly controlled by the French, to ascertain the destination of a large expeditionary force which was reported to be preparing to leave Toulon and other nearby ports, including Marseilles, under the command of General Buonaparte, as Nelson still spelled and always would spell the name of 'the Corsican scoundrel', in the original Italian manner.

There was as yet no indication as to where this fleet of French warships and numerous transports was bound. Likely destinations mentioned were Spain and Portugal, Naples and Ireland; but an invasion might take place almost anywhere along the Mediterranean coast, or on the Atlantic coast of the Iberian peninsula, or even in the West Indies; and it was for Nelson to discover where. He had been chosen for this difficult task, so Lord Spencer said, because his 'acquaintance with that part of the world, as well as his activity and disposition' qualified him 'in a peculiar manner' for a service upon which 'the fate of Europe' might 'be stated to depend'. 'I am very happy to send you Sir Horatio Nelson again,' he wrote to the Commander-in-Chief, Lord St Vincent, 'not only because I believe I cannot send you a more zealous, active and approved officer, but because I have reason to believe that his being under your command will be agreeable to your wishes.'[13] Lord St Vincent fully concurred with the First Lord's choice, which had been pressed upon the Admiralty by the unsolicited testimony of Sir Gilbert Elliot, soon to be created Lord Minto. 'The arrival of Admiral Nelson has given me new life,' St Vincent wrote to the Admiralty. 'You could not have gratified me more than in sending him.'[14] When orders came for Nelson's small reconnaisance squadron of three seventy-four-gun ships and three frigates to be reinforced as a fighting fleet, the Commander-in-Chief hastened to send ten other seventy-four-gun ships to the Mediterranean after him.

Nelson, 'exhilarated beyond description' to be at sea again with 'a small but very choice squadron', was given his first clue as to Bonaparte's intended destination on 17 May when one of his frigates captured a French corvette, *La Pierre*, which had set sail from Toulon the night before. Prisoners brought to him from this French ship informed him that over 10,000 troops had been embarked on transports, and many more, almost 40,000, were being marched down to the quays. The escorting warships were under the command of Vice-Admiral François Brueys d'Aigalliers, a brave, experienced and conscientious officer whom Bonaparte trusted despite his royalist past. But if the prisoners knew the destination of Brueys's fleet, they did not divulge it; nor did they tell Nelson when the French fleet was due to sail. So the British fleet would have to be patient and alert. The lookouts kept careful watch for three days; and then suddenly one night after a bright warm day on which they had still not sighted the enemy ships, a storm struck their own. Nelson recounted the consequences in a letter to his wife:

Figure to yourself a vain man, on a Sunday Evening at sun set, walking in his cabbin with a Squadron about him, who looked up to their Chief to lead them to glory ... Figure to yourself this proud, conceited man when the sun rose on Monday Morning, his Ship dismasted, his Fleet dispers'd and himself in such distress that the meanest Frigate out of France would have been a very unwelcome guest ... I ought not to call what has happened to the vanguard by the cold name of accident: I believe firmly that it was the Almightys goodness, to check my consummate vanity. I hope it has made me a better Officer, as I feel confident it has made me a better Man. I kiss with all humility the rod.[15]

The roaring storm had not only brought the *Vanguard*'s topsail yard crashing on to the deck, killing two men and injuring several others, it had split the main topmast, which went hurtling over the side, and cracked the mizzen topmast which was carried off into the raging sea 'with a most tremendous crash'. The dismembered ship, its broken masts thumping against its bottom, was driven helplessly away towards the shore and would almost certainly have been lost on the rocks had not Captain Alexander Ball in the *Alexander* and Sir James Saumarez in the *Orion* come to her rescue. Nelson went aboard the *Alexander* to thank Captain Ball for what he had done – and encountered the well-connected officer from an old Gloucestershire family whom he had come across years before at St Omer, the 'great coxcomb' with the non-regulation epaulettes. He found he liked the reflective, learned and reasonable Ball very much, after all, and was to write to him for the rest of his life in terms of the most affectionate friendship.[16]

The furious tornado had not spared the French ships either. Tearing them out of Toulon, it had sent them rushing in the darkness way past the British fleet, so that by the time the carpenters and riggers aboard the *Vanguard* had resourcefully repaired the damage and the flagship was seaworthy once more, Admiral Brueys's fleet was nowhere to be seen; and Nelson was as much in the dark as ever as to its destination. His captains, taking it for granted that he would not attempt to find out until his ships had been more thoroughly prepared, set sail for Gibraltar. But he had no such intention. 'I thought,' he said, 'that they would have known me better.'[17]

On 5 June, a fortnight after the gale had come so close to wrecking his fleet, Nelson was at last given some news about the French. The crew of a passing merchant ship reported that they had been sighted to the north of Corsica sailing on a south-easterly course. They were making perhaps for Naples or Sicily or, possibly, for Malta. Constantinople was another possible destination; so were Corfu and the Levant; and so, indeed, as Nelson concluded in a letter to Lord Spencer, was Egypt, where French troops might be landed for a march into India and a dangerous alliance with Haidar Ali's son, Tippu Sahib, Sultan of Mysore, the leading opponent of British interests in the subcontinent.

'If they pass Sicily,' Nelson wrote to the Admiralty, 'I shall believe they are going on their scheme of possessing Alexandria and getting troops to India – a plan concerted with Tippu Sahib, by no means so difficult as might at first be imagined; but [even if they are] bound for the Antipodes, your lordship may rely that I shall lose not a moment in bringing them to action.'[18]

Joined now by the ships of the line which Lord St Vincent had sent after him, by his friends Ralph Miller and Samuel Hood, Benjamin Hallowell, George Westcott and the four Thomases, Foley, Troubridge, Thompson and Hardy, all one day to be admirals, he sailed after the enemy in cheerful and confident mood, knowing that he could trust every one of these men to engage Brueys's fleet closely once they caught up with it.

14

Abū Qîr

Before this time tomorrow I shall have gained a peerage or
Westminster Abbey.

After passing through the Straits of Messina, Nelson was told by
the master of a Genoese brig that Malta had surrendered and that
the French were now making for Italy. Crediting the first of these
assertions but doubting the second, he summoned a council of war
aboard the *Vanguard* and with four captains in whom he placed
'great confidence' – Troubridge, Ball, Saumarez and Henry Darby
– he discussed once more the likely objective of Bonaparte's
armada.

The problem had been discussed also in London; and had been
much in the thoughts of Henry Dundas, William Pitt's shrewd and
uncouth Scottish friend, a former Treasurer of the Navy, who was
now Secretary of State for War. 'My dear Lord,' Dundas had
written to Spencer on 10 June, '*India* has occupied my thoughts all
night.' He had heard that the admittedly not always reliable
Captain Sidney Smith, who had recently escaped after two years
as a prisoner in France, had brought home stories of French
officers being landed in the Levant *en route* to India and of an
intended landing of French troops in Egypt. 'Did the instructions
to Lord St Vincent mention that *Egypt* might be in the contemplation of Bonaparte's expedition?' Dundas asked. 'It may be whimsical, but I cannot help having a fancy of my own on that subject.'[1]

Nelson shared this fancy. Reports that there were 'naturalists,
astronomers and mathematicians etc aboard the French fleet'
confirmed him in his belief that its most probable destination was
Egypt; and, the captains agreeing that he was doubtless right, he
gave orders for his own ships to make fast for Alexandria. Captain
Saumarez for one felt thankful that the responsibility for making

this decision did not rest with him. 'Some days must now elapse before we can be relieved of our suspense,' he wrote, 'and if at the end of our journey we find we are upon a wrong scent, our embarrassment will be great indeed.'[2]

When Alexandria hove into view on 28 June it appeared that they were undoubtedly upon a wrong scent. In the harbour beneath the lighthouse and the minarets of the town there were no craft to be seen other than one Turkish ship of the line, two Turkish frigates and various merchantmen of indeterminate nationalities. Nelson gave orders for his fleet to sail eastwards along the coast. He was beginning to feel extremely apprehensive. He knew that his appointment to his command in the Mediterranean had led to widespread annoyance amongst more senior officers who felt themselves slighted. One of these, Sir John Orde, a brother of the first Lord Bolton, had protested to Lord Spencer about a 'junior officer, just arrived from England' being preferred to older and more experienced admirals. He 'would not conceal from his Lordship' how much he felt hurt. Orde protested also to Lord St Vincent, expressing himself in such angry terms that he was sent home, where he challenged St Vincent to a duel.

Nelson was not only concerned by the jealousy of senior officers. He feared that his operations were being criticized in newspapers in England, as, indeed, in some of them they were. 'It is a remarkable circumstance,' one paper suggested to its readers, 'that a fleet of nearly 400 sail, covering a space of so many leagues, should have been able to elude the knowledge of our fleet for such a long space of time.'

Nelson thought it as well to compose a lengthy dispatch explaining his failure to find the French after so long a search. Captain Ball advised him not to send it: it was better 'never to make a defence' before actually being 'accused of error'. Nelson sent the letter all the same.

Still there was no sign of the enemy, though once on a murky, damp day, the two fleets passed so close to each other that the French could hear the British firing signal guns to help them maintain stations. Nor were the French to be seen when, having passed the mouths of the Nile delta, the British fleet sailed northwards by the coast of Palestine and then towards Crete. Nelson began to fear that while he was making for Alexandria, they had, perhaps, invaded the Kingdom of the Two Sicilies after all. But upon approaching Syracuse, he discovered that the enemy were not there either. He was so anxious and worried by now that any unexpected sound set his heart racing, as it was ever afterwards to do whenever he was 'startled, either by pleasure or pain'. This frustrating voyage, he thought, 'had taken years off [his] life'.[3]

He turned towards Greece; and it was off the small town of Koroni in the Gulf of Messenia, having sent Captain Troubridge ashore to question the Turkish Bey, that he learned that the French fleet had at last been sighted sailing, so it seemed, for Egypt. In unconcealed excitement, Nelson raced back across the Mediterranean after it; and by 1 August the British fleet was once more in sight of Alexandria. Now its harbour was packed with vessels. Excitement turned to dismay, however, when, approaching closer inshore, the lookouts saw that the masts were those of transports and that there were no enemy ships of the line to be seen. Bitterly disappointed, Nelson sailed eastwards once more. At half-past one in the afternoon dinner was served. Captain Saumarez sat down to eat in gloomy mood. But then, some fifteen miles from Alexandria, beyond the small town and fort of Abū Qīr, Nelson's search ended: he had found the French fleet of sixteen warships at last. Saumarez's dismay was transformed in a moment to exhilaration as cheers rang out on his quarterdeck: 'Imagine what a change took place when, as the cloth was being removed, the Officer of the Watch came running in saying, "Sir, a signal is just now made that the enemy is in Aboukir Bay and moored in line of battle."

'The utmost joy seemed to animate every breast on board the squadron at sight of the Enemy,' continued Edward Berry; 'and the pleasure which the Admiral himself felt was perhaps more heightened than that of any other man.'[4]

Nelson stood up from his table. 'Before this time tomorrow,' he declared to the officers who had shared the meal with him, 'I shall have gained a peerage or Westminster Abbey.'[5]

Admiral Brueys could but hope that Nelson would not risk an action by night in waters of which he surely had no reliable charts. Many of the sailors from the French ships were on shore, gathering provisions, digging wells and filling water casks, or acting as guards to protect the men performing these tasks from being attacked by Bedouin. Had he not been so short of provisions, he might have been able to follow Bonaparte's advice and taken shelter in Corfu. As it was, his flagship, the huge *L'Orient* of 120 guns, still had army stores on board, as well as – so it was rumoured – gold ingots and diamonds worth some £600,000 plundered from Bonaparte's victims in Switzerland and Rome, and the treasure of the Knights of St John of Jerusalem looted in Malta. It would be late evening before the British ships had drawn close enough to engage the French fleet; and Brueys hoped that in the darkness he might perhaps contrive to escape, or at least draw his ships up closer to the shore and get his men aboard, for their absence would mean that his crews would be fighting dangerously under strength.

Nelson, of course, had no intentions of delaying the action. As soon as the French fleet had come in sight he viewed it, in Berry's words, 'with the eye of a seaman prepared for attack'.[6] From time to time, so he later told a friend, he could not help popping his head out of the window to look at the French ships, although he had 'a damned toothache'. 'And once,' he added, 'as I was observing their position, I heard two seamen near me, talking, and one said, "Damn them, look at them. There they are, Jack, if we don't beat them, they will beat us." I knew what stuff I had under me, so I went in to the attack.'[7] As Brueys suspected, he had no charts to guide him safely past the treacherous shoals and reefs of Abū Qîr Bay. Captain Hallowell of the *Swiftsure* had sent him a sketch-map of the bay which had been seized in a captured French ship; but this showed little detail and was of scarcely more use than an English map which Samuel Hood had taken with him aboard the *Zealous*. Thomas Foley of the *Goliath* had a more useful chart taken from a recently published French atlas; but even this was not considered altogether trustworthy; and in Nelson's plan of attack – which was to overwhelm the van and centre of the enemy line before dealing with the rear – reliance would have to be placed on sailors taking soundings by means of their lead lines.

It would be a dangerous operation in which one ship, Troubridge's *Culloden*, by sailing too close to the shoals was to ground on them and lie stranded under the guns of the island off Abū Qīr point. But Nelson determined to attempt it, hoping that the landward guns of the French ships would not be adequately manned, that the shore batteries would not prove too troublesome and that the British sailors, in firing their guns at the enemy ships lying between them, would not hit each other.

Nelson, hailing the *Zealous* as she passed close on the *Vanguard*'s bow, asked Hood if he thought he could get through between *Le Guerrier* at the end of the French line and the shoals to starboard. Hood called back that he had no chart, but he was in eleven fathoms and if the Admiral would allow him the honour of leading him into battle he would certainly attempt it. 'You have my leave,' Nelson called back, waving his hat in the air. 'I wish you success.' Hood took off his own hat to wave it in return; but it was torn out of his hand by a sudden gust of wind and carried away to fall into the sea. 'Never mind, Webley,' he said to his first lieutenant. 'There it goes for luck. Put the helm over and make sail!'[8]

As it happened, however, Hood did not have the honour of leading the British squadron into battle, for Captain Foley's *Goliath* came dipping past to overtake the *Zealous*. 'This will never do,' said Hood to Webley, but then added, 'Well, never mind. Foley is a fine, gallant fellow. Shorten sail and give him time to take up his berth.' So the *Goliath* shot ahead, passing *Le Guerrier*, which Foley left to be dealt with by Hood. Giving a terse order – 'Sink that brute!' – when a French frigate, *La Sérieuse*, tried to block his progress, Foley then took up position at the head of the British line. *La Sérieuse* was duly sunk; *Le Guerrier* was dismasted by the guns of the *Zealous* and Ralph Miller's *Theseus*; while the immense flagship, *L'Orient*, was engaged by Darby's *Bellerophon* and Thompson's *Leander*, the darkness of the warm night lit by the ceaseless flash of the guns.

Aboard the *Vanguard*, Nelson was examining the map which

Hallowell had sent him when he suddenly stumbled and fell to the quarterdeck, his face covered in blood which poured into his eyes. 'I am killed,' he murmured to Berry who knelt beside him. 'Remember me to my wife.'[9]

A fragment of shot had struck him on the forehead above his right eye, cutting the flesh to the bone. But when he was taken down the ladder to the cockpit – where, in an atmosphere thick with the smell of sweat and smoke, the surgeons and their assistants were busy cutting and stitching and applying bandages and tourniquets in the light of the swaying lanterns as they had been off Santa Cruz the year before – the wound was pronounced not as serious as it looked. The Admiral refused to have it attended to before the other sailors in the cockpit had been treated. 'Do not identify me to the surgeons,' he told Berry. 'I will await my turn.' So Berry left him and climbed back on deck to send a boarding party aboard a crippled French ship, the *Spartiate*. When he returned to the cockpit, where Nelson sat on a chest with a large bandage around his stitched wound, he brought with him her captain's sword. He presented it to Nelson with what he called the 'pleasing intelligence' that two other French ships had been captured and at least three more, including the flagship, *L'Orient*, were 'completely in our power'. 'It appears, Sir,' Berry added complacently, 'that victory has already declared itself in our favour.'[10]

Although concussed and in pain, Nelson, having been removed from the cockpit to the quieter bread-room in the hold, began immediately to think about the wording of his dispatch. He sent for his secretary so that he could start dictating it. But when the secretary came into the bread-room it was clear that, having been slightly wounded, the man was in too great a state of shock to be of any use; and Nelson, pale, bandaged and alarming in his impatience, was in no mood to tolerate such weakness: he dismissed the man from his presence and, later, from his appointment, having him transferred as purser to the *Franklin*. The chaplain, Mr Comyn, was then summoned to act as amanuensis; but he too was found wanting; so Nelson began to draft the dispatch himself.

He was thus engaged when, at about a quarter past nine, Berry appeared once more to announce that the enemy flagship was on fire. Nelson put down his pen at once and demanded to be helped on deck. The burning *Orient* was a terrible sight. On her lower deck some brave crews were still fighting the guns, but flames were spreading fast above them, licking into the jars of oil and buckets of paint which had been left there when the painting of the ship had been interrupted by the arrival of the British fleet. Sailors were leaping into the sea in an attempt to escape the fire; and, although orders were given to 'save as many as possible' and a boat was put out from the *Vanguard* for this purpose and several men were saved, many others, three hundred or more, trying to swim in the luridly lit water or clutching desperately to bits of floating debris, sank exhausted into the depths.

Admiral Brueys, sitting in a chair on deck, both his legs shot off and tourniquets bound round the stumps, was spared further pain and misery when a shot knocked him to the deck and killed him. His flag-captain, Louis de Casabianca – whose sufferings were to be commemorated a generation later by that prolific poet, Felicia Dorothea Hemans – refused to leave the quarterdeck while his ten-year-old son, Jacques, who had been wounded, was trapped by the fire below. The boy was later glimpsed in the sea, clinging to part of the splintered mainmast; but neither he nor his father survived the night.

As Ralph Miller watched what he called the 'most grand and awful spectacle' of the giant ship ablaze, he and several other captains cut their cables to get clear of what they knew would be a tremendous explosion when the flames reached *L'Orient*'s powder magazine. Benjamin Hallowell, however, kept the guns of the *Swiftsure* firing into the heart of the roaring conflagration. Hoping that when *L'Orient* did blow up, the shattered timbers would be carried by the blast over his mastheads, Hallowell ordered the decks to be soaked with water and full buckets to be placed ready to extinguish any burning debris that might fall on them.

Soon after ten o'clock the French flagship burst apart in an explosion so tremendous that French soldiers ten miles away at Rosetta looked at each other in questioning surprise. Broken spars and broken bodies, rigging and guns, shattered chests and bits of metal were hurled into the sky and splashed into the sea or crashed and tumbled down on to the decks of nearby ships.

For a few moments there was silence; then the British guns opened up again before falling into silence once more, afterwards firing desultorily and intermittently until about three o'clock in the morning. The men were utterly exhausted. 'My people were so extremely jaded,' Captain Miller wrote, 'that as soon as they had hove our sheet anchor up, they dropped under the capstan bars and were asleep in a moment in every sort of posture, having been working then at their fullest execution or fighting, for nearly 12 hours.'[11]

Nelson gave orders for the ships still operational to continue the fight; but few were now in a state to do so. The *Culloden* was still stranded on the shoals; the *Franklin* was dismasted; the *Bellerophon* was utterly crippled, with two hundred of her crew killed or wounded. Aboard the *Majestic* Captain Westcott lay dying with his throat shattered by a musket ball. By the time *Le Généreux* and *Le Guillaume Tell*, with two frigates, cut their cables and stood out to sea, only the *Zealous* was in a fit state to pursue them, and she was soon recalled. So the battle ended, and 'an awful sight it was', a man aboard the *Goliath* recorded. 'The whole bay was covered with dead bodies, mangled, wounded and scorched, not a bit of clothes on them but trousers.'[12] Over two hundred British sailors had been killed and seven hundred wounded; the French losses, so Nelson estimated, were six times as heavy − 1,700 killed, many drowned or burned to death, 1,500 wounded and 3,000 taken prisoner. 'The slaughter on board [*Le Conquérant*, of which he had taken possession] is *dreadful*,' reported Captain Davidge Gould of the *Audacious* in a characteristic report; 'her Captain is dying. Our fore and mainmast are wounded . . . They tell me the foremast is the worst. I give you joy. This is a glorious victory.'[13] So it was: of the thirteen French sail of the line which had been engaged, nine had been taken, two had been burnt and only two had escaped; of the four frigates one had been burnt and one sunk.

Having appeared early on the morning of 2 August, looking pale, drawn and bandaged, to acknowledge the cheers of his men,

Nelson returned to the dispatch which he had begun the night before with the words, 'My Lord, Almighty God has blessed His Majesty's Arms in the late Battle by a great Victory over the Fleet of the Enemy, whom I attacked at sunset on 1st August off the mouth of the Nile.' Apart from Berry and the mortally wounded Westcott, he named no captains in this report, contenting himself with the observation that their judgement 'together with their valour, and that of the officers and men of every description was absolutely irrisistible. Could anything from my pen add to the character of the captains, I could write it with pleasure, but that is impossible.'

The Almighty, to whose grace Nelson attributed his victory, was given thanks on the afternoon after the battle. 'At two o'clock accordingly on that day,' Captain Berry recorded, 'public service was performed on the quarter-deck of the *Vanguard* by the Rev Mr Comyn, the other ships following the example of the Admiral [who, before leaving London, had asked the Society for the Propagation of Christian Knowledge for as many Bibles and Prayer Books as they could let him have for the sailors under his command] . . . This solemn act of gratitude to Heaven seemed to make a very deep impression upon several of the prisoners.'[14]

Having completed his dispatch, Nelson, in his always conscientious way with correspondence, had a copy made in case the original failed to reach its destination; and it was fortunate that he did so, since while the Hon. Thomas Capel, captain of the *Mutine*, succeeded in landing at Naples, and, having handed over command of his ship to William Hoste, in travelling from there overland to London with one copy of the dispatch, Captain Berry lost the other copy when Captain Thompson's fifty-gun *Leander*, in which he was sailing, was attacked by the seventy-four-gun *Généreux*, one of the two ships that had escaped from Abū Qīr Bay. The *Leander* was captured after a hard fight in which both Thompson and Berry were severely wounded, and taken to French-occupied Corfu.

As well as his dispatches for the Admiralty, Nelson wrote a letter to the Governor of Bombay with the welcome news that, with the French fleet destroyed, their army stranded in Egypt and the

Mediterranean once more safely under British control, there was no immediate danger to India. This letter he entrusted to Lieutenant Thomas Duval of the *Zealous*, an officer fluent in French and competent in several other languages, who was to make his way to Bombay by way of Aleppo, Basra and the Persian Gulf. Captain Saumarez was ordered to take the *Orion*, together with several other ships of the squadron when repaired and all the French prizes, across the Mediterranean to Gibraltar; Captain Hood was dispatched with the *Zealous* to blockade Alexandria and to intercept a convoy of supplies which was expected there shortly for the French army. Nelson himself remained for the moment where he was, writing on 11 August to Lady Hamilton:

My dear Madam,

I may now be able to shew your ladyship the remains of Horatio Nelson, and I trust my mutilations will not cause me to be less welcome. They are the marks of honour. I beg leave to introduce Captain Capel, who is going home with my dispatches, to your notice. He is a son of Lord Essex, and a very good young man. And I also beg your notice of Captain Hoste, who to the gentlest manners joins the most undaunted courage. He was brought up by me, and I love him dearly. I am afraid you will think me very impertinent in introducing all these young men, but you and Sir William have spoiled [me].[15]

By day there was the constant hammering of the carpenters as they worked on their repairs; by night insects fluttered about Nelson's cabin as, coughing perpetually and intermittently feverish, he gazed across the water to the fires of the Arabs and Mamelukes along the shoreline.

The shore, to the extent of four leagues, was covered by wrecks [wrote Baron Denon, the artist and archaeologist who had accompanied the French expedition], which enabled us to form an estimate of the loss which we had sustained. To procure a few nails, or a few iron hoops, the wandering Arabs were employed in burning on the beach the masts, gun-carriages, boats, etc., which had been constructed at so vast an expense in our ports.[16]

As he had done in the past, Nelson omitted all reference to his wounds in his official dispatch, a cause for added congratulations when the omission became known, as it was bound to do. But he did not attempt to hide his suffering from his visitors or correspondents. His head, he told Lord St Vincent, was 'splitting, splitting, splitting'. He wrote as much to Fanny. The officers who came to see him to congratulate him on his victory, to discuss the formation of an Egyptian Club and a portrait of the admiral to be painted for its dining-room, found him strangely uneasy. 'My head is so upset,' he wrote one evening, 'really I know not what to do; but by tomorrow I will arrange matters in my mind, and do my best.' 'On the day Hoste left me, I was taken with a fever, which has very near done my business,' he continued in another letter to St Vincent;

for eighteen hours my life was thought to be past hope; I am now up, but very weak both in body and mind, from my cough and this fever. I never expect, my dear Lord, to see your face again; it may please God that this will be the finish to that fever of anxiety I have endured from the middle of June; but be that as it pleases His goodness – I am resigned to His will.[17]

Nelson displayed no eagerness to return to England. Letters had arrived intermittently from his wife. They contained the usual humdrum information about the weather, fashions in Bath, the price of gloves, the progress of improvements at Roundwood, the problems of preserving fruit, titbits from the Norwich papers, news of friends, relations and acquaintances in East Anglia, belated apologies for not taking more care with his packing, hopes that in future they would have 'proper servants', complaints about being unsettled in his absence, about her ill health, her colds and 'rhumitism', the high cost of everything since he had left England – she had had to pay £342 for his new carriage – longings for peace when he would be able to return to live 'quietly at home', apologies for being such 'a poor creature' when her spirits were so low. She was 'enervated' in one letter, 'fagged' in another, 'fretful' in a third. Her eyes were 'very weak', her hearing at times 'very indifferent'; she thought herself 'a little nervous'. 'I wish I knew some cheerful story to tell you,' she ended one long letter rather pathetically. 'My mind and ideas will brighten up when I can get a letter from my dear husband.' Roundwood was not proving a very satisfactory house: it was 'rather exposed being reckoned the highest spot within ten miles'. The neighbours were unfriendly; the 'Middletons [were] the only country family who [had] been attentive'. The expense of housekeeping was very great, although she dined on 'cold roast beef not being able to procure fish or fowl'. She was 'obliged to keep three women servants, could not get on with two'. She had tried to do so but could not manage.

Far more welcome to Nelson was news that engravings of the Lemuel Abbott portrait were selling so well that one bookseller had sold a whole load of them and had ordered more, and that upon visiting a nursery garden, and asking the name of a dianthus she much admired, Fanny had been told it was called the 'Admiral Nelson'.[18]

15

Naples

All Naples calls me 'Nostro Liberatore'.

Making up his mind to go to Naples, and giving as his reason the
need for the *Vanguard* to be extensively repaired in the nearby
shipyards at Posillipo, Nelson set sail from Abū Qīr Bay for Italy
with a few other ships, including the *Culloden* and the *Alexander*, on
the evening of 19 August. It was an unpleasant voyage – during
which the *Vanguard* was further damaged in a squall and several
men lost their lives – and Nelson 'detested' it. Suffering from a
recurrence of malaria and stabbing pains, his head 'ready to split',
and feeling 'always so sick', he announced, as he so often did when
ill, that he was about to die and was resigned to death.[1]

The *Culloden* and the *Alexander* reached Naples first. Bands played
to welcome them; barges filled with courtiers and foreign ministers
were rowed out to the ships to the uncertain strains of Thomas
Arne's 'Rule Britannia' and 'God Save the King'. The King was in
one of the barges with Sir William Hamilton, who, 'observing some
seamen looking earnestly out of the port-holes, said to them, "My
lads, this is the King whom you have saved" . . . Several of the
men answered, "Very glad of it, Sir – very glad of it." '[2]

Lady Hamilton was awaiting Nelson's arrival in what she
confessed was an agony of excitement. She was now thirty-three
years old, and had become undeniably fat. Sir Gilbert Elliot, who
had come to live in Naples after the British evacuation of Corsica,
described her figure as being 'nothing short of monstrous in its
enormity and growing every day'. 'She tries hard to think size
advantageous to her beauty, but is not easy about it,' Elliot added.
'Her face is beautiful . . . She is the most extraordinary compound

I ever beheld . . . She is all Nature and yet all Art; that is to say, her manners are perfectly unpolished, of course very easy, though not with the ease of good breeding, but of a barmaid.' She was 'excessively good humoured', wished 'to please and be admired'. Her conversations with men were 'exaggerations of anything' Elliot had 'ever heard anywhere'.[3]

No longer given to self-doubt, she had, indeed, become extremely self-confident, quick to contradict those who disagreed with her, unduly conscious of the importance bestowed upon her by her intimacy with the exploitative Queen Maria Carolina, as eager as ever to be the centre of attraction and as ready as ever to entertain the company with her loud soprano voice, which was not to everyone's taste: Lady Holland described it as 'vile discordant screaming', Lady Palmerston as 'powerful but perfectly without harmony'. Yet no one could deny Lady Hamilton was still as kind as she was good-natured.

Earlier that summer the *Vanguard* had been briefly anchored in the Bay of Naples, and Admiral Nelson had sent Troubridge and Hardy ashore with instructions to pay respects to Sir William Hamilton and Sir John Acton, and to deliver a letter to Lady Hamilton in which he had written, 'As soon as I have fought the French fleet, I shall do myself the honour of paying my respects to your Ladyship at Naples and I hope to be congratulated on a victory.'[4]

To this she had written in reply, 'God bless you, my dear Sir, and send you victorious . . . I shall be in a fever of anxiety . . . I will not say how glad I shall be to see you. Indeed, I cannot describe to you my feelings of your being so near us.'[5]

Near as he was, however, Nelson had not gone ashore at Naples, contenting himself with assurances that, in a favourite phrase of his, he would return 'to be presented to her crowned with laurels or covered with cypress'. When she heard, a month later, that he had won his great victory at Abū Qīr, she fainted in the most theatrical manner, falling heavily to the floor and badly bruising her side.[6] 'How shall I begin what shall I say to you,' she wrote when she had recovered.

Tis impossible I can write for since last Monday I am delirious with joy & assure you I have a fevour caused by agitation and pleasure Good God what a victory. Never never has there been anything half so glorious, half so complete . . . How I felt for poor Troubridge. He must have been so angry on the sandbank. In short, I pity those who were not in the battle. I wou'd have been rather an English powder monky or a swab in that great Victory than an emperor out of it . . . I should feel it a glory to die in such a cause no I would not like to die till I see & embrace the *Victor of the* NILE . . . How I glory in the Honner of my country and my *countryman*. I walk and tread in air with pride, feeling I was born in the same land with the victor Nelson and his gallant band . . . My dress from head to foot is *alla Nelson*. Even my shawl is in blue with gold anchors all over. My earrings are Nelson's anchors; in short we are be-Nelsoned all over.[7]

Since she could not embrace the heroic Admiral, she kissed the two young officers who had brought the marvellous news to Naples, the attractive eighteen-year-old Lieutenant William Hoste, Nelson's favourite pupil, and Lieutenant the Hon. Thomas Capel. She whisked them off in her carriage, so as, Hoste said, to parade them through the streets till dark. She was wearing a bandeau round her forehead with the words 'Nelson and Victory' emblazoned upon it. 'The populace saw and understood what it meant and "*Viva Nelson*" resounded through the streets.' The Hamiltons' house, the Palazzo Sessa, was brilliantly illuminated that night, and covered, so Lady Hamilton assured her hero, with his 'glorious name. There were three thousand lamps and there should have been three million.' Sir William wrote to say that history did not record an action that did more honour to the heroes that gained the victory. 'You have now completely made yourself, my dear Nelson, immortal . . . God be praised . . . You may well conceive, my dear Sir, how happy Emma and I are in the reflection that it is you, Nelson, our bosom friend, that has done such wondrous good.'[8]

Lady Hamilton's friend, Queen Maria Carolina − who had 'walked frantic about the room' on hearing of Nelson's victory, embracing 'every person near her' and crying out, 'Oh! Nelson!

Oh! Saviour of Italy!' – wrote to him in equally excited tones,
telling him that she had hung his portrait in her room and asking
him to give '*un hip hip hip*' and to sing in her name 'God Save die
King et puis God Saeve Nelson et marine Britannique'. 'My
gratitude is engraven on my heart,' she told Lady Hamilton. 'Live!
Long live this brave nation and her honoured navy. It is a glory in
which I participate . . . *Hip! Hip!* my dear Miledy. I am wild with
joy! With what pleasure I shall see our heroes . . . My children are
mad with joy.'[9]

Sir William Hamilton wrote more soberly to invite Nelson to
stay at the Palazzo Sessa when he arrived: 'A pleasant apartment
is ready for you in my house and Emma is looking out for the
softest pillows to repose the few wearied limbs you have left.'[10]

When Nelson did arrive aboard what he described somewhat
fancifully as 'the wreck of the *Vanguard*', the Hamiltons and the
King and Queen were all rowed out to greet him, the court
orchestra accompanying them and bands in other boats playing
what passed for 'See the Conquering Hero Comes', which had
been practised rather uncertainly for days past. The Hamiltons'
boat reached the *Vanguard* first; and, so Nelson wrote, 'up flew her
ladyship exclaiming, "Oh God is it possible!" She fell into my arm
more dead than alive.'

'Tears, however, soon put matters to rights, when alongside
came the King . . . He took me by the hand, calling me "Deliverer
and Preserver" with every other expression of kindness. In short all
Naples calls me "Nostro Liberatore" . . . I hope one day to have
the pleasure of introducing you to Lady Hamilton. She is one of
the very best women in the world. How few could have made the
turn she has. She is an honour to her sex.'[11]

Also on board the *Vanguard* that morning was a forty-one-year-
old English lady, Miss Ellis Cornelia Knight, author of a two-
volume novel, who was then living in Naples with her mother, the
formidable, dogmatic and rather stupid widow of an admiral. Miss
Knight had been brought out to the ship in the Hamiltons' barge
and was a witness of the dramatic collapse of Lady Hamilton into
the arm of her hero, whom Miss Knight described as 'little and not
remarkable in his person either way'. When they all sat down to

breakfast, however, she was struck by 'the great animation of [his] countenance and activity in his appearance'. A little bird hopped about the table; she was told it had flown into the cabin just before the battle, 'to the joy of the crew who superstitiously regarded it as an excellent omen'.[12]

'With boyish enthusiasm', the King wished to see everything and was shown all over the ship, taking particular interest in the sick-bay, where a sailor was reading to a wounded friend, and in the hat which Nelson was wearing when he was wounded in the head.[13]

Nelson had suggested that on landing in Naples he had 'better be at a hotel' and had asked Sir William to order his servants to get him 'some apartments'. But the Hamiltons had insisted that he must stay with them. So, greeted by hundreds of birds released from their cages by fishermen, he was taken up to the Palazzo Sessa, where he was given a room with a wide window overlooking the bay and plied with ass's milk, while Lady Hamilton immediately began to prepare a splendid party to celebrate his fortieth birthday. Although this was only a week after his arrival, Nelson was feeling much better and could look forward to the celebrations with pleasure; he could not, however, be prevailed upon to visit his wounded adversary, Admiral Blanquet du Chayla, who had been dreadfully wounded in the face in the recent battle and had had most of his nose shot off. 'Seeing me will only put him in mind of his misfortune,' Nelson protested. 'I have an antipathy to Frenchmen, which is so powerful that I must, I think, have received it from my mother at my birth.'[14]

'The preparations of Lady Hamilton for celebrating my birthday are enough to fill me with vanity,' he told his wife. 'Every ribbon, every button has *Nelson* etc., and the whole service are "*H. N. Glorious 1st August!*" Songs and sonnets are numerous, beyond what I ever could deserve.' 'The whole city is mad with joy,' Miss Knight confirmed. 'The Neapolitans have written up "*Vittoria*" and "*Viva Nelson*" at every corner of the street.'

Pressing invitations to 'the great Nelson's birthday' were dispatched to the captains of British ships in the bay, who were asked to bring with them 'as many officers and midshipmen' as could be spared from their duties on board. A column was inscribed with the names of all those captains who had fought under Nelson at the Nile; and this was to be unveiled during the course of the evening by Lady Hamilton, who was to sing a song composed by Cornelia Knight:

> The British Nelson rivals Caesar's fame,
> Like Him, he came, he saw, he overcame.
> In conquest modest as in action brave,
> To God the glory pious Nelson gave.[15]

On the appointed day, 29 September 1798, so Nelson wrote home, '80 people dined at Sir William's, 1,740 came to a ball, 800 supped, conducted in such a style of elegance as I never saw, or shall again probably.' He sent a copy of a verse composed by Miss Knight as an addition to the National Anthem, which had been sung most lustily by Lady Hamilton:

> Join we great Nelson's name,
> First on the roll of fame,
>   Him let us sing;
> Spread we his fame around,
> Honour of British ground,
> Who made Nile's shores resound –
>   God save our King.[16]

Nelson also sent his wife a ballad, which he felt sure Fanny would 'sing with pleasure', beginning, 'Brave Nelson fought and scorned the frowns of fate, his tranquil bosom fearless of surprise.'

The one unpleasant episode in the evening was Josiah Nisbet's uncouth behaviour. Drunkenly complaining of the unseemly attentions which his stepfather was paying to Lady Hamilton, he had to be hurried out of the room by Captain Troubridge and other officers. Nisbet was not much liked in the Navy. Although the same age as the capable and popular Lieutenant Hoste, who did not at all care for him, he was already a captain and had been given command of the captured French sloop, *Bonne Citoyenne*, an appointment considered solely due to the influence of a stepfather who did not, in fact, rate his talents very highly. Certainly Nelson admitted privately that Nisbet was 'ungracious in the extreme'; yet the lad was not considered past redemption. Lady Hamilton, he told his wife – who was no doubt growing rather tired of hearing so much of this woman's remarkable talents – Lady Hamilton 'would fashion him in six months in spite of himself . . . Her ladyship, if Josiah were to stay, would make something of him and, with all his bluntness, I am sure he likes Lady Hamilton more than any female.'*[17]

It was becoming plain by now that this was true of Nelson himself. Openly admiring her talents, her amusing and occasionally witty remarks, obviously delighting in her lush and voluptuous beauty, responding to her sensuality, deeply gratified by her wholehearted admiration of him as a hero and comforted by her attentive kindness to him as a convalescent invalid, he did not trouble to disguise the emotions she stirred in him. Writing to St Vincent, he apologized for 'the glorious jumble' of the letter; but it was written, he explained, while he was sitting opposite Lady Hamilton. 'Were your Lordship in my place,' he commented, 'I much doubt if you could write so well; our hearts and hands must all be in a flutter.'[18]

Lord St Vincent confessed himself somewhat alarmed by such observations, and by reports reaching him from other correspondents. In a letter to Lady Hamilton, thanking her for all she was doing in helping to restore the health of their 'invaluable friend', he added, 'Pray, do not let your fascinating Neapolitan Dames approach too near him; for he is made of flesh & Blood & cannot resist their temptation.'[19]

---

* This was evidently not the case. Informed by Lady Hamilton that Josiah was 'much improved in every respect', that, although they quarrelled sometimes, they really loved each other, and assured by Nelson that, although his manners were 'so rough', his heart was 'as good and as humane as ever was covered by human breast', the young man's mother noted on the back of her husband's letter, 'My son did not like the Hamiltons' (Naish, 462, 479).

16

Palazzo Reale

It is a country of fiddlers and poets, whores and scoundrels.

In the week that Lord St Vincent's letter to Lady Hamilton was written, Captain Capel arrived in London bringing news of the great victory which had been won off the coast of Egypt two months before.

Earl Spencer was given the exciting news as he was leaving his office at the Admiralty. He listened to the brief account; then, without saying a word in reply, he 'fell on the floor insensible'.[1] 'Capel has arrived! Joy, joy, joy to you, brave, gallant immortalised Nelson!' wrote Lady Spencer when she in turn was given the news.

May that great God, whose cause you so valiantly support, protect and bless you to the end of your brilliant career! ... My heart is absolutely bursting with different sensations of joy, of gratitude, of pride, of every emotion that ever warmed the bosom of a British woman, on hearing of her country's glory – and all produced by you, my dear, good friend ... This moment, the guns are firing, illuminations are preparing, your gallant name is echoed from street to street ... London is mad – absolutely mad – Capel was followed by a mob of several thousands from the Admiralty, huzzaing the whole way ... I am half mad and I fear I have written a strange letter but you'll excuse it.'[2]

The King, apparently, received the news less excitedly. Indeed, he was said to have remained silent for a few minutes, which was, perhaps, so the naval historian Oliver Warner commented, 'one of the most astonishing effects of the battle'.[3]

All over the country, as reports of the victory spread, sentiments as effusive as Lady Spencer's were expressed and celebrations held to mark so notable an achievement. Bonaparte, the dreaded

'Boney', with whom nurses frightened their little charges into obedience, had been soundly defeated and humiliated at last. England, which had sometimes appeared almost on the verge of revolution that summer, so widespread had discontent become, seemed to give itself entirely over to patriotic rejoicing. It was said that a messenger galloping down to Weymouth to take the news to the King was challenged by a highwayman who, on being told the contents of the dispatches the rider was carrying, waved his intended victim on his way, declining to rob him. At Weymouth, the King, having found his voluble tongue again, 'read Admiral Nelson's letter aloud four times to different noblemen and gentlemen on the esplanade'.[4]

Newspapers which had been censorious of Admiral Nelson's failure to find the French fleet now praised his acumen and daring. The month before caricatures had shown the fleet sailing pointlessly all over the Mediterranean; now they depicted the hero, the 'gallant Nellson', 'extirpating the Plagues of Egypt' with his club of British oak, 'destroying the Revolutionary Crocodiles' and the 'Old Cock Deviles', 'cleansing ye mouth of ye Nile'.[5]

Bonfires were lit; cannon fired salutes; church bells rang; balls were held in assembly rooms; two new dances, 'the Vanguard' and 'the Breaking of the Line', became all the rage. Bumper after bumper was drunk in taverns; schoolchildren were given holidays; coaches flew flags as they rattled down the roads, their postillions shouting the good tidings to the toll-keepers at the turnpikes; villagers marched from church to alehouse bearing aloft portraits or silhouettes of 'our single-handed Conqueror'. In churches and chapels special prayers were said; songs were composed and rhymes repeated. Immense quantities of souvenirs were produced – pictures and mugs, engraved glasses, mechanical toys, naval uniforms for children, illustrated books, models of British ships. In Norfolk the celebrations in honour of the county's 'most valiant son' were particularly joyous. 'Great rejoicings at Norwich to day on Lord Nelsons late great & noble Victory over the French,' the Rev. James Woodforde, parson at Weston Longeville, recorded in his journal.

An Ox rosted whole in the Market-Place etc. This being a day of general Thanksgiving Mr Cotman read Prayers this Morning at Weston-Church, proper on the Occasion. Dinner today Leg of Mutton rosted etc. I gave my servants this Evening after Supper some strong-Beer and some Punch to drink Lord Nelson's Health on his late grand Victory and also all the other officers with him and all the brave Sailors with them.[6]

At Swaffham a grand ball was held. William Nelson's daughter, Charlotte, described the occasion in a letter to her aunt:

It was as full as could be expected ... Young Mrs Hoste danced the first Two dances with me ... We sent to London for all the songs which are published and we had them and sung, and I am learning them all to play ... Mrs Hoste's ribbands which she had from London were half Navy Blue and half red to signify the Knights of the Bath, and of the Navy. She gave me a medallion of my uncle which I wore round my neck ... Mrs Micklethwaite had a very handsome cap from London inscribed in Gold Spangles: 'The Hero of the Nile.'[7]

At Burnham Thorpe, Edmund Nelson's neighbour, Sir Mordaunt Martin, presided over the roasting of a sheep and the rendering of an 'excellent song formed for the occasion from the old Rule Britania & sung by Mr Carter & the Burnham Ulph Band'.[8]

At Roundwood House, Lady Nelson found herself the centre of attraction and much courted by the members of the grand families who had not taken much notice of her hitherto. But this did not please her. 'Truly I don't thank them,' she wrote.[9] Her brother-in-law, Maurice, however, was delighted and flattered to be asked as guest of honour to a splendid dinner in London by the Prime Minister, who had described Horatio in the House of Commons as 'that great commander whose services fill every bosom with rapturous emotion, and who will never cease to derive from the gratitude of his countrymen the tribute of his worth'.

The City of London – to whose Lord Mayor Nelson had given the sword of the French commander-in-chief's flag officer – presented Nelson and his captains with swords, while the King presented them with medals. Medals of gold were also made for them, at a cost of over £2,000, by Alexander Davison, who supplied further medals for lieutenants, and for 'warrant and inferior officers Copper Gilt medals and for the men Copper Bronzed'.* Medal ribbons were manufactured by the yard. Numerous gifts were bestowed upon the hero, his officers and his men, including 2,000 sequins from the Sultan of Turkey for distribution among the wounded. For Nelson personally the Sultan dispatched a dress sword, a pelisse 'of the finest scarlet cloth, lined with most beautiful sable fur', a canteen, a scimitar with a gold hilt, a musket mounted in silver and ivory, and a diamond ornament known as a *chelengk* taken from one of the Grand Signior's turbans, which Nelson was to stick in his hat, having been informed by the donor, extolling the virtuosity of his lavish gift, that this 'blaze of brilliants, crowned with vibrating plumage and a radiant star on the middle', turned 'on its centre by means of watch-work which winds up behind'. From Russia came a miniature of the Tsar and a gold box set with diamonds; from other sovereigns silver-studded boxes; from the East India Company a reward of £10,000 for Nelson; from his brother officers 'a magnificent sword, the hilt of which most appropriately represented a crocodile, very finely executed in gold'.[10] It seemed that only the King and the Government seemed reluctant to give the hero his due, as though they wished to add no further fuel to his vanity or give offence to senior officers.

Lord Hood had whispered to Fanny Nelson that she could expect shortly to become a viscountess: Mr Pitt, the Prime Minister, had said so. After all, Admiral Jervis had been created Earl of St Vincent following his defeat of the Spanish fleet the year before, and Admiral Duncan a viscount after the battle of Camperdown. Yet, as Lord Spencer explained to him, on the grounds that Nelson had not been commander-in-chief at Abū Qīr Bay, only

---

* Davison's gesture was not quite as generous as it seemed. It was in acknowledgement of the highly profitable benefits granted to him as a prize agent, 'the truly flattering manner in which [Nelson and the officers under his command] had conferred upon [him] the sole Agency for the sale of the French ships of War taken at the ever memorable Battle of the Nile' (Llangattock Papers, March 1799, E.67).

detached in command of a squadron, and that any higher rank would create an unwelcome precedent – in Lord Hood's opinion, 'a more flimsy reason never was given' – the Government announced that Admiral Nelson was to be created a baron with a pension of £2,000 a year for three lives.[11]

In the House of Commons, Nelson's distant kinsman, Major-General George Walpole, Member for Derby, suggested that the hero should be offered 'a higher degree of rank'; but Pitt thought it 'needless to enter into the question of rank'. Admiral Nelson had obtained a great victory, 'and no man would think it worth while to ask whether he had been created a baron, a viscount or an earl'.[12]

With his friends and family, Nelson did not hide his disappointment. He was 'known to have frequently expressed his grief and indignation at receiving the title of baron only. Had they left him as he was, he was heard repeatedly to say, he would not have complained; but, he thought, his services merited more than a barony.'[13]

Lady Hamilton gave vent to her outrage. 'Hang them, I say!' she wrote to Lady Nelson towards the end of October;[14] and in a letter to her hero she told him, 'If I was King of England, I would make you the most noble puissant DUKE NELSON MARQUIS NILE EARL ALEXANDER VICOUNT PYRAMID BARON CROCADILE, and PRINCE VICTORY, that posterity might have you in all forms.'[15]

In this and other long, excited, rambling, in places incoherent letters she grew feverishly excited about the honours and presents which had been and ought to be bestowed upon him, about the high esteem in which the King and Queen of Naples held him, about her own feelings towards him which she 'would leave [him] to guess'.

I must see the present [the pelisse] touch it put [it] over my shoulders look in the glass & say vivo il Turk ... May you live long long long for the sake of your country your King your family all Europe Asia Affrica 2 Americas & for the scourge of Franc but particularly for the happiness of Sir William & self who love you admire you & glory in your friendship ... I told her Majesty we onely wanted Lady Nelson to be the female *tria juncta in uno* for we all love you & yet all three differently & yet all equally if you can make that out ... I [am] not a luke warm friend for the world I am no one's enemy & unfortunately am difficult & cannot make friendship with all but the few friends I have I would die for them ... We love you so dearly he is the best husband friend ... I wish I could say father also but I would be too happy if I had the blessing of having children so must be content.[16]

In Naples, Lady Hamilton and her husband were doing all they could to make Nelson's stay there as enjoyable as possible. 'I have had the singular satisfaction of having one of the first men in the world and our Friend Sir Hor: Nelson [by then Lord Nelson] in my house,' Sir William Hamilton wrote to Charles Greville, 'and although necessary Fetes, Illuminations etc have ruined me for the present, I had rather live on bread and cheese the rest of my life than not have done what was right for me to do on this great occasion.'[17]

Nelson was still not very well, with occasional headaches and symptoms of malaria; and although letters of congratulation poured into the Palazzo Sessa from government ministers, senior officers and younger friends alike, for weeks he could not hide his disappointment at not being granted the viscountcy he had expected and being 'cut off £1,000 a year less than either St Vincent or Duncan'. But the pride which Lady Hamilton took in his achievements and the affection she showed him, the companionship of the agreeable Sir William, the confidence placed in him by the King's minister, Sir John Acton, and the flattering attentions bestowed upon him by the King and Queen, all helped to cheer and comfort him and to make his time in Campania so enjoyable. He drove in the Hamiltons' carriage along the coast, acknowledging the acclamations of the people in the streets; he dined at the Palazzo Reale; he was taken to the other royal palace at Caserta, which had been completed to the designs of Vanvitelli in 1774; he sat reading in the shade of the trees in the gardens of the Hamiltons' villas of Torre del Greco at the foot of Vesuvius and the Villa Emma outside Naples on the beach at Posillipo. He was accompanied on excursions to Herculaneum and Pompeii; he went sailing in the bay; he climbed the slopes of Vesuvius. Above all, he enjoyed the company of Emma Hamilton, so exuberant, so responsive, so plumply beautiful, so admiring of his fame, so kind and attentive as a nurse, so exciting and voluptuous as a woman. He was now obviously and deeply in love with her; and, perhaps, was also by now her lover. 'Naples is a dangerous place,' he had written in a letter to Lord St Vincent not long after his arrival, in a letter confessing his desire for her. 'We must keep clear of it.'[18] But he had no intention of keeping clear of such intoxicating excitement; and, according to some reports, his attentions to her in public were already becoming too obvious to ignore.

Even so, he began to think of going home, drawn by the enticing lure of the acclamations which would undoubtedly greet his arrival, the further honours which might be bestowed upon him. His orders from the Admiralty were to blockade the French in Alexandria and Malta; but his own presence was not required for these duties. Samuel Hood was perfectly capable of blockading Alexandria; and, having sailed himself to accept the surrender of the island of Gozo, he could safely leave Captain Ball to conduct the blockade of the larger, neighbouring island of Malta, a tedious assignment which was to occupy the *Alexander* for two years. Besides, powerfully as he was attracted to Lady Hamilton, he did not care for the unremitting social life of the Neapolitan circles in which she moved, or for the company of the courtiers and the ladies who hung about the dark, scented, over-decorated rooms of the Palazzo Reale.

The morning after the dinner given for his birthday, he had written grumpily to Lord St Vincent, 'I am very unwell, and the miserable conduct of this Court is not likely to cool my irritable temper. It is a country of fiddlers and poets, whores and scoundrels.'[19] He had not since had reason to change his mind.

Yet he could not leave Naples just yet. Sir William Hamilton had for long been pressing King Ferdinand to abandon his pretence of neutrality and to declare war on the French. Nelson had added his voice to Sir William's, strongly urging the King to remember that, as Lord Chatham had said, the 'boldest measures are the safest',[20] and doing all he could to counteract the cautious advice of the aloof and courtly Foreign Minister, the marchese di Gallo, whom he disliked intensely, aware that the blunt ways of an

English sailor were not at all to a wily diplomat's taste. 'He admires his Ribbon, Ring, and Snuff-box, so much,' Nelson commented sardonically, echoing an opinion previously expressed by Lady Hamilton, 'that an excellent Petit-Maitre was spoil'd when he was made a Minister.'[21] The Queen, 'the only man in Naples', as Bonaparte had described her, was more insistent than either Sir William or Nelson that war should be declared, castigating the marchese di Gallo as 'a frivolous, ignorant, self-conceited coxcomb'. Ever since her sister had been guillotined in Paris, the Queen had been longing for revenge, and had already asked her son-in-law, the Austrian Emperor, to send her a good general who could put some energy into what passed for the Neapolitan army, a motley collection of 'peasants in uniform' as one of their officers described them. The Emperor responded by dispatching to Naples the Bavarian Baron Karl Mack von Leiberich, a sturdy soldier of forty-six with 'an intelligent eye', who struck Nelson as being a good choice. 'General,' the Queen said to him across the dinner table at the Palazzo Reale, 'be to us on land what my hero, Nelson, has been at sea.' Nelson, who was there and took pleasure in the royal appeal, returned the compliment by observing that her majesty was truly a daughter of Maria Theresa.[22]

The more he saw of General Mack, however, the less Nelson thought of him, eventually deciding that he was 'a Rascal, a Scoundrel and a Coward'.[23] He appeared most reluctant to inconvenience himself in any way; he could not move 'without five carriages'; and his conduct of a military exercise – which began by his declaring that he 'only regretted such a fine army should not have to encounter an enemy more worthy of its prowess', and which ended in his being attacked and surrounded by men who were meant to be on his own side – inspired no confidence in his ability to lead the Neapolitan army to victory in the campaign which he had been employed to organize.[24]

This was an attack upon Rome, which the French General Berthier had recently occupied, billeting his officers in Roman palaces, his soldiers in Roman convents, arresting or expelling several cardinals, disarming the Pope's soldiers, sending the frail and mortally ill Pius VI, 'Citizen Pope', as French officials referred

to him, into exile, and declaring Rome a republic. To throw the
French out of this so-called republic, General Mack was to march
on Rome with a Neapolitan army of 30,000 men under the
nominal leadership of King Ferdinand, while Admiral Lord Nelson
was to land a further four to five thousand troops to the north of
Rome at Leghorn to cut across the French line of communications.
'The King of Naples quits his boars,' Sir William Hamilton
reported to Greville, 'and puts himself at the head of his army as he
ought to have done long ago.'[25]

At first all went well: the soldiers of the King of Naples marched
into Rome through the Porta S. Giovanni on the south side of the
city, while the French, greatly outnumbered, withdrew through
the Porta del Popolo on the north; and, during the next few days,
the Romans grew accustomed to the sight of King Ferdinand
emerging from the Palazzo Farnese to ride around the city with an
escort of resplendently uniformed dragoons. As a proud conqueror
he invited the Pope to return and, 'borne on the wings of the
cherubim, to descend into the Vatican and purify it with [his] holy
presence'.[26]

His duties off the Tuscan coast accomplished satisfactorily, Nelson
returned to Naples; and once again he considered going home,
tempted by reports of the protracted celebrations which continued
to reach him. There was, after all, not much now for him to do in
Naples except take pleasure in the company of Lady Hamilton.
'There can be no occasion for a Nelson here,' he told his wife, who
had more than once proposed coming out to Naples to join him, a
visit that would 'never do' and must at all costs be put out of her
mind. He told her to look for a house in London, a 'neat house
near Hyde Park' if they could afford it, but on no account on the
other side of Portman Square. 'I detest Baker Street,' he added.
'In short, do as you please; you know my wishes and income. . .
Get good servants. You will take care I am not let down.'[27]

All thoughts of returning home, however, had to be abandoned
for the time being when news arrived from the north that the
proud liberators of Rome were no longer in the city. Routed by a
reinforced French army outside its walls, the Neapolitans had

withdrawn, taking with them as much plunder as they could conveniently carry; and the King had ridden hastily after them, asking an equerry to stay close by his side since, as he readily confessed, he was terrified.[28]

'It is reported and, indeed, is certain,' Nelson wrote to Troubridge, 'that the Neapolitan officers, and many of their men are running away even at the sight of the enemy. I know not the extent of the disaster, but I believe it is very bad.' He himself had noticed how reluctant the Neapolitan officers had been to go ashore in Tuscany, and could well believe that in Rome they had behaved no better. 'The Neapolitan Officers have not lost much honour, for God knows, they had but little to lose,' he told Lord Spencer. 'But they lost all they had.'[29]

'It is impossible in the hurry that we are in at this moment to enter into any particulars,' Sir William Hamilton wrote hastily to the Foreign Secretary in London, conscious that the advice which he and Nelson had so strongly urged upon the King had not been wise. 'The fine army of [King Ferdinand] from treachery and cowardice is fading away ... It needs no great penetration to foresee that in a very short time ... the Kingdom is lost. However, fortunately Lord Nelson is here ... which will secure us a retreat.'[30]

Lord Nelson, with the help of Admiral Francesco Caracciolo of the Neapolitan navy, was already preparing for the evacuation by night of the royal family, and of numerous other fugitives, with his customary care, well aware that his advice to the King was to a large extent responsible for their present plight. He arranged for boats from the *Vanguard* and another British ship the *Alcmene*, to be at the landing-stage on the small quay, the Mola Figlio, at 'half-past seven o'clock precisely', for the sailors aboard them to be armed with cutlasses, for the barges to have four to six soldiers in each.

It was essential that the whole operation should be carried out quickly and discreetly since, if it were known that the King was leaving, the *lazzaroni*, who were clamouring for a stand against the heathen French, might well endeavour to prevent him. Already hundreds of them were milling about outside the Palazzo Reale and a royal messenger trying to get through the crowds had been clubbed to death directly beneath the King's windows when the cry went up that he was a Jacobin spy.

It being impossible to get the royal family's treasured possessions, including the crown jewels, down to the quay from the Palazzo Reale without arousing suspicion, they were packed into covered wagons and sent by night to the Palazzo Sessa, where Lady Hamilton – 'living' as she confessed, 'in fear of being torn to pieces by the tumultuous mob who suspected our departure' – had them conveyed aboard the *Vanguard* by British sailors. At the same time her husband was busily supervising the packing of his best remaining pictures and the last of his two thousand vases which were to be taken to safety in England in the British ship *Colossus*.

In the days before their departure the atmosphere in Naples grew ever more tense, as crowds of *lazzaroni* marched menacingly through the streets, threatening to slit the throats of the upper classes, many of whom were known to have Francophile and anti-monarchial sympathies. At court there were signs of increasing panic. Count Carlo Vanni, the widely disliked Inquisitor of State, who feared that he would be lynched if there were to be a Jacobin uprising, shot himself. Admiral Caracciolo, distressed that his own navy was considered incapable of looking after the royal family, who were to be taken aboard the *Vanguard*, and that British sailors were being sent aboard Neapolitan ships, seemed as though he might follow Count Vanni's example. Cornelia Knight, who met him at a dinner party, 'never saw any man so utterly miserable. He scarcely uttered a word, ate nothing, and did not even unfold a napkin.' After this dinner party Miss Knight and her mother thought it as well not to leave their apartments, since Lord Nelson had promised that Commodore Stone would take care of them and they dared not be out when the message to board the ships came.[31]

No one was yet sure when this would be. Nelson had hoped that he might have got the *Vanguard* under way by 18 December; but a stream of letters from Sir John Acton, mostly contradictory, and offering such reasons for delay as the sea being too rough and the difficulties of feeding the Hereditary Princess's recently born baby daughter, had induced him to put off the time of sailing until the night of the twenty-first.

That evening there was to be a grand reception held by Kelim Effendi, the Minister of the Grand Turk, who had arrived in Naples with the presents which had been given to Nelson to honour his victory at Abū Qīr Bay. If Sir William and Lady Hamilton were known to be attending this reception with Admiral Nelson, their departure that night would be considered improbable. So, having made a show of telling their servants to send the coach to fetch them back for supper in two hours' time, they drove from their palace with Mrs Cadogan for Kelim Effendi's party, which they soon left on foot to make their way down to the quay. Nelson – clearly enjoying the excitement and feeling 'never better' in his mind and with his heart 'in the right trim' – also left the party, walking fast for the Palazzo Reale, which he entered, in Lady Hamilton's words, by 'a secret passage'. He 'got up the dark staircase that goes in to the Queen's room & with a dark lantern, cutlasses, pistols etc, brought off every soul'.[32]

Also hurrying down to the mole, muffled against the bitter cold of the night, were Sir John Acton and Prince Esterhazy, the Austrian ambassador, and numerous courtiers, diplomats, ladies-in-waiting, French émigrés, British merchants, servants, cooks, the King's confessor, his treasurer with money and valuables worth £2,500,000, and of course, his head gamekeeper. Also there were Miss Knight and her mother, who had decided to go to bed when the summons came. They had been aroused by a knock on their door and the appearance of a party of sailors armed with cutlasses who hoisted the ladies' trunks on to their shoulders and escorted them down to the shore. 'The night was cold,' Miss Knight remembered,

and it was between twelve and one before we were in the boat. There were several persons already in it, and an English child fell in the water, but was taken out unhurt. We had a long way to go, for the ships had cast anchor at a great distance from the city, to be beyond the range of the forts in the event of treachery or surprise. When we came alongside the Admiral's ship [the *Vanguard*], the captain, Sir Thomas Hardy, stepped into the boat and told my mother that the ship was so full there was no room for us. In vain we entreated to be taken on board.[33]

The Knights were handed over to the care of a midshipman who was 'constantly jumping about in the boat to keep himself from falling asleep'. He explained that he had been on duty without a moment's rest for the past forty-eight hours, 'getting the baggage and numerous attendants of the Royal Family on board'. He took them to a Portuguese ship commanded by an Englishman, which was as crowded with refugees as the *Vanguard*, the cabins being crammed with women talking in a variety of languages, including a rich Russian, who alone amongst them had been able to take possession of a bed. The captain of the ship was extremely rude to them, Miss Knight complained, and his crew were 'an unsavoury mixture of mulattos and jail-birds, gathered up from various ports round the globe and . . . completely without order, discipline, or cleanliness'.[34]

Aboard the *Vanguard* sail-makers had been hard at work for the past three days making canvas cots, while such sailors as could be spared for the task had been slapping paint on the walls of the wardroom, the Admiral's quarters and all the other places in the ship which were being prepared for the royal family and their courtiers and attendants, who now began to clamber aboard, seeking what comfort they could find. Those, like the Knights, for whom there was no room were directed to other craft, to the seventy-four-gun *Archimedes*, to one or other of three British transports, to two Greek polaccas chartered for the purpose, to the Portuguese ship in which the Knights had found shelter, or to a Neapolitan corvette in which several British sailors had had to take the place of members of her usual crew who refused to leave their homes and families even though offered twice their normal rates of pay. The *Alcmene* was not available as the Admiral had decided to leave her behind under the command of the Portuguese Admiral, the Marquis de Niza, who was ordered to get as many Neapolitan ships as he possibly could away to Sicily, and − much to the consternation of the King, who was aghast to remember what they cost − to burn the rest rather than allow them to fall into the hands of the French or Neapolitan rebels. Captain Troubridge had been told to come to Naples and 'for God's sake [to] make haste'; but the *Culloden* had not yet arrived.[35]

After an uncomfortable night, the refugees aboard the ships were aroused by the timbers creaking in a rising storm. Many of them were sick, as they had been in the boats that had taken half an hour to bring them across from the quay; and the King's confessor fell out of his canvas cot and fractured his arm. The next day was calmer; and delegation after delegation came out from the town to the *Vanguard* to beg the King not to leave Naples. When Baron Mack came aboard, however, looking, so Nelson thought, 'worn to a shadow', he urged him to leave as soon as possible.[36] This advice was much more to the King's taste. 'We shall have plenty of woodcocks, Cavaliere,' he said contentedly to Sir William Hamilton after the Austrian general had returned to his broken army, and satisfactory news had reached his majesty that his favourite hounds were being brought to him from Caserta. 'This is just the season. The wind will bring them in . . . We shall have rare sport; you must get your *cannone* ready!'[37]

The King's fellow passengers were not so cheerful. The stench of vomit and unwashed bodies, overlaid with the smell of paint, was nauseating; and when the ships and transports began to roll and dip again on 24 December – the day after the convoy at last set sail for Palermo – most of the refugees aboard were sick again, while those not feeling too ill to care were in fear of losing their lives. Many of the Neapolitan servants sank to their knees in prayer. 'It blew harder than I have ever experienced since I have been at sea,' said Nelson, who ordered sailors on to the tossing decks with axes to hack free the already tattered shrouds and stays if the masts broke and the ship was in danger of capsizing.[38]

Passengers were thrown to and fro, many having abandoned the struggle to keep on their feet on the lurching deck. Princess Castelcicala, whose husband was to be Neapolitan ambassador in London, fell over and cut her head open on the Admiral's sideboard; the six-year-old Prince Alberto fell into convulsions; Prince Esterhazy flung into the raging sea, as a propitiation for his sins, a precious snuffbox decorated with a portrait of his naked mistress. Sir John Acton evinced his distaste at the sight of a wet-nurse suckling the royal baby; Lady Hamilton, looking around for her husband, who was nowhere to be seen, 'discovered that he had

withdrawn to his sleeping cabin,' one of the ship's officers recorded,
'and he was sitting there with a loaded pistol in each hand. In
answer to her Ladyship's exclamation of surprise, he calmly told
her that he was resolved not to die with the "guggle-guggle-guggle"
of salt-water in his throat; and therefore he was prepared, as soon
as he felt the ship sinking, to shoot himself!'[39]

Lady Hamilton herself, assisted by her mother, behaved
admirably, comforting the sick, wrapping the Queen's feet in a
cashmere shawl — a present from the Porte, which Nelson had
passed on to her — giving the royal family all her own bedlinen
when it was discovered that, in the haste of packing, the royal
sheets had been left at the Palazzo Reale, declining to go to bed
herself, holding Prince Alberto in her arms, where he was to die
the next day.

In the early morning of 26 December 1798 the *Vanguard*, flying King
Ferdinand's standard and followed by Admiral Caracciolo's flagship, sailed into Palermo harbour. The Queen, in an agony of grief
over the loss of her child, hurried ashore and, accompanied by
Nelson, was driven in a closed carriage through the fast-falling
snow to the Colli Palace just outside the city. She found the place
gloomy, dark, very cold and almost bereft of furniture. There were
no carpets in her bedroom, nor even a fireplace; the windows did
not fit and the door would not close. She said she wished she were
dead.[40]

Her husband followed her ashore later, looking forward eagerly
to hunting in the palace park and to the opportunity of escaping
from his wife, whom he blamed for urging upon him the misguided
attack on the French, and from his wife's friend, Lady Hamilton,
whom he had come to dislike so much that he threatened to have
her thrown out of a window. 'As far as he is concerned,' the Queen
told her daughter, the Empress, 'Naples might be the land of the
Hottentots. He does not give it another thought.'[41]

The Hamiltons and Nelson, after an uncomfortable time at the
Colli Palace, were taken to the Villa Bastioni where Sir William,
having gone to bed with what he complained was 'a fever from
cold and bile', was distraught to learn that the ship carrying the

best of his vases to England had been wrecked off the Isles of Scilly, the only part of the cargo to be salvaged being a coffin containing the pickled corpse of Admiral Lord Shouldham.* The Knights found room in a squalid inn immediately opposite the prison from which, throughout most of the night, emanated the groans of convicts accompanied by the mournful strumming of a guitar.[42]

* On his return to England, Hamilton, 'quite beyond all expectations', discovered that it was 'some cases of the worst vases' that had been taken on board the *Colossus*. Many of the best had been put on board the *Foudroyant* by mistake and had arrived safe and sound. Hamilton was able to put his finances on a sounder footing by selling them for £4,000 (Morrison, 544; Fothergill, *Sir William Hamilton*, 402–3; Naish, 581).

17

Palermo

I can neither Eat or Sleep for thinking of You my dearest love.

It passed more than once through Lord Nelson's mind in the early weeks of 1799 that he would be better off dead himself. 'I am ready to quit this world of trouble,' he wrote to Alexander Davison, 'and envy none but those of the estate of six feet by two.'[1] Lady Parker was informed that his health was 'such that, without a great alteration,' he would 'venture to say a very short space of time would send him off to that bourne from whence none return, but God's will be done'.[2] 'After the action [at Abū Qīr Bay],' he added, 'I had nearly fell into a decline . . . I am [now] worse than ever: my spirits have received such a shock that I think they cannot recover from it . . . you would hardly believe the change in me.' 'Palermo is detestable,' Admiral Goodall was told, 'and we are all unwell and full of sorrow . . . where is all this to end?'[3] Suffering from nausea, biliousness and indigestion as well as palpitations and attacks of breathlessness – which, in his hypochondriacal way, he took to be heart attacks – he was irritable as well as depressed.* He was also troubled by persistent headaches, the result perhaps, so it has often been suggested, of his recent wound which, combined with late nights and an unaccustomed diet, may

---

* Palpitations and attacks of breathlessness, irritability and depression and the feeling that a 'girth were buckled taut' over the breast, as Nelson described it, are all symptoms of Da Costa's syndrome or disordered action of the heart. This condition, also known as soldier's heart because of the frequency with which it was encountered in the First World War, has been diagnosed by recent medical opinion as Nelson's complaint, rather than the heart disease he feared (Pugh, 5). It arises under conditions of great anxiety and physical strain (William A. R. Thomson, *Black's Medical Dictionary* (31st edition), 288, 783).

1. A drawing by Thomas Rowlandson of seamen climbing on board the 74-gun *Hector* in Portsmouth Harbour

2. The scene on a gun deck of the *Hector* while the ship is still in port

5. A newly arrived young gentleman is shocked by the rowdyism of the midshipmen's berth

3. (*opposite above*) Helped by his tearful mother, the boisterous Master William Blockhead packs his sea chest before embarking in HMS *Hellfire* for the West Indies

4. (*opposite*) Sailors gambling and dancing while waiting in port for their ship to set sail

6 and 7. Rowlandson's drawings of a seaman and a cabin boy with mop and pail

8. Samuel Scott's drawing of ships in the Royal Dockyard at Deptford

9. The Royal Dockyard at Portsmouth in the 1790s

10. Miniatures of King Ferdinand of Naples, known as *il Re Nasone* because of his large ill-shaped nose, and Queen Maria Carolina, whose nickname was *Polpett Mbocca*, 'Mouthful of Rissole', because of the way she gabbled her words

11. Sir William Hamilton, British minister in Naples, and his first wife, a Welsh heiress who died in 1782, from a portrait by David Allan

12. A drawing by Thomas Rowlandson of Emma, Lady Hamilton, than whom, in her lover Charles Greville's opinion, 'a cleaner, sweeter bedfellow did not exist'

13. Nelson and his boarding party leap on to the deck of the Spanish ship, the *San Nicolas*, at the Battle of St Vincent on 14 February 1797

14. Nelson accepting the sword of surrender from the Spanish captain on the quarterdeck of the captured *San José*

15. HMS *Theseus*, Nelson's flagship, sailing with the fleet in a strong wind off Cadiz in July 1797, from a painting by Thomas Luny

16. The first letter written by Nelson after the loss of his right arm, dated 27 July 1797 aboard the *Theseus*. Gradually letters written with his left hand became more distinct and neater than those previously written with his right.

have been responsible for the errors of judgement and instances of erratic behaviour which were to be noticed in the months to come.* Sir William Hamilton, still ill himself and mourning the supposed loss of his precious vases, was no companion; and even the presence of Lady Hamilton, who seemed to spend much of her time weeping with the inconsolable Queen, was occasionally an embarrassment rather than a pleasure.

This at least was the opinion of the Scot, Captain Pryse Lockhart Gordon, who was in Palermo that year acting as travelling tutor to the invalid Lord Montgomerie. Gordon was put out that he and his companion were not invited to stay at the Palazzo Palagonia, though there were already several people living here apart from the Hamiltons, Mrs Cadogan and Lord Nelson. Gordon and Montgomerie were, however, asked to dinner, and so they were able to observe Nelson, who spent part of the evening writing at a table in the corner, as well as Lady Hamilton, who came into the room leaning on her husband's shoulder, 'her raven tresses floating round her expansive form and full bosom'.

'The ceremony of introduction being over,' Gordon related,

she rehearsed in a subdued tone a *mélange* of Lancashire and Italian, detailing the catalogue of her miseries, her hopes, and her fears with lamentations about the dear Queen, the loss of her own charming Palazzo and its precious contents, which had fallen into the hands of the vile republicans. But here we offered some consolation, by assuring her Ladyship that every article of the ambassador's property had been safely embarked in an English transport, and would be despatched in a few days. All this we afterwards learned she knew . . . During this interesting conversation the Lady discovered that she was Lord Montgomery's

---

* It has also been suggested that Nelson was a manic depressive, a diagnosis which has not found wide agreement amongst medical historians. As for his head wound, the surgeon, T. C. Barras, has observed that 'although alarming and spectacular because of the profuse bleeding', head wounds such as that suffered by Nelson are 'trivial from a surgical aspect . . . It is emphasized that there is nothing in any available evidence to suggest that the cut in Nelson's forehead was other than a simple minor injury' (T. C. Barras, 'Nelson's Head Injury at the Battle of the Nile', *Journal of the Nelson Society*, vol. 2, part 11, July 1987, 217).

cousin, 'A'nt us, Sir William?' His Lordship made his bows and acknowledgements.

Then Nelson came up to Gordon and, after a few 'trifling queries', said to him, 'Pray, Sir, have you heard of the battle of the Nile? . . . *That*, Sir, was the most extraordinary one that was ever fought, and it is *unique*, Sir, for three reasons; first, for its having been fought at night, secondly, for its having been fought at anchor; and thirdly, for its having been gained by an admiral with one arm.'

To each of these reasons, Gordon made 'a profound bow'. But, he commented, 'had the speech been made *after* dinner, I should have imagined the hero had imbibed an extra dose of champagne'.[4]

After dinner the next day it was Lady Hamilton who behaved in a rather disconcerting manner. A Turkish messenger had arrived with a message from the Tsar. Lady Hamilton suggested to Nelson that he put on the pelisse and the *chelengk* which the Sultan had given him. 'This was done in a moment,' Gordon continued '. . . and the Mussulman entered. The moment he caught a glance of his Lordship's costume the slave was prostrate on the earth, making the grand salaam . . . Lady H. by means of a Greek interpreter belonging to the Embassy, flirted with the Turk, a coarse savage monster, and he was invited to dinner the following day.'

At this dinner the Turk, 'drunk with rum which does not come under the prohibition of the prophet', entertained Lady Hamilton with an account of his exploits. 'With this weapon,' he told her, 'I cut off the heads of twenty French prisoners in one day! Look, there is their blood remaining on it!' 'The speech translated,' Gordon went on,

her Ladyship's eye beamed with delight, and she said, 'Oh let me see the sword that did the glorious deed!' It was presented to her; she took it into her fair hand covered with rings, and looking at the encrusted Jacobin blood, kissed it and handed it to her hero of the Nile! . . . Mrs C[harles] L[ock], the beautiful and amiable wife of our consul-general, was sitting *vis-à-vis* to the Turk, and was so horrified at the scene (being near her accouchement) that she fainted and was taken out of the room. Her Ladyship said it was a piece of affectation, and made no efforts to assist her guest; the truth is, she was jealous of her beauty, and insinuated that being the sister of the late Lord E. F. [Edward Fitzgerald, the Irish rebel, who had recently died of wounds in Newgate prison] she must necessarily be a Jacobin.

Lady Hamilton's action was applauded by the toad-eaters, so Gordon said, 'but many groaned and cried "shame" loud enough to reach the ears of the Admiral, who turned pale, hung his head and seemed ashamed. Lord M[ontgomerie] got up, and left the room, and I speedily followed. Poor Nelson was to be pitied.'[5]

Mrs Lock's husband Charles, the recently appointed touchy and self-opinionated consul-general, entertained an even lower opinion of Lady Hamilton than Captain Gordon did. To Lock she was a 'superficial, grasping and vulgar minded woman', who possessed an 'unbounded power' over Lord Nelson. As for Nelson himself, his 'extravagant love' for her had made him 'the laughing stock of the whole fleet'.[6]

It could certainly no longer be doubted now that Nelson was helplessly and passionately in love with her, as excited by her sensuality as he was enthralled by the motherly care she took of a man whose own mother had died when he was nine years old. While Sir William spent much of his time ill in bed, they were seen together constantly. He watched her with unconcealed admiration and adoration as she performed her 'Attitudes', rather less enticingly now that her figure had become so very rounded. He sat beside her, drinking glass after glass of champagne, while she gambled for such high stakes, sometimes as much as £500 a night, that her husband was reported to have remarked that when he was dead she would be a beggar.

Away from her, Nelson clearly thought of her constantly. 'Last Night I did nothing but dream of You, altho' I woke 20 times in the Night,' he told her once when he was at sea '20 leagues farther' from her than he had been 'Yesterday noon'.

I can neither Eat or Sleep for thinking of You my dearest love, I never touch even pudding You know the reason. No I would Starve sooner. My only hope is to find You have Equally kept Your Promises to Me . . . but I rest perfectly confident in the reallity of Your love and that You would die sooner than be false in the smallest thing to Your Own faithful Nelson who lives only for his Emma . . . I shall run Mad . . . In one of my dreams I thought I was at a large Table You was not present. Sitting between a Princess who I detest and another. They both tried to Seduce Me and the first wanted to take those liberties with Me which no Woman in this World but Yourself ever did. The consequence was I knocked her down and in the moment of bustle You came in and, taking Me to Your embrace wispered 'I love nothing but You My Nelson.' I kissed You fervently And we enjoy'd the height of love. Ah Emma I pour out my Soul to You . . . no love is like Mine towards You.[7]

With his sexuality so deeply and turbulently aroused, Nelson was naturally distressed to hear through Alexander Davison that unless he returned home in a few months his wife intended coming out to join him. He replied immediately to put such ideas out of her mind: she would certainly regret it if she left England to come to 'a wandering sailor who would be quite unable to look after her properly. I could, if you had come,' he told her,

only have struck my flag, and carried you back again, for it would have been impossible to set up an establishment at either Naples or Palermo. Nothing but the affairs of this country has kept me from England; and if I have the pleasure of seeing their Sicilian Majesties safe on their throne again, it is probable that I shall yet be home in the summer. Good Sir William, Lady Hamilton and myself, are the mainsprings of the machine which manages what is going on in this country. We are all bound to England when we can quit our posts with propriety.[8]

The situation in King Ferdinand's realm undoubtedly needed careful handling. News had arrived in Palermo that Prince Pignatelli, King Ferdinand's representative in Naples, had entered into negotiations with the French, who had finally defeated the royalist forces outside the city, and that, in obedience to the orders given him, the Marquis de Niza had scuttled three ships of the Neapolitan navy. This capitulation to the French and the 'patriots', as the Neapolitan Jacobins called themselves, had enraged the *lazzaroni* who had rioted outside the Palazzo Reale, demanding weapons with which to defend their city and the honour of their King against the educated classes and the liberal aristocracy, who were united in condemning Bourbon autocracy. The *lazzaroni* had looted the houses of known liberals and Jacobin sympathizers, tied the intellectual duca della Torre and his brother to chairs and shot them both, stripped ladies supposed to be in sympathy with the ideas of the pagan French and dragged them naked through the streets. On the arrival of the French army under General Jean-Etienne Championnet, the uprising had been crushed in a matter of hours. Hundreds of *lazzaroni* had been killed, the royalist garrisons had been thrown out of the castles of Sant'Elmo, Nuovo and dell'Ovo, and a republic, known as the Parthenopean Republic, after the ancient Greek city which had been founded in the shadow of Vesuvius, had been established. Street names had been changed, puppet shows and religious services provided with republican undertones, Trees of Liberty – later to be cut down by Captain Troubridge – erected, and men named Ferdinand told that it would be advisable to call themselves something else.[9]

King Ferdinand himself listened in Palermo to the advice of a loyal Bourbonist, who, having been Treasurer and War Minister in the administration of Pope Pius VI, had been rewarded with a cardinal's hat, though he was only in minor orders. This was Fabrizio Ruffo, a brave and resourceful man of noble family, who had been born in Calabria and was much respected by the *contadini* of the region. He proposed going to Calabria, enlisting the support of the clergy and leading families of the area, arousing the patriotism and religious faith of the *contadini* and persuading them to serve under a banner bearing the royal arms on one side and a cross on the other and to follow him in a holy war against the French.

The King gave his blessing to Cardinal Ruffo, who received a letter from the Queen assuring him of her heartfelt gratitude. 'Order is to be re-established in that monstrous city [Naples],' she wrote, 'by rewarding the faithful and inflicting exemplary punishment on the wicked ... Order must be evolved from this atrocious disgrace.' Justifying the Queen's faith in him, Ruffo soon had almost 20,000 men under more or less primitive arms in what he called a Christian Army of the Holy Faith.

Nelson, encouraged by the news that Austria had declared war against the French and that both Russia and Turkey were prepared to lend naval support, was persuaded to commit his own ships to the defeat of what he called the Vesuvian Republic, though he did not disguise his low opinion of the Calabrese army and of Ruffo, 'the Great Devil', the 'swelled-up priest' who commanded it.[10]

He ordered Troubridge to the Bay of Naples with four ships including the *Vanguard*, giving him instructions to blockade the city and seize the islands in the bay. He removed his own flag to the *Culloden*, and then to the transport, the *Samuel and Jane*, while continuing to live ashore in the Palazzo Palagonia.

The welcome opportunity to use his fleet to some useful purpose did not, however, improve Nelson's ill temper. He wrote to the Duke of Clarence to tell him that he was 'seriously unwell' and to assure him that two of King Ferdinand's incompetent generals were to be court-martialled and if found guilty to be shot or hanged. 'Should this be effected,' he added, doubtless to the approval of the royal martinet, 'I shall have some hopes that I have done good. I ever preach that rewards and punishments are the foundation of all good government.'[11]

Nelson was equally pugnacious when replying to Troubridge, who had taken the islands of Ischia and Capri but had been obliged to accept on board his ships various men handed over to him as having collaborated with the French. Troubridge asked for some native troops and a judge to conduct these men's trials. Nelson, having consulted Acton and the Queen, dispatched both soldiers and judge immediately with the curt request, 'Send me word some proper heads are taken off; this alone will comfort me.'[12] Troubridge acknowledged receipt of the judge, but did not think much of him. He was, said Troubridge, 'the poorest creature I ever saw; frightened out of his senses ... talks of it being necessary to have a bishop to degrade the priests, before he can execute them. I told him to hang them first, and if he did not think the degradation of hanging sufficient, I would.'[13]

The judge was not the only Neapolitan to arouse Troubridge's scorn. 'I have a villain by name Francesco on board, who commanded the castle at Ischia,' he told Nelson in another letter. 'The moment we took possession of the castle, the mob tore this vagabond's coat with the tricoloured cape and cap of liberty button to pieces, and he then had the impudence to put on his Sicilian Majesty's regimentals again; upon which I tore his epaulette off, took his cockade out and obliged him to throw them overboard. I then honoured him with double irons.'[14] 'The villainy we must combat is great indeed,' Troubridge reported the next day. 'I have just flogged a rascal for loading bread with sand. The loaf was hung round his neck in sight of the people.' The head of 'another rascal', one Carlo Granozio, had been presented to him with a basket of fruit by a man he described as 'a jolly fellow', who asked Troubridge 'kindly to accept the head as proof of his attachment to the Crown'. Troubridge apologized for not sending it on to Nelson: the weather was too hot.[15]

Nelson himself was urgently prompted by the Queen and Lady Hamilton to go to Naples himself. The Queen 'begs, entreats and conjures you, my dear Lord . . . to go to Naples,' Emma wrote to him on 12 June. 'For God's sake consider it and go.'[16] Nelson left that same day, taking with him 1,700 royalist infantry. But, warned that a French fleet from Brest had managed to get past the British blockade and enter the Mediterranean, he put back into Palermo to disembark his cumbersome cargo of soldiers so that his gun decks could be cleared for fighting.

While looking out for the French fleet off the west coast of Sicily, and hoping to intercept it should it be making for Egypt to the relief of the army stranded there, Nelson received a message from Sir William Hamilton which urged him to leave his present post and make for Naples where Cardinal Ruffo's horde of irregulars, 'all ferocious men' as their leader admitted them to be, had swarmed down towards the city, forcing the French to withdraw most of their men, leaving only a garrison in the castle of Sant'Elmo to support the men of the Parthenopean Republic militia.

Mindful of the importance of preventing the French fleet getting through to Egypt, Nelson had already apologized to Lord St

Vincent for not joining the main British fleet in the western Mediterranean. 'You may depend upon my exertion,' he had written from Sicily, 'and I am only sorry that I cannot move to your help; but this Island appears to hang on my stay. Nothing could console the Queen this night but my promise not to leave them.' But although it meant abandoning a station from which he could cover the approaches to Sicily, Malta and Egypt, and although it entailed disregarding the Commander-in-Chief's known intentions, Nelson did not hesitate for long before deciding to sail for Naples at Hamilton's request.

On his way he called at Palermo where he was told that Cardinal Ruffo's men were fighting in the streets of Naples and approaching the castles where the outnumbered defenders of the Parthenopean Republic still held out. He was also told that the royalists were now firmly in control of the islands in the Bay of Naples and that they were taking ferocious revenge on those whom they accused of Jacobin sympathies, including three priests who were being sent to Sicily to answer a charge of treason. 'Your news of the hanging of thirteen Jacobins gave us great pleasure,' he assured Captain Edward Foote, commander of the *Seahorse* and the senior British officer in the bay. 'And the three priests, I hope, return in the *Aurora* to dangle on the tree best adapted to their weight of sins.' As for Cardinal Ruffo, Nelson did not consider him any more trustworthy than King Ferdinand's enemies. He told Lady Hamilton that he was going to Naples so 'that their Majesties might settle matters there and *take off* (if necessary the head of) the Cardinal'.[17]

Both Lady Hamilton and Sir William were taken aboard his ship for the voyage from Palermo to Naples, Sir William as diplomatist, his wife as interpreter and the Queen's deputy. The passage was a calm one; and when they arrived in Naples the city appeared to be *en fête*: windows were ablaze with light; shouts of '*Viva il Re!*' could be heard from the shore; numerous boats were rowed out with passengers eager to welcome Nelson's ship. Aboard one of them was Egidio Pallio, chief, so he claimed, of 90,000 *lazzaroni* prepared to fight for the King if only they had arms. These Nelson recklessly undertook to supply for as many men as he could.

Ashore the city was in turmoil. Cardinal Ruffo's uncontrollable troops were plundering houses and murdering those they singled out as enemies. 'The streets were full of scattered dead bodies, stripped naked and white, for they were gentlemen,' one eyewitness told his son. 'In the Via di Porto suddenly a whole wave of the populace is upon me, crying "a Jacobin!" I feel them snatch off the false *queue* of tow that I had put on [to hide the fact that he had followed the fashion of those who supported the Republic by cutting his hair short]. They seize me, they strip me, they prick me with bayonets.' Saved from death by a friend, he was thrown into prison where his sister visited him and fainted at the sight of him. 'Oh it's nothing,' said a Calabrese officer, 'I'll make her come to,' cutting the girl twice across the face with a whip.[18]

'We met swarms of brigands and armed *lazzaroni*,' another survivor reported.

They were all intent upon a remorseless sacking of those houses which, from their being well furnished, the people judged to belong to Jacobin patriots ... Bodies lay here and there, mostly mutilated ... women and girls were borne by the populace naked, in procession, and that because they were supposed to belong to the family of some Jacobin. Heads and mutilated limbs were scattered in the street corners ... A great number of victims were all shot, one after the other ... This done those butchers, not caring whether they were alive or dead, proceeded to cut off their heads, some of which were borne in procession on the ends of long poles and others served them to play with, rolling them along the ground like balls.[19]

Anxious to avoid further bloodshed, worried by the excesses of his men – and fearful that the French fleet, now joined by Spanish warships, would soon appear in the bay – Ruffo had accepted the surrender of the French troops and their Neapolitan allies in the city's strongholds on the understanding that the French would be shipped home to France and any Neapolitans who wished to do so would be allowed to accompany them, so as to be spared the ferocious attentions of the *lazzaroni* and the Calabrese. Neapolitans who had supported the short-lived Parthenopean Republic would be allowed to return to their homes under a general amnesty.

Nelson, unwavering in his opinion that there was 'no way of dealing with a Frenchman but to knock him down', was outraged by what he took to be the leniency of such 'infamous terms'.[20] A messenger who came aboard his flagship from Naples described him as being 'in a violent passion' as he burst out furiously, 'Tell the people on shore when you return that I will batter down their city.' Sir William caught the messenger before he climbed down into his vessel, and asked him not to repeat the Admiral's remarks. 'I hope,' Sir William added, 'he will be calmer tomorrow and think differently.'[21] Without waiting to be informed of the details of the treaty, Nelson sat down to write a condemnation of it, which he headed, 'Opinion delivered before I saw the treaty of armistice, etc., only from reports at sea.' This long paper concluded, 'Therefore the British admiral proposes to the Cardinal to send, in their joint names, to the French and rebels that the arrival of the British fleet has completely destroyed the compact . . . that as to rebels and traitors, no power on earth has a right to stand between their gracious King and them: they must instantly throw themselves on the clemency of their sovereign.'[22]

Confident of the support of the King, who, indeed, strongly condemned the 'infamous Capitulation to the rebels', Nelson uncompromisingly stood his ground when that 'worthless fellow' Ruffo came aboard his ship, clambering past the open gun ports beneath which were boats unloading supplies of lemons and beef. Nelson met him on the quarterdeck and immediately let it be known, through Sir William Hamilton, acting as interpreter, that, as he had already said by letter, 'the treaty entered into with the Rebels [could not] be carried into execution without the approbation of his Sicilian Majesty'.[23] The French must surrender unconditionally, while the 'rebellious subjects of His Sicilian Majesty, in the Castles of Nuovo and Uovo' must not be allowed to leave them for the boats which were waiting to take them to safety. Cardinal Ruffo – 'the very quintessence of Italian finesse', in Hamilton's words – explained that the polaccas for the French and those Neapolitans who wished to accompany them to France were ready for departure. The Cardinal had given his word that they could leave and he could not go back on it now. The most sensible, as well as the most just policy, was one of forgiveness for all but a few of the worst offenders. When he left the ship Hamilton decided that it was only his diplomatic intervention which had 'prevented an open rupture between Cardinal Ruffo and Admiral Nelson'; while Nelson himself told Admiral Duckworth, who had been detached to reinforce him at Naples, 'As you will believe, the Cardinal and myself have begun our career by a complete difference of opinion.' An admiral was 'no match in talking with a Cardinal'.[24]

The differences remained unresolved after a second meeting between the two men, as cold and unproductive as the first. Nelson, his overbearing, irritable manner much exacerbated by 'persistent head-aches, sickness and want of sleep', demanded that the forts should be surrendered unconditionally: Ruffo could not agree. Indeed, if the terms he had negotiated were not to be implemented, he would withdraw his men and leave it to the British to deal with the problem on their own. It was he, after all, who had defeated the King's enemies without any help from the British admiral now presuming to dictate terms to him. On his return to the city, the cardinal let it be known that Lord Nelson was about to break the armistice and foretold a night of violence.

His fears were realized: hundreds of people fled headlong from the city, terrified that their homes were about to be destroyed, either by the guns of the French in the castle of Sant'Elmo or those of the British ships in the bay, probably both. Suspected Jacobins were set upon by Calabrese and many were murdered; Egidio Pallio's *lazzaroni* made eager use of the muskets with which, at Lady Hamilton's instigation, Nelson had supplied them. Throughout the night, from the ships in the bay, firing could be heard and fires seen breaking out in the city.

The next day Nelson decided that order must be restored while formal instructions were awaited from Palermo. He informed Cardinal Ruffo that he was, for the moment, 'resolved to do nothing which might break the armistice'. Refugees would be allowed to board the polaccas; and to help the cardinal in the restoration of order 1,500 marines would be sent ashore. The cardinal went to a service of thanksgiving in the church of the Carmine.[25]

18

The Bay of Naples

The most notorious of the rebels I have in irons on board, and I hope they will meet the same fate as Caraciollo.

On the morning of 28 June 1799 the expected instructions from Palermo arrived in Naples. Sir John Acton had written to say that nothing less than unconditional surrender would be considered. There was also a letter from the Queen to Lady Hamilton:

The following conditions ought to form the basis, in the King's opinion and in mine, and we submit them to the excellent judgement and heart of our dear Lord Nelson. The rebel patriots must lay down their arms and surrender at discretion to the pleasure of the King. Then, in my opinion, an example should be made of some of the leaders . . . [with] a rigorous severity . . . The females who have distinguished themselves in the revolution to be treated the same way and without pity . . . This is not pleasure but absolutely necessary for, without it, the King could not for six months peacefully govern his people . . . Finally, dear Milady, I recommend Lord Nelson to treat Naples as if it were an Irish town in a similar state of rebellion. France will be none the better for all these thousands of rascals; we shall all be better off without them. They merit being sent to Africa or to the Crimea . . . They deserve to be branded that others may not be deceived by them. I recommend to you, dear Milady, the greatest firmness, vigour and severity.[1]

Soon after his wife's receipt of this letter, Sir William Hamilton wrote to Cardinal Ruffo:

My Lord Nelson desires me to inform your Eminence that in consequence of an order which he has just received from his Sicilian Majesty, who entirely disapproves of the capitulation made with his rebellious subjects in the castles of Ovo and Nouvo, he is about to seize and make sure of those who have left them and are on board the vessels in this port . . . and, at the same time, to warn the rebels who have escaped to Naples from the said castles, that they must submit to the clemency of his Sicilian Majesty within the space of twenty-four hours under pain of death.[2]

On the same day Nelson wrote to Sir John Acton:

I approve of no one thing which has been and is going on here. In short, if the cardinal was an angel, the voice of the people is against his conduct. I see nothing but little cabals and complaints, which in my humble opinion nothing can remove but the presence of the King, QUEEN, and the Neapolitan Ministers that the regular government may again go on.[3]

Boats were accordingly sent from the British ships to escort the crowded polaccas to moorings beside the fleet; and the refugees aboard these polaccas, having spent a dreadfully uncomfortable night in the most insanitary conditions, were placed under armed guard. Many of them were convinced that the English admiral had intended this all along, that he had allowed them to leave the forts and embark only to get them all securely under his control. Certainly his behaviour over the next few hours confirmed them in the belief that they were at the mercy of an oppressor.

Among the men aboard the polaccas was Francesco Caracciolo, duca di Brienza. Having returned to Naples from Palermo to safeguard his estates from confiscation, Caracciolo had been prevailed upon by the leaders of the Parthenopean Republic to take command of the disintegrating Neapolitan navy which he had, in a short time, brought to a state of some efficiency. He had ordered his gunboats to fire both on British ships and on those whose Neapolitan crews had remained loyal to the Bourbon dynasty; he had also fired upon the *Minerva*, which had been his flagship while he had been in command of King Ferdinand's navy. Deemed, therefore, a traitor to the King, he had fled from Naples at the approach of the British and, dressed in the clothes of a peasant, he had made his way to a remote villa on the estate of his uncle, the Duke of Calvirrano. Warned that he had been betrayed and was in danger of capture, he had crept from the villa by night and, having sheltered for a time in a hut, was concealed by faithful servants in a well when pursued by a party of Ruffo's *sanfedisti* led by one Scipione La Marra.

Informed of his capture, Nelson wrote to Cardinal Ruffo to say that if Caracciolo and any other leading rebels were to be handed over to him, he would undertake to 'dispose of them'.[4]

Captain Hardy was on deck aboard the *Foudroyant* when the prisoner was brought up to him. Caracciolo was only forty-seven but he looked much older, 'pale, with a long beard, half dead and with downcast eyes', in Sir William Hamilton's description. Feeling compassion for him, Hardy ordered him to be released from his irons, taken to a cabin in the care of a lieutenant and two marines, and offered food and drink. The prisoner said he wanted nothing. A midshipman, George Parsons, also took pity on him: he was 'haggard with misery and want; his clothing in wretched condition but his countenance denoting stern resolution to endure that misery like a man'.[5]

Seizing the opportunity for making an example of the quick punishment he always advocated in such cases, Lord Nelson ordered the convening of an immediate court martial of the 'miserable Caraciollo' in the *Foudroyant*'s wardroom.[6] The prisoner's request for a trial by British officers having been refused, Count Thurn, an Austrian commodore in King Ferdinand's service, was appointed president of the court. Five other senior officers of the Neapolitan navy were elected to serve with him in the questioning of the prisoner, which lasted from ten o'clock until noon. The accused was not allowed an advocate; nor was he permitted to call witnesses in his defence. Caracciolo, exhausted as he was, answered the questions in what Parsons described as 'a deeply manly tone'. He explained that he had taken command of the Parthenopean fleet under compulsion: he was threatened with a firing squad had he not done so. But the verdict of the court was never in doubt. By four votes to two the court decided upon a capital sentence. 'Admiral Prince Caracciolo,' Count Thurn declared, putting on his hat, 'you have unanimously been found guilty ... You have repaid the high rank and honours conferred on you by a mild and confiding sovereign with the blackest ingratitude. The sentence of the court is that you shall be hanged by the neck at the yard-arm of your own flagship in two hours' time and may God have mercy on your soul.'[7]

Nelson confirmed the sentence, ordering Count Thurn to 'cause the said sentence to be carried into execution upon the said Francisco Caraciollo by hanging him at the foreyard arm of his Sicilian Majesty's frigate La Minerva at five o'clock this evening; and to cause him to hang there until sunset, when you will have his body cut down, and thrown into the sea'.[8]

Count Thurn proposed delaying the execution for twenty-four hours to allow Caracciolo to prepare himself for death; but Nelson was adamant: the man must be hanged that day. He had been 'fool enough to quit his master when he thought his cause was desperate'. Sir William Hamilton, having accepted without question Nelson's stern, unyielding stand up till now, 'wished to acquiesce with Thurn's opinion', so he told Sir John Acton. He did not, however, press the point. 'Lord Nelson's manner of acting must be as his conscience and honour dictate,' he wrote as though anxious to justify his reluctance to oppose the Admiral's intransigence, 'and I believe his determination will be found best at last . . . All is for the best.'[9]

Caracciolo himself asked the lieutenant in charge of his escort to intercede with Lady Hamilton on his behalf. He begged that he might be shot rather than meet an ignominious death by hanging and having his body cast into the sea, as Nelson had decreed. But apparently Lady Hamilton could not be found.[10]

Shortly before five o'clock, therefore, Caracciolo was handed over by the British to Neapolitan sailors, who drew him up to the foreyard arm of the *Minerva*. Some of the spectators in the polaccas were in tears; others turned their heads away. They had heard that the British admiral was full of pique because, when he was taking the royal family from Naples to Palermo, he had almost lost his ship in a storm while Caracciolo had sailed through easily, a feat of seamanship which the King had warmly praised.[11]

Hundreds of British sailors clambered up the rigging of their ships to watch the hanging. They were clustered there 'like bees',

Midshipman Parsons reported. They 'consoled themselves that it was only an Italian prince, and an Admiral of Naples, that was hanging – a person of very light estimation compared with the lowest man in a British ship'.[12]

Nelson and the Hamiltons were at dinner aboard the *Foudroyant*. According to Charles Lock, the British consul-general at Naples, who greatly disliked her – and who, having failed to obtain the privilege of victualling the British fleet, had annoyed Nelson by spreading rumours about the corruption of captains and pursers – Lady Hamilton fainted at the table when the Admiral's secretary, carving a roasting pig, cut off its head. 'On recovering she said, sobbing, that it put her in mind of Caracciolo. "Her Ladyship, however, who was an amateur of this savoury dish, ate heartily of it – aye! and even of the brains." '[13]

A signal gun announced that the sentence had been carried out. As the sun fell the rope was cut and the body plunged feet first into the waters of the bay. 'Your Majesty may always rely on my faithful services,' Nelson reported to King Ferdinand. 'The most notorious of the rebels I have in irons on board, and I hope they will meet the same fate as Caraciollo ... That your Majesty's whole Kingdom may be very soon liberated from these murderers and thieves is the fervent prayer of your Majesty's most faithful servant.'[14]

Two days later King Ferdinand sailed into the bay to the sound of gunfire from the shore, where the French were still besieged in the castle of Sant'Elmo. Escorted by the British frigate, the *Seahorse*, the King had made the voyage in a Neapolitan ship as though mindful of Cardinal Ruffo's observation that the Neapolitans, even the Bourbonists among them, hated the British because they had been responsible for burning their fleet. The King had been reluctant to leave Sicily, where he had been enjoying the pleasures of a sporting life; and did not once step ashore in the city which he had abandoned in such secrecy six months before. His bed was set up in the Admiral's cabin in the *Foudroyant* and he held levees on the quarterdeck. Although in later life Captain Troubridge looked back upon those days without pleasure, his officers were pleased to have the King aboard since, so George Parsons said, 'never did midshipmen fare so sumptuously'. What did distress them, however, was the sight of Neapolitans, women as well as men, both poor and well-to-do, 'patriots' to each other, 'rebels' to the Bourbonists, being brought aboard the British ships in chains. 'Many, very many of Italy's beauteous daughters, and those of high rank, have I seen prostrate on our deck imploring protection,' Midshipman Parsons recorded

... Their graceful forms bent with misery ... their clear, olive complexion changing to a sickly hue from anguish of mind. How could men, possessing human hearts, refrain from flying to their relief? Yet, I am sorry to say, they were placed (without regard to their feelings) in *polaccas*, under the guidance of young English midshipmen [and many were taken to overcrowded prison-ships] ... I grieve to say that wonderful, talented and graceful beauty, Emma Lady Hamilton, did not sympathise in the manner expected from her generous and noble nature.[15]

Lady Hamilton, relishing her position as the Queen's *soi-disant* deputy, was bombarded with pleas for mercy and with letters from erstwhile friends. She also received numerous letters from the Queen herself, in some of which her majesty recommended forbearance and put in a good word on behalf of a well-born 'rebel' whom she had known in the past, but generally urged the 'firmness, vigour and severity' she had recommended to Nelson.[16]

Nelson considered Lady Hamilton spent far too much time bothering with 'excuses from Rebels, Jacobins and Fools' and thus tiring herself out. The King, in Nelson's opinion justifiably stern, was dealing with his rebellious subjects 'in a most proper manner'.[17] There was no need for Emma to trouble herself about them. 'We are restoring happiness to the Kingdom of Naples,' Nelson reported, 'and doing good to millions.' She should preserve her energies so that she was not too exhausted to play her harp after dinner and, in the evenings, to listen with him to the musicians playing their serenades in the gently swaying boats alongside.[18]

In the daytime he himself was constantly busy, so Lady Hamilton said, 'here, there and everywhere'. She had never seen 'such zeal and activity as in this wonderful man'. Every day boats were sent ashore with prisoners for questioning by the tribunal sitting in the Castel dei Carmini. Some prisoners were dispatched from there to one or other of the city's gaols – compared to which Troubridge thought 'death a trifle' – others were set down for public execution in the Piazza del Mercato.

Week after week, month after month, these executions continued. Some of the victims were beheaded, others, women as well as men, were hanged in front of jeering and frequently drunken crowds as the executioners tugged at their legs and a dwarf pranced about on their shoulders. When Michele Natale, Bishop of Vico, was executed, 'the hangman performed all sorts of antics, saying he might never again have the good luck to ride a bishop'.[19]

'The trials of the principal Neapolitan rebels having been carried on without intermission,' Sir William Hamilton wrote to Charles Greville, 'many of all classes have suffered death by having been beheaded or hanged; among the latter we have seen with regret the name of Doctor Domenico Cirillo [Professor of Botany at Naples University and a Fellow of the Royal Society of London], one of the first physicians, botanists and naturalists in Europe.'[20]

This man, who had been court physician – and of whom the Queen was said to have been so fond that she knelt before her husband to plead for his life after the King's return to Palermo – was not only a most distinguished but also a most kindly man. He confessed to having collaborated with the French, and to having signed various anti-Bourbon documents; but he had done so, he said, because he had been made to do so. He wrote to Lady Hamilton, who had been a friend and one of his grateful patients, to explain his conduct, pleading that he had saved the English Garden in Naples from destruction and had attended the wounded in hospitals, Jacobins and Royalists alike. Lady Hamilton seems to have appealed to Nelson on Cirillo's behalf, though she did not usually care to bother him with the many applications which came her way. But Nelson did not believe he should be spared the punishment inflicted on others who had been basely disloyal to their sovereign. The man had chosen 'to play the fool and lie, denying that he ever made any speeches against the government, and that he only took care of the poor in hospitals'.[21]

Considering the case of another prisoner condemned to death, a marine who had struck an officer when drunk, Nelson wrote, 'You will, in obedience to my orders, prepare everything for the execution of the Court Martial on John Jolly; but when all the forms, except the last, are gone through, you will acquaint the prisoner that . . . I have reason to hope that the sparing of his life will have as beneficial an effect for the discipline of the Service as if he had suffered death.'[22]

So John Jolly was spared. Domenico Cirillo was taken to the Coccodrillo prison, and from there to the gallows.

Another of the victims of Bourbon revenge had recently reappeared in the most gruesome circumstances. At dawn one day a fisherman reported that Prince Caracciolo had risen from the bottom of the sea and was coming back to Naples. Midshipman Parsons was woken up and told to go at once to the King, who was already on deck and in a state of the utmost consternation. 'I hurried up,' Parsons wrote,

and found his Majesty gazing with intense anxiety on some distant object. At once he turned pale and, letting his spyglass fall on deck, uttered an exclamation of horror. My eyes instinctively turned in the same direction and, under our larboard quarter, with his face full upon us, much swollen and discoloured by the water, and his [eyes] started from their sockets by strangulation, floated the ill-fated Prince.[23]

The corpse, the legs weighted by irons, seemed to be standing half in and half out of the water and making its sightless way towards the shore. 'The priesthood, who were numerous on board, were summoned,' Parsons went on, 'and one, more adroit than his sovereign, told the King that the spirit of the unfortunate admiral could not rest without his forgiveness, which he had risen to implore.'[24] The priest added that Caracciolo had risen from the waves to demand Christian burial. "Let him have it," said the King and turned away; but afterwards he rallied from his fright and laughed and said the corpse had come to beg his pardon.'[25]

'On being wakened from his uneasy slumbers by the agitation of the court Lord Nelson ordered a boat to be sent, from the ship to

tow the corpse on shore.'²⁶ This was done; the body was hastily
buried in the sand, and later removed to the church of Santa
Maria delle Grazie a Catena, where the sailors and fishermen of
the coast 'laid him in the grave with tears'.²⁷

When the boat which had taken Caracciolo's body ashore
returned to the *Foudroyant*, the coxswain brought with him the
shots which had been used to weight it. 'A portion of the skin was
still adhering to the rope by which they had been fixed. They were
weighed by Captain Hardy, who ascertained that the body had
risen and floated with the immense weight of 250 lbs. attached to
it.'²⁸ The 'unlooked for appearance of Caracciolo's corpse', George
Parsons commented, 'did not lessen our appetite for the good
things in the King's larder, or our zest for the evening's opera'.²⁹

On the anniversary of the battle in Abū Qīr Bay the evening's
entertainments aboard the *Foudroyant* were especially lively. Nelson
described them to his wife. His recent letters to her had been few
and short. 'You must not think it possible for me to write to you as
much as I used to,' he had written in one rather distant letter in
April. 'In truth, I have such quantities of writing public letters,
that my private correspondence has been, and must continue to
be, greatly neglected.' Yet now, as if anxious to assure and remind
her how highly he was still regarded, he gave her a most detailed
account of the celebrations of 1 August:

The King dined with me; and, when His Majesty drank my health, a
Royal salute of 21 guns was fired from all his Sicilian Majesty's ships of
War, and from all the Castles. In the evening there was a general
illumination. Amongst other representations, a large Vessel was fitted out
like a Roman galley; on its oars were fixed lamps, and in the centre was
erected a rostral column with my name; at the stern were elevated two
angels supporting my pictures ... More than 2,000 variegated lamps
were suspended round the Vessel. An orchestra was fitted up; and filled
with the very best musicians and singers. The piece of music was in a
great measure to celebrate my praise, describing their previous distress,
*'but Nelson came, the invincible Nelson, and they were preserved and again made very
happy.'* This must not make you think me vain; no, far, very far from it.³⁰

*

The torture in the prisons and the executions went on remorselessly. On one day that month, so Thomas Troubridge reported, princes, dukes and ladies were amongst those to be hanged. He hoped that the tribunals would 'soon finish, on a great scale, and then pass an act of oblivion'; but the gallows were not dismantled for months. On windless nights the commotion in the Piazza del Mercato could clearly be heard aboard the ships of the fleet. When the polaccas were at last permitted to sail to Toulon with the French troops who had survived at Sant'Elmo, scarcely a third of the Neapolitan refugees originally aboard were still alive. Sir William Hamilton believed 'more than 8,000 persons' remained imprisoned as Jacobins and rebels in the gaols of Naples. Others, including 'the heads of two of the first families of Naples', were incarcerated in the subterranean cells on the island of Marittimo off Sicily's west coast, where confinement was 'a punishment worse than death'.[31]

In his letter to his wife describing the celebrations in which his name had featured so prominently, Nelson had told her, 'I return to Palermo with the King.'

He set sail the next day in contravention of the orders he had received from Lord Keith, who had been confirmed Lord St Vincent's successor as commander-in-chief in the Mediterranean. Keith, believing that Minorca was threatened by the French, had already told Nelson to send him as many ships as could be spared from Naples. Nelson had ignored this order as well as a subsequent command which soon followed it. 'It is better,' he wrote, 'to save the Kingdom of Naples and risk Minorca, than to risk the Kingdom of Naples to save Minorca.' He would 'not part with a single ship'.[32] A third order, worded so as to tolerate no such insubordinate opposition, was handed to Nelson, requiring him to send 'the whole or the greater part of the force' under his command to join the main fleet without delay. Reluctantly, he sent John Duckworth with three ships of the line and a corvette, continuing to maintain that they would be of far more use where they were. He was also of the strong opinion that King Ferdinand, while admittedly no paragon of virtue or intellect, must be strongly supported as the rightful monarch of his country and that those who had risen up against him must be mercilessly crushed if the dreadful events that had taken place in revolutionary France were not to be repeated elsewhere. When the King offered to reward his support by bestowing upon him a title of Sicilian nobility, Nelson decided that he might accept it before receiving permission from his own monarch, which was, in fact, not granted until 1801. 'The bounty of your Majesty has so overwhelmed me that I am unable to find words adequate to express my gratitude,' he wrote to King Ferdinand. 'That the Almighty may pour down his choicest blessings on your sacred person, and on those of the Queen and the whole Royal Family, and preserve your Kingdom in peace and happiness, shall ever be the fervent prayer of your Majesty's faithful servant, Bronte Nelson.'[33]

The title, which came with the gift of a diamond-hilted sword which had once belonged to Louis XIV, was that of the Duke of Bronte. The name was that of a town on the western slope of Mount Etna in the province of Catania, now an agricultural centre known mainly for its pistachio nuts. The ducal seat was the Castello di Maniace, and the estate had originally belonged to the monastery of Maniacium.* Its 30,000 acres were not then notably productive, being strewn with the debris of primeval volcanic eruptions; and the dilapidated *castello* was uninhabitable. There was a smaller house on the estate which might have been lived in, but its name, *La Fragila*, was not inviting. However, Nelson was assured that rents and other income from the estate would produce about £3,000 a year; and, with his usual generosity in financial matters, he wrote immediately to his father to say that, 'as a Mark of Gratitude to the Best of Parents from his Most Dutiful Son', he was now in a position to offer him £500 a year and that sum, equivalent to about £30,000 a year today, 'in succession' to his

---

* The title and estate of Bronte passed to Nelson's niece, Charlotte, Lady Bridport, in 1835. The house at Bronte was acquired by the local Sicilian commune in 1981 and several of its contents were sequestrated. There was an intention to create a museum and conference centre here. But most of the money allocated for the creation of the museum has disappeared; and at the time of writing the house was becoming derelict.

'nearest relations'.[34] He would have offered more; but he had refused to accept any money from the King and Queen for the considerable expenses incurred while their majesties had been on board the *Foudroyant*, and he was not sure yet whether or not the Admiralty would reimburse him. Also he wanted to invest most of the income for the first year or so in improvements on the estate; and with this in mind he appointed John Graefer – supervisor of the English Garden in Naples – to act as his agent.[35] He was determined, so he told his wife, to make the estate 'the happiest place in Europe'. 'I have directed the building an *English* farm house,' he added, 'and I hope to make all Sicily bless the day I was placed amongst them.'

But it was neither the income nor the estate which pleased Nelson so much as the title and the decoration which went with it, a decoration which at first he wore above the Star of the Order of the Bath.[36] He experimented with a new signature, at first subscribing himself 'Bronte Nelson', as he had done to King Ferdinand, then 'Bronte, Nelson of the Nile', before deciding that his English title should come first and settling upon 'Nelson and Bronte', an inscription which he habitually used thereafter and with which he was to sign his final will.* Lady Hamilton now added to the other titles which she had already bestowed upon him, such as 'Marquis Nile' and 'Prince Pyramid', that of 'Lord Thunder', in allusion to Bronte, the mythological blacksmith, one of the Cyclopes, who, so her husband told her, forged the thunderbolts for Jupiter. This was an epithet deemed particularly appropriate for an admiral whose flagship was the *Foudroyant*.

---

* The name Bronte so appealed to Patrick Brunty, an Ulsterman of humble birth who identified himself 'almost obsessively with the heroes of the age', that, on arrival at Cambridge, he 'repudiated with magnificent dash the plebeian name of Brunty in favour of Brontë as a tribute to Nelson' (Rebecca Fraser, *Charlotte Brontë*, London, 1988, 9).

The Colli Palace

I am prepared for any fate which may await my disobedience.

The royal party and their English saviour were welcomed back to Palermo on 9 August 1799 with great rejoicing. The Queen was rowed out to meet the arrivals, upon whom she bestowed the most generous presents, among them a fine gold chain with her miniature, set in diamonds and inscribed with the words *Eterna Gratitudine*, which she fastened around Lady Hamilton's neck.[1]

Palermo's notabilities were lined up on the quayside to congratulate the royal party upon their safe return. Cannon boomed in a twenty-one-gun salute; a thanksgiving service was held in the ornate Arab–Norman cathedral; as darkness fell fireworks flashed and exploded in the sky. A week later it was the feast-day of Palermo's patron saint, an event to which Nelson was looking forward without enthusiasm. 'We are dying of heat,' he told John Duckworth, 'and the feast of St Rosalia begins this day. How shall we get through it?' It was one of the most important dates in the Palermitan calendar. The streets were bright with flowers. A chariot, drawn by twenty-eight mules, carried the saint's bones and relics to the cathedral, which was lit by 20,000 candles.

To the British officers, the celebrations, splendid though they were, were not nearly so exciting as the *fête champêtre* held by night three weeks later in the grounds of the Colli Palace. Aboard the *Foudroyant* the midshipmen called out to each other for clean shirts and stockings, breeches and pipe clay. Fifteen of them rowed ashore, took a carriage for the ride uphill to the palace, arrived in time for a magnificent firework display, which included a representation of the blowing-up of *L'Orient*, and, walking along avenues lit by strings of coloured lamps, mingled longingly with what George Parsons, in his most grandiloquent manner, called 'Italy's nut-brown daughters, their lustrous black eyes and raven tresses, their elegant and voluptuous forms, gliding through the mazy dance'. The *pièce de résistance* was 'a temple erected to the goddess of Fame, who, perched on the dome, was blowing her trumpet above statues of Nelson supported by figures of Sir William Hamilton and his statuesque wife'. Then, Parsons continued,

as a band struck up *Rule Britannia*, Prince Leopold [the nine-year-old Crown Prince] crowned the statue with a laurel wreath inlaid with diamonds and the band played *See the Conquering Hero Comes!*

Lord Nelson's feelings were greatly touched and big tears coursed down his weather-beaten cheeks, as on one knee he received the young Prince in his only arm, who, with inimitable grace embraced him, calling him the guardian angel of his papa and his dominions ... Many a countenance that had looked with unconcern on the battle and the breeze now turned aside, ashamed of their womanly weakness.

Parsons himself was overcome with emotion and reached for his handkerchief, only to find that he had put a rolled-up white stocking in his pocket by mistake. But other witnesses of the scene, who also wiped their eyes, did so, he had to admit, 'from a contrary feeling of mirth'.[2]

The next day Lord Nelson was back at work. Lord Keith had left the Mediterranean to pursue the French and Spanish fleets into the Atlantic; and Nelson, as senior officer in his absence, had much to do and much to worry about, not least the problem of Malta, where Alexander Ball, who had been appointed Governor, did not have the means to drive 'the accursed French' out of Valletta. Nelson was, he himself admitted, 'almost in desperation about Malta'; and this was but one of the numerous difficulties about which he complained. To deal with these difficulties, so he told the secretary to the Admiralty, he had to be at his writing-table at half-past five in the morning, and he could not 'relax from business' until after eight o'clock at night.

The lethargy of the King now utterly exasperated him. The Queen urged her husband to return to Naples but, no longer obedient to her wishes, he refused to do so. Nelson confessed himself 'sick and tired of this want of energy'; he was 'almost mad with the manner of going on here'.[3] Then there came news that, having abandoned his army in Egypt and slipped through the British blockade, Bonaparte had landed in France, where he was soon, as First Consul, to direct the aggressive policies of his government. Above all, Nelson was concerned by the slackening discipline of the men of his inactive fleet in the oppressively hot climate of a summer in which the thermometer still registered over 80 degrees at eight o'clock at night as the sultry, humid scirocco blew across the bay from the sands of the Sahara. On the evening of the Queen's fête the boisterous midshipmen of the *Foudroyant* had charged King Ferdinand's footguards, brandishing their dress daggers and provoking one of the soldiers to open fire and shoot one of the midshipmen through the thigh. 'For this notable and ill-timed feat,' George Parsons commented, 'Lord Nelson stopped our leave for six months.'[4]

The Earl of Elgin, who was passing through Palermo on his way to take up his duties as minister in Constantinople, reported the Admiral as looking 'very old'. He 'has lost his upper teeth,' Elgin added, 'sees ill of one eye and has a film coming over both of them.' Young Lady Elgin, who had been married only six months before, had heard reports of Nelson at Gibraltar. 'Never was a man turned so *vain glorious*,' she was told. 'He is now completely managed by Lady Hamilton.'[5] On landing at Palermo, she was handed an invitation from Lady Hamilton to stay at the Palazzo Palagonia; but she had no desire to do so. Besides she was overcome by the heat – the air felt as though 'it came from an oven' – and the captain of the ship in which she had come out reported a strange interview at the Palazzo Palagonia.:

A little old Woman with a white bed gown and black petticoat came out and said, 'What do you want Sir?' 'Lord Nelson, M'am?' (Old woman), 'And what do you want to say to Lord Nelson?' Captain laughing, 'Oh, M'am, you must excuse me telling you that.' Upon this a servant said to him, 'Sir, I fancy you don't know that is Lady Hamilton's mother.' The Captain was surprized and said, 'What! Does she act as housekeeper?' 'Why, yes Sir, I believe she does sometimes.'[6]

Intrigued by such reports, Lady Elgin decided to accept an invitation to dine at the *palazzo*. In a letter to her mother she reported on the *ménage* she found there:

I must acknowledge she [Lady Hamilton] is pleasant, makes up amazingly and did all she could to make me accept of an apartment there . . . She looked very handsome at dinner, quite in an undress; – my Father would say, 'There is a fine woman for you, good flesh and blood.'

She is indeed a Whapper! and I think her manner very vulgar. It is really humiliating to see Lord Nelson. He seems quite dying and yet as if he had no other thought than her. He told Elgin privately that he had lived a year in the house with her and that her beauty was nothing in comparison to the goodness of her heart.[7]

One day Lady Hamilton invited Lady Elgin to accompany her to a fête which was to be attended by the King and Queen. It would be perfectly all right to go in 'a common morning dress', Lady Hamilton assured her. Lady Elgin took her at her word; but, when the time came, Lady Hamilton appeared in a magnificent gown of coloured silk covered with diamonds which the Queen had given her. This, Lady Elgin commented, was 'a common trick'. 'You never saw anything equal to the fuss the Queen made with Lady H.,' she continued 'and Lord Nelson, wherever she moved, was always by her side. I am told the Queen laughs very much at her to all her Neapolitans, but says her influence with Lord N. makes it worth her while making up to her. Lady H. has made him do many very foolish things.'[8]

It was not only Nelson's dancing attendance upon Lady Hamilton that Mary Elgin found exasperating but also the fuss made of her by the Queen, who, indeed, was quite as assiduous in her attentions to Lord Nelson, to whom her compliments were 'the most fulsome thing possible'.[9]

Others remarked upon the way in which Lord Nelson would sit beside Lady Hamilton while she played faro, gambling for high

stakes, long after Sir William had gone to bed. Nelson often looked
as though he ought to have been in bed, too. Frequently he was
fast asleep as his companion helped herself to the gold pieces piled
in front of him. Troubridge thought it as well to warn the Admiral
how people were gossiping about all this. 'If you knew what your
friends feel for you,' Troubridge wrote to him, 'I am sure you
would cut out all the nocturnal parties; the gambling of the people
at Palermo is talked of everywhere. I beseech your Lordship, leave
off. Lady H—'s character will suffer; nothing can prevent people
from talking; a Gambling Woman in the eyes of an Englishman is
lost.'[10]

Troubridge also took it upon himself to write to Lady Hamilton
to warn her 'of the ideas that [were] going about. You may not
know that you have many enemies. I therefore risk your displeasure
by telling you . . . The construction put on things may appear to
your Ladyship innocent, and I make no doubt done with the best
intentions. Still your enemies will, and do, give things a different
colouring.'[11] The stories circulating about her and Lord Nelson
went far beyond her gambling, though Troubridge refrained from
mentioning the tales of sexual excesses. Some stories, such as that
Sir William had challenged the Admiral to a duel, were patently
absurd. Nor was it in the least likely that Lady Hamilton and her
paramour frequented taverns along the waterfront in disguise. Yet
all manner of such rumours were repeated and many were believed,
not only in Palermo and Naples and aboard the fleet, but also in
London drawing-rooms. 'Some person about Sir William's house
sends accounts,' Troubridge told Nelson. 'I have frequently heard
things which I know your Lordship meant to keep secret.'[12]

Certainly it was true that Sir William was now finding the
Admiral's continuing presence in his house rather irksome. Ever
since he had returned from Naples, where his houses had been
badly damaged in the bombardment and thoroughly plundered,
Sir William had been feeling far from well, 'plagued with bilious
attacks and diarrhoea continually owing to the intense heats and
damps of this climate'. Besides, having the Admiral for so long as a
guest was proving extremely expensive. He had already given a
home to Miss Knight, in obedience to her mother's dying wish;

and the additional cost of having Lord Nelson living in his house, not to mention 'the numerous train of officers' that came to see the Admiral, was one he could 'by no means afford'. He would be better off at home; but it was 'impossible to quit Lord Nelson, who doesn't understand any language but his own and fairly said that if we went he would not stay'.

'The whole and sole confidence of their Sicilian Majesties appears to be reposed in Lord Nelson,' Hamilton explained to Charles Greville. 'Their Majesties are not easy if His Lordship is absent from them one moment and as Lord Nelson seems to think that my going home at this moment would distress them, I have let the *Goliath* [put at his disposal by Lord Keith] go down to Gibraltar without me.'[13]

The Admiral continued to complain of the amount of business he was expected to undertake. By Lord Keith's withdrawal from the Mediterranean he had been 'thrown into a more extensive correspondence than ever, perhaps, fell to the lot of any Admiral, and into a political situation, I own, out of my sphere . . . You must make allowances for a worn-out, blind, left-handed man . . . Plain commonsense points out that the King should return to Naples, but nothing can move him.'[14]

To Alexander Davison, Nelson repeated his readiness to die, provided he could do so with honour. 'Ah my Dear friend,' he wrote towards the end of September, 'if I have a morsel of bread & cheese in comfort, it is all I ask of kind heaven, until I reach the Estate of 6 feet by 2 which I am fast approaching . . . If the war goes on I shall be knocked off by a Ball or killed with *chagrin*.'[15] In less mournful mood he comforted himself with thoughts of retiring to Bronte and made lists of 'Seeds and Instruments' to be supplied to John Graefer, the manager there, instructing Davison to send him 'Early York Cabbages, White Dutch Clover . . . 1 French plough . . . 12 large garden spades . . .' But then gloom would overcome him again and in later letters he told his friend, 'I am so fagged and worn out that the Nelson you know is gone, and but a shadow remains . . . You will see an old man.'[16]

Lord Elgin, confirming that Nelson looked ill and prematurely old, conceded that he worked extremely hard, refusing to be daunted by his difficulties, by what he took to be the obtuseness of his nominal Commander-in-Chief, and by the misjudgements of their Lordships at the Admiralty, with whom he had been constantly at odds ever since the Levant had been detached from his command and given to that 'mountebank', Rear-Admiral Sir Sidney Smith, an appointment which he had taken as a personal slight.

'I am fully aware of the act I have committed,' he told Lord Spencer, after declining to obey Lord Keith's orders to send ships to Minorca; 'but sensible of my loyal intentions, I am prepared for any fate which may await my disobedience . . . Do not think, my dear Lord, that my opinion is formed from the arrangements of any one. *No*, be it good, be it bad, it is all my own.' 'Much as I approve of strict obedience to orders,' he added later, '. . . yet to say that an Officer is never, for any object, to alter his orders, is what I cannot comprehend . . . Do not, my dear Lord, write harshly to me – my generous soul cannot bear it, being conscious it is entirely unmerited.'

Their Lordships, however, were not convinced by Admiral Nelson's excuses. They did not 'see sufficient reason to justify [his] having disobeyed orders'. Nelson remained unrepentant. 'My conduct,' he declared, 'is measured by the Admiralty by the narrow rule of law when I think it should have been done by common sense.'[17]

When Lord Keith returned to the Mediterranean at the beginning of 1800 he was determined to ensure that his disrespectful subordinate paid proper attention to the instructions he chose to give him. He ordered him to meet him at Leghorn, then to accompany him back to Palermo.

Lord Keith, a son of the tenth Lord Elphinstone, was fifty-four years old, a reliable, rather dour, cautious and unimaginative Scotsman, whose only child, Margaret Mercer Elphinstone, was the intimate friend and bossy confidante of Princess Charlotte, daughter of the Prince of Wales. He was not a man likely to appeal to Nelson; and he did not do so. Nor did Nelson appeal to him, although he did find common ground with him in his insistence on the wearing of pigtails, condemned by younger officers as archaic.

The few days that Lord Keith spent with the Hamiltons and Nelson in Palermo were predictably unpleasant for all concerned, the only person there having a good word to say for the unwelcome visitor being Miss Knight, whom he delighted by saying how pleased he was to see the daughter of Sir Joseph Knight, an admiral he had always held in high regard.[18] 'The whole was a scene of fulsome Vanity and Absurdity all the long eight days,' Keith complained. 'I was sick of Palermo and its allurements, and much as I was made up to (their hours are beyond belief) I went to bed at ten.' In his opinion Nelson and Lady Hamilton were 'just a silly pair of sentimental fools',[19] Nelson himself, so Keith told his sister, 'cutting the most absurd figure possible for folly and vanity'.[20]

Keith was only too thankful to get away to the ships blockading French-occupied Malta, taking Nelson with him. Nelson also seemed relieved to be at sea; and, sailing south of Sicily on the deck of the *Foudroyant* on 18 February 1800, he was excited to hear a lookout's shouted warning of enemy sails in sight. They proved to be those of the French ship *Le Généreux* from Abū Qīr Bay; and Nelson gave orders to his flag-captain, Sir Edward Berry, for a general chase: 'Sir Ed'ard [the Nelsonian pronunciation of Edward] make the *Foudroyant* fly!'

The *Foudroyant* surged ahead; but not as fast as another ship in the flotilla, the *Northumberland*, which threatened to overtake her. 'This will not do, Sir Ed'ard. She is certainly *Le Généreux* and to my flagship she can alone surrender. Sir Ed'ard, we must and shall beat the *Northumberland*.'

Sir Edward noticed the twitching stump of Nelson's right arm, a sure sign of the stress and impatience which broke out in an angry reprimand of the apparently careless quartermaster at the wheel: 'I'll knock you off your perch, you rascal, if you are so inattentive. Sir Ed'ard, send your best quartermaster to the weather wheel.' But when the *Généreux*'s guns opened fire and the British guns replied, Nelson was calm again and, as Midshipman Parsons recorded, displayed that kindliness – so little in evidence during the past months – which made him so much loved by those who served under him at sea:

As a shot passed through the mizzen stay-sail, Lord Nelson, patting one of the youngsters on the head, asked him jocularly how he relished the music; and, observing something like alarm depicted on his countenance, consoled him with the information that Charles XII ran away from the first shot he heard, though afterwards, he was called 'The Great', and deservedly from his bravery. 'I therefore,' said Nelson, 'hope much from you in future.'[21]

The British guns, 'firing coolly and deliberately at her masts and yards', forced the *Généreux* to surrender. Captain Berry climbed aboard and came back with the sword of the mortally wounded French admiral.

The next day Nelson gave his report to a characteristically unresponsive Lord Keith, who listened in what appeared to be disapproving silence. But when writing his dispatch for the Admiralty, Lord Keith, as generous in spirit as he was severe in manner, gave Nelson full credit for what he had achieved.

It was not long, however, before Lord Keith had further cause to feel annoyed with his uncooperative subordinate. The Commander-in-Chief had intended leaving him in charge of the blockade of Malta while he himself went to Genoa. But Nelson had other ideas. 'I could no more stay fourteen days longer here than fourteen years,' he wrote. 'My state of health is such that it is impossible I can remain ... I must ... request your permission to go to my friends in Palermo.' And, despite the pleas of Commodore Troubridge, go to Palermo he did.

Nelson's behaviour distressed Captain Hardy as well as Troubridge, though Hardy, a more reserved and temperate man, was less outspoken about Lady Hamilton, believing Nelson's relationship with her was his own affair, except when it affected the Navy, as sometimes, regrettably, it did. On one such occasion a recalcitrant boat's crew from Hardy's ship approached Lady Hamilton in the hope that she would use her influence to get them excused punishment for their misbehaviour. She went to see Hardy, who was characteristically noncommittal. The next day he had the men flogged and then ordered another dozen lashes because they had applied to Lady Hamilton. He told her what he had done, adding that he would do the same should she intercede for miscreants again.[22]

Nelson's undutiful behaviour, attributed to his passion for Lady Hamilton, was causing widespread concern in England as well as in the Mediterranean fleet. His old friend, Admiral Goodall – recalling the romance of Rinaldo, Charlemagne's knightly paragon, who was lured by the beautiful sorceress, Armida, into a life of voluptuous pleasure – wrote to him from London:

My Good Lord,

I hope, as the sailor says, 'this will find you well, as I am at this present' ... They say you are Rinaldo in the arms of Armida, and that it requires the firmness of Ubaldo and his brother Knight to draw you from the enchantress. To be sure 'tis a very pleasant attraction, to which I am very sensible myself. But my maxim has always been – *Cupidus voluptatum, cupidior gloriae* [Much as I desire pleasure, I desire glory more]. Be it as it will, health and happiness attend you.[23]

A sterner letter than this reached him from Lord Spencer:

It is by no means my wish to call you away from service, but having observed that you have been under the necessity of quitting your station off Malta, on account of the state of your health, which I am persuaded you could not have thought of doing without such necessity, it appeared to me much more advisable to come home at once than to be obliged to remain inactive at Palermo ... You will be more likely to recover your health and strength in England than in any inactive situation at a foreign Court, however pleasing the respect and gratitude shown to you for your services may be.[24]

Nelson's concern about his health was not feigned. He had pains in his chest and believed, as he often did, that he might be suffering from some perhaps fatal disease of the heart. Alexander Ball wished he 'could be prevailed upon to write less' because he was 'very apprehensive he [impaired] his health by leaning so much'. Yet the prospect of returning to England did not appeal to Nelson. 'Greenwich Hospital seems a fit retreat for me,' he grumbled to Lord Minto, 'after being *evidently* thought unfit to command in the Mediterranean.'[25]

20

Germany

Mrs Siddons be damned!

The replacement of Sir William Hamilton as British envoy at the Neapolitan court put a completely different complexion upon Nelson's own return to England. He persuaded himself that he could no longer perform his duties in the Kingdom of the Two Sicilies without the Hamiltons to act as interpreters and counsellors; so, since they were going home, he would go home with them. First, however, they would go on a short sea voyage; and so, without consulting Lord Keith, Nelson took his friends aboard the *Foudroyant* for a cruise towards Malta by way of Syracuse. Before sailing he held a party aboard the ship to celebrate the recent capture of another French ship, the *Guillaume Tell*, whose wooden figurehead, an enormous tricoloured plume, was displayed in the admiral's Great Cabin. In reporting the capture of this ship by Captain Berry to his Commander-in-Chief, Admiral Keith, Nelson was at his most tactless: 'I thank God I was not present; for it would finish me, could I have taken a sprig of these brave men's laurels. They are, and I glory in them, my darling children; served in my school; and all of us caught our professional zeal and fire from the great and good Earl of St Vincent.'[1]

As well as the capture of the *Guillaume Tell*, the party aboard the *Foudroyant* was celebrating the marriage of Sir John Acton, whose choice of bride had led to much disapproving talk in Sicily. He had seemed perfectly content to remain a bachelor and to bequeath his estate in Shropshire to his younger brother Joseph. But Joseph had served in the French army and was disbarred from inheriting. So Sir John asked him for the hand of his daughter, who was not yet fourteen. Joseph had no objection: a papal dispensation for Sir

John to marry his young niece was forthcoming. But the girl herself was naturally reluctant to marry an uncle sixty-four years old. She hid under the sofa while he and her father discussed her disposal, and then attempted to escape from the house in boy's clothing. Caught as she was running across the courtyard, she was brought back and married in the Hamiltons' house by Lord Nelson's chaplain.[2]

The *Foudroyant* was gaily bedecked to celebrate this strange alliance. Her guns were removed from sight, her masts clad in silk, and silk awnings were arranged on deck to make two reception rooms.

The ship was decorated for another celebration on 26 April. This was Emma Hamilton's thirty-fifth birthday. She looked no more happy than Sir John Acton's bride. Apprehensive about returning to England, where she would no longer be the intimate friend of a queen and 'the toast of a fleet', she was evidently also concerned that her love affair with Nelson might well not prosper once he had returned to his family, though they had by now become regular lovers: indeed, it seems that it was on this voyage that she conceived their child. Certainly their daughter was born nine months later.

The voyage to Malta was pleasant enough. Miss Knight was of the party, looking forward to visiting the archaeological sites in Sicily, where the ship was to stop on the way. She was intrigued by Nelson's cabin and its mementoes – the flagstaff of the *Orient*, four muskets from the *San Joséf*, the huge plume of feathers from the *Guillaume Tell*. Also there was a table, on which there was a pile of new books,* apparently unread, sent to Nelson by his wife, and a coffin which Captain Hallowell had had made for the Admiral from the main mast of the *Orient*.†[3]

---

* Nelson appears to have confined his reading almost entirely to newspapers, periodicals and books about naval strategy and tactics. His letters show that he was as familiar with the Bible and Shakespeare as a man of his time and background was expected to be; but there seems to be no record of his having read for pleasure anything else, other than accounts of sea voyages. His enormous correspondence would, in any case, have afforded him little time, while in later years his poor eyesight would have been a disincentive.

† This coffin had come to Nelson accompanied by a letter: 'My Lord, Herewith I

Two enjoyable days were spent visiting the antiquities of Syracuse. But soon after joining the blockading squadron off Malta, the *Foudroyant* dragged her anchor at night and came within range of the French batteries in Valletta. 'Lord Nelson was in a towering passion, and Lady Hamilton's refusal to quit the quarter deck did not tend to tranquillize him.'[4]

Once the *Foudroyant* had sailed round the island to anchor in the small bay of Marsaxlokk, however, calm and amity were restored; dinner parties were held both on shore and at sea; and Lady Hamilton was created a Dame Petite Croix by the Grand Master of the Order of St John, and was thus entitled to wear a splendid enamelled cross, a privilege of which she later availed herself as readily as Nelson wore his own larger and more numerous decorations.

On their return journey to Palermo she felt ill; and so that she might not be kept awake at night by unnecessary noise, Nelson ordered silence to be observed throughout the ship. By the time Sicily was in sight again, she was better, sufficiently recovered to oversee the arrangements for Sir William's farewell banquet and to comfort the Queen, now on exceptionally bad terms with her husband, to whom she was no longer 'either agreeable or necessary'. She had decided to go to stay with her daughter, the Empress, in Vienna and to take with her Prince Leopold and her three younger daughters, the future Queens of Spain, France and Sardinia. Much to the annoyance of Lord Keith, who wrote

---

send you a Coffin made of part of L'Orient's Main mast, that when you are tired of this life you may be buried in one of your own Trophies – but may that period be far distant, is the sincere wish of your obedient and much obliged servant, Ben. Hallowell, Swiftsure, May 23rd 1799' (Nicholas, iii, 89). A paper stuck to the bottom of the coffin read, 'I do hereby certify that every part of this Coffin is made of the wood and iron of L'Orient.' At first this coffin was placed upright behind Nelson's chair in his cabin in the *Foudroyant*, and then removed to the *Vanguard* where it remained for many days on the gratings of the quarterdeck. It was then sent to England 'to be lodged with Peddieson, the upholsterer in Brewer Street, who was desired by Nelson to get the attestation of its identity engraved on the lid, at the same time saying, "I think it highly probable that I may want it on my return."' (Pettigrew, i, 132).

exasperatedly of the care which he lavished upon his women while neglecting other duties, Nelson offered to take the Queen as far as Leghorn in the *Foudroyant*, accepting on board a large suite of about fifty persons, as well as the five members of the royal family, trunks of dresses and jewels, and crates of plate, and giving his instructions for his own cabin as well as Captain Berry's to be prepared for her majesty and the Hamiltons. The King, declining to make up their quarrel, did not come to see his wife off; while Charles Lock did not hide his pleasure at the departure of Lady Hamilton. '*She* is now gone,' he commented. 'Thank my stars.' 'Her wish to engross the conduct of affairs entirely,' he continued in a letter to his father, 'prompted her to poison Sir William's mind against me. To this was joined a female vanity which could not bear that any English woman should be admired by her countrymen but herself.'[5]

The Queen's daughter, Princess Maria Amalia, would have been delighted if Lady Hamilton had been left behind. The passage to Leghorn was a stormy one; and, according to the Princess, her ladyship's behaviour was far from as stoic as it had been during the voyage from Naples to Sicily in 1798. 'We found Miladi on a mattress in the middle of the room,' the Princess wrote in her diary. 'Toto [her sister, Princess Marie Antoinette] cried out, "We are finished ... submerged."' The Queen told them to brace themselves against the beds; and this is how Nelson found them when he came to reassure them that all would be well and that they would soon be safe in harbour. At that moment, the ship gave a fearful lurch and Nelson went 'white as a sheet', while 'Miladi began to wail and roll about on the ground.'[6]

Several weeks pregnant by now, she was reported by others to be in a gloomy mood, apprehensive no doubt about her reception in England, where she would give birth to a child which she would have to conceal since nobody would believe it was her husband's. Nelson, also, was not at his best, suffering from a bad cold and with good reason to fear that his welcome at the Admiralty would not be a warm one. Midshipman Parsons, however, thoroughly enjoyed the crossing when the storm abated. Princess Maria Amalia, eighteen years old and most attractive, climbed up on the

quarterdeck where Parsons and his fellow midshipmen took great
pleasure in teaching her to use a speaking-trumpet. He was sorry
when, on 14 June 1800, the guns at Leghorn fired a royal salute,
and the time to say goodbye drew near. While they were waiting
to land, the Queen and her children composed a letter in faltering
English which was handed to Lord Nelson:

My dear and respectable Lord Nelson. To the numerous obligations,
wich all Europa and we particularly have to you is to be added our
gratitude for the care that you have taken [of us] from Palermo to
Leghorn. We return you our most sincere thanks and pray you may be
quite sure, that all you have done for us will be truly ingraved in our
heart. Nothing [we] desire more than to have frequent occasions to
prouve you our feelings . . . and the great regard with wich we are and
will be till the Last moment of our Life respectable Lord Nelson.[7]

The Queen drew forth farewell presents from her piles of baggage,
handing to Lady Hamilton a diamond necklace with locks of the
royal children's hair displayed in a silver pendant, to Sir William a
gold snuffbox and to Lord Nelson a green enamel medallion
appropriately set with silver anchors. The royal children again
politely expressed their thanks to Nelson for bringing them thus far;
he, at a loss for words in their language, bowed to the Prince and
kissed the Princesses' hands. The sea still being too rough to go
ashore, mass was celebrated on deck for the royal suite. Nelson
and Lady Hamilton attended it, Princess Maria Amalia was
pleased to note, but, as Protestants, they stood apart from the
rest of the congregation, 'Miladi' bareheaded, dressed demurely in
white.[8]

On landing at Leghorn, the Queen was driven to the Governor's
palace; the Hamiltons were taken to the house of the British
consul, the Hon. William Frederick Wyndham; and Nelson, having
accompanied them there, returned to the *Foudroyant*, where he
found his cabin 'truly a hog-stye', with some of his things floating
about in the water which the high seas had thrown aboard a ship
still badly in need of repair since her fights with the *Généreux* and
the *Guillaume Tell*. Even so, he settled down to write a letter to
Lady Hamilton, whom he would be seeing again the next day.

That night he was given disturbing news. Bonaparte, whose army had crossed the Brenner Pass and invaded Italy again, had routed the Austrians at Marengo on 14 June, obliging them to sign a convention by which they agreed to give up almost all of northern Italy. Following hard upon this news came orders from Lord Keith for Nelson to send all his ships to reinforce the British fleet at Genoa, with the exception of the *Foudroyant*, which was to be sent to Minorca for refitting.

Nelson, who had been hoping to take the Hamiltons and Miss Knight home to England in the *Foudroyant*, submitted to the order that this ship should go to Minorca. But, having transferred his flag to the *Alexander*, he kept that ship at Leghorn.

His orders once more disobeyed, Lord Keith left immediately for Leghorn to ask for an explanation and to land fugitives from Genoa. He was, as he had expected – and as he reported to the First Lord of the Admiralty – plagued upon his arrival by 'Lord Nelson for permission to take the Queen back to Palermo, and princes and princesses to all parts of the globe'.[9] The Queen herself added her entreaties to Nelson's, weeping, so William Wyndham, the consul, reported, in the belief that 'royal tears were irresistible'. But Keith 'remained unmoved'. There were three Neapolitan frigates at Leghorn, he told her. That was as may be, she retorted. She did not trust them; she must sail in a British ship. The French, who were even now advancing south, had executed her sister; they would not hesitate to murder her. Lord Keith stood his ground; and, so Lady Minto was told by Wyndham, who had never got on well with Sir William, he added, 'Lady Hamilton has had command of the fleet long enough.'[10] The Queen thereupon fell into a 'sort of convulsive fit'. 'Nelson is trying to nurse her,' Lady Minto wrote to her sister. 'He does not intend going home till he has escorted her back to Palermo. His zeal for the public service seems entirely lost in his love and vanity, and they all sit and flatter each other all day long.'[11]

Nelson assured the Queen that nothing would make him leave her until her plans were 'perfectly settled'. But all her plans seemed likely to be disrupted when, on 8 July, the people of Leghorn – hearing that the French were now less than thirty miles away at

Lucca – invaded the Arsenal, armed themselves with all the weapons to be found there, surrounded the Governor's palace and threatened to keep the Queen and her children prisoners there unless Lord Nelson led them against the French. Nelson, accompanied by the Hamiltons, hurried to the palace, pushed his way through the crowds and, entering the building, appeared on the balcony with Lady Hamilton at his side. Speaking in his name, she admonished the crowds below for thus surrounding 'an amiable and illustrious queen', and 'positively declared that his Lordship would not hold the least communication' with them, unless they immediately returned their weapons to the Arsenal. The Livornese, until then so bellicose, seem to have dispersed at her bidding, obediently taking back their arms. The Queen was so alarmed, however, that she and her children fled for their lives to the *Alexander*; they were then persuaded, with difficulty, to disembark and to make their way overland to Florence, where the Grand Duke Ferdinand III would surely offer them his protection. She, her children and a large retinue left in a long procession of coaches and baggage wagons, praying that the French would not intercept them on the way.

Nelson and the Hamiltons had also decided to continue their journey by land, going by way of Florence to Ancona and from there taking an Austrian ship to Trieste. Lord Keith, having decided that the *Alexander* should go to Puerto de Mahon, had offered them berths in the frigate *Seahorse* or in a troopship from Malta. But, as a disgruntled Cornelia Knight, still mourning the death of her mother, told Captain Berry:

Lady Hamilton cannot bear the thought of going by sea; and, therefore, nothing but impracticality will prevent us going to Vienna . . . I fear all the dangers and difficulties to which we shall be exposed. Think of us embarking on small Austrian vessels at Ancona, for Trieste, as part of a land journey! To avoid the danger of being aboard an English man-of-war where everything is commodious and equally well arranged for defence and comfort; but the die is cast, and so we must . . . Sir William appears broken, distressed and harassed . . . [He] says *he* shall die by the way . . . I should not be surprised if he did . . . If I am not detained in a

French prison or do not die upon the road you shall hear from me again
. . . Lady Hamilton hates the sea, and wishes to visit the different courts
of Germany.[12]

So, since Lady Hamilton so strongly wished to go by land, there
was no further question of going by sea.

The Hamiltons and Mrs Cadogan, Miss Knight and Nelson all
left for Florence on 13 July. It was a most uncomfortable journey.
Despite the heat, the windows of the carriage had to be kept shut
to keep out the dust that rose in clouds from the rattling wheels
and the horses' hooves. Miss Knight's fear that they might find
themselves in a French prison was not an idle apprehension: on
occasions their road passed within a mile or two of the enemy's
outposts.

They arrived in Florence, however, without mishap; and, after a
short rest there, drove on after the Queen, who had already left the
relative safety of the Pitti Palace for the road to Arezzo and
Trieste. At Arezzo the Hamiltons' coach, in which Nelson was also
travelling, was overturned for the second time with a cracked
wheel. It was then decided that Miss Knight and Mrs Cadogan
should be left with the broken-down carriage, it being considered,
in Miss Knight's resigned words, 'of less consequence' that they
should be taken than the other three more important travellers. So
these two women were abandoned, and had to wait for three days
for the Hamiltons' carriage to be repaired. Sir William had obviously been distressed at leaving them behind; but 'his wife and
Nelson were too much wrapped in each other to care'.[13]

When they reached Ancona they found that the Queen had
refused to go aboard the Austrian frigate which had been prepared
for her voyage across the Adriatic, as there had recently been a
mutiny on board; and she had decided to travel instead in a
Russian ship, even though this was so jammed with beds that it
looked like a hospital. Poor Sir William was by now looking as
though he were close to death. He caught a dreadful cold aboard
the ship; so did his wife. While the others tried to change the
subject, Nelson reminded them continually of the comforts of the
Foudroyant, whose boat's crew, he told them, had, in a touching

petition asking him to 'pardon the rude style of Seamen little aquainted with writing', begged him to allow them to return to England with him 'in any way that might seem most pleasing to his Lordship'.[14]

Nelson's mood brightened, however, when Trieste hove into view, even though his nose was blocked and reddened by another streaming cold. The city was *en fête* for the second anniversary of the Battle of the Nile, lights glittering everywhere and shouts of '*Evviva* Nelson!' At Laibach (Ljubljana), where a symphony was performed in celebration of his great victory, his reception was equally gratifying. So it was at Klagenfurt, where he was greeted with loud cheers, at Bruck an der Mur and Baden, and at Vienna where he and his companions alighted outside an inn near the Graben Square, the Gasthof Aller Biedermänner.

By the time they arrived in Vienna, most of them were worn out. Poor Sir William, Miss Knight reported, 'had been so ill that the physicians had almost given him up'; she herself was 'dreadfully fatigued, far from well, and uneasy on many accounts, besides being a good deal injured by the carriage being overturned'. 'You can form no idea of the *helplessness* of the party,' she told Berry. 'How we shall proceed on our long journey is to me a problem.'

Apart from feeling tired and ill, Miss Knight was much concerned by the cool and even disdainful reception accorded to the Admiral and Lady Hamilton by the British residents, the consuls and their wives, in the towns through which they passed. She could not but feel that her own respectability was being compromised by the lack of theirs.[15]

They remained for three weeks in Vienna. They were invited to Schönbrunn; they were taken to the Leopoldstadt Theatre; they went to a breakfast in the garden of the Augarten Palace and to a grand banquet at the Esterhazys' country estate, Eisenstadt, where, accompanied by Joseph Haydn, who had a house near by, Lady Hamilton sang a cantata in what was described as a 'clear strong voice'. They went shooting; they went fishing; they attended firework displays and concerts and a naumachia on the Danube. Nelson, who presented copies of Miss Knight's *Ode on the Battle of the Nile* to both the university and the imperial library, was received in audience by the Emperor, and was loudly cheered as he drove in an open carriage down the Prater. At St Veit, the country house of Lord Minto, the British ambassador, Lady Minto, so she told her sister, Lady Malmesbury, found him not 'altered in the least'. He had 'the same shock head, and the same honest simple manners'. She could not speak so highly of Lady Hamilton, to whom he was obviously 'devoted'. 'He thinks her quite an *angel*,' she wrote, 'and talks of her as such to her face and behind her back, and she leads him about like a keeper with a bear. She must sit by him at dinner to cut his meat; and he carries her pocket handkerchief. The aigrette the Grand Signor gave him is very ugly and not valuable, being rose diamond . . . He is a gig from ribands, orders and stars.'[16] Another observer noted that she even carried his hat. The ambassador himself thought that he did not seem 'at all conscious of the sort of discredit he had fallen into'. 'But it is hard,' Minto added charitably, 'to condemn and ill use a hero, as he is in his own element, for being foolish about a woman who has art enough to make fools of many wiser than an admiral.'[17]

Lady Minto's nephew, Lord Malmesbury's eldest son, James Harris, was even more critical of Lady Hamilton than was his aunt. It was 'really disgusting' to see her with Lord Nelson, whose health was drunk with 'a flourish of trumpets and a firing of cannon'. She was 'without exception the most coarse, ill-mannered, disagreeable woman' he had ever met.

The Princess [Princess Esterhazy] had got a number of musicians, and the famous Haydn who is in their service to play, hearing Lady Hamilton was fond of music. Instead of attending to them she sat down at the Faro table, played Nelson's cards for him, and won between 300 L and 400 L . . . I could not disguise my feeling, and joined in the general abuse of her.[18]

A Swedish diplomat was quite as censorious:

Muladi Hamilton, once considerd the most beautiful woman in Europe . . . is [now] the fattest woman I've ever set eyes on, but with the most beautiful head . . . [She] wears the Maltese Cross so that she now has all the titles that can impress people.[19]

An Austrian observer, Franz Cullenbach, drew an equally unflattering portrait:

Lady Hamilton never stopped talking, singing, laughing, gesticulating and mimicking while the favoured son of Neptune appeared to leave her no more than did her shadow, trying to meet with his own small eyes, the great orbs of his beloved, and, withal, as motionless and silent as a monument, embarrassed by his poor figure and by all the emblems, cords and crosses with which he was bedecked.* In a word, the Lord of the Nile seemed as clumsy and dim on land as he is adroit and notable at sea.[20]

'His hair is combed onto his forehead,' wrote a journalist who had seen him walking through the streets of Graz with Lady Hamilton on his arm, followed by Fatima, her ladyship's Nubian maid, whom Nelson had bought for her in Egypt. 'The loss of an eye is less noticeable than that of the right arm as he . . . fastens the empty sleeve across his buttoned tunic . . . His face is pale and sunk.'[21]

The blunt Tom Allen – who had warmly shaken King Ferdinand's hand with the greeting, 'How do you do, Mr King', when his Majesty extended it to be kissed – warned his master that he was drinking too much champagne: 'You will be ill if you take any more.' Nelson had certainly obtained a good supply, though it was proscribed in Vienna. An Englishman living in the city, Francis Oliver, whom Nelson had employed as his secretary and translator, had gone to a wine merchant to buy some when the cellars of the Gasthof Aller Biedermänner ran dry. The merchant warily denied he had any in stock; but, when told they were for the great admiral, he offered several cases and refused payment for them.

---

* Before leaving Vienna, Nelson wrote to Sir Isaac Heard at the College of Arms: 'I shall be very much obliged if you will have the goodness to inform me whether I am permitted to wear the *Star* of the order of the Bath,, which I am allowed to under the King's Sign Manual on my coming abroad, or whether I am to cut it off my coat on my arrival in England, also whether I may wear the *Star* of the Crescent and the *Star* of the Order of St Ferdinand and Merit, all of which at Present adorn my coat' (Llangattock Papers, E.79, 20 Sept. 1800).

Much exercised as to the wearing of his foreign decorations, which, as well as the Orders of the Crescent and of St Ferdinand, were, in 1802, to include the Equestrian Order of St Joachim of Leiningen, Nelson was also concerned that he should be allowed to wear in England the pelisse and the *chelengk* presented to him by the Sultan of Turkey and he had already written to Heard about this:

The Admiral's forty-second birthday on 29 September 1800 was celebrated in Prague where his inn, the Rothes Haus, was brilliantly illuminated in his honour, a gesture which was less appreciated, so Miss Knight observed, when the cost of the lighting appeared on the bill. The Rothes Haus's distinguished guest created a disappointing impression upon at least one German onlooker, although 'his bold nose, the steady eye and the solid worth revealed in his whole face [did betray] in some measure the great conqueror':

[He] was one of the most insignificant figures I ever saw in my life . . . a more miserable collection of bones and wizened frame I have yet to come across . . . He speaks little, and then only English, and he hardly ever smiles . . . Lady Hamilton behaved like a loving sister towards him; led him, often took hold of his hand, whispered something into his ear, and he twisted his mouth into the faintest resemblance of a smile . . . He was almost covered with orders and stars.[22]

A dinner was held for him at the Archduke's palace where Lady Hamilton entertained the guests by singing 'God Save the King', a national anthem which had become popular in the time of George III's grandfather as a demonstration of loyalty to him and opposition to the Jacobites. Lady Hamilton also sang some verses written by Miss Knight, who was always more than ready to oblige with lines on such occasions and who, according to an unfriendly observer, never opened her mouth except to flatter her friends.

At the end of September the Admiral's party left Prague for Dresden, where they took rooms at the Hotel de Pologne. The British minister in Dresden was Lord Minto's snobbish younger brother, Hugh Elliot, who entertained a very low opinion of Lady Hamilton and a not much higher one of her lover. 'She will

---

'As the Pelise given to me . . . [is] novel, I must beg you will turn in your mind how I am to wear it when I first go to the King; and, as the Aigrette is directed to be worn, where am I to put it? In my hat, having only one arm, is impossible, as I must have my arm at liberty; therefore, I think, on my outward garment' (Nicolas, iv, 81).

captivate the Prince of Wales, whose mind is as vulgar as her own,'
Elliot foresaw, 'and will play a great part in England.' His opinions
were fully endorsed by an Englishwoman visiting Dresden at that
time, Melesina St George, a pretty young widow who was one of
the guests at Elliot's table the day after the Admiral's party arrived
in the city. 'It is plain that Lord Nelson thinks of nothing but Lady
Hamilton, who is totally occupied by the same subject,' Mrs St
George observed. She had to concede that her fellow guest had fine
features, that her teeth were 'tolerably white', her figure, though
'colossal', 'well-shaped', and that her light blue eyes had a certain
beauty of expression despite the defect of a brown spot in one of
them. But she was 'exceedingly *embonpoint*'; her feet were 'hideous',
her movements 'ungraceful', her hair ('by-the-bye never clean')
was 'short, dressed like an antique', her dress 'tasteless, vulgar,
loaded and unbecoming'; her waist 'absolutely between her
shoulders'. Her six months' pregnancy had evidently gone
unnoticed.

'She is bold, forward, coarse, assuming and vain,' concluded
Mrs St George, who was in no way more kindly disposed to the
woman on closer acquaintance. She was 'vain even to folly, and
stamped with the manners of her first situation much more strongly
than one would suppose, after having . . . lived in good company
fifteen years. Her ruling passions seem to me vanity, avarice, and
love for the pleasures of the table. She shows a great avidity for
presents, and has actually obtained some at Dresden by the
common artifice of admiring and longing.' As for Lord Nelson:

[He] is a little man, without dignity . . . Lady Hamilton takes possession
of him, and he is a willing captive, the most submissive and devoted I
have ever seen. Sir William is old, unfirm, all admiration of his wife and
never spoke today [3 October] but to applaud her . . . Mrs Cadogan,
Lady Hamilton's mother, is – what one might expect. After dinner we
had several songs in honour of Lord Nelson, written by Miss Knight, and
sung by Lady Hamilton. She puffs the incense full in his face; but he
receives it with pleasure, and snuffs it up very cordially.[23]

At the subsequent dinner at the Elliots' it appears that the
guests drank rather too many bumpers and that, irritated by the

disapproval of their boring and disapproving hosts, they behaved with provocative high spirits. Lady Hamilton announced that she was 'passionately fond of champagne' and drained an astonishing number of glasses. Lord Nelson having drunk almost as many, 'called more vociferously than usual for songs in his own praise'. 'The songs all ended in the sailor's way, with "Hip, hip, hip, hurra", and a bumper with the last drop on the nail', a ceremony which Mrs St George had not come across before.

'Poor Mr Elliot, who was anxious the party should not expose themselves more than they had done already,' Mrs St George continued, 'endeavoured to stop the effusion of champagne, and effected it with some difficulty; but not till the Lord and Lady, or, as he calls them, Antony and *Moll* Cleopatra, were pretty far gone.'

After Mrs St George had left the party, Lady Hamilton 'acted Nina intolerably ill', so Hugh Elliot told her, 'and danced the *Tarantala*. During her acting Lord Nelson [punctuating the perform-ance with cries of 'Mrs Siddons be damned!'] expressed his admiration by the Irish sound of astonished applause, which no written character can imitate ... Sir William also this evening performed feats of activity, hopping round the room on his backbone, his arms, legs, star and ribbon all flying in the air ... Lady Hamilton expressed great anxiety to go to Court, and Mrs Elliot assured her it would not amuse her, and that the Elector never gave dinners or suppers – "What?" cried she – "no guttling [guzzling]."' Since the Electress declined to receive Lady Hamilton because of her former 'dissolute life', it had been thought as well that no formal receptions would be held throughout the period of the English people's visit. 'If there is any difficulty of that sort,' Nelson declared with mock pugnacity, 'Lady Hamilton will knock the Elector down.' But, in the event, he went to court on his own, 'a perfect constellation of stars and Orders', so Mrs St George said; and Lady Hamilton had to be content with dinners, concerts, visits to the theatre and parties, at one of which, in her good-natured way, she was especially pleasant to Mrs St George, who wrote of the encounter: 'Lady Hamilton loading me with all marks of friendship which I always think more extraordinary than love of the same kind.'[24]

The Elliots and Mrs St George were not at all sorry when Lady Hamilton and her entourage returned to their canopied barge for the next stage of their journey down the Elbe. Mrs St George 'went to congratulate' the Elliots on the woman's departure. She found them 'very sensible of it. Mr Elliot would not allow his wife to speak above her breath, and said every now and then, "Now, don't let us laugh tonight; let us all speak in our turn, and be very, very quiet."' Hugh Elliot went down to the riverside to watch the visitors depart.

'Lady Hamilton's maid began to scold in French about some provisions which had been forgot,' he told Mrs St George, no doubt making the most of the story, 'in language quite impossible to repeat, using certain French words, which were never spoken but by *men* of the lowest class, and roaring them out from one boat to another. Lady Hamilton began bawling for an Irish stew, and her old mother set about washing the potatoes ... They were exactly like Hogarth's actresses dressing in the barn.'[25]

The barges drifted down river to Dessau, Nelson and Sir William passing the time by playing cribbage. At Dessau, Prinz Franz von Anhalt-Dessau invited them to his palace and renamed a feature of the place the *Nelsonberg*; then they moved on to Magdeburg where they put up at the König von Preussen and where Nelson dined 'with open doors and had wine and refreshments handed out to the crowd of onlookers of every standing'. Some of these onlookers were English, and Nelson 'busied himself a good deal amongst them,' a German officer noted sardonically, 'assuring them that he was nothing less than a great man. They must be loyal and industrious, then they would do equally well. He urged upon them, above all, an eternal hatred of the French.' When he left Magdeburg – where, so Alexander von Dalwick said, Lady Hamilton 'showed the Admiral off to the people like a curiosity, telling them of his hundred engagements'[26] – he stood up on the barge, raising his hat to the crowds on the river bank and in the surrounding boats.[27]

At Hamburg he was welcomed with equal enthusiasm and curiosity. General Dumouriez, the former French Minister of War who had gone over to the Austrians, came to see him; so did the diplomatist, Baron de Breteuil, an intimate friend of Marie Antoinette, who had retired into private life in Germany after the Queen's execution; so did the elderly poet, Friedrich Gottlieb Klopstock, who had been living in Hamburg for the past thirty years; so, too, did an old pastor, who brought from his village church some forty miles distant a Bible which he asked Nelson to sign as a Christian hero, 'the Saviour of the Christian World'; and so did the British merchants resident in Hamburg, who honoured him with a dinner, concert, ball and supper.[28]

Journalists in England, however, seemed at this time less eager to praise the hero than to condemn him for his conduct at Naples and the irregularity of his private life. The Whig *Morning Chronicle* commented, 'There is indeed a terrible scene to be unfolded of what has passed in Naples these last twelve months. We can assert from the best information, that the British name has suffered a reproach on the Continent by the transactions at Naples.' The *Morning Post*, which had earlier rebuked the Admiral for 'signing himself Bronte Nelson' and thus indicating his preference for the Neapolitan over the English title, informed its readers on 15 September: 'The German State Painter, we are assured, is drawing Lady Hamilton and Lord Nelson at *full length together*. An Irish correspondent hopes the artist will have delicacy enough to put Sir William *between* them.'[29]

Nelson had hoped that a British frigate would be waiting at Hamburg to take him and his friends home across the North Sea; but no ship was there for that purpose. Nelson wrote to the Admiralty asking for one to be sent; and while they were waiting, Miss Knight suggested he should buy some lace trimmings for a court dress as a present for Lady Nelson, the last expense of a journey which had cost him no less than £1,349, in today's terms about £80,000.[30]

Nelson had clearly not been giving much thought to his wife of late. Until falling in love with Lady Hamilton he had seemed quite content with his marriage, however disappointed he was by Lady Nelson's failure to bear children and however exasperated he was

from time to time by her restrained comments on his brilliant
victories, her failings as a housekeeper, her lack of sparkle and
confidence in society. Certainly he had liked it to be thought that
he was a happily married man. He had told Lord Lansdowne that
he was blessed with 'everything that is valuable in a wife', and had
assured Lady Spencer that Fanny was 'an angel'. When Miss
Knight observed that his victory in Abū Qīr Bay must have been
the happiest day of his life, he had replied, 'No, the happiest was
that on which I married Lady Nelson.'[31]

All this was now in the past. His letters to his wife, affectionate
in the early years of their marriage, had become shorter and more
infrequent. She had written to him more often, and more affectionately, imparting such less than engrossing information as
that the weather was so cold in England that she was 'clothed in
two suits of flannel' and hoped to be better for it, endeavouring to
please him by sending Lady Hamilton 'a cap and a kerchief such
as are worn this cold weather', and persistently asking for news of
her son, Josiah.

In the past she had had no reason to ask about Josiah. His stepfather's letters had at that time rarely omitted a reassuring report:
'Josiah is well, teeth good, 5 feet 4 inches in height', 'Josiah is very
well and is daily threatening to write you a letter', 'Josiah is very
well', 'I can only say Josiah is well, indeed he is never sick.' At
Santa Cruz, Josiah, she had been reminded, had been 'principally
instrumental' in saving his life.

But now, regrettably, Nelson had no good news of Josiah to send
his wife. While in Naples in 1798 he had been fairly reassuring even
though the mother cannot have taken kindly to her son's supposed
fondness for Lady Hamilton being forced upon her attention. 'The
improvement made in Josiah by Lady Hamilton is wonderful,' the
young man's stepfather had written at that time. 'She seems the only
person he minds and his faults are not omitted to be told him but in
such a way as pleases him. Your and my obligations are infinite on
that score . . . His manners are so rough but, God bless him, I love
him with all his roughness.' 'Josiah is so much improved in every
respect,' Lady Hamilton confirmed, 'I love him much and, although
we quarrel sometimes, he loves me and does as I would have him.'

Later reports, however, were not so encouraging. 'I wish I could say much to your and my satisfaction about Josiah,' Nelson wrote bluntly from Palermo. 'But I am sorry to say and with real grief, that he has nothing good about him; he must sooner or later be broke, but I am sure neither you nor I can help it.'

In the hope of improving his behaviour, Nelson used his influence to get him the command of a frigate, the *Thalia*. 'Josiah is now in full possession of a noble frigate,' he reported. 'I *wish* he may deserve it, the thought half kills me. He has sent to say he is sensible of his youthful follies and that he shall alter his whole conduct. I sincerely wish he may for his and your sake . . . He has had done for him more than any young man in the service and made, I fear, the worst of his advantage.'

Nelson's fears were justified. He heard that Josiah had brought two women on board the *Thalia* who were up to 'no good' and that, feeling lonely as a captain, he had taken to having his meals in the gunroom. Conscious that he had over indulged the young man in the past, he felt it necessary to apologize to Admiral Duckworth for having sent him the *Thalia*, of which he could say nothing complimentary 'inside or out'. 'Perhaps you may be able to make something of Captain Nisbet,' he had added. 'He has, by his conduct, almost broke my heart.' But Admiral Duckworth had not been able to make anything of Captain Nisbet; and, nine months later, he had felt obliged to complain that the *Thalia* was an exceptionally ill-disciplined ship, on which the principal medical officer was under arrest and demanding a court martial on his captain, and the first lieutenant was also bringing charges against him. Duckworth diffidently suggested that it might have been a mistake of his lordship to authorize this first lieutenant to give advice to his less experienced captain, a touchy character of uncertain temper. Be that as it may, he hoped to be able to deal with the problem without an embarrassing public inquiry, and it might be best if the *Thalia* were paid off, once the warring parties had been separated.[32]

Little of this was passed on to Captain Nisbet's mother, though she was soon to be made aware that her husband considered her son to be beyond redemption. She was also very soon to be made

painfully aware of other bitter truths too. For, tired of waiting for
the frigate that the Admiralty failed to send to Hamburg, Nelson
and his party boarded the *King George* mail packet bound for Great
Yarmouth where, 'not without a horrible grating of the ship's
bottom while forcing its way through the sands', they landed in
cold and windy weather on 6 November.[33]

London and Fonthill

Take care, Fanny, what you say . . . I cannot forget my obligations to
Lady Hamilton.

Although it was raining steadily, Lord Nelson's welcome in Great
Yarmouth was as enthusiastic as he had come to expect. Church
bells rang as men of the town pulled his carriage up from the
harbour where all the boats were flying colours; a band played
patriotic tunes as the hero appeared on the balcony of an inn to
loud applause and cheers, Lady Hamilton standing by his side in a
muslin gown which, made for her in Sicily, had the words 'Nelson'
and 'Bronte' surrounded by oak leaves and acorns embroidered on
the hem. 'I am a Norfolk man,' he assured the admiring crowd,
'and glory in being so.'[1]

He was sworn in as a freeman of the borough and had seemed
pleased when, complying with an injunction to place his hand on
the Bible, the town clerk, drawing attention to his disabled state,
had said, 'Your *right* hand, my Lord.' Also, when the landlady of
the Wrestlers' Arms asked permission to change its name to the
Nelson's Arms, he seemed delighted to remark that the name
would be absurd since of those particular limbs he had only the
one. From the inn he was escorted to church by the mayor and
corporation and as he entered the porch, the organ struck up 'See
the Conquering Hero Comes'.

That evening he wrote to his wife to say that he would leave for
Ipswich at noon the following day and be with her on Saturday for
dinner. 'Sir and Lady Hamilton beg their best regards,' he added,
'and will accept your offer of a bed . . . I beg my Dear Father to be
assured of my Duty and every tender feeling of a son.'[2]

He and the Hamiltons were escorted to the county boundary by
the cavalry of the Norfolk Volunteers; but, when they arrived at

Roundwood, there was no one at home. The Rev. Edmund had left for London a short time before to join Lady Nelson who, so Nelson thought, in agitation at the prospect of seeing her husband again after an absence of three years, had confused the arrangements, though she had in fact gone to London so as not to delay his attendance at the Admiralty. Annoyed by what he evidently took to be yet another example of his wife's incompetence, Nelson, a model of exactitude himself, gave orders to the coachman to drive off, leaving a house in which he was never to spend the night.

He did not, however, immediately leave for London. 'Notwithstanding all the newspapers, his Lordship has not arrived in town and when he will God only knows,' wrote Captain Thomas Hardy on 8 November. 'His father has lost all patience, her Ladyship bears up very well as yet but I much fear she also will soon despond. He certainly arrived at Yarmouth on Thursday last and there has been no letter received by anybody. Should he not arrive tomorrow, I think I shall set off for Yarmouth *as I know too well the cause of his not coming*.'[3]

Nelson arrived the next day, a Sunday, and the meeting between husband and wife took place at three o'clock in the afternoon in the hall of Nerot's Hotel, King Street, St James's, on the site of the future St James's Theatre. The rain had been pouring through the windswept streets and the people who had gathered to watch the arrival of the great Admiral and his friends were soaked. Among the crowd was a journalist from the *Courier*, who reported that Lord Nelson was wearing full uniform with two medals and two stars as he emerged from 'Sir William Hamilton's German travelling carriage'. He looked thin but well; Lady Hamilton appeared to be 'a very fine woman'. A black female servant, 'a Copt perfectly black', followed her mistress into the hotel.

Inside, the atmosphere was strained. Lady Nelson's nervousness struck Lady Hamilton, who had every reason to feel nervous herself, as an 'antipathy not to be described'. They all had dinner together at five o'clock, Nelson's father being also of the company. But Nelson himself had to leave early for an appointment at the Admiralty; and soon after his departure the Hamiltons also left for 22 Grosvenor Square, a house lent to them by the inordinately rich dilettante, William Beckford, Sir William's second cousin, who had not long since returned from a prolonged Grand Tour on which he had been dispatched by a family concerned by his emotional entanglements with both a young boy and a married female cousin.

Miss Knight and Mrs Cadogan had already departed for a more modest hotel in Albemarle Street, where Thomas Troubridge had called upon them. He had taken Miss Knight aside and warned her that if she wished to be received by polite society in London, she would have to distance herself from Lord Nelson and the Hamiltons. Reluctant to be accused of ingratitude for such behaviour towards the Hamiltons, who after all had brought her back to England at their own expense, she consulted another friend, Margaret Nepean, the wife of the Secretary to the Admiralty. Mrs Nepean, the granddaughter of a most respected general, endorsed Troubridge's advice; so did other friends to whom Miss Knight spoke.[4] She thought it advisable to follow their counsel and was afterwards referred to by Nelson in a letter to Lady Hamilton as 'that Bitch Miss Knight'.[5] As for Lady Hamilton, her fury with Miss Knight was limitless. She took up a copy of Molière which the woman had given to her and wrote on the flyleaf, 'Given to me by Miss Knight whom I thought good and sincere . . . When Lady K. died my poor mother took Miss K. to our house . . . We gave shelter to Miss K. for near two years. We brought her free of expense to England. What has she done in return? . . . She is dirty illbred ungrateful bad mannered false and deceitful.'[6]

There could be no doubt how most of London society would behave after Nelson had accompanied Sir William Hamilton to a levee at St James's Palace. He was tactless enough to present himself wearing his usual glittering collection of medals and decorations, not only the Star of the Order of the Bath and his battle medals but what might well have been left at home on this occasion, his spray of Turkish diamonds presented to him by the Sublime Porte and the King of Naples's Order of St Januarius. The King of England, whose wife had made it clear that she would not receive Lady Hamilton, was not pleased to see his adulterous

Admiral thus arrayed. His reception was 'not very flattering', Cuthbert Collingwood reported, having been told by Nelson what happened. 'His Majesty merely asked him if he had recovered his health; then turned to General — and talked to him near half an hour in great good humour. It could not have been about *his* success.'[7]

Nelson's reception by the people of London was much more gratifying. When he was recognized – and it was, of course, difficult to miss him since, as Sir John Moore said, he looked, with his stars and medals and ribbons, 'more like the Prince of an Opera than the Conqueror of the Nile'[8] – he was quickly surrounded by a crowd, from whose attentions on one occasion he was saved by Alexander Davison, who took him off as guest of honour to a banquet given by the Lord Mayor. Dragged to the Guildhall by excited men taking the place of horses, he was detained outside the building by a group of sailors anxious to shake his hand, some of them 'old Agamemnons', whom he delighted by remembering their names. After the meal he was presented with a sword, a weapon which, he said in his speech of thanks, he hoped to use soon against the French.

Again as guest of honour, the Admiral also attended a dinner given by the East India Company at the London Tavern, Bishopsgate Street Within, a large hostelry renowned for the excellent meals provided in a dining-room that could accommodate 355 guests; on this occasion it was decorated with transparencies depicting scenes from the battle of Abū Qīr Bay, a victory for which the East India merchants had reason to feel particularly grateful.

Yet another grand dinner was given for Nelson by Alexander Davison at his splendid house in St James's Square. Here Nelson met the Prime Minister, William Pitt, whose father had lived next door, four other Cabinet Ministers and the Prince of Wales, whom Nelson, to his fury, glimpsed ogling Lady Hamilton and ever afterwards intensely disliked.

Lady Nelson was not present on this occasion, but she had attended a dinner at Admiralty House as guest of the First Lord of the Admiralty and Lady Spencer. This had been a most embarrassing evening, an extraordinary contrast, so Lady Spencer said, to that previous dinner when Nelson had upset her seating plan by asking to sit next to his wife. During this later evening, the evening of the King's rebuff at St James's Palace, Nelson had been in a sour and silent mood, treating his wife 'with every mark of dislike and even of contempt'. 'Her conduct during his absence had been most exemplary,' Lady Spencer continued, 'but even in public he treated her ill. He never spoke during dinner and looked blacker than all the devils.'

Lady Nelson, perhaps inadvisedly, but with good intention, shelled some walnuts for him – a service which, with his one arm, he could not perform for himself – and handed them across the table in a wine glass. Her husband pushed the glass irritably aside with such force that is smashed against a dish. Lady Nelson burst into tears. When the ladies had risen from the table and retired to the drawing-room she confided in Lady Spencer 'how she was situated'.[9]

Her situation was also made clear at the Theatre Royal, Drury Lane, one evening later that month during a performance of R. B. Sheridan's *Pizarro* with John Kemble playing the part of Rolla, which he had first performed the year before. Lady Hamilton appeared in a flamboyant dress with many feathers and plumes and with a fashionably high waist which helped to conceal her pregnancy, Lady Nelson comparatively demure in white and purple satin. Nelson's appearance was greeted with cheers.

All went well for the first and second acts, during which Nelson applauded Kemble's performance vigorously. But in the third act lines passionately enunciated – 'How a woman can love, Pizarro, thou hast known . . . How she can hate thou hast yet to learn . . . thou, who on Panama's brow . . . wave thy glittering sword, meet and survive an injured woman's fury' – were greeted by a scream from Beckford's box. Lady Nelson had fainted and had to be taken home. Some reports, including that in the *Morning Herald*, say that she returned later 'to the great satisfaction of all present'. All reports agreed that Nelson remained until the end of the play.[10]

The house to which Lady Nelson was taken that evening was No.17 Dover Street, to which she and her husband had recently moved from Nerot's Hotel, where they had had to stay since the rented Dover Street house had not been available earlier – more evidence, so Nelson apparently thought, of his wife's incompetence. As soon as they were settled there, with what Nelson's father described as many servants comprising 'the long suite of nobility', Lord Nelson told his wife to invite the Hamiltons to dinner. He was bound to be attentive to Lady Hamilton, he said, because he 'felt irritated' by the remarks he knew were being made about his regard for her and was obliged to devote himself to her 'for the purpose of what he called supporting her'.[11] The evening was not a success. A few evenings before Lady Hamilton had felt faint at the theatre and had had to be helped by Lady Nelson to the cooler air outside. During the dinner at Dover Street, Lady Hamilton again felt ill, and hurried from the table. On this occasion Lady Nelson did not immediately follow her. When, reprimanded by her husband for failing in her duties as a hostess, she went out after her guest, she found her being sick into a basin which she took from her hands and held for her. Their host surprised his other guests by leaving the dining-room himself to go to his mistress's side.[12]

According to one early biographer, it was upon this night that Nelson left the house in Dover Street to walk about London till four o'clock in the morning. 'In a state of absolute despair and distraction', he strode as far as the City, wandering into Fleet Market and across Blackfriars Bridge, until, 'exhausted with fatigue, as well as overpowered by mental suffering', he arrived at the Hamiltons' door in Grosvenor Square. He knocked; a sleepy servant admitted him; he went upstairs and sat down as though worn out on the edge of the Hamiltons' bed, asking them to take him in. 'What say you?' Lady Hamilton is said to have asked her husband dubiously, concerned by what society would think. Sir William maintained that he personally did not care 'a fig for the world'. Nelson, however, went back to Dover Street.[13]

It was as well that Sir William did not care a fig for the world, as all who knew him gossiped endlessly about him, and about his wife and their mutual and intimate friend. Before their arrival in London there had been anxious discussions as to how best to receive Lady Hamilton, indeed whether or not to receive her at all. Sir William's successor in Naples, the Hon. Arthur Paget, wrote to his mother, the Countess of Uxbridge, 'I hear that Lady Hamilton is moving Heaven and Earth to be received at Court but I trust without any chance of succeeding; pray don't let that be if you can help it.'[14] Charles Greville implausibly insisted that there was no reason in the world not to receive her since all the reports about her affair with Lord Nelson were false; others, however, maintained that the woman was by now so compromised that she could not possibly expect society to accept her. Sir William Hotham, for many years a gentleman-in-waiting at court, considered that Nelson's vanity had led him to 'unpardonable excesses, and blinded him to the advantages of being respected in society ... His conduct to Lady Nelson was the very extreme of unjustifiable weakness, for he should have at least attempted to conceal his infirmities, without publicly wounding the feelings of a woman whose conduct he well knew was irreproachable.'[15]

Lord St Vincent was of much the same opinion: 'It is evident from Lord Nelson's letter to you on his landing, that he is doubtful of the propriety of his conduct,' he wrote to Evan Nepean.

I have no doubt he is pledged to getting Lady H. received at St James's and everywhere, and that he will get into much brouillerie about it. Troubridge says Lord Spencer talks of putting him in a two-deck ship. If he does he cannot give him a seperate command, for he cannot bear confinement to any object; he is a partisan; his ship always in the most dreadful disorder, and never can become an officer fit to be placed where *I* am.[16]

St Vincent made similar comments to Lady Elizabeth Foster:

That foolish little fellow Nelson has sat to every painter in London. His head is turned by Lady Hamilton, who sometimes writes him four letters a day. I conceal some of them when I can ... Nelson is a brave man but a partizan. Troubridge is the best officer we have.[17]

It was eventually decided by Greville's family at least that, as his sister Frances told a friend, it would not be possible to avoid noticing '*Ly H*. without offence to *Sr Wm*. or at least *affecting his feelings*'; and, as he had been ill and had 'met with much *Vexation & disappointment*, as to *His Recall* [from Naples]', it would be unkind to turn their backs on his wife, even though his '*Idolatory*' of the woman was lamentable.[18]

Others, however, were not prepared to see her, much to her chagrin, since she had brought home with her a letter of commendation from the Queen of Naples to Queen Charlotte and had hoped moreover that her husband's relationship to such noblemen as the Earl of Warwick, the Marquess of Queensberry and the Marquess of Abercorn would surely in itself gain her social acceptance. When Sir William went by himself to court, Nelson, less well versed in these matters than his friend, was outraged. 'I would not in Sir William's case have gone to court without my wife,' he protested, 'and such a wife, never to be matched.'[19]

'Few ladies visit Lady H except those have been at Naples,' Greville's sister subsequently related. 'They have continual Company [at Grosvenor Square],' she added. 'But I don't know their set. Prince Augustus [the Duke of Sussex who had infuriated his father by marrying Lady Augusta Murray] is one, & Foreigners.'

This kind of company was assembled by William Beckford, who asked the Hamiltons and Nelson to spend Christmas at his country house in Wiltshire, assuring Lady Hamilton that they would enjoy 'a few comfortable days of repose – uncontaminated by the sight and prattle of drawing-room parasites'.[20] By these he meant the families from other great houses in Wiltshire, from Wilton, Stourhead and Longleat, none of whom were to be present. Lady Hamilton's mother was included in the invitation but not Lady Nelson.[21] She was to remain in London with her father-in-law, who had not seen much of his son since his return – the Admiral being always 'on the wing' – and with her brother-in-law the Rev. William Nelson and his wife, Sarah, who had come up from Norfolk to see how they might profit from their connection with the Admiral, now in the House of Lords.

On their way to Fonthill Splendens, the magnificent Palladian mansion built for Beckford's father – the merchant and Lord Mayor of London who had left his son a fortune which today would be worth about £60,000,000 – Nelson was greeted at Salisbury by the familiar cheering crowds, by bands and volunteer cavalry, and by the city fathers who bestowed upon him the freedom of the municipality, accompanied by long orations celebrating the hero's character and achievements. As elsewhere the sight of the small, thin, mutilated figure was a disappointment to those who had expected a latter-day Drake or Ralegh. 'As he alighted from his carriage,' one observer commented, 'I could not help asking myself if that one-armed, one-eyed man could really have scattered destruction among the fleets of France. I felt all my conception of what constituted a grammar-school hero utterly discomforted.'[22]

Among the other guests at Fonthill were Madame Brigida Banti, the opera singer whose voice was even more powerful than Lady Hamilton's; Benjamin West, the American painter and Sir Joshua Reynolds's successor as President of the Royal Academy; John Wolcot, a former physician, the composer of satirical verses under the pseudonym 'Peter Pindar'; William Hamilton, the son of one of Robert Adam's assistants who was painting a series of pictures for Beckford; and James Wyatt, the architect, son of a farmer and timber merchant, who was helping his host design the astonishing Gothic folly, Fonthill Abbey, whose octagonal tower, eventually to collapse, was to be seen rising to a height of 276 feet in the park.

Welcomed by a military escort and a thirty-piece band playing 'Rule Britannia', Nelson and his fellow guests were escorted up the drive to be attended upon by thirty servants, including a dwarf whom Beckford had acquired in Portugal. They were met by their host standing, so his daughter told her cousin, 'on the Landing of the grand flight of steps to the Marble Hall'. Dinner was then served; and 'during the Dessert Lady Hamilton [and Madame Banti] sang "God Save the King" and "Rule Britannia", the company joining in chorus. There followed some charming duets by the two ladies.'[23]

Of this Christmas at Fonthill Splendens, little is known apart from the host's taking of Nelson for a brisk drive in a phaeton around the grounds and plantations, a drive cut short by Nelson who, alarmed and rather giddy, exclaimed, 'This is too much for me: you must set me down,' and jumped off the box as soon as Beckford – who, 'singular to say', 'had noticed a peculiar anxiety' in his companion's countenance – slowed his well-trained horses down.[24] There is, however, a detailed description of a 'monastic fête' in the Abbey on the night before Christmas Eve.

After the sun had set, Beckford's guests were driven to the Abbey up a winding drive beneath lanterns and flambeaux glittering in the branches of the trees above their heads, while hidden musicians played a variety of instruments, 'the more distant players providing an eerie echo effect which reverberated in the darkness ... Everything was provided to steal upon the senses, to dazzle the eye, and to bewilder the fancy.'[25]

The guests were conducted through the hall into the Cardinal's Parlour where pine cones were burning in the immense fireplace. On the long refectory table were laid all manner of 'enormous silver dishes' filled with the most exotic food – 'unmixed with the refinements of modern cookery' – to give the 'authentic monastic flavour'. The walls were draped with purple hangings; the chairs were of ebony.[26]

A room upstairs, to which the guests were taken after the meal – climbing stairs lit by torches held by attendants in hooded gowns – was hung with yellow damask. Here Lady Hamilton gave an inspired performance of her 'Attitudes', presenting the tragic story of Agrippina in mime and gesture, with such pathos, so Miss Beckford said, that several of the company were in tears. After this performance – which was depicted for Beckford by Benjamin West – the guests, 'as if waking from a dream', as one of them put it, 'or just freed from the influence of some magic spell', were taken to an octagonal room to admire John Charles Felix Rossi's statue of St Anthony of Padua placed on an altar and surrounded by reliquaries, candlesticks and other jewelled objects. They then returned to Fonthill Splendens for supper.

By now their host had decided that he did not really much care for Lady Hamilton. 'She affected sensibility,' he thought, 'but felt none, was artful; and no wonder, she had been trained in the court of Naples – a fine school for an Englishwoman of any stamp. It was a hell of corruption. Nelson was infatuated. She would make him believe anything – that the profligate Queen was Madonna. He was her dupe.'[27]

*

The next day Beckford's guests went home.[28] For Nelson, though, No. 17 Dover Street could scarcely be called a home any more. His passion for Lady Hamilton painfully exacerbated his irritation with his wife, for whom he had by now conceived a positive dislike. When he heard of rumours that she was considering renting Shelburne House as a place for them to live together, he commented sharply, 'If she was to take Shelburne House, I am not, thank God, forced to live in it.'[29] He could hardly bear to be in the same room with her; nor could she herself bear any longer her husband's praise of the beauty, virtues and astonishing talents of Lady Hamilton. One day at breakfast, according to the rather shaky memory of William Haslewood, Nelson's solicitor, who provided this account forty-five years later, she suddenly burst out in protest: 'I am sick of hearing of dear Lady Hamilton and am resolved that you shall give up either her or me.'

'Take care, Fanny, what you say,' Nelson replied, so Haslewood reported. 'I love you sincerely but I cannot forget my obligations to Lady Hamilton or speak of her otherwise than with affection and admiration.' 'Without one soothing word or gesture, but muttering something about her mind being made up, Lady Nelson left the room, and shortly after drove from the house. They never lived together afterwards.'[30]

'I believe,' Haslewood added, 'that Lord Nelson took a formal leave of her Ladyship before joining the Fleet.' It seems that this leave taking was a brief one. According to Sir Andrew Hamond, Comptroller of the Navy, Nelson, calling at the house in Dover Street, went upstairs, where he found his wife in bed. She held out her hand to him and said, 'There is not a man in the world who has more honour than you. Now tell me, upon your honour, whether you have ever suspected or heard from anyone anything that renders my own fidelity disputable.' No, Nelson said, there never had been. He then left the house and did not see her again. That night he wrote a letter of twenty-five words to say he had arrived in Southampton and asking her to give his kindest regards to his father and 'all the family'. He had arranged for his agents to pay £400 into her account immediately and for a 'handsome quarterly allowance'.[31] Roundwood, the house in Suffolk, had by then been sold; but he had taken 17 Dover Street for a year so she would not be homeless.

22

The Channel

Kiss and kiss our dear Horatia . . . a love-begotten child.

Immediately upon arriving at Great Yarmouth two months before, Nelson had written to the Secretary of the Admiralty before letting anyone else know of his return to England: 'I trust that my necessary journey, by land, from the Mediterranean [a leisurely journey that had taken sixteen weeks], will not be considered as a wish to be a moment out of active service.' Bitterly recalling Lord Spencer's letter of reproof written to him when he was in Italy, he told Sir Edward Berry that he hoped it would not 'be an *inactive* service'.[1] He had heard from Alexander Ball that there was talk in the Mediterranean that he would be recalled to that theatre to succeed Lord Keith; but Nelson himself thought it more likely that he would be appointed second-in-command of the Channel Fleet under the Earl of St Vincent. He was not sure how this appointment would be received by St Vincent since there was disagreement between them about prize-money, St Vincent claiming that he was due for a share of the amounts received from captures while he was temporarily absent from his command, Nelson arguing that, as he was the *de facto* commander for part of that time, he was due a sum which he estimated at £20,000. 'My Commander-in-Chief runs away with all the money I fight for,' Nelson complained acrimoniously. 'So let them. I am content with the honour. But damn me if I suffer any man to swindle me out of my property whilst he is at his ease in England . . . I have only *justice*, *honour*, and the custom of the service on my side; he has *partiality*, *power*, *money* and *rascality* on his.'*[2]

* Judgement in Nelson's suit against St Vincent was eventually given on 14 November 1803. The action had been brought to recover 'a share of the prizes

When the appointment he had expected was confirmed and he went down as a newly promoted vice-admiral of the Blue to the south coast to join the Channel Fleet, the dispute was not mentioned on his meeting Lord St Vincent. It was, however, on Nelson's mind; and, as the Commander-in-Chief reported to the Secretary of the Admiralty, 'Nelson was very low when he came here . . . appeared and acted as if he had done me an injury and felt apprehensive that I was acquainted with it . . . Poor fellow! He is devoured by vanity, weakness and folly; was strung with ribbons, medals, etc., yet pretended that he wished to avoid the honour and ceremonies he everywhere met with on the road.' Such pretended modesty was absurd in 'the foolish little fellow'.[3] 'We parted good friends,' St Vincent added in another letter, 'and as he owes all the fame, titles, badges and distinctions he wears to my patronage and protection I will continue kind to him in the extreme. He is vain and weak and therefore open to flattery and all its concomitants.'[4] St Vincent did remain kind to him, and took pains to assure him that, whatever faults he found in him as a man, he had a very high opinion of him as a sea officer: 'I never saw a man in our Profession, excepting yourself and Troubridge, who possessed the magic art of infusing the same spirit into others, which inspired their own actions . . . Your Lordship's whole conduct, from your first appointment to this hour, is the subject of our constant admiration. It does not become me to make comparisons: all agree there is but one NELSON.'[5]

Busy as he had been since getting back from the Continent, and much as his time had been taken up with Lady Hamilton, Nelson,

---

taken by Captain Digby of Lord St Vincent's squadron, after his Lordship had left his station and returned to England, and when Lord Nelson had the command. Judgement was given for Lord St Vincent in the Court below; but upon Writ of Error, Lord Ellenborough delivered it as the opinion of the Court, that the moment a Superior Officer left his station, the right of the next Flag Officer commences; and, consequently, that Lord St Vincent having returned to England, the enterprise and conduct of the Fleet devolved on Lord Nelson. Judgement was, accordingly, given in favour of Lord Nelson, who thereby becomes entitled to the whole of the Admiral's share of the Prize-money' (*Naval Chronicle*, X, 432).

as St Vincent said, spent hours sitting to both Sir William Beechey and John Hoppner.* He had also been painted, bedecked with his decorations and medals, by F. H. Füger; had been sketched by the Dutch artist Simon de Koster, engravings of whose drawings had been sold at Brydon's, the printseller's; and had sat for a bust to Field Marshal Conway's daughter, Mrs Anne Damer, to whom he presented the coat he had worn during the Battle of the Nile, telling her that he had never worn it since 'nor even allowed it to be washed in order that [his] Naval as well as other friends may know, from the streaks of perspiration and hairpowder which are still to be seen on it, the exertions which [he] made and the anxiety which [he] felt on that day to deserve the approbation of [his] King and Country'.†[6]

Nelson had other worries on his mind, besides his strained relationship with Lord St Vincent. Although her baby was due to be born any day now, he was still desperately concerned that Lady Hamilton might in his absence fall prey to the lust of the Prince of Wales. His dreadful anxiety about this made him all the more angry to discover that his trunks had once again been carelessly packed and nails had been driven into the top of his mahogany table. And, as before, he blamed his wife. 'I find myself without anything comfortable or convenient,' he complained to her. 'Half

---

* Beechey also painted Nelson's father. Lady Nelson told her husband how she had persuaded him to do so. 'I was to [go to] Sir W. B. to ask his price, look at his pictures and then enquire whether he would go to an invalid. The answer "No" puzzled me, however I said sometimes general rules were broken thro'. Sir W. finding I was rather anxious about this picture said, that really he never went to any person excepting the King and Royal Family, the Duke and Duchess of York had that instant left the house. I knew that. "But Madam may I ask who is the gentleman?" "Yes Sir, my Lord Nelson's father." "My God, I would go to York to do it, yes Madam directly." He was as good as his word, and has been here twice. I think the likeness will be an exceedingly good one' (Naish, 552).

† Nelson had also had a marble bust made in Vienna by Franz Thaler and Matthias Ranson. For this purpose, it seems, a plaster cast was taken from his face. There are three such masks in existence; two are at the Royal Naval Museum, Portsmouth, one at the National Maritime Museum, Greenwich. Formerly believed to be death-masks, they are now accepted almost certainly to be life-masks (Michael Nash, ed., *The Nelson Masks*, 1933).

my wardrobe is left behind, and that butler, a French rascal ought to be hanged . . . I am forced to buy everything, even a little tea, for who would open a large chest? . . . In short I only regret that I desired any person to order things for me. I could have done all in ten minutes and for a 10th part of the expense . . . It is now too late to send half my wardrobe, as I know not what is to become of me, nor do I care.'[7]

The thought of the Prince of Wales enjoying himself at 99 Piccadilly, to which the Hamiltons had moved from Grosvenor Square, drove Nelson almost frantic with rage and jealousy. Letter after admonitory letter was dispatched to that address, some taken there by Oliver, Davison, Troubridge or Captain Edward Parker, others entrusted to the ordinary post. 'Does Sir William want you to be a whore to the rascal?' he demanded. 'I see clearly you are on SALE.' It was 'shocking conduct' to have invited a man who associated with 'a set of whores, bawds and unprincipiled lyars'.

He wondered how Sir William 'could have had a wish for the Prince of Wales to come under [their] roof'. Could this be 'the great Sir William Hamilton?' He blushed for him. Even one visit would stamp her as his *chère amie*. He was dotingly fond of such women as herself. Of course, he knew she could not be 'seduced by any Prince in Europe'; she was 'the pattern of perfection'. Yet if Sir William knew as much of the Prince's character as the world did, he would rather let the lowest wretch that walked the streets dine at his table than that 'unprincipalled lyar'. Lady Hamilton's 'hitherto unimpeached character' would be ruined. 'No modest woman would suffer it.' The Prince was 'permitted to visit only people of *notorious ill fame*'; it had been reported that he had said he would make her his mistress; he was a 'false lying scoundrel'.

DO NOT let the lyar come. Be firm May God blast him . . . Do not let the rascal in . . . Oh God Oh God Keep my sences . . . Hush, hush my poor heart keep in my breast be Calm, Emma is true but no one not even Emma could resist the Serpent's flattering tongue . . . What will they all SAY & think that Emma is like other Women when I would have killed anybody who had said so must now *hang* down my head and admit it . . . but forgive me I know my Emma and don't forget that you had once a

Nelson a friend a dear friend but alas he has his misfortunes he has lost his only friend his only LOVE, don't forget him poor fellow he is honest ... don't scold me indeed I am not worth it ... Oh I could thunder and strike dead with my lightening ... I am in tears, I cannot bear it.[8]

Nelson longed to get her away by herself. 'What must be my sensations at the idea of sleeping with you,' he told her in a letter to be taken to her by Francis Oliver and, therefore, safer from prying eyes than correspondence sent by other means.

It setts me on fire, even the thoughts, much more would be the reality. I am sure my love & desires are all to you and if any woman were to come to me, even as I am this moment from thinking of you, I hope it might rot off if I would touch her even with my hand. No, my heart, person and mind is in perfect union of love towards my own, dear beloved Emma ... My own dear wife, for such you are in my eyes and in the face of heaven ... I long to get to Bronte, for, believe me, this England is a shocking place; a walk under the chestnut trees, although you may be shot by a banditti, is better than to have our reputations stabbed in this country.[9]

Their reputations had been stabbed deeply enough already. In November the year before one of the first of several caricatures alluding to their affair had appeared in the print-shop windows. It was by Isaac Cruikshank, George Cruikshank's father, and shows Nelson looking at Lady Hamilton keenly as he smokes a hookah. She says, '*Pho, the old mans pipe is allways out, but yours burns with full vigour.*' Other caricaturists ridiculed her 'Attitudes', as Rowlandson did in his celebrated drawing of her naked beauty being exhibited by her elderly husband to a young gentleman with artistic inclinations. James Gillray portrayed her as Cleopatra to Nelson's Mark Antony, with a volcano erupting in the background, and as an immensely fat Dido rising from a curtained bed in which her husband is still asleep. She is in despair at the departure of a fleet seen through an open window. Below her outstretched foot is a garter inscribed 'The Hero of the Nile'. At the foot of the print is a verse:

Ah, where, & ah where, is my gallant Sailor gone?
He's gone to Fight the Frenchmen, for George upon the Throne,
He's gone to fight ye Frenchmen, t'loose t'other Arm & Eye,
And left me with the old Antiques, to lay me down, & cry.[10]

Balladeers as well as caricaturists found inspiration in the excessively bulky figure of Lady Hamilton. This offering was sung to the tune of the National Anthem:

> Also huge Emma's name
> First on the roll of fame,
> Now let us sing.
> Loud as her voice, let's sound
> Her faded charms around,
> Which in the sheets were found –
> God save the King.
>
> Nelson, thy flag haul down,
> Hang up thy laurel crown,
> While her we sing.
> No more in triumph swell,
> Since that with her you dwell,
> But don't her William tell –
> Nor George your King.[11]

Fearing that his letters to Lady Hamilton might be opened and made public, Nelson had suggested that he write to her as though he were an ordinary sailor named 'Thompson' who was concerned about his sweetheart, a woman in Lady Hamilton's service who was about to have a baby and whom 'Thompson' would marry were it not for an uncle who stood in the lovers' way. As 'Thompson', or sometimes 'Thomson', Nelson wrote to Lady Hamilton regularly, sometimes in cheerful mood, more often frustrated and sad, on occasions forgetting to maintain the pretence of being the sailor and writing as the lovelorn admiral: 'He wishes there was peace, or, that if your uncle [Sir William] might die, he would instantly then come and marry you ... I was sure you would not go to Mrs Walpole's, it is no better than a bawdy house

... I own I sometimes fear that you will not be so true to me as I am to you, yet I cannot, will not believe you will be false. No, I judge you by myself; I hope to be dead before that will happen, but it will not . . .'[12]

He was still worried to distraction about the Prince of Wales and the threatened dinner to be given by the Hamiltons in the Prince's honour:

Do not have him *en famille* . . . Do not sit long at table . . . He will put his foot near you . . . telling you soft things. If he does, tell it out at table, and turn him out of the house . . . Don't let him touch you . . . God strike him blind if he looks at you – that is high treason and you may get me hanged by revealing it . . . I shall that day have no one to dinner; it shall be a fast day for me . . . Oh God, that I was dead . . . I am gone almost mad . . . I know his aim is to have you for a mistress. The thought so agitates me that I cannot write. I had wrote a few lines last night, but I am in tears, I cannot bear it.[13]

I am well aware of the danger that would attend the Prince's frequenting our house [Sir William told Nelson in an effort to allay his anxiety], not that I fear that Emma could ever be induced to act contrary to the prudent conduct she has hitherto pursued . . . This dinner must be, or the Prince would be offended . . . I have been thus explicit as I know well your Lordship's way of thinking.[14]

As it happened, the dinner was cancelled because Lady Hamilton had been suffering from what Sir William called a 'foul stomach' as well as intermittent headaches ever since she had given birth to her baby, a girl, on or about 29 January 1801.[15]

Soon after the birth – of which Sir William with the utmost tact appeared to be oblivious – the baby's mother, carefully concealing the child in the folds of her muff, took her to be looked after by a Mrs Gibson at 9 Little Titchfield Street. The financial arrangements were settled: Mrs Gibson – who was promised that she would be 'handsomely rewarded' – undertook to bring up the child with her own, slightly deformed daughter, Mary; and Lady Hamilton was driven back in a hackney carriage to Piccadilly. It seems that the baby may have been a twin, that the other child was taken to the Foundlings' Hospital, and that Nelson was told that this baby had died.[16] If this was so, the sad news of its death did not overcast the pleasure he felt at becoming a father for the first time. As soon as he was given the news, almost hysterically overjoyed, he began to rewrite his will and to make plans for the christening. Writing excitedly to 'Mrs Thompson', believing he would 'go mad with joy', he proposed a ceremony at St George's, Hanover Square, where Lady Hamilton had been married, and, as sponsors, Lady Hamilton and himself.[17] 'Its name will be Horatia, daughter of Johem and Morata Etnorb! If you read the surname backwards and take the letters of the other names, it will make, very extraordinarily, the names of your real and affectionate friends, Lady Hamilton and myself.' He had at first proposed the name of Emma for the baby, not knowing that Lady Hamilton already had a daughter of that name, the girl known as Emma Carew, twenty-one years old now, short and rather plain, with what Charles Greville considered a most unsuitable accent. Greville thought 'a little money might be an inducement for a clergyman to marry her'; but if she did not 'make an impression on a good sort of man', he was sure he could not find one for her. The existence of this girl had also been kept from Sir William Hamilton until Hamilton married her mother, when Greville, in pique, forwarded the bills for her keep.

Emma or Horatia, Nelson did not mind which name it was to be. His delight in being a father overflowed in letters to the child's mother, his 'only, *only*, love' whom he 'swears he will marry as soon as it is possible'. 'I believe poor dear Mrs Thompson's friend will go mad with joy,' he wrote. 'He cries, prays and performs all tricks, yet dare not show all or any of his feelings ... He does nothing but rave about you and her. I own I participate of this joy and cannot write anything ... He charges me to say how dear you are to him and that you must, every opportunity, kiss and bless for him his dear little girl.'[18]

Lady Hamilton was as alarmed by Nelson's lack of discretion, as she was annoyed by his wild jealousy and fears of her faithlessness. She scolded him for it and he replied:

As for the P. of W., I know his character, and my confidence is firm as a
rock till you try to irritate me to say hard things, that you may have the
pleasure of scolding me; but recollect it must remain 4 days before it can
be made up, not, as before, in happy time, 4 minutes ... Let us be
happy, that is in our power. Do you know how I am amusing myself this
evening? Troubridge is gone to bed, and I am alone with all your letters
except the cruel one, that is burnt, and I have scratched out all the
scolding words, and have read them 40 times over, and if you were to see
how much better & prettier they read I am sure you would never write
another scolding word to me.[19]

In her reply, she pointed out the scandal which might ensue
were his will, as he intended, to contain codicils linking her name
with that of a child born out of wedlock, and the embarrassment
they might have to face should the vicar of St George's be curious
as to such extraordinary names as Johem and Morata Etnorb and
ask questions about them. Nelson was persuaded to leave his will
as it was for the moment and to postpone the christening.

Yet the letters, sometimes four of them a day, protesting love
and eternal devotion, repeating his desire to marry her as a
woman 'more suited to [his genius]' than his legal wife, though
never mentioning the previous necessity of his own divorce,
continued to pour from his pen late at night aboard his ship.

If you was single, and I found you under a hedge, I would instantly
marry you ... I hope one day to carry you there [to Norfolk] by a nearer
tie in law, but not in love and affection. I wish you would never mention
that person's [Lady Nelson's] name ... Aye, would to God our fates had
been different ... I have been the world around, and in every corner of
it, and yet never saw your equal or even one which could be put in
comparison with you ...

I love, I never did love any one else, I never had a dear pledge of love
till you gave me one, and you, thank my God, never gave one to anyone
else. You, my beloved Emma, and my country, are the two dearest
objects of my fond heart – a heart susceptible and true ... My longing
for you ... you may readily imagine. I am sure my love and desires are
all for you ... My love, my darling angel, my heaven-given wife, the

dearest only true wife of her [*sic*] till death ... kiss and kiss *our* dear Horatia, think of that.

Other women were of no interest to him now. Those he liked, such as Sarah Collingwood – with whom he sat by the fire in the Fountain Inn, Plymouth, while her little daughter taught her dog, Phyllis, how to dance – made his longing for domestic happiness with Emma all the harder to bear. The rest were dismissed as of no interest, like one admiral's 'old wife dressed ewe lamb fashion', and the wife of another officer who was overfond of the bottle and looked 'like a cook-maid', and a certain 'Mrs D.', a 'damned pimping bitch', and Lady Abercorn, likewise 'a damned bitch' who 'would pimp for her husband that she might get at her lovers for ... not one satisfies her'. 'All other [women] except your-self,' he assured Emma, 'are pests to me ... for who can be like my Emma?' 'I will dine nowhere without your consent,' he promised her, 'although with my present feelings I might be trusted with fifty virgins naked in a dark room.'[20]

He had gone to Plymouth by way of Exeter, where he received the freedom of the city on 17 January, and Honiton, where one of his 'Band of Brothers', Captain George Westcott of the *Majestic*, had been born. Westcott, who had been killed at the Nile, was the son of a baker in the town and had joined the service as a master's mate. Nelson invited his widow and daughter to breakfast. He asked Mrs Westcott if she had received her husband's gold medal and, when she said she had not, he removed his own which hung on a blue ribbon round his neck and presented it to 'the poor thing' with the words, 'You will not value it less because Nelson has worn it.' Writing to tell Lady Hamilton of this encounter, he added, 'The brother is a tailor, but had they been chimmney sweeps, it was my duty to show them respect.'

At Plymouth, where he was granted the freedom of the city on 22 January, he saw another of his captains' relations, Troubridge's sister, whom he dismissed in a letter to Lady Hamilton as being pock-marked and as deaf as her brother, so there was no cause for Emma to feel jealous.[21] He hated Plymouth, he said, and when he got aboard his flagship the weather was horrid and he was frequently seasick. Besides, his eyes were troubling him so much he consulted the physician of the fleet, who told him he was writing too many letters and that an operation might be necessary. 'He has directed me not to write,' he told Emma, 'not to eat anything but the most simple food; not to touch wine or porter; to sit in a dark room; to have green shades for my eyes − (will you, my dear friend, make me one or two? − nobody else shall) − and to bathe them in cold water every hour . . . My eye is like blood; and the film so extended, that I only see from the corner furthest from my nose.'[22] His ship's decks were leaking, he added, and 'it is truly uncomfortable but it suits exactly my present feelings, which are miserable in the extreme. I have not closed my eyes all night and am almost blind and far from well.'

He had been told that the Admiralty were making plans for operations in the Baltic and he had consequently been ordered to move his flag from the *San José* to a new flagship, the *St George*, a seventy-four-gun ship more suited to Baltic waters. He did not like the look of her. 'You cannot think how dirty the *St George* is compared to my *San José*,' he complained to Lady Hamilton, 'and probably her inside is worse than her outside appearance.'[23]

Before moving his things, he wrote to the Society for Promoting Christian Knowledge, which had been founded over a hundred years before, reminding them that they had presented Bibles to the crews of the *Agamemnon* and the *Vanguard* and trusting that the men's subsequent conduct had been such 'as to induce a belief that good to our King and Country may have arisen from the seamen and marines having been taught to respect the established religion'. He hoped, therefore, that the Society would present a further consignment of Bibles to the crew of the *San José* ('the number near 900') and that the ship would be 'as successful as the former ships [they] gave them to'.[24]

There had been a time when he had been concerned that his adultery could not be readily reconciled with his religious beliefs. But gradually he had somehow persuaded himself that his love for Lady Hamilton was not susceptible to such consideration. 'I know you are so true and loyal an Englishwoman,' he wrote to her at this time, 'that you would hate those who would not stand forth in defence of our King, Laws, Religion and all which is dear to us.' As for himself, he had, years ago, been granted a vision of his future mission in life. Emma Hamilton was clearly a part of that mission. 'As truly as I believe in God I believe you are a saint,' he told her, 'and in this age of wickedness you set an example of real virtue and goodness . . . How can I thank you sufficiently for all your goodness and kindness to me, a forlorn outcast except in your generous soul.' It was as though he had been granted a dispensation from God to ignore the rules by which other men must consider themselves bound. That winter he composed a prayer, a copy of which he sent to the woman divinely ordained to be his partner:

O God, who knows the purity of my thoughts and the uprightness of my conduct, look down, I beseech Thee, on me; one, I own, of the most unworthy of Thy servants, help and support me, for Thou, O Lord, art my only comfort and to Thy infinite mercy alone do I look for support through this transitory life, and I beseech Thee, O most merciful God, that in Thy good time Thou will take me to Thyself and remove me from this world, where I have no friends to comfort or relieve me even on the bed of sickness. Relieve me, O Lord, from the miseries of this world, speedily, speedily, speedily. Amen, amen, amen. Nelson and Bronte.[25]

The morose mood that led to the composition of this prayer was suddenly transformed to one of burning excitement when he heard from the Admiralty that he had been granted three days' leave.

'Poor Thompson seems to have forgotten all his ill health and all his mortifications and sorrows in the thought that he will soon bury them in your dear, dear bosom,' he wrote hurriedly before leaving for London. 'I dare say twins will again be the fruit of your and his meeting. The thought is too much to bear. Have the dear thatched cottage [contemporary slang for female genitals] ready to receive him and I will answer that he would not give it up for a queen and a palace. Kiss dear H. for me.'[26]

He arrived in London before dawn, had breakfast at Lothian's Hotel in Albemarle Street, then dashed off to Piccadilly. From there he and Emma went to Little Titchfield Street where he decided the baby's eyes and 'upper part of her face' were just like her mother's: 'a finer child was never produced by any two persons. It was in truth a love-begotten child.'[27]

To Emma it seemed that her lover was gone almost as soon as he arrived. 'My heart is fit to Burst quite with grief,' she told her new friend, Nelson's sister-in-law Sarah, the Rev. William's wife. 'Oh, what pain, God only knows . . . Oh God only knows what it is to part with such a *friend, such a one* . . . I shall go mad with grief . . . We were truly called [in Naples] *Tria Juncta in Uno* for Sir W., *he* and I have but one heart in three bodies.'[28]

Nelson had heard that his wife, who had gone to Brighton, proposed returning to London to talk to him. He had immediately written to tell her not to do so: he was in town 'on very particular business' only for a day or two; she must 'rest quiet' where she was; he would 'not on my account' have her come to London; nor must she think of going to Portsmouth where he 'never came on shore'. He signed himself 'as ever your affectionate Nelson'.[29]

Lady Hamilton was delighted to hear of this rebuff. 'Tom Tit does not come to town,' she told Sarah Nelson. 'She offered to go down but was refused. She only wanted to do mischief to all the *great JOVE'S* relations. 'Tis now shewn, all her ill-treatment and bad-*heart* − *JOVE* has found it out.'[30]

Certainly Nelson had made up his mind that he must make it clear to his wife that he did not want to see her again and wanted nothing more to do with her tiresome son, 'the Cub', as Lady Hamilton derisively referred to him, telling Sarah Nelson that she 'only' hoped he did not come near her when he came to London and that, if he did, '*not at home* shall be the answer.'[31] 'I have done all for him,' Nelson wrote to his wife − sending a copy to Lady Hamilton − at the beginning of March,

and he may again, as he has often done before, wish to break my neck, and be abetted in it by his friends, who are likewise my enemies. But I have done my duty as an honest, generous man, and I neither want or wish for anybody to care what becomes of me, whether I return or am left in the Baltic. Living, I have done all in my power for you and, if dead, you will only find I have done the same; therefore my only wish is to be left to myself; and wishing you every hapiness, Believe that I am, Your affectionate Nelson and Bronte.[32]

At the top of this letter, Fanny noted: 'This is my Lord Nelson's letter of dismissal, which so astonished me that I immediately sent it to Mr Maurice Nelson, who was sincerely attached to me, for his advice; he desired me not to take the least notice of it as his Brother seemed to have forgot himself.'[33]

Unable to bear the thought of being dismissed from his life in this way, and what she called 'the silence you have imposed', Fanny wrote to ask him to reconsider his decision. She received no reply.

23

The Kattegat

I know the Chief is fond of good living, and he shall have the turbot.

No sooner had he returned to Portsmouth than Nelson fell ill again. 'A pain immediately seized my heart,' he told Lady Hamilton, parting from whom was 'literally tearing one's own flesh'. The pain 'kept increasing for half an hour,' he added, 'that, turning cold, hot, cold, etc., I was obliged to send for the surgeon'. He felt little better when he set sail in the *St George* for Yarmouth to join the fleet assembling there under Sir Hyde Parker.

Lieutenant-Colonel the Hon. William Stewart, the twenty-seven-year-old son of the Earl of Galloway and Member of Parliament for Wigtonshire, who was in command of the marines aboard the *St George*, noted Lord Nelson's fussy ill temper. Instead of leaving such matters to his flag-captain, Thomas Hardy, 'his Lordship was rather too apt to interfere with the working of the Ship, and not always with the best judgement', Stewart recorded. 'The wind, when off Dungeness, was scanty and the Ship was to be put about. Lord Nelson would give orders and caused her to miss stays. Upon which he said rather peevishly to the Master, or Officer of the Watch (I forget which), "Well now, see what we have done. Well, Sir, what do you mean to do?" The officer saying with hesitation, "I don't exactly know, my Lord, I fear she won't do," Lord Nelson turned sharply towards the cabin and replied, "Well, I am sure if you don't know what to do, no more do I either." He then went in, leaving the Officer to work the Ship as he liked.'*[1]

* 'Anyone who has ever handled a ship under sail will read that passage with some amusement,' the naval historian, Dudley Pope, himself an experienced sailor, has written. 'The occasional wilfulness of a sailing vessel of any size with a

The Admiral's temper was not improved when the *St George* reached Yarmouth and he found that his Commander-in-Chief, Sir Hyde Parker, was not with his fleet but was living ashore at the Wrestlers' Arms with the nineteen-year-old girl whom he had recently married as his second wife. Sir Hyde himself was nearly sixty-four, the son of an admiral, the son-in-law of an admiral, and the father of a midshipman who was one day to be an admiral too. He had been sent to sea as a boy and had seen service on the North American station, in the West Indies, in the Mediterranean and in the North Sea. An experienced sailor, he had little imagination and less verve. To Collingwood he seemed 'a good-tempered man, full of vanity, a great deal of pomp, and a pretty smattering of ignorance'. Kindly, fussy, stout, rubicund and very rich, he looked more like a yeoman farmer than a naval officer, and was evidently as much concerned that his fat and jolly second wife, one of Sir Richard Onslow's four daughters, known as 'the batter pudding', should have a happy time ashore as he was to ensure that his fleet was made ready for sea. He was much occupied with plans for a ball to be given in her honour.[2]

Nelson was naturally predisposed to condemn the faults of such a man, considering 'how nice it must be lying in bed with a young wife, compared to a damned cold, raw wind', and comparing the Commander-in-Chief's comforts with his own separation from a woman who would surely be the object of other men's attentions in

---

"scanty" wind usually provokes more surliness than Nelson displayed; and to use the episode to doubt the Admiral's ability is to forget the years he had spent at sea' (Pope, *The Great Gamble*, 182). Colonel Stewart was not, however, the only observer to comment upon Nelson's interference with his ship's quartermaster. Recalling the chase after the *Généreux* in 1800, Sir Henry Duncan commented upon his being 'always fidgety' upon such occasions: 'Lord Nelson put his head up on deck. "Quarter Master, you can put her head a little more to the wind." "No, my Lord." Went down. In a few minutes up again. "Quarter Master, can't you put her head a little more to the wind?" "No, my Lord." Down again. Up again. "Quarter Master, I think you can put her head a little more to the wind." "No, my Lord." "Then I lie?" "Yes, my Lord." "Then you're a pig"' (Sir Henry Duncan to H. L. Long, 'written down by Lady Catherine Long', quoted in Matcham, 175).

his absence, particularly of those of the Prince of Wales, to whose imagined designs his thoughts kept returning in renewed agonies of jealousy: 'My senses are almost gone tonight; I feel as I never felt before. My head My Head . . . But I will lay down and try to compose my spirits, miserable wretch that I am . . . Goodnight, I am more dead than alive, but all yours till death . . . My God My God . . . You are on SALE . . . Good God my blood boils.'[3]

Disturbed as his nights were, Nelson was always up and about at daylight, so Colonel Stewart said, and had breakfast soon after six o'clock. So, 'choosing to be amusingly exact to that hour, which he considered to be a very late one for business', he presented himself, with Stewart, at the Wrestlers' Arms at eight o'clock one morning and sent up his compliments to the Commander-in-Chief's room. Sir Hyde appeared, spoke briefly to his subordinate and went back to bed without giving any orders.[4]

This was too much for Nelson. He immediately wrote to Thomas Troubridge, who had become a Lord of the Admiralty under the new First Lord, the Earl of St Vincent, and asked for sailing orders so that 'we shall not be tempted to lie abed till 11 o'clock'. Nelson's complaints soon elicited a firm reproof from St Vincent to Parker:

I have heard by a side wind that you have intention of continuing at Yarmouth on account of some trifling circumstances [the projected ball]. I really know not what they are, nor did I give myself the trouble of inquiring into them, supposing it impossible . . . that there could be the smallest foundation for this report. I have, however . . . sent down a message purposely to convey to you my opinion, as a private friend, that any delay in your sailing would do you irreparable injury.[5]

Spurred by this reproach, the fond husband reluctantly sent his 'batter pudding' home and hurried aboard his flagship, the *London*, much to the satisfaction of Nelson, who expressed his pleasure at the ball's having been 'knocked up' and 'gentlemen being sent to sea instead of dancing with nice white gloves'. Yet, even now, so he complained, he did not know exactly upon what duty the fleet was bound. 'I declare solemnly that I do not know that I am going to the Baltic,' he told Alexander Davison, 'and much worse than that

I could tell you. Sir Hyde is on board sulky. Stewart tells me his treatment of me is now noticed. Dickson came on board today to say all were scandalized at his gross neglect. Burn this letter; then . . . you can speak as if your knowledge came from another quarter.'[6]

Nelson had, of course, read in the newspapers of the formation of the so-called 'Armed Neutrality of the North', an alliance inspired by Bonaparte's admirer, the deranged Tsar, between Russia, Sweden, Prussia and Denmark, which then included Norway. These countries – exasperated by British ships stopping and searching their merchant vessels and occasionally seizing cargoes intended for unloading in French ports – had joined together with the intention of breaking the British blockade of France. But Nelson did not know that Sir Hyde Parker had been ordered to make for Copenhagen and to do his utmost to persuade the Danes, either by force or by 'amicable arrangement', to withdraw from the Armed Neutrality of the North before sailing on to attack the Russian fleet. And Sir Hyde was in no hurry to discuss these orders with his subordinate, who, he feared, would press for some reckless action that might end in disaster. Caution, in Sir Hyde's opinion, was essential: he had a strong fleet admittedly, with fifteen sail of the line and three more expected; but the northern nations could bring many more than this against him and – while their fleets were said to be not nearly so well equipped or well manned as his own – their numbers were formidable. Besides, one of the ships due to join him had run aground off the Norfolk coast and, lashed by heavy seas, had sunk with nearly all hands.

In what proved to be a successful attempt to be admitted to the Commander-in-Chief's confidence, Nelson, according to Lieutenant William Layman of the *St George*, sent over to the *London* a splendid turbot which one of the ship's other officers had caught upon his instructions. Nelson had appeared delighted by the catch and called out, 'Send it to Sir Hyde.' 'Something being said about the risk of sending a boat, from the great sea, lowering weather, and its being dark, his Lordship said with much meaning, "I know the Chief is fond of good living, and he shall have the turbot." '[7]

Sir Hyde, a noted gourmet, responded by asking Nelson to attend his next conference. 'Now that we are sure of fighting, I am sent for,' Nelson told Lady Hamilton. 'When it was a joke I was kept in the background; tomorrow will, I hope, be a proud day for England.'[8]

In fact, as he discovered, having climbed aboard the *London*, fighting was not yet a certainty. Attending the conference was Nicholas Vansittart, a young barrister and Member of Parliament for Hastings, who was one day to become Chancellor of the Exchequer. He had been chosen to conduct a diplomatic mission to Copenhagen, to make England's position clear to the Danish court and to persuade the Danes to abandon their allies in the Armed Neutrality. His mission, he reported, had not been successful, as Nelson had hoped and foreseen. The Danes were prepared to fight for their right to exercise their legitimate trade and were already hard at work strengthening the defences of Copenhagen and Elsinore. This intelligence increased Sir Hyde Parker's natural caution. He was inclined to believe the wisest plan was for the fleet to remain where it was in the Kattegat and from there to maintain a blockade of the Baltic. The officer who had brought Nelson's gig over from the *St George* to the *London* observed that 'all the heads were very gloomy'.[9]

Nelson was himself exasperated. 'I hate your pen and ink men,' he told Lady Hamilton. 'A fleet of British ships are the best negotiators in Europe . . . Your Nelson's plans are bold and decisive – all on the great scale.'[10]

In counselling immediate action, however, Nelson kept his temper and, on returning to his ship from the *London*, he put forward his reasons for advocating positive action in a long, forthright, persuasive yet, for all its hyperbole, temperate letter to the Commander-in-Chief:

The more I have reflected, the more I am confirmed in my opinion, that not a moment should be lost in attacking the Enemy. They will every day and hour be stronger; we shall never be so good a match for them as at this moment . . . You are with almost the safety, certainly with the honour of England more entrusted to you than ever yet fell to any British Officer. On your decision depends, whether our country shall be degraded in the eyes of Europe, or whether she shall rear her head higher than ever.

Again I do repeat, never did our Country depend so much on the success of any Fleet as on this . . . I am of opinion the boldest measures are the safest; and our Country demands a most vigorous exertion of her force directed with judgement. In supporting you, my dear Sir Hyde, through the arduous and important task you have undertaken, no exertion of head or heart shall be wanting from your most obedient and faithful servant, Nelson and Bronte.[11]

The Commander-in-Chief felt obliged to give way to this pressure. Authorizing a direct attack upon Copenhagen, he gave orders for the fleet to make for the narrow strait between Elsinore and the Swedish coast of Kristianstad and for Nelson to take the shallow-draught ships through the channel between the shoals in front of Copenhagen while Parker himself sailed with the other half of the fleet and took up position to the north of the city in support. Before the fleet divided in this way, Parker and Nelson went out together in a schooner to reconnoitre Copenhagen's natural and man-made defences. They appeared, indeed, to be formidable, even more so than Nicholas Vansittart had reported them to be: a long line of moored ships, hulks and floating batteries lay beneath the shore batteries and the seventy-odd guns of the Trekroner fort by the northern end of the Danish fleet. The guns were heavier than the British and some were known to fire a shot of almost forty pounds. Yet Nelson professed himself unimpressed. His own gun crews had been trained to fire a broadside every minute, a rate which the shore batteries surely could not match. The defences looked redoubtable, he conceded, 'to those who are children at war, but to my judgement, with the sail of the line I think I can annihilate them'. In the event he was to have two more ships of the line allocated to him by Parker, who would thereby be peril-ously weak should the Russians or Swedes appear while the fleet was thus divided.[12]

Nelson himself was to sail in the *Elephant*, a ship of lower draught than the *St George* and therefore less likely to run aground in the narrow channel to the east of the shoals where the Danish ships were moored. 'Sir Hyde Parker has by this time found out the worth of your Nelson and that he is a useful sort of man in a pinch,' he wrote complacently to Lady Hamilton. 'Therefore, if he has ever thought unkindly of me, I freely forgive him. Nelson must stand among the first or he must fall.'[13]

On the afternoon of 1 April 1801 he invited his captains to dinner. At his table on that occasion were Thomas Foley, his flag-captain in the *Elephant*, who had led the English line into action at the Battle of the Nile; Thomas Thompson, captain of the *Bellona*, who had also distinguished himself at the Nile; Thomas Hardy of the *St George*; Thomas Fremantle of the *Ganges*, another of Nelson's 'Band of Brothers'; and Rear-Admiral Thomas Graves, like Nelson a parson's son and one of four brothers in the Navy, who had hoisted his flag in the *Defiance* and was Nelson's second-in-command. Also dining that day in the *Elephant* were Colonel Stewart, the commander of the Marines; Colonel Hutchings, commanding a detachment of the 49th Regiment; and a sea officer with whom Nelson was serving for the first time, Edward Riou of the *Amazon*, a man of renowned seamanship who had achieved fame as captain of a ship which, carrying convicts from Newfoundland to Sydney, had been struck by an iceberg and had been brought, crippled as she was, a distance of more than four hundred leagues to the Cape of Good Hope. Nelson was immediately struck by Riou's knowledge and character and he asked him to remain behind after dinner to help him and Foley draft the orders for the following day.

Nelson was in cheerful mood, so Colonel Stewart reported; but some of his companions harboured doubts as to the success of the imminent and dangerous enterprise. Captain Fremantle feared that they might have left their attack too late, having given the Danes enough time to make their defences impregnable; Admiral Graves expressed the opinion that they might be 'playing a losing game, attacking stone walls'. Even Nelson seemed apprehensive about the pilots who had been pressed into service to guide the ships past the shoals in which the Danes had misplaced the buoys. These pilots were for the most part seamen from the ports of Scotland, Northumberland and Yorkshire whose ships were engaged upon the Baltic trade, carrying out coal and tea, sugar and tobacco and bringing back timber, copper and iron. But, familiar though they were with these waters, they showed what Nelson called a 'very unpleasant degree of hesitation' in coming forward to help their countrymen. Having 'no other thought than to keep their ships clear of danger, and their own silly heads clear of shot', they were united in mournfully declaring that to sail down the channel proposed would be an extremely hazardous operation.[14] Despairing of finding a pilot among these men, Nelson entrusted the task to the master of the *Bellona*, who had seen action at the Nile as master of the *Audacious* and 'declared himself prepared to lead the fleet'.

Meanwhile Captain Hardy was himself sent out with a long pole to take soundings in the channel as close as he dared to the enemy's ships. A midshipman, W. S. Millard of the *Monarch*, who had come on board the *Elephant* to take one of the Admiral's dinner guests, Colonel Hutchings, back to his ship, heard Lord Nelson giving his orders to the sounding party. He had earlier seen Nelson being rowed towards the *Monarch* in a gig:

On directing my spying-glass towards [the gig], I observed several officers in her, but at the end of the boat was a cocked hat put on square, with a peculiar *slouch*, so as to be at right angles to the boat's keel. I immediately ran to the officer of the watch and assured him Lord Nelson was coming aboard, for I had seen his hat.

My information did not receive much credit until . . . a squeaking little voice hailed the *Monarch* and desired us, in true Norfolk drawl, to prepare to weigh.[15]

Millard now heard Nelson's voice again as he gave orders to the sounding party: 'Are your oars muffled?'

'Yes, my lord.'

'Very well, should the Danish guard boat discover you, you must pull like devils and get out of his way as fast as you can.'

'On our way to the *Monarch*', Millard continued,

Colonel Hutchinson informed me that Lord Nelson intended to attack the enemy in the morning, and that he [Colonel Hutchinson] was to storm the Crown Batteries at the head of a division of the 49th . . . As soon as we came on board I hastened to communicate the intelligence to the two midshipmen's berths, where it was received with three cheers, and [I was] rewarded with grog [I] would gladly have refused . . . having to turn out again at midnight to walk the deck till four in the morning. The joy expressed on this occasion was unfeigned, which may be easily believed when it is remembered that we had been in sight of our opponents three days, and knew that sooner or later the bloody day must come.[16]

It was one o'clock in the morning before Nelson was ready to dictate his final and most detailed orders to a group of clerks. Earlier he had been suffering from the nervous dyspepsia which so often afflicted him at times of stress and he was now very tired. Foley and Riou, worried by his obvious weariness, suggested that his cot be brought up so that he could lie down while dictating. He brushed this idea aside; but when Tom Allen, without being asked to do so, produced the cot, he agreed to get into it and took without demur the hot drinks which were brought to him. It was very cold. Large pieces of broken ice floated past the ship in the dark waters, parts of the mass of ice melting farther up the Baltic and slowly releasing the Russian fleet.[17]

When he had finished dictating, the six clerks moved to a cabin near by where they scratched away with their quills to produce copies of the orders for the various ships under Nelson's command. The Admiral, calling from his cot every half-hour, urged them to hurry, since the wind was veering round favourably and he was anxious not to miss his opportunity.

He was up and dressed by six o'clock and at half-past nine the expected signals were drawn up the *Elephant*'s halyards and soon afterwards the leading ship made her way through the channel. 'Not a word was spoken throughout the ship save by the pilot and the helmsman, and their commands, being chanted in the same manner as the responses in a cathedral service, added to the solemnity.'[18]

Aroused by the drum beating to quarters, Midshipman Millard 'bustled on deck', passing 'the dreadful preparations of the surgeons'. One table was 'covered with instruments of all shapes and sizes,' he recalled, 'another, of more than usual strength, was placed in the middle of the cockpit: as I had never seen this before, I could not help asking the use of it, and received for answer "that it was to cut off arms and wings upon". One of the surgeon's men, called loblolly boys, was spreading yards and yards of bandages about six inches wide, which he told me was to clap on my back.'

Having examined the guns under his command, Millard reported to the first lieutenant, John Yelland, who had 'taken care to have the decks swept and everything clean and nice before we went into action. Yelland was dressed in full uniform with his cocked hat set on square, his shirt-frill stiff-starched, and his cravat tied tight under his chin.'[19]

24

Copenhagen

I really do not see the signal.

Before the morning of 2 April was long advanced it seemed that Foley's worst fears would be realized. The *Agamemnon* had run aground; so had the *Bellona*; while the *Russell*, endeavouring to follow the *Defiance* to her prescribed berth, lost sight of her in the thick gun smoke already heavy in the air, sailed after the *Bellona* instead and was herself soon stranded on the shoals. The other ships, anchoring by the stern as they reached their berths and presenting their broadsides to the Danish batteries, came under so unexpectedly fierce a fire that Admiral Parker began to wonder whether the fleet should be ordered to break off the action, though he could see little of it through the billowing smoke. Robert Southey was told by his brother, Tom, who was serving as a lieutenant in the *Bellona*, that Parker, having caught glimpses of two of Nelson's ships flying distress signals and another apparently run aground, said, 'I will make the signal for recall for Nelson's sake. If he is in a condition to continue the action he will disregard it; if he is not, it will be an excuse for his retreat, and no blame can be attached to him.' The flag-captain advised the Admiral not to send the signal yet, but to send Captain Otway of the *London* across to the *Elephant* to find out how desperate the situation was. But, before Otway reached the *Elephant*, Admiral Parker decided that the fire was 'too hot for Nelson to oppose' and ordered the signal to discontinue action to be made.

Aboard the *Elephant*, Nelson appeared to be relishing the excitement of the bombardment as the guns roared around him and the shot crashed through wood and canvas. 'It is warm work,' he said with a smile to Colonel Stewart as a shot from either the shore batteries or the Danish flagship, the *Dannebrog*, with which his own flagship was furiously engaged, struck the mainmast, scattering splinters about them. 'This day may be the last for us at any moment. But mark you,' he added, 'I would not be elsewhere for thousands.'[1] The *Elephant*'s signal lieutenant, Frederick Langford, his telescope trained on the Commander-in-Chief's flagship, saw Parker's Signal Number 39, signifying 'Discontinue action'. Langford called out to Nelson to report this signal; Nelson took no notice as though he had not heard; Langford shouted again. 'Mr Langford,' Nelson shouted back angrily, 'I told you to look out on the Danish commodore and let me know when he surrendered. Keep your eyes fixed on him.'

Langford bravely persisted: should he pass on the Commander-in-Chief's signal to the other ships? No, he should not; he was merely to acknowledge it. Was the *Elephant*'s own signal for close action still flying? Yes, said Langford, it was. 'Well, mind you keep it so.'

Nelson resumed his pacing up and down the deck, walking faster now, working the stump of his right arm, so Colonel Stewart noticed, a sure sign of his agitation. Suddenly he stopped and demanded 'in a quick manner', 'Do you know what's shown on board the Commander-in-Chief's? Number 39.' What did it mean, asked Stewart. 'Why to leave off action. Now damn me if I do.' Then turning to Foley, Nelson delivered himself of words which were to be repeated in various forms for generations to come, 'You know, Foley, I have only one eye. I have a right to be blind sometimes.' Raising the spyglass to his right eye, he added, 'I really do not see the signal.'

For nearly three hours now the bombardment had continued remorselessly in what Nelson called 'no manoevring . . . downright fighting'. Yet the Danes showed no signs of relaxing their efforts. Their gunners, killed or wounded in the batteries and in the Trekroner fort and aboard the ships, were replaced by reinforcements from the city. Nor had the fire from those British ships still capable of returning it slackened in the least. If two or three hours' bombardment was not enough, an army officer aboard the *Elephant* heard Nelson declare, then they must take four hours to do it.[2]

By two o'clock the rate of fire began to slow down. Several British ships were critically damaged; many of the Danes' floating batteries and hulks were smoking silently. The waters around both were littered with splintered debris and bodies floating face downwards amidst the wreckage. The Danish flagship, the *Dannebrog*, was burning fiercely, having slipped her moorings; members of her crew were throwing themselves into the sea to escape death in the imminent explosion. Yet when British boarding parties rowed towards ships which were thought to have surrendered they were fired on. Provoked by this, Nelson called for writing materials and, with the ship's purser by his side to take a copy, composed an ultimatum addressed to 'the Brothers of Englishmen the Danes':

Lord Nelson has directions to spare Denmark when no longer resisting; but if the firing is continued on the part of Denmark Lord Nelson will be obliged to set on fire all the floating batteries he has taken without having the power of saving the brave Danes who have defended them. Dated on board His Britannick Majestys ship *Elephant*, Copenhagen Roads, April 2nd, 1801.

> Nelson and Bronte, Vice admiral under the
> command of Sir Hyde Parker.[3]

Having signed his name, on which his pen spattered a blob of ink, he sent a sailor to the cockpit to fetch a candle and wax to make a seal. The sailor did not return. When he was told the man's head had been blown off by a cannon shot, Nelson merely ordered, 'Send another messenger for the wax.' Someone more daring than the others directed the Admiral's attention to a packet of wafers, one of which could perfectly well seal the missive. 'Send for the sealing-wax,' Nelson said again. At length the wax and candle were found, a large drop was dabbed on the folded sheet and Nelson pressed into it his own seal incised with his coat of arms. Colonel Stewart afterwards asked him why, 'under so hot a fire and after so lamentable an incident', he should have been so particular about the wax. 'Had I made use of a wafer,' Nelson replied, 'the wafer would have been still wet when the letter was presented to the Crown Prince; he would have inferred that the letter was sent off in a hurry; and that we had some very pressing reasons for being in a hurry. The wax told no tales.'[4]

The letter was handed to an officer who spoke Danish, Commander Frederick Thesiger, the son of a German who had settled in England and had become secretary to the Marquess of Rockingham. Thesiger took it ashore under a flag of truce tied to an oar and held aloft by a sailor in the *Elephant*'s gig. He handed it to the twenty-three-year-old Crown Prince Frederick, son of the mentally unstable King Christian VII who was married to the daughter of King George III's sister, Caroline Matilda.* The Crown Prince turned to an aide-de-camp, Hans Lindholm, whom he told to go over to the English flagship to ask Lord Nelson 'the particular object of sending his flag of truce'.

Nelson received Lindholm on the *Elephant*'s quarterdeck and asked him to put his question in writing. This Lindholm did, remarking in English as he did so on the bluntness of the quill he was offered. 'If your guns are no better pointed than your pens, you will make little impression on Copenhagen.' The guns, in fact, had already been silenced on both sides; and Nelson's written reply to Lindholm's note was friendly enough:

Lord Nelson's object in sending ashore a Flag of Truce is humanity: he therefore consents that hostilities shall cease ... Lord Nelson, with humble duty to His Royal Majesty, begs leave to say that he will ever esteem it the greatest victory he ever gained if this Flag of Truce may be the happy forerunner of a lasting and happy union between my most gracious Soverign and his Majesty the King of Denmark.[5]

If it could be called a victory it was one won at great cost. Most of the British ships were seriously damaged and six, including by now the *Elephant*, were aground. Almost a thousand sailors had been killed or wounded. Captain Mosse of the *Monarch* was dead; Captain Riou had been cut in half by a shot from the Trekroner fort; Captain Thompson of the *Bellona* – in which Tom Southey had been wounded – had lost his left leg.

Nelson, however, appeared in good spirits as he was rowed over

* He was to become King Frederick VI in 1808 and, as a consequence of this British bombardment, a supporter of Napoleon. Too faithful in this support, he was obliged to cede Norway to Sweden at the Peace of Kiel in 1814.

to the *London* to report to the Commander-in-Chief. 'I have fought contrary to orders,' he remarked insouciantly, 'and I shall perhaps be hanged. Never mind, let them.'[6]

Admiral Parker, who had not the least intention of taking him to task and was to praise his actions highly in his dispatch, greeted Nelson warmly; and suggested that, as the silencing of the Danish guns had been his doing, he should go to Copenhagen next day and conduct negotiations with Crown Prince Frederick for an extension of the truce. Tired as he was, Nelson agreed. He then returned to his ship to go to bed, not to the *Elephant*, in which the hammering of the carpenters would have kept him awake, but to his old flagship, the *St George*. Here, before climbing into his cot, he took up his pen to write to Lady Hamilton. Inscribing the sheet, 'St George, April 2nd, 1801, at 9 o'clock at night very tired after a hard fought battle', he reported, 'Of eighteen sail, large and small, some are taken, some sunk, some burnt, in the good old way.' He placed in the packet a verse headed, 'Lord Nelson to his Guardian Angel.'[7]

The next morning, Good Friday, Nelson was up early as usual and dressed for his encounter with the Crown Prince. Around him as he rowed over in his barge to the quay, sailors were already hard at work with hammer and bodkin, mending broken timbers and torn sails and rigging, clearing blood off decks with swabs soaked in vinegar. Danish prisoners were being distributed between the ships of the line beneath an overcast sky. Accompanied by the tall, bulky, reassuring figure of Captain Hardy, and the linguist Frederick Thesiger, he made his way to the rococo Amalienborg Palace, which had been built in the 1750s and occupied as a royal residence in 1796. A closed carriage and escort had been provided for him as it was feared he would be jeered or even assaulted by a populace which, as Colonel Stewart said, had never before seen a shot fired in anger in their native country. But Nelson preferred to walk past the crowds lining the Amaliegade, which leads up to the palace from Nyhavn, expecting to be well received. The people who had gathered to see him were, indeed, polite, if not as welcoming as Nelson reported them to be. Colonel Stewart was told they displayed 'an admixture of admiration, curiosity and displeasure'; while a Danish observer said that the English Admiral was received by the people 'neither with cheers nor murmurs – they did not degrade themselves with the former, nor disgrace themselves with the latter'.[8] Yet Captain Hardy reported that 'extraordinary to be told', Nelson 'was received with as much acclamation as when we went to the *Lord Mare's Show*',[9] while Nelson himself assured Troubridge that the crowds cheered him. 'My reception was too flattering,' he wrote, 'and landing at Portsmouth or Yarmouth could not have exceeded the blessings of the people.'[10] He said as much to Fremantle, who told his wife, 'He was received by the Multitude with Cheers and *Viva* Nelson. On his going to the Palace they were [even louder] in their Applause.'

Nelson reported the Crown Prince as being much put out by this; so also apparently was Graf von Bernstorff, the Foreign Minister. 'I hate the fellow,' Nelson decided after a few moment's conversation. He got on rather better with the Crown Prince, by whom he sat as guest of honour at a state banquet that evening. Nelson told him he had been in 105 engagements but that the bombardment the day before had been the most severe. Mostly he had fought against the French, who behaved well, but they could not have withstood for one hour what the Danes had endured yesterday for four.*

During the discussion that followed the meal, Nelson was firm but polite, once contradicting the Crown Prince sharply yet for the most part playing the part of the negotiator – which he admitted was 'out of my line' – with commendable skill. 'The more I see of his Lordship,' Hardy commented, 'the more I admire his great character, for I think his Political Management was *if possible*

---

* Thereafter Nelson often referred to the Battle of Copenhagen as the hardest he had fought, and was, accordingly, all the more bitterly disappointed by the government's declining to recognize his victory by the usual distribution of medals. Upon being congratulated by a fellow guest at a dinner on his victory in the Battle of the Nile, he replied, 'Poh, that was nothing. I always did beat the French, and I always will. But I have had a harder day since . . . at Copenhagen, that was a terrible day indeed' (Charles Heath, *The Excursion down the Wye from Ross to Monmouth* (1808), entry for 19 August 1802).

greater than his bravery.'[11] After two hours' conversation he left the Crown Prince with no doubt that the Danes must rescind the treaty with Russia or face the most indescribable consequences: Denmark must understand that their interests lay in friendship with Britain, not Russia.

For almost a week after his return to his ship Nelson was busily engaged in writing to London to report upon the progress of the negotiations. 'All here,' he said 'hang on my shoulders.' He was also busy supervising the removal of prizes, though this difficult operation came to an end when Admiral Parker, anxious about the possible arrival of a Swedish or Russian fleet – and having himself accumulated a very large amount of prize-money in a long career – decreed that all prizes must be burned with the exception of one which had been converted into a hospital ship and was to be sent to England.

On 9 April, taking with him an agreement which it was hoped the Danes would accept, Nelson went ashore again. This time he was accompanied by Colonel Stewart, Captains Foley and Fremantle, the Rev. Alexander John Scott, a convivial linguist who was the Commander-in-Chief's chaplain, and Edward Thornborough Parker, a young officer – prouder, so he said, to be called a Nelsonite than he would have been to be created a duke – whom Nelson had removed from his command of a sloop and appointed his aide-de-camp.

The discussions were held as before in the Amalienborg Palace and, although the Danish commissioners were perfectly friendly, the conference almost broke up over an article which provided for an armistice lasting as long as sixteen weeks. This term was essential, Nelson insisted with what Colonel Stewart called 'a candour not quite customary in diplomacy', because the British needed that length of time to deal with the Russian fleet before returning to Copenhagen Roads. This admission provoked one of the Danish commissioners to protest in French to a colleague that there would presumably be a renewal of hostilities. To the obvious consternation of the Dane, who had supposed that the English Admiral who could not speak French could not understand it either, Nelson exclaimed, 'Renew hostilities!' Then, turning sharply to the interpreter, he said, 'Tell him that we are ready at a moment; ready to bombard this very night.'[12]

He repeated the threat in different words and as a muttered comment to Stewart as they climbed the staircase to the palace dining-room, 'Though I have only one eye, I see all this will burn very well.'[13] He was clearly frustrated by the prolonged discussions, all the more so because it had been raining hard when he had been rowed over to the quay and his uniform was 'half-wet through'. During dinner, however, the atmosphere was more relaxed as the Danes and their guests talked of other things. Although, so Stewart supposed, 'thinking more about the bombardment than about dinner', Nelson joined in the general conversation. At one point he commented on the exploits of a young Danish officer whose courage made him worthy of promotion to the rank of admiral. 'If I were to make all my heroes admirals,' the Crown Prince replied, 'there would be no lieutenants or captains left.'[14]

After the meal the negotiations were resumed, and Nelson, in an effort to get the matter settled, offered to reduce the duration of the armistice from sixteen to fourteen weeks. This was accepted by the Danes and the armistice was signed at last.

'I received, as a warrior, all the praises which could gratify the ambitions of the vainest man and the thanks of the nation from the King downwards for my humanity in saving the town from destruction,' Nelson wrote to Lady Hamilton in self-congratulation. 'Nelson is a warrior, but will not be a butcher. I am sure, could you have seen the adoration and respect, you would have cried for joy; there are no honours can be conferred equal to this.'[15]

If only Admiral Parker would behave with as much forthright determination as himself! The Commander-in-Chief had at least consented to sail into the Baltic to see what could be done about the Swedes now that the Danes had been brought to heel. But, having got as far as the Swedish port of Karlskrona in Hanö Bay, he contented himself with sending a boat into the town to ask the Swedes to follow the Danish example; and then, instead of advancing north to deal with the Russians at Revel (Tallinn in Estonia), he brought the fleet back to Copenhagen, fearing that it would be foolhardy to leave the Swedes free to corner him in the eastern

Baltic and trusting that the recent assassination of the Tsar Paul I
in his bedchamber in the Mikhaylovsky Palace and the accession
of his son, Alexander I, might entail a reversal of Russian policy.

Nelson, who had chased after Parker in a boat when the *St
George* had been becalmed, had caught a chill in the process,
having refused the offer of a greatcoat with the characteristic
comment, 'My anxiety for my Country will keep me warm.'[16] A
cold struck me to the heart,' he told Lady Hamilton. 'I had one of
my terrible spasms of heart-stroke [and vomiting and I] brought
up what everyone thought was my lungs and I was emaciated
more than you can conceive.'[17]

The illness, severe though it was, was not prolonged; and, before
the end of the first week in May, he had recovered sufficiently to
make plans for sailing to Tallinn himself. He was now Commander-
in-Chief, having been appointed to succeed Sir Hyde Parker, who
had been recalled in disgrace. Nelson could not but feel sorry for
him. The old man was reported to be facing a court martial and
certainly he saw no more service and died a few years later in quiet
retirement. Nelson hoped he would not have to face a trial: his
friends in the fleet wished 'everything to be forgot'; yet, it had to
be said, 'the dearer his friends, the more uneasy they have been at
his *idleness*'. The new Commander-in-Chief asked Sir Hyde's
chaplain and interpreter, Alexander Scott, to come over to the *St
George*; but Scott was grateful to Parker for past kindnesses and
'could not bear to leave the old admiral at the very time when he
stood most in need of his company'.

Before leaving for England, Scott and Admiral Parker both
attended a party aboard the *St George* to celebrate Lady Hamilton's
thirty-sixth birthday, the 'Birthday of Santa Emma' as their host
called it in an unwelcome invitation dispatched to Thomas
Fremantle: 'If you don't come here on Sunday ... Damn me if I
ever forgive you.' A similar invitation was sent to Captain Foley:

Sunday the 26th being the birthday of our guardian angel Santa Emma,
whose prayers I can answer were offered to the throne of heaven both at
the Nile and on the 2nd for our success & it is my firm belief that they
had much more influence than any ever offered either to a heathen

goddess or any saint ever made by the best Pope, so it is our duty to express our gratitude were [sic] due, therefore I have to request that as her kindness was spread over you as well as all other your Med friends now in the fleet that you will be on board the St George on Sunday.[18]

He had already written to 'Santa Emma' to tell her about this party he was giving in her honour:

I am in expectation every moment for the removal of the fleet from the Baltic: be that as it may, I will not remain, *no* not if I was *sure* of being made a DUKE with £50,000 a year. I wish for happiness to be my *reward* and not titles or money. Tomorrow is the birthday of *Santa Emma*. She is my guardian angel ... I have invited the Admirals and all the Captains who had the happiness of knowing you and experiencing your kindness when in the Mediterranean. You may rely my saint is more adored than all the saints in the Roman Calendar. I know you prayed for me both at the Nile and here, and if the prayers of the good, as we are *taught* to believe, are of avail at the throne of Grace, why may not yours have saved my life? I own myself a BELIEVER IN GOD, and if I have any merit in not fearing death, it is because I feel that his power can shelter me when he pleases, and that I must fall whenever it is His good pleasure.[19]

The absent Emma, toasted in bumpers of champagne, seemed a ghostly presence in the Admiral's quarters on her birthday. The green morocco armchair had been chosen by her for the Admiral; the blue satin cushion was a present from her;[20] there were – as Queen Charlotte's brother, the Duke of Mecklenburg-Strelitz was later to notice when the *St George* put into Rostock – three portraits of her in the cabin; and there would have been a fourth had Colonel Stewart, who had taken a copy of the armistice back to London, been able as asked to bring back with him a picture of her as Saint Cecilia by George Romney.*

* This portrait, formerly hanging in the Palazzo Sessa, now in the Music Room at Kenwood and known as *Lady Hamilton at Prayer*, had been bought for Nelson by Alexander Davison for £300 at a sale of Sir William Hamilton's pictures in March. If the price had been 300 drops of blood Nelson would, he said, have given it with pleasure.

'My dearest beloved friend,' Nelson wrote to her while waiting for her picture to arrive.

A santa you are if ever there was one in this world . . . As truly as I believe in God do I believe you are a saint and in this age of wickedness you sett an example of real virtue and goodness . . . and may God's curse alight upon those who want to draw you my dearest friend from a quiet home into a company of men & women of bad character, and I am one of those who believe that in England the higher the class the worse the company . . . How can I sufficiently thank you for all your goodness & kindness to me a forlorn outcast except in your generous soul.[21]

Much to Nelson's disappointment, Colonel Stewart returned without the portrait. He explained he had had to leave London in a great hurry and had not even had time to pick up letters for Lord Nelson at the Hamiltons' Piccadilly house, let alone the Romney portrait. Nelson was also disappointed that the order for Admiral Parker's recall did not include permission for his own return to England, which he had requested of Lord St Vincent, believing that the fleet would not be required to fire another shot in the Baltic. His appointment as Parker's successor as Commander-in-Chief did not please him in the least; and in a series of letters to Alexander Davison he gave voice to his frustration:

I hope another admiral is on his way to superseed me for why am I here to die a natural death. I did not bargain for that when I came to the Baltic, it is now 16 days that I have not been able to get out of my cabin . . . I am very unwell . . . If I do not see you in 14 days probably I never may . . . Why have I been kept here, when for anything which could be known I ought long since to have been dead, unless indeed the Admiralty thought I had as many lives as a cat or was it a matter of indifference to them [whether] I lived or died . . . I am *used* and *abused* and so far from making money I am spending the little I have . . . The Baltic expedition cost me full 2000l. since I left London, it has cost me, for Nelson cannot be like others, near 1000l. in 6 weeks. If I am continued here ruin to my finances must be the the the consequence.[22]

In one of his replies, Davison informed him that he had heard that Nelson was to be rewarded for his important services at

Copenhagen with a mere viscountcy which he 'ought to have had long ago'. It was Davison's 'humble opinion' that 'any additional distinction short of an Earldom would be degrading'.[23] Nelson himself was not hopeful that justice would be done to him. 'We shall see whether the new Administration [that of Henry Addington] treats me as ill as the old,' he wrote to his brother Maurice. 'How they will manage about Sir Hyde I cannot guess. I am afraid much will be said about him in the public papers; but not a word shall be drawn from me, for God knows they may make him Lord Copenhagen, it will not offend me. I only want justice for myself which I have never had yet.'[24] 'I have given up in reason everything to my country,' he continued in another letter of complaint to Lady Hamilton, 'but the late Ministers have done less for me than any other man in my situation. The Commanders-in-Chief made fortunes by their victories, for which Ministers gave them 1,000 a year more than poor Nelson, higher title in the Peerage, and promoted their followers, whilst mine were all neglected, and now, what even the custom of the service and common justice gives me, is attempted to be withheld.'*[25]

Since he was obliged for the moment to be Parker's successor, Nelson determined to do what the old man had failed to do. As already planned, he sailed for the Russian base of Tallinn. Here he went ashore and, so he wrote with pride, 'hundreds came to look at Nelson, *"that is him, that is him,"* in short, 'tis the same as in Italy and Germany, and I feel that a good name is better than riches, not amongst our great folks in England; but it has its fine feelings to an honest heart. All the Russians have taken it into their heads that I am like *Suwaroff, Le jeune Suwaroff*' (Aleksandr Suvorov, the great Russian military commander to whom he certainly did bear some resemblance).[26]

---

* 'Nelson is made a viscount,' wrote Lady Malmesbury when the honour was confirmed. 'Sir Hyde passed over. The cause is supposed to be his having made repeated signals during the engagement to Nelson to desist in the attempt . . I feel very sorry for Sir Hyde; but no wise man would ever have gone with Nelson or over him, as he was sure to be in the background in every case' (Minto, iii, 219).

At Tallinn, however, he was handed a cross letter from the new Tsar, protesting that no discussions would be held with his Britannic majesty's representatives so long as his warships remained uninvited in Russian waters. Nelson's natural inclination was to order an immediate bombardment of the port. But, restraining this impulse, he returned a soft answer, and was gratified to learn soon afterwards that the Armed Neutrality of the North had been disbanded. He was even more gratified to be told, on his return to Copenhagen Roads on 12 June, that he might go home as soon as he was relieved by Vice-Admiral Charles Pole, whom he had first met when they were both young captains at Portsmouth.

A week later Admiral Pole arrived and Nelson prepared to depart. Before doing so he sent one of his stock of Nile medals to the commandant of the Danish Naval Academy with a 'short account' of his life. This brief biography, so he claimed in a covering letter which, were it not for the writer's lack of a sense of humour, might have been taken for self-parody, 'cannot do harm to youth and may do good, as it will show that perseverence and good conduct will raise a person to the very highest honours and rewards'. Perseverance, he had emphasized in his 'Sketch of My Life' which he had provided for his early biographer, John M'Arthur, would probably meet its reward in any profession. 'Without having any inheritance,' he wrote of his own case, 'or having been fortunate in prize money, I have received all the Honours of my Profession, been created a Peer of Great Britain, and I may say to the Reader, "Go thou and do likewise." '[27]

Nelson had already sent a present to the Hamiltons' house in Piccadilly, entrusting it to Captain William Bligh, formerly of the *Bounty* and the *Glatton*, now commanding the *Monarch*, an officer whose seamanship and worthy character were commended by Nelson in a covering letter. This present was one of Copenhagen porcelain and was sent in the hope that it would 'bring to your recollection that here your attached Nelson fought and conquered'.[28] Nelson himself left for England on 19 June, arriving in Yarmouth after an uneventful voyage on 1 July.

25

The Thames Valley and Boulogne

You will ... signify to Lady N. that I expect ... to be left to myself, and without any inquiries from her.

Immediately upon landing Nelson made his way to the naval hospital where a number of sailors brought home from Copenhagen were recovering from their wounds and amputations. One of the hospital's doctors, observing 'his demeanour to the sailors', paid tribute to the way in which he endeared himself to them. 'He stopped at every bed and to every man he had something kind and cheery to say.' The doctor recorded one characteristic exchange:

Nelson: 'Well, Jack what's the matter with you?'
Sailor: 'Lost my arm, your honour.'
Nelson [glancing down at his empty sleeve before turning again to the sailor]: 'Well, Jack then you and I are spoiled for fishermen; cheer up, my brave fellow.'[1]

Having distributed guineas to the nurses, he left for London in a post-chaise and stepped down at the door of Lothian's Hotel in Albemarle Street. There had been talk of his buying a house. A few weeks before his sister, Susannah Bolton, had written to Lady Nelson, who had never felt altogether at home with her sister-in-law,

Will you excuse what I am going to say? I wish you had continued in town a little longer, as *I have heard* my Brother regreted he had not a house he could call his own when he returnd. Do, whenever you hear he is likely to return, have a house to receive him. If you should absent yourself entirely from him, there can never be a reconcilliation ... I hope in God I shall have the pleasure of seeing you together as happy as ever. He certainly, as far as I hear, is not a happy man.[2]

Lady Hamilton had heard rumours that his wife was, indeed, looking out for a house for them; but this was strongly denied by Nelson, who had already written to Davison to complain of such 'nonsensical reports'.[3] Writing now to Lady Hamilton as the sailor 'Thompson', he assured her that he had never written to 'his aunt' since he sailed, 'and all about the house is nonsense. He has written to his father, but not a word or message to her. He does not, nor cannot, care about her; he believes she has a most unfeeling heart.'[4]

He had made it clear to Alexander Davison that he did not want to hear from his wife when he returned to England. 'You will,' he instructed him,

at a proper time, and before my arrival in England, signify to Lady N. that I expect, and for which I have made such a very liberal allowance for her [£1,600 a year], to be left to myself, and without any inquiries from her; for sooner than live the unhappy life I did when I last came to England, I would stay abroad for ever. My mind is as fixed as fate; therefore you will send my determination in any way you think proper.[5]

He was true to his word. When his wife wrote to congratulate him on his victory, to 'intreat' him to believe that 'no wife ever felt greater affection for a husband' than she did, to assure him that she had tried 'invariably' to do everything he desired, and to say that she was sorry if she had not, he did not bother to reply to her letter.[6] She tried again a few months later:

My dear Husband, It is some time since I have written to you. This silence you have imposed is more than my affections will allow me and in this instance I hope you will forgive me in not obeying you ... Do my dear husband, let us live together. I assure you again I have but one wish in the world to please you. Let everything be buried in oblivion it will pass away like a dream. I can now only intreat you to believe I am most sincerely and affectionately your wife, Frances H. Nelson.

The letter was returned to her marked 'opened by mistake by Lord Nelson but not read'.[7]

His father was deeply distressed by the failure of his son's marriage and all the talk about his liaison with the Hamiltons. He wrote to his son to say that he had received the 'joyous news' of the Copenhagen victory, but 'all things have their alloy': Lady Nelson was 'heavily affected with her personal feelings at not receiving a line from your own hand'. Other members of their family were less upset. Nelson's sister-in-law, Sarah, now stood firmly in Lady Hamilton's camp and was made much of there as an extremely useful and respectable chaperone. His sister, Susannah Bolton, had also forsaken Lady Nelson and wrote disparagingly of her to Lady Hamilton: 'A *certain* lady is at Bath so *condescendingly humble* to those who formerly she would not *notice*, all to *be thought* amiable.'[8] Even Kitty was soon to write to Lady Hamilton, 'I have seen Tom Tit once. She called in her carriage at Lady Charlotte Drummond's, who lives next door. The lady was not at home, but she got out of her carriage, walked stiff as a poker about half a dozen steps, turned round, and got in again. What this Manoeuvre was for I cannot tell, unless to show herself. She need not have taken so much pains if nobody wanted to see her [any] more than I do. She is stiffer than ever.' Kitty was to assure Horatia that her father's separation from his wife was Lady Nelson's fault; and Horatia herself commented, 'He was treated with coldness by his wife. His home was not made happy . . . He felt the want of someone to love and be loved by in return.'[9]

Nelson's family was shrinking; so were the number of his old friends. William Locker, who, had been in poor health for some time, had died the previous Boxing Day, while Lieutenant-Governor of Greenwich hospital. William Suckling had died the year before; so had Lord Howe. Maurice Nelson who, after working so long as a clerk in the Navy Office, was at last, thanks to his brother's influence, on the point of taking up duties as a commissioner of the Customs and Excise, had died that April of what was called 'a brain fever', leaving a middle-aged and nearly blind mistress, Mrs Sarah Ford, upon whose behalf Nelson, remembering his brother's past kindnesses, wrote to Davison, asking him to do what he could, and be as liberal as he could, for the poor woman.*

* Like the rest of his family, Maurice had been much disappointed when Nelson had not been granted the expected viscountcy after the Battle of the Nile. Lady

I have heard of the death of my Dear Brother Maurice. As the dead cannot be called back it is no use dwelling on those who are gone. I am sure you will do everything which is right for his poor blind wife . . . for such I shall always call her . . . I hope he has left her well provided for if not I beg you will take the trouble to arrange a proper & ample subsistance and I will make it up, it is the only true regard I can pay to his memory he was always good & kind to me . . . I am very unwell since April 27.[10]

Nelson wrote also to 'poor Blindy' himself, urging her to stay on at Maurice's house 'with horses, wiskey . . . and every convenience to make your stay comfortable'. 'By Michaelmas,' he added, 'you can determine as to the mode and manner of your future residence. Nothing, be assured, shall be wanting on my part to make your life as comfortable and cheerful as possible.'[11] He sent her £100 and also took the trouble to provide for Maurice's black servant, James Price, 'as good a Man as ever lived', as he described him. 'He shall be taken care of and have a Corner in my house as long as he lives.'[12]

This generosity was characteristic. The daughter of the vicar of the parish in which he was soon to live told Sir Harris Nicolas, 'I cannot refrain from telling you of Lord Nelson's unlimited charity and goodness. His frequently expressed desire was that none in that place should want, or suffer affliction that he could alleviate; and this I know he did with a most liberal hand, always desiring it should not be known from whence it came.'[13]

To his family he was equally generous. 'My small income shall always be at [his sister Kitty's] service,' he had told his brother William in his bachelor days, 'and she shall never want a protector and sincere friend while I exist.'[14] To his other sister, Susannah

---

Nelson told Lord Hood that when Nepean called him in to tell him that 'his brother was to be created a baron – he was so much hurt and surprised that he never made any reply, but bowed and took his leave' (Naish, 458). It was not, of course, that Maurice wanted any honours for himself. 'William may have all the Honours,' he had written. 'It will be my wish and request to my Brother not to put my Name in the patent . . . I move in too humble a sphere to think of such a thing' (Llangattock Papers, E.667).

Bolton, he made an allowance of £100 a year for her children's education and helped to pay her son Tom's fees at Cambridge, to which he went after Norwich Royal Grammar School.[15]

Deeply saddened by his brother's death, Nelson was also dispirited by the reception he was accorded in London. Bombarding the Danes at anchor was clearly not to be considered a victory to be compared with that won over the French at the Nile. The King evidently did not think it so. 'Lord Nelson, do you get out?' he asked when the Admiral attended a levee at St James's Palace. Nelson was, he confessed, 'tempted to say, "Sir, I have been out and come in again. Your Majesty has perhaps not heard of Copenhagen?"'[16]

On hearing this story, Lady Elizabeth Foster commented:

This truly great hero has his weaknesses, but his love of praise has led to such glorious actions to obtain it that one must forgive him, and his love for Lady Hamilton I feel inclined to excuse also. She was beautiful when he first saw her, and he thought that she had contributed to his glory by influencing the Court of Naples to give him those supplies that enabled him to go and attack the French at Aboukir – from that moment Lady Hamilton was associated with all his ideas of Victory and triumph. She fed his vanity by every art that could gratify it. Crawford described how she sat by him and said, 'I would wish with all my heart to die in two hours, so I might be your wife for one.' Nelson, delighted, kissed her hand; and it is by this enthusiasm that she keeps up his love and vanity.[17]

At the Hamiltons' house in Piccadilly, he was given a far warmer welcome than he had received at court and just such a one as Lady Elizabeth might have expected. The news from Copenhagen had so excited the lady of the house that she had sprung from the dining-table and, while one of her guests, the Admiral's parson brother, had performed a jig about the room, she had danced a tarantella with her husband, then with the duca di Noja and, when he was worn out, with selected servants, including Fatima, the lively Nubian maid. 'It would be difficult to convey any idea of this dance,' commented one of the guests, Sir Nathaniel Wraxall. 'We must recollect that the two performers are supposed to be a Satyr and a Nymph, or, rather, a Fawn and a Bacchante.

It was certainly not of a nature to be performed except before a select company as the screams, attitudes, starts and embraces with which it was intermingled gave it a peculiar character.'[18]

After a few days in London, Nelson left with the Hamiltons and young Captain Parker, the ever-attentive aide-de-camp, for a holiday in the country, moving from inn to inn as fancy dictated, and paying a visit to 'Poor Blindy' at Laleham. They spent a week or so at the Fox and Hounds between Dorking and Walton on the Hill, then went on to the Bush at Staines, where Sir William fished in the Thames and Nelson's brother William joined them and, in his loud voice and boisterous manner, plagued the Admiral to use his influence to get him a canonry or even a deanery, giving rise to a verse by a mutual friend, Lord William Gordon:

> But, to return to this same worthy Vicar,
> Who loves, you say, good eating and good liquor,
> Know, Lady, that it is our earnest wish,
> That we, ere long, may greet him – Lord Archbish:
> For this, no common pains, or I'm mistaken,
> Our best of friends, the Duke [Nelson], hath lately taken,
> And, if a mitre fall not on his head
> Justice and gratitude are gone to bed!*[19]

* The Rev. William Nelson had for a long time persistently pressed both his brother and Lady Hamilton to use their influence to gain his preferment. 'A Prebend in *any* Cathedral and of *almost any* value is my wish,' he had written to his brother in one characteristic letter in 1797. 'When I say a Prebend I mean a Presidentiary, for there are many *Prebends* which are not *Presidentiaries* & have only a small stipend of ten or twenty pounds a year & no stall, they are not what I mean; it must be a *Stall* . . . and *larger* of income the better. I have some notion there is one *now* vacant at Rochester . . . but Bristol, Worcester, Gloucester or any other would not be refused by me. I am confident you have sufficient interest' (Llangattock Papers, E. 656, 30 Nov. 1797). To Lady Hamilton, who declared that he 'ought to be in the palace of Lambeth', William wrote, '*Now* we have secured the Peerage, we have only *one* thing to ask, and that is, my promotion in the Church, handsomely and honourably, such as becomes Lord Nelson's brother and heir apparent to the title. No put off with small beggarly stalls. Mr Addington must be kept steady to that point' (Pettigrew, ii, 153). The Admiral did his best for his brother, but did not hide his irritation from Lady Hamilton. 'I have a letter from William – he is as big as if he was a Bishop . . . I hope you

The jaunts of the party travelling about in Surrey and the Thames Valley did not, of course, escape the notice of the press. 'The gallant Lord Nelson,' ran one report, 'the terror of the French, Spaniards and the Danes, is now amusing himself with Sir William and Lady Hamilton at *catching gudgeons* at Shepperton.' Nelson's father, distressed by such reports and innuendoes, came to see his son on his way back to Burnham Thorpe and distressed him in turn by his obvious sympathy for the plight of his neglected daughter-in-law.

The holiday was brought to a sudden end when Nelson, who later assured Lady Hamilton that he would 'never forget' their happiness together at Laleham, was recalled to his duties.[20] There were growing fears that Bonaparte was planning an invasion of England: large numbers of ships and landing-craft were being assembled off the French coast under the command of one of France's most enterprising naval officers, Rear-Admiral Louis de la Touche-Tréville, and a formidable army, which some reports put at 40,000 strong, was being assembled around Flushing and in the Pas de Calais. Nelson was required to take command of a squadron being formed to protect the English shores from Suffolk to Sussex against the French wherever they might try to land. Lord St Vincent had amused his fellow-countrymen by declaring, 'I do not say that the French cannot come. I only say they cannot come by sea.' Nelson's duty was to ensure that the First Lord's assurance was justified.

Hoisting his flag at first in a frigate, captured from the French, the *Unité*, then in the *Medusa*, he confidently informed the government that, although in calm weather the enemy, crowded into numerous landing-craft, might row across the Channel in twelve hours, making for beaches on either side of Dover, they would not get through. The fleets of the enemy would 'meet the same fate which [had] always attended them'.

---

ordered something good for him, those bigwigs love eating and drinking . . . He has not patience, and now thinks that what would have satisfied him before, and which he has neither got, or is likely to get, is not worth his acceptance' (*Nelson's Letters to Lady Hamilton*, 40; Pettigrew, ii, 101; NMM CRK 18/251). Eventually, in May 1803, William Nelson was appointed to a prebendal stall at Canterbury.

Edward Parker testified to the energy he displayed and the sense of urgency and confidence he instilled in the ships under his command, giving orders, reading reports, making his rounds, and, though 'half sea-sick', writing replies to letters of which, so he told Lady Hamilton, he received over a hundred in a single day. 'Not one moment I have to myself,' he told her. 'My business is endless.' Even so, she would hear from him 'every day if possible'. 'I feel all the affection which it is possible for man to feel towards *Woman* and such a Woman . . . Be where I may you are always present in my thoughts not another thing except the duty I owe my Country ever interferes with you, you absorb my whole soul.'[21]

Three days after this letter was written, on 1 August 1801, Nelson made a reconnaissance of the French coast around Boulogne, sending in his bomb-ketches to throw a few shells into the assembled brigs and gunboats by way of warning. Two days later a crowd standing on the cliffs of Dover cheered at the sight of some of Nelson's ships engaging the enemy.

The Admiral was, however, anxious to deal the French a blow more crippling than such insignificant strikes as these. He proposed an attack upon the French fleet and port at Flushing and, when he was told by the Admiralty that the currents and sandbanks of the Scheldt estuary made this too risky an enterprise, he put forward plans for a night attack on the French ships moored at Boulogne. This was to be launched by fifty-seven boats, mostly flat-boats armed with howitzers or carronades, divided into four divisions. While the sailors from two boats from each division cut through the cables of the enemy ships, which were then to be brought away as prizes or burned, other sailors and marines would board the ships and attack the crews with musket fire and bayonets, cutlasses, pikes and even tomahawks. The Admiral stamped the bold plan as his own by decreeing that the password would be 'Nelson' and the answer 'Bronte'. But it was not a well-conceived plan: and in the event the tides ran too fast for the assault craft to maintain their positions, some boats being swept a long way past Boulogne by the strong current, while the French Admiral had taken precautions against such an attack upon his fleet by reinforcing his crews with soldiers armed with muskets, by mooring his ships with chain cables which the British sailors could not cut through with their axes, and by hanging heavy nets between the yards and the gun-wales of the ships to prevent landing parties clambering on deck.

The attack was, accordingly, a disastrous failure. Forty-five lives were lost, including those of several promising young officers, and nearly 130 sailors and marines were wounded. Among the wounded was 'dear little Parker'.

Nelson – while acknowledging that 'no person [could] be blamed' for authorizing the attack other than himself – suggested that the result would have been different had he led the attack in person;[22] but the 'personal exertions of a vice-admiral', he had promised Lady Hamilton, were not necessary for 'services on this coast'. He might also with truth have acknowledged that had his thoughts been less occupied with 'Fair Emma, Good Emma, Great Emma, Virtuous Emma,' his 'own dear friend Emma,' he might, perhaps, have been able to plan the attack with more concentrated care. It had, though, been difficult to concentrate when visions of Emma kept rushing into his mind. 'My heart is ready to flow out of my eyes,' he had written to her a week or so before. 'Who can tell what passes in my mind? Yes, you can; for I believe you are feeling as I do.' He supposed being at sea made their separation seem all the more terrible, for 'terrible it is'. His thoughts turned constantly to the prospect of being with her ashore. She must look out for a house where they could be happy together; in the meantime she must take lodgings at Dover, Deal or Margate, at any port along the Kentish coast where he might be alone with her for a few hours. 'What place would you like to come to, Margate or Deal? ... The Three Kings [at Deal], I am told, is the best house (it stands on the beach) if the noise of constant surf does not disturb you ... You can bathe in the sea, that will make you strong and well ... [there were bathing machines to be hired on the beach]. Your interest with Sir William is requested to come and see a poor forlorn sailor.' A few hours before the ill-fated attack upon Boulogne he had written:

From my heart I wish you could find me a good comfortable home, I should hope to be able to purchase it. At this moment I can command

£3,000; as to asking Sir William, I could not do it; I would sooner beg
. . . You may fairly calculate £2,000 for furniture . . . As you may
believe, my dear Emma, my mind reels at which is going forward this
night . . . After they have fired their guns, if one half of the French do not
jump overboard and swim on shore, I will venture to be hanged . . . If
our people behave as I expect, our loss cannot be much. My fingers itch
to be at them. What place would you like to come?[23]

After the defeat at Boulogne, he was stung by the comments of
contributors to the *Naval Chronicle*, a journal illustrated with prints
and largely composed of articles written by serving naval officers.
In the number which appeared at this time there were veiled hints
that Nelson should have directed the operation personally. In
another an old salt was depicted as asking a fellow Greenwich
pensioner, 'I say, Ben, do you know who this Bronte is that Nelson
has got hold on?' 'No, I don't,' the other replies. 'All I can say is
that he is a d—d fool, begging his pardon, for *taking a partner*, for,
depend on it, no one will ever do so well as Nelson himself.'[24]

Nelson, as he told Emma, longed to mount another attack on
the French to make amends for this failure, to pay them the 'debt
of a drubbing', though how or where this was to be done it was
impossible for 'mortal man to say'. In the meantime he had
funerals to attend and wounded men to visit. For Parker and the
other young wounded officer, Frederick Langford, who had been
with him in the *Elephant* at Copenhagen, he took rooms in a
lodging-house in Deal, where he went to see them twice a day.
'How is it possible for me ever to be sufficiently thankful for all his
attentions,' Parker told Lady Hamilton. 'He is now attending me
with the most parental kindness; comes to me at six in the morning
and ten at night . . . I would lose a dozen limbs to serve him . . .
my friend, my nurse, my attendant, my protector.' Nelson seemed
almost distracted by the suffering of the young man, who clung to
his hand and said he could not bear him to leave him and 'cried
like a child'. On returning to his ship, Nelson felt the need for
Lady Hamilton's comforting presence more sharply than ever. 'I
came on board,' he told her, 'but no Emma. No, no, my heart will
break. I am in silent distraction. My dearest wife, how can I bear

our separation? Good God! What a change. I am so low that I cannot hold up my head.'[25]

Frederick Langford survived, but Parker, who was only twenty-two, did not. 'His thigh very much shattered', he had to suffer the agonies of having a gangrenous leg amputated. 'The operation was long, painful and difficult ... his groans were heard far off.' If Nelson had been his father, he 'could not have suffered more'. Towards the end he could not bring himself to see 'Dear Good Little Parker' in his agony; and when told of his death, he felt his heart was 'almost broke'. He slept 'not a wink' that night, and the next morning was 'very low' and miserable, 'grieved almost to death'. He asked for some of the young man's hair so that it could be buried with him and for long afterwards sealed his letters with black wax.[26]

The young man's father, a mealy-mouthed sponger, turned out to be 'a very different person from his son', Nelson observed. 'He has £72 more in his pocket than when he came to Deal ... He is worse than a public thief ... I wish for his own sake that his conduct had been more open and generous, like mine to him ... I am so vexed that he should have belonged to our dear Parker!'[27]

The young man's funeral, conducted to the sound of minute guns and muffled drums, was the saddest of ceremonies. Nelson, who had been seen with tears in his eyes at the burials of other men, was overcome by grief, weeping openly at the graveside, supporting himself with his hand on the trunk of a tree.[28]

He had been frequently depressed that summer and autumn. 'Tis but a life of sorrow and sadness,' he had lamented on one occasion. 'I am really this day very low indeed,' he had confessed to Lady Hamilton on another. He had felt that St Vincent and Troubridge were conspiring at the Admiralty to keep him away from her by objecting to his going to London to be with her, even for a short visit. St Vincent had told him that since 'the public's mind [was] so very much tranquillis'd' by his being at his post, it was 'extremely desirable' that he should continue there. Troubridge agreed; and – so Nelson commented bitterly of an old friend who had taken Lady Nelson's part – Troubridge would. It was 'all his doing'; he and St Vincent were both 'so cruel as to object to [his

going to London]'. He had 'dreadful pains' in his teeth, he told
Lady Hamilton, and a terrible cold which had settled in his
bowels. 'I wish the Admiralty had my complaint; but they have no
bowels; at least for me . . . what a set of beasts . . . None of them
cares a damn for me or my sufferings.'[29]

At least a house had been found. There had been talk of one at
Turnham Green of which Lady Hamilton was to 'have the whole
arrangement'; but then they had heard of a property at Merton in
Surrey which was almost as convenient for the Admiralty and
even more so for the Portsmouth road.

17. A drawing by Rowlandson showing Nelson with bandaged head celebrating the victory off the mouth of the Nile with the seamen of the *Vanguard*

18. The chaplain of the *Vanguard* preaching to Nelson, his officers and the crew of the ship after the Battle of the Nile

19. *Extirpation of the Plagues of Egypt*, James Gillray's caricature depicting Nelson cleansing the mouth of the Nile of its weeping, tricoloured crocodiles

20. (*opposite above*) James Gillray's caricature of the resplendent Hero of the Nile, who wears the star of the Order of the Bath beneath 'the pelisse of the finest scarlet cloth' and, in his hat, the *chelengk* awarded him by the Sultan. In the burlesqued arms, in place of proper emblems, Gillray has drawn a full purse and a scroll reading '£2000 pr Ann'

21. (*opposite*) James Gillray's caricature, *Dido in Despair*, shows the tear-stained Lady Hamilton rising from the bed in which her elderly husband is still asleep, and lamenting the departure of the fleet seen through the open window. Below her outstretched foot is a garter inscribed 'The Hero of the Nile'; on the floor are objects from Sir William Hamilton's collection, including statues of Venus and a satyr and a figure of a headless monster, the base inscribed 'Pri[apus]'

The HERO of the NILE.

Portraits of eight of Nelson's fellow sea officers:

22. John Jervis, Earl of St Vincent, from the studio of Lemuel Abbott

23. Cuthbert, Lord Collingwood, by Henry Howard

24. Sir Thomas Masterman Hardy, by Domenico Pellegrini

25. Sir Thomas Troubridge, by Sir William Beechey

26. Sir Hyde Parker, by George Romney

27. Sir Thomas Fremantle, from an engraving after Edmund Bristow

28. Sir Thomas Foley, by Henry Edridge

29. Sir William Beatty, by Arthur Devis

30. Nelson deep in thought in his cabin before the Battle of Trafalgar, from an engraving by C. W. Sharp after the painting by Charles Lucy

31. Lord Nelson's funeral procession passing the Royal Naval Hospital, Greenwich, from a drawing made by C. A. Pugin, a witness of the scene

32. The interment of Lord Nelson beneath the dome of St Paul's Cathedral on 9 January 1806, from a lithograph by C. A. Pugin

33. Lady Hamilton as Britannia crowning a bust of Lord Nelson, from the painting by Thomas Baxter

26

Merton Place

None of the great shall enter our peaceful abode. I hate them all.

Merton was a village on the river Wandle which had been celebrated in the Middle Ages for its large Augustinian priory where Thomas Becket and Walter de Merton, Chief Justice of England and founder of Merton College, Oxford, had both been educated. The house, Merton Place, just to the south of what is now Merton High Street, had been built in 1690. It was a neoclassical house on two floors approached by a drive which crossed an ornamental canal by way of an attractive single-span bridge with ironwork railings. On the other side of the road were stables partially concealed by shrubberies. There was work to be done both to the house and grounds: an underpass would have to be built beneath the road to connect the house with its outbuildings; and the ground-floor rooms, while large enough, would have to be made to appear more spacious, Lady Hamilton decided, by adding windows opening on to the garden. The parlours must have verandas, and interior doors would have to be fitted with looking-glass. Lady Hamilton was also to install new kitchens, new bathrooms and several modern water closets.[1]

The place was being offered furnished for £9,000. This, roughly equivalent to £550,000 today, was a good deal more than Nelson had intended to pay, having regard to the many and expensive improvements Lady Hamilton had in mind. But, since she so warmly recommended it, he did not hesitate, agreeing to offer the price asked without attempting to negotiate a lower one, making arrangements for a surveyor to inspect it, and instructing his solicitor to settle with the vendor for a down payment of £3,000 and the remaining £6,000 in two instalments within three years.

'The place I wish much to have,' he told Haslewood, the solicitor, 'and sailor-like a few pounds more or less is no object. I never knew much got by hard bargains . . . I approve of the Gentleman's plan that went to see an estate, bought it as it stood, Dinner on Table, the former owner sat as his guest.'[2] The purchase would severely strain his resources, since his expenses of late had been very heavy, much being expected of him, it being a well-known fact, as he sardonically observed, that Nelson was *'amazingly rich'*.[3] His anxiety to settle down with the Hamiltons on what he called his 'farm' overcame all prudence, however; and, if the worst came to the worst, he could rely upon the generosity of Alexander Davison, who had offered to lend him any sum he needed. 'Can your offer be real?' Nelson had replied facetiously to this munificence. 'Can Davison be uncorrupted by the Depravity of this world. I almost doubt what I read; I will answer, my dear friend, you are the only person living who would make such an offer . . . When you come down you shall know all my pecuniary affairs and if in arranging them I should want your kind assistance I will accept it with many thanks.'[4]

If only, he thought, his 'lords and masters' at the Admiralty were as generous and understanding. But they seemed determined to keep him afloat: 'What a set of beasts.'[5] The refusal to grant a medal for the victory over the Danish fleet constantly rankled, fuelling his resentment. He would rather have that medal than be created a duke, he told St Vincent. But the medal was not forthcoming. 'For what reason,' he commented bitterly, 'Lord St Vincent knows.'[6]

His application for leave on the grounds of ill health had been met by Troubridge's advice to wear flannel next to his skin. 'Does he care for me?' he asked rhetorically, knowing how strongly his erstwhile friend, whom he had once described as 'the very best sea officer in His Majesty's Service', disapproved of his relationship with Lady Hamilton.[7] '*No*; but never mind.' All the same, 'he ought to have recollected that I got him the medal of the Nile,' he told Emma. 'Who brought his character into notice? . . . Who placed him in such a situation that he got by my public letters, *Titles, the Colonelcy of Marines, Diamond Boxes*, 1000 ounces in money for *no* expenses that I know of? Who got him £500 a year from the King of Naples? ... Nelson, that he now *lords* it over. So much for gratitude. I forgive him but, by God, I shall not forget it.'⁸ 'I left Lord Nelson three days ago very much displeased with the Admiralty for refusing him leave of absence,' Captain Hardy commented. 'But I think [they] seem Determined to oppose him in every thing he wishes. I begin to think Ld. St V. wishes to Clip his Wings a little & certainly has succeeded a little in the affair of Boulogne. Troubridge like a true Politician forsakes his old friend who has procured him all the Honors he has got.'⁹

William Pitt, who had recently been obliged to resign as Prime Minister over his thwarted intention of bringing in a Relief Bill for the benefit of Irish Roman Catholics and had become Master-General of the Ordnance in Henry Addington's new administration, offered Nelson his sympathy and agreed that it did seem 'very hard' that he should be kept at sea, now that the war was, for the time being anyway, almost over.¹⁰

'I should have got well long ago in a warm room, with a good fire and sincere friends,' Nelson complained. As it was he had got a nasty cold, was seasick on and off in the cold cabin of his lurching frigate, and was troubled by dreadful toothache. Also, as he told Emma gloomily, he could not get his bowels in order and was occasionally feverish. He sometimes felt he would never get warm again: he could not feel his pen. Pitt had asked him to dine at Walmer but, as he told Emma, 'I refused, I will dine nowhere till I dine with you ... for ever my Dearest only friend ... If I am cross you must forgive me I have reason to be so by Great Troubridge.'¹¹

He had more than his health to worry about. The terms which the government were negotiating with the French seemed to him outrageously advantageous to the enemy. What had England been fighting for all this time? 'Although it is peace, I wish all Frenchmen to the devil.' Then there was his constant fretting about what people were saying about his failure at Boulogne, the heavy casualties suffered there. 'A diabolical spirit is still at work,' he wrote to the Admiralty.

Every means, even to posting up papers in the streets of Deal, has been used to set the seamen against being sent by Lord Nelson to be butchered ... At Margate it was the same thing, whenever any boats went on shore, '*What*, are you going to be slaughtered again?' ... The subject has been fully discussed in the wardrooms, midshipmen's berths, etc ... I must probably be, from all the circumstances I have stated, not much liked by either officers or men ... I really think it would be better to take me from this Command.[12]

His thoughts kept returning to the house at Merton and the worrying cost of buying and running it. The surveyor's report had been damning: the place was 'very slightly built'; an 'old paltry, small dwelling', it was in poor repair and had not 'the least privacy as a place for pleasure'. Public roads surrounded it; the grounds were 'worn and out of condition', and through them ran 'a dirty, black-looking canal' which kept the whole place damp; indeed, all in all, it was the worst place that the surveyor had ever seen 'pretending to suit a gentleman's family'. But Emma had set her heart on it, and if 'after all [his] labour for the Country', he could not 'get such a place as this', he was 'resolved to give it all up and retire for life'. Emma was to be 'Lady Paramount of all the territories and waters of Merton,' he told her, 'and we are all to be your guests and obey all lawful commands.' He was to own everything in the house, since he refused to approach Sir William for anything other than his share of household expenses when the time came. 'To you I may say that my soul is too big for my purse, but I do earnestly request that all may be mine, even to a pair of sheets, towels, etc.' He made it clear that he did not want to give house room to any of Sir William's books or, indeed, servants. He left her to deal with the lawyers and the agents and with the owner, who seemed reluctant to move out. Yet he bombarded her with instructions: she was to take care he was not cheated; she must have netting put along the banks of the canal so that Horatia did not fall in; the canal must be stocked with fish, and she must be careful what kind of fish she put in, since, as Sir William would tell her, 'one sort destroys the other'.[13] Emma must also 'take care not to be beset' by discharged seamen, since 'every beggar will find out your soft heart and get into your house'. She was also, of course, to keep out the Prince of Wales. 'I am sure you will not let any of royal blood into your house,' he told her in one letter; 'they have the impudence of the devil.' 'We will eat plain, but will have good wine, and a hearty welcome for all our friends,' he wrote in another. 'None of the great shall enter our peaceful abode. I hate them all ... But let us turn our thoughts to the dear farm Whatever you do about it will be right and proper ... We can get rid of bad furniture and buy others, all will probably go to Bronte one of these days.'[14]

'I admire the pigs and poultry,' he continued in yet another long letter. 'Sheep are certainly most beneficial to eat off the grass ... I intend to have a farming book ... I expect all the animals will increase where you are, for I never expect you will suffer any to be killed ... Take care that they are kept on the premises all night, for that is the time they do good to the land ... Have we got a nice church at Merton? We shall set an example of goodness to the under-parish ... We shall employ the tradespeople of our village in preference to any others [he was later to learn their pleasantly rustic names – Greenfield, the butcher, Peartree, the stable-keeper, Woodman, the chandler, Wyld, the cheesemonger, Mr Stone, the brandy merchant, and Mr Foottit 'for malt, hops, etc.'] and give them every encouragement to be kind and attentive to us.'[15]

A letter from Sir William, written a few days after he and his wife moved into the house, reassured him of his choice, despite the surveyor's opinion:

We have now inhabited Your Lordship's premises some days & I can now speak with some certainty. I have lived with our dear Emma some several years. I know her merits, have an opinion of the head & heart that God Almighty has been pleased to give her; but a seaman alone could have given a fine woman full power to chuse and fit up a residence for him without seeing it himself. You are in luck, for, on my conscience, I verily believe that a place so suitable to your views could not have been found & at so cheap a rate ... The proximity of the capital and the perfect retirement of this place are for your Lordship, two points beyond estimation . . . You have nothing but to come and enjoy it immediately. You have a good mile of pleasant dry walk around your farm. It would make you laugh to see Emma & her mother fitting up pig-sties and hen-coops and already the canal is enlivened with ducks and the cock is strutting with his hens along the walks. Your Lordship's plan as to stocking the Canal is exactly mine. I will answer for it, that in a few months you may command a good dish of fish at a moment's warning.[16]

Evidently encouraged by this letter, Nelson wrote to Emma excitedly telling her how they would take a boat on this canal which he called 'the Nile', the name which was also given – in its Latin form – to a little dog, a present for Emma. 'How I should laugh to see you, my dear friend, rowing in a boat: the beautiful Emma rowing a one-armed Admiral in a boat it will certainly be caricatured. Well done, farmer's wife I'll bet your turkey against Mrs Nelson's.'[17]

More than once in the recent past, he had written of the possibility of their one day leaving Merton for Bronte and he had sent William Hoste with a frigate to Sicily carrying a cargo of what Hoste called 'ploughs, harrows and garden stuff'. But now all his thoughts and hopes for the future were centred upon Merton. He longed to see the place; and one October morning at eight o'clock he did. Emma was overjoyed. 'He is better than I expected in looks,' she told Sarah, her sister-in-law. 'We are all so joyous, we do not know what to do. Believe me, my heart is all convulsed seeing him again *safe on shore*, safely *moored with we* – I must not say *me*.'[18] It had been intended that the horses would be taken out of his carriage and that he would be drawn to his house by the men of the village through a triumphal arch; but he had arrived earlier than expected and there was no one there to welcome him. The coach-man asked him the way to the house, but he could not tell him.[19]

When he did arrive, he was delighted with his purchase, so Lady Hamilton said. He walked about the place exclaiming endearingly, 'Is this, too, mine?' Inside, the house was, or was shortly to become, a kind of museum dedicated to the Admiral's fame. There were portraits of him and mementoes and trophies of his victories: a bust of him stood in the hall besides the topmast of the French flagship at the Battle of the Nile. Everywhere there were pictures of other battles, models of ships, flags, facsimiles of his honours, framed maps and plans and charts.

As well as the Hamiltons and Mrs Cadogan, Sarah Nelson's daughter, Charlotte, a fourteen-year-old girl on holiday from a boarding-school, Whitelands House, in Chelsea, was at Merton to greet its new owner; and this niece of his, in letters to her mother, described her uncle's arrival, the volunteers firing their muskets in salute, the celebratory fireworks falling into the canal. She also described the drive, on the following Sunday, to St Mary's Church, where she was allowed to turn the pages of her uncle's prayer-book. At the bottom of her letters Lord Nelson or Lady Hamilton occasionally added a postscript. To a letter describing a ring she had been given by her uncle – a diamond ring, chosen for her by Lady Hamilton, of which she was so proud she was 'always looking at it' – a note was added by the lady of the house: 'You must not think Charlotte's ring much, but it is pretty . . . a little simple Diamond and well set.' To a letter informing her mother that she had been fishing with Sir William and had caught some carp, her uncle added, 'For carp read pike. We caught some very fine fish.'

Charlotte thought her 'dear uncle' so kind, such a 'glorious, Victorious, virtuous uncle'. He took the trouble to write to the headmistress of her school to ask that the girls might have a holiday. Miss Veitch obliged him. The girls had apple pie and custard for dinner and drank a toast in negus to Lord Nelson – 'May his future years be as happy as his past have been glorious.'[20]

At Merton Place there were dinner parties, too, but not large ones. Lord Nelson had decided that, since the unconventional trio were unlikely to be asked to certain houses in the district – protest as Lady Hamilton so often and so embarrassingly did that her regard for Lord Nelson was 'the purest flame' – it would be best if they did not accept invitations to dinner at all. 'No person can take amiss our not visiting,' Nelson explained. 'The answer from me will always be civil thanks, but that I wish to live retired. We shall have our sea friends; and I know Sir William thinks they are the best.' 'We *could* have plenty of visiting in the neighbourhood,' Lady Hamilton told Sarah Nelson, 'but none of us like it.'[21]

The people in the village, among them Mr Halfhide, the next-door neighbour, Thomas Lancaster, the vicar, and Dr Parrett, the local physician, were perfectly friendly and welcoming. But so far as grander people were concerned, there was little if any hospitality to return.

In the early days of his life at Merton, Nelson would not have much enjoyed it if there had been, since, as he complained, he was 'not yet well'. The cold of the Downs had given him 'a severe shake'. Lady Hamilton professed herself worried about him. 'I am sorry to tell you I do not think our Dear Lord well,' she wrote to Sarah Nelson. 'I hope we shall get him up. He has been *very very* happy since he arrived, and Charlotte *has* been very attentive to him. Indeed, we *all* make it our constant business to make him *happy* . . . [But] he has frequent sickness and [is] low, and he throws himself on the sofa, *tired, and* says "*I am worn out.*"'[22]

It seemed an indication of his exhaustion that, instead of the much-decorated uniform he had almost invariably worn in the past, he could occasionally be seen at Merton in a plain, more comfortable black suit.

Although it was given out that the new owners of Merton Place did not accept invitations, there were nevertheless one or two houses of middle-class families in which they were known to be welcome. One of these was Southside House near Wimbledon Common, the house of John Pennington, a cloth merchant who had business connections in France and claimed to have helped several émigrés escape from Paris during the Terror. Here Emma performed her 'Attitudes' in the Music Room, where the platform erected for her and the ceiling hooks for drapery can still be seen.

Nelson and the Hamiltons were also occasional guests at Wandle Bank House, the home of James Perry, a Scottish journalist, the son of a builder, who had been an assistant in a draper's shop in Aberdeen and an actor, then a clerk, before taking up writing. He had edited the *European Magazine* and the *Gazetteer*, and in 1789 had borrowed money to buy a share in the *Morning Chronicle*, a Whig newspaper of which he was editor and to which Charles Lamb and William Hazlitt were both contributors. A stooping figure with a quick, darting glance, who 'not unwillingly turned his eyes upon the ladies', Perry was celebrated for his fund of anecdotes as well as his generosity. He had been imprisoned in Newgate for three months in 1798 for a libel upon the House of Lords.

Another unconventional character who received the Merton Place ménage into his house, Morden Hall, was Abraham Goldsmid, a Jewish financier and bullion broker of Dutch descent, renowned alike for his riches, his genial temperament and his generosity: upon his death it was said that his drawers were found to be filled with IOUs to the amount of £100,000, the backs of which were used for making notes. Nelson and the Hamiltons were fond of him and of his homely Dutch wife, though they did not care for the kosher food served at his table and considered his house decorated in rather vulgar taste. So did Nelson's nephew, George Matcham, who, after a visit there with his cousins, Charlotte and Horace, recorded in his diary: 'Fine house ... Grounds poor. Very polite. Did not like their dinner; jewish. The hall the height of the house, very gaudy; as are all the rooms, but tasteless.'[23]

There were those who thought Merton Place might also be described as tasteless. One of these was Lord Minto, who told his wife:

I went to Lord Nelson's on Saturday to dinner and returned today in the forenoon. The whole establishment and way of life is such to make me angry as well as melancholy; but I cannot alter it and I do not think myself obliged or at liberty to quarrel with him for his weakness, though nothing shall ever induce me to give the smallest countenance to Lady Hamilton. She looks ultimately to the chance of marriage, as Sir W. will not be long in her way and she probably indulges a hope that she may survive Lady Nelson; in the meanwhile she and Sir William and the whole set of them are living with him at his expense. She is in high looks, but more immense than ever. Not only the rooms, but the whole house, staircase and all, are covered with nothing but pictures of her and him, of all sizes and sorts, and representations of his naval actions, coats of arms, pieces of plate in his honour, the flagstaff of *L'Orient*, etc. – an excess of vanity which counteracts its purpose. If it was Lady H.'s house there might be a pretence for it; to make his own a mere looking-glass to view himself all day is bad taste. [John] Braham, the celebrated Jew Singer, performed with Lady H. She is horrid, but he entertained in spite of her.[24]

Lord Minto was a guest at Merton Place during the Christmas holidays of 1801. Also in the house then were Charlotte Nelson; one of her school friends, a Miss Furse; Nelson's former secretary, John Tyson, once purser in the *Badger*, and his wife; and the grandson of Lord Hood, Samuel Hood, who was to succeed his great-uncle as second Baron Bridport in 1814. Charlotte was much attracted to this young Sam Hood, who, in turn, so Lady Hamilton noticed, 'seemed to devour her with his eyes'. '*That*,' so Emma suggested to the girl's mother, 'would be a *good match*.'[25] So, indeed, it was to prove, the marriage taking place in 1810.

Apart from this budding romance, however, the dinner party at Merton Place that Christmas was not altogether a success. Miss Furse, who had, so her hostess said disapprovingly, 'not grown a Bitt', ate so much she was sick at table and had to be escorted from the dining-room by her friend, Charlotte; Mrs Tyson got drunk and began to talk nonsense until her husband tipped her the wink and she held her tongue.[26] Lady Hamilton, so Minto said, persisted in 'cramming Nelson with trowelfuls of flattery', which he went on 'taking as quietly as a child does pap'. 'The love she makes to him,' Minto added, 'is not only ridiculous but disgusting.'[27]

There were times, it seems, when Sir William thought so, too, accommodating as he was and professing as he did that Nelson was the 'best man and friend' there was in the world and that, so he chose to assure his wife, he had no doubt of the '*purity of* [her] *connection with him*'. He complained to Charles Greville of the 'nonsense' to which he was obliged to submit at Merton so as to avoid the 'explosion which would otherwise be provoked and be attended with many disagreeable effects totally destroying the comfort of his best friend'. He was 'determined' that his quiet should not be disturbed by any such explosion, 'let the nonsensical world go on' as it might.[28] Sir William also later complained to Emma of her extravagance, her 'passion' and 'nonsense' in a letter which clearly indicates that all was not now so well between them. 'It gave me much uneasiness to leave you and I did in a most uncomfortable state,' he wrote to her in a long and pained and muddled letter.

There is no being on earth that has a better understanding or better heart than yourself, if you would but give them *fair play* and keep down the passions that make you see everything thro' an improper and false medium . . . Our dear Ld. N. is noble, generous, open and liberal to all and I wish to God he could afford it . . . The greatest fortunes will not stand the total want of attention to what are called trifling *Expenses* . . . It is not my fault if by living with a great *Queen* in *intimacy* for so many years that your *ideas* should so outrun what my means can furnish.[29]

He was paying a third of the household expenses at Merton Place while still maintaining the Piccadilly house complete with servants. The garden statuary which had been bought with the house had so much offended his aesthetic sensibilities that he had suggested it all be removed and he had replaced it with an antique statue of the River Nile. He was still feeling the loss of the works of art which had not survived the uprising in Naples, while the pictures he had since sold had not fetched as much money as he had hoped. Moreover, like many old men, he considered himself much poorer than he was. As Nelson told Emma, he had become used to thinking that 'a little candle-light and iced water would ruin him'. His straitened circumstances were not altogether imaginary, though. He was still owed money by the government for expenses incurred while he had been their envoy in Naples; and he felt aggrieved, as he told Greville, that, 'having fagged' all his life, his last days should not 'pass off agreeably and comfortably'. Admittedly, he could do a bit of fishing at Merton, which he did quite like; but it now entailed a tedious journey up to London to do the things he really enjoyed, going to the salerooms in Pall Mall, Covent Garden and Leicester Square, and to meetings of the Royal Society in Somerset House, and pottering about the British Museum, where the French plunder captured after Bonaparte's defeat at Alexandria, including the Rosetta Stone, had recently been put on display.

27

The West Country

I have received an overflowing measure of the Nation's gratitude.

On occasions Nelson accompanied Sir William to London after a walk around the garden and a chat with Thomas Cribb, the head gardener. Sometimes Nelson would go to the Admiralty, often he would go to a painter's studio – to the large number of portraits of him already in existence there were added at this time a half-length by Sir William Beechey and a full-length by Hoppner. Fairly regularly he attended the House of Lords. He had been eager to make his mark there ever since his being raised to the peerage had put an end to his ideas of becoming a Member of the House of Commons. One of his first concerns on being granted leave to relinquish his command off the Kentish coast had been to write to ask if Mrs Cadogan had had his peer's robes altered to those of a viscount. He had no strong party allegiances, but he did hope to become a respected figure in the Lords and thereby advance his own career and reputation and that of his persistently ambitious brother, William, for whose preferment Emma so constantly solicited. William had been granted the honorary degree of Doctor of Divinity by Cambridge University (and consequently insisted upon being addressed as Dr Nelson); but he had not yet got his deanery. He thought it as well to point out that the Dean of Exeter had just died; perhaps there might be some hope for him there. Failing that there were vacant stalls at Durham and York. In any event, in the Lords his brother's influence must surely count for something.

Nelson greatly derided his brother's pretensions. 'His being a Doctor is nonsense,' he thought, 'but I must write tomorrow and congratulate him, or else the fat will be in the fire.'[1] But Nelson indulged him. Their father's laconic comment on his son's viscountcy was that he 'liked him as well *plain Horace* as with all these high-sounding titles'.[2] For Doctor Nelson, though, the higher the better. His brother gratified his ambition by having his patent worded to extend to the name of the Norfolk parish where William lived.[3]

Viscount Nelson of the Nile and of Burnham Thorpe in Norfolk, Baron Nelson of the Nile and of Hilborough, Norfolk, had made his maiden speech on 30 October 1801, the day after he had taken his seat in the Lords in his new style. A simple oration, seconding a motion of thanks to Admiral Saumarez and complimenting Lords Hood and St Vincent for having been masters of the school in which Saumarez had been so well taught, the speech was well received. A second speech, delivered a few days later, however, was not. This was made at the prompting of Henry Addington, the Prime Minister, and contradicted much that he had been saying in private about the terms of the peace treaty to be signed with the French. Addington had approached both St Vincent and Nelson in the hope that favourable comments upon the terms by two distinguished naval officers might help to quieten the adverse criticism of the proposed treaty. St Vincent's speech caused little offence, even to the government's leading opponents, since he contented himself with emphasizing the undeniable advantages of certain of the treaty's provisions. But Nelson unwisely chose to discount the importance of the territories which England stood to lose, Malta, Minorca and the Cape of Good Hope among them, dismissing the last of these as little more than an outmoded tavern on the way to the East Indies.[4] 'I was obliged to Lord Nelson for giving me anything that could create a smile on such a grave and awful subject,' commented William Huskisson, who had recently resigned as Under Secretary at War, in a letter to his former superior, Henry Dundas. 'His Lordship's experience might have convinced him that a seaman could find a tavern nearer home than the Cape of Good Hope, and if Malta is not to be considered because it does not serve to block Toulon, we must be obliged to conclude that no station in the Mediterranean is a good one. How can Ministers allow such fools to speak in their defence?'[5]

Nelson's fellow officers shared the view of the politicians, most of them believing, as Captain Hardy did, that '*Sailors* should not *talk* too much.' Nelson himself seems to have considered his speech a small price to pay for what he hoped would be the goodwill of the government to which, in any case, he professed himself obliged for past favours – and for these he was 'never ungrateful'.

Encouraged by Lady Hamilton, who foresaw a great future for him in politics and was, indeed, 'quite mad for him as an orator', Nelson was not to be dissuaded by his friends from making further speeches in the Lords. He apologized 'for the imperfect manner', the 'plain seamanlike manner', in which he delivered them; but he felt he should not have done his duty had he remained silent when drawn to speak.[6]

Lady Hamilton 'could hear him for ever', she said. He spoke 'like an angel'. Her great regret was that she could not hear him speak in the chamber and had to be content with his repeating the words at Merton Place just as he had delivered them in the House. 'How my heart would throb and beat high,' she told Sarah Nelson, 'how should I exult to see him standing up with his manly look and honest, dear, innocent, energetic-looking face, speaking truth to people who hardly speak it . . .'

He had not been 'rewarded a quarter part he deserves', she considered. '*Shame on them all* . . . If another Blenheim were built five times as large with five times the income, it would be only right; it would be no favour.'[7]

Although she had no doubt that she would have been asked to share such a place with him, Lady Hamilton could still not overcome her jealousy and dislike of her hero's wife, 'that vile Tom Tit'. 'You & I liked each other from the moment we met our souls were congenial,' she told Sarah Nelson, 'not so with Tom Tit . . . Tom Tit might go to the *devil* for what I care.'[8]

'I wonder where Tom Tit goes?' she asked Mrs Nelson in another typical letter. 'I dare say by today's papers that she is arrived in town. She must give five shillings to put in the papers such insipid stuff.' In London, where she had rented a house in Somerset Street on the Portman Estate, the woman would no doubt have her father-in-law to stay, and the two of them would,

Emma thought, discuss her and Nelson's supposed misbehaviour *ad nauseam.*[9]

The old parson had, indeed, told his son that gratitude required that he should sometimes be with his daughter-in-law if he could be of any comfort to her; and Lady Nelson had herself gone to Norfolk to see him. She had not stayed with him at Burnham Thorpe, offering to spend the nights at either Holkham or Burnham Market, since she knew 'Lord Nelson's friends' would not like her staying in the parsonage; and, on her return to London, she had written to say that, having thought over all they had discussed, she had concluded that it would not be practicable for him to come to live with her. She did not want to exacerbate the difficult relationship between Lord Nelson and his father, who had already written his son a letter of gentle reproach. Edmund Nelson replied to Fanny that 'the opinion of others must rest with themselves and not make any alteration with *us*'; he was still ready to join her in her London house when the servants were installed there.[10] He felt sorry for her, he confessed. There were no prospects of better times for her, he told his daughter, Kate Matcham – 'nay, I think worse'. The thought that he might go to stay with her in London distressed Nelson and Lady Hamilton alike. 'I am sure he will not stay in that damned Somerset Street,' Nelson told Emma. 'If he ever mentions her name I shall stop that directly. I shall never go there to see him.'[11]

For her part, Lady Hamilton was almost distracted, and let forth her feelings in a passionate diatribe to Sarah Nelson about 'that vile Tom Tit', her 'squinting brat' and 'dirty tribe':[12]

His poor father is unknowing and taken in by a very wicked, artful woman acting a bad part. He would, if this designing woman had had her way, have put you all aside. *Your* father, Nelson's father, protects this woman and gives a mortal blow to his son. The old man could never bear her until now and he conspires *against the saviour* of his Country and his darling, who has risen to such a height of fame and for whom a *wicked, false, malicious* wretch, who rendered his days wretched and his nights miserable ... And the father of Nelson says, 'I will stab my son to the heart.' But indeed he says, 'My poor father is old now – he does not know what he does.' But oh how cruel shocking it is.[13]

The Matchams and the Boltons could not 'escape their share of
the guilt'. They were 'as close-tongued about *her* as they [were]
close-fisted'. They had 'pushed the dear old gentleman to act this
bad and *horrible part* to support a false, proud, bad woman [with] a
cold heart and infamous soul . . . But let her own wickedness be
her own punishment; her sins be on her head . . . What do you
think my dearest friend, of her impudence? . . . My patience is
gone . . . Tom Tit is despised and hated even by those that pretend
to protect her.'[14]

'Tom Tit's' father-in-law, having assured his 'dearest son' of a
'warm, joyful and affectionate welcome if [he] could find an
inclination to look once more at [his father] in Burnham Parsonage', nervously and reluctantly accepted an invitation to Merton
Place.
    'Pray let him come to your care at Merton,' Nelson had asked
Emma. 'If he remains at Burnham he will die . . . Your kindness
will keep him alive for you have a kind soul. She [Lady Nelson]
has none.'[15] Having obtained Emma's agreement, Nelson issued a
warm invitation:

On the 23rd I shall be at Merton with Sir William and Lady Hamilton
and them with myself shall be happy to see you, my beloved father, that
is your home. My brother and sister, the dear children will soon be with
us and happy shall we all be, but more so if you will come. Plenty of
room for you and your servant. Allen's wife is the dairy maid.
                    Ever my dear father's dutiful son, N. and B.[16]

    The Rector arrived in the middle of November to find his son
'in better Health and Happier in himself than in good truth' he
had 'in any passed Time observed Him to be'.[17] Emma was as kind
as Nelson had hoped she would be, even though she thought the
old man might deliver some unwelcome message for his son from
that horrid, duplicitous 'Tom Tit'. He 'contradicts *a little* every
now', she told Sarah Nelson, but the old gentleman seemed tolerably well content. Certainly she fed him well − that night they

were having 'a turtle dress'd and a haunch of venison. Don't your mouth water?' But he was *very feeble* indeed and inclined to sleep'. She thought he had not long to live.[18]

Five months later news arrived at Merton that the old man was indeed dying at Bath. Lady Nelson left London immediately to be with him. But her husband wrote, 'I have no hopes that he can recover. God's will be done. Had my father expressed a wish to see me, unwell as I am, I should have flown to Bath, but I believe it would be too late. However, should it be otherwise and he wishes to see me, no consideration shall detain me a moment.'[19]

His father died the day this letter was written, on Lady Hamilton's birthday; and arrangements were made for taking the body from Bath to Burnham Thorpe for burial. Unwilling to meet his wife at the funeral, Nelson pleaded his continuing indisposition for not attending it himself. Instead he attended the baptism of Lady Hamilton's maid, Fatima, now to be known as Fatima Emma Charlotte Nelson Hamilton and entered in the parish register as 'from Egypt, a negress, about 20 years of age'. Lady Nelson had tactfully left Bath, having said goodbye to the father-in-law who had always been kind to her. She was thanked for her attention to the old man by her husband's sister, Susannah Bolton, who, the last of the family to drop Lady Nelson, told her that her 'going to Bath was all of a piece with her conduct towards [their] beloved father'.[20] Susannah added that she was going to London shortly but that, although she would always be her sister-in-law's sincere friend, they could not meet since reports of a visit to Somerset Street would certainly reach Merton. Her other sister-in-law, Sarah Nelson, had already got into trouble for not going with her husband to join the other mourners at Merton Place. 'My uncle is very much hurt at your not being here this morning,' Charlotte Nelson told her mother,

and he begs me to say it would be indecent for me to be at school and has ordered Lady Hamilton to write to Miss Veitch the reason for my not coming. We are all going into deep mourning as my uncle is very particular that all possible respect should be paid to my dear Grandpapa's memory. He would not let Horatio [her thirteen-year-old brother] go a-fishing . . . this morning, nor do we see anybody. A written paper is shown at the gate to everyone that comes . . . My spirits are worn out seeing my uncle's suffering.[21]

The funeral was well attended, the church crowded; six clergy-men of the diocese acted as bearers; the farmers of Burnham Thorpe and Burnham Westgate followed the coffin to the grave. It gave Nelson comfort to think, so he told a friend, that his own bones would 'probably be laid' in that same grave, in 'Dear, Dear Burnham', the village that gave him birth. 'The thought of former days,' he added, 'brings all my Mother to my heart, which shows itself in my eyes.' Characteristically he wrote to Davison to ask him to persuade the chairman of the East India Company to give his father's faithful servant, Abraham Cook, 'a place about their warehouses of 50l. a year'.[22]

Soon after the death of his father, Nelson decided to accompany the Hamiltons on a visit to Wales to look over Sir William's estates, which were being supervised for him by Charles Greville. They first went to Oxford, staying at the Star Inn. They were shown over the prison and were received at the town hall, where Nelson was made a freeman of the city. The next day it was the university's turn to honour the distinguished visitors. Dr William Nelson, so gratified to be a Doctor of Divinity of Cambridge University, was granted that degree in the University of Oxford at the hands of Dr Septimus Collinson, Provost of The Queen's College and Lady Margaret Professor of Divinity and author of learned lectures on the Thirty-nine Articles. Lord Nelson and Sir William were both honoured with the honorary degree of Doctor of Civil Law, conferred upon them by Dr William Blackstone, Principal of New Inn Hall, Vinerian Professor of Civil Law and son of the distinguished and irascible jurist whose *Commentaries on the Laws of England* had made the family rich. The ceremony was performed in full Congregation with appropriate dignity, though it was later mildly ridiculed in some sections of the press, the *Morning Post* facetiously commenting that Lord Nelson's degree should have been the same as his brother's since he was renowned for his knowledge of *cannon* laws, and the *Morning Herald* snidely commenting that it was not known whether Sir William Hamilton had been granted the degree of LLD or ASS.[23]

From Oxford, 'Lord Nelson's tourists', as other newspapers referred to them, set out for Woodstock to pay their respects to the Duke of Marlborough, whose great ancestor had been rewarded for his military services by the grant of royal land upon which Sir John Vanbrugh had built for him the grand palace which looked to Horace Walpole the sort of place that might have been designed for an auctioneer who had been elected King of Poland. The then incumbent of Blenheim Palace was the fourth Duke of Marlborough, aged sixty-three and the husband of the only daughter of the fourth Duke of Bedford. Reserved and aloof, he had been much distressed of late by the publication of love letters written by his son and heir to the wife of a Member of Parliament. Unwilling to receive a fellow member of the House of Lords who was himself involved in a dubious relationship with a married woman, the Duke declined to see the Hamiltons and Lord Nelson when they presented themselves at the palace door. A servant offered refreshments which would be brought out to the visitors' carriage or to some place in the park should they prefer to eat alfresco.

This was curtly rejected and the party drove away, Nelson commenting that he had always expected no better treatment from 'the great'.*

Lady Hamilton angrily maintained that the reward of the first Duke of Marlborough's services was 'because a woman reigned, and women had great souls'. Then she added, and these are 'her own matchless words', as she recounted them to Nelson's early biographer, James Harrison, who said that she spoke them 'with a spirit and energy forcibly depicting the grand character of that superlative mind which renders her, at once, the idol and idolizer of transcendent genius and valour':

---

* Half a century or so later, as a pleasantly ironic postscript to this rebuff, the Duke's great-granddaughter married the Rev. the Hon. John Horatio Nelson, grandson of Lord Nelson's sister, Mrs Bolton.

I told Nelson that if I had been a queen after the battle of Aboukir, he should have a principality, so that Blenheim Park should have been only a kitchen garden to it The tears came into his eyes and he shook Sir William and me by the hand; saying that he was content to have done his duty by the country and the people and he hoped we should ever approve his conduct; but that yet he had not half done, for there were two or three beds of laurels in the Mediterranean to be gathered.[24]

The travellers' reception at Gloucester was in comforting contrast to their dismissal at Woodstock. Here to welcome the 'Noble Visitants and the gallant Hero of the Nile' there were cheering crowds, parades of yeomanry, blaring bands and loud peals from the cathedral bells. They were taken on a tour round the city, and, as at Oxford, shown the cathedral and the prison, 'with both of which his Lordship expressed himself highly pleased, particularly with the extent and convenience of the latter'. Their programme of visits completed, Gloucester's guests were driven on west through the Forest of Dean to Ross-on-Wye.[25]

As a naval officer, interested in the building of ships, Nelson cast a keen eye on the woodlands through which their road passed, and he was concerned to notice how neglected they were. When he reached their next inn, he settled down to write to the Prime Minister to tell him so, maintaining that the state of the Forest of Dean was 'deplorable', that, if the information he had been given was true, there were fewer than 3,500 loads of timber in over 33,000 acres fit for shipbuilding, whereas, if 'brought to a high state of cultivation of oak', the forest 'would grow in full vigour 920,000 oak trees', capable of providing well over 9,000 loads 'fit for building ships of the line every year'.[26]

At Ross, Nelson and his friends went aboard a boat that took them down river to Monmouth past the ruins of the grey and red sandstone Goodrich Castle perched upon its bedrock and beneath the towering Symond's Yat Rock. As the boat approached Monmouth its passengers could hear the sound of cheering, a brass band playing 'See the Conquering Hero Comes', and the occasional thud of a cannon firing in salute from Kymin Hill, a mile to the east of the town.

In the town, where the river Wye joins the Monnow, 'Nelson's tourists' took to the road again and drove towards Abergavenny, then, by the banks of the Usk, to Brecon and Carmarthen and on to Milford Haven. Villagers came out to greet them as they passed, hands were waved, flowers thrown; and at Milford, where they stayed at the New Inn, ever afterwards to be known as the Lord Nelson, Charles Greville was there to meet them with announcements of a series of engagements, including attendance at a ceremony at which Nelson was to be granted the freedom of the town, at a fair and a banquet, at a regatta, a cattle show and the laying of the foundation stone of a new church, St Katherine's, which was to be consecrated in 1808.[27] Nelson's friend, Captain Thomas Foley, whose family had lived not far away at Ridgeway in Pembrokeshire for centuries, would be coming; so would his bride of a few weeks, the youngest daughter of the Duke of Leinster. So would Lord Kensington, Lord-Lieutenant of the county, whose father, the first Baron, had been Member of Parliament for Haverfordwest; and so also would Lord Cawdor, formerly Member for Cardigan, whose son was to be created an earl and whose wife – a daughter of the fifth Earl of Carlisle, and a close friend of Greville – had invited them all to Stackpole Court. These notabilities were not quite so grand as those who had rebuffed Nelson at Blenheim; but their presence would surely indicate that he was not to be slighted in Wales as he had been in Oxfordshire. He appeared to be particularly gratified by his reception at the banquet given in the assembly room of the hotel where his party were staying. He spoke warmly of the town's harbour which Greville and Sir William had good reason for hoping would be developed as a dockyard and arsenal rather than the harbour at Pembroke on the other side of the estuary; and, after he had finished speaking, Sir William presented to the owners of the hotel a copy of the portrait of Lord Nelson painted after the Battle of the Nile by Leonardo Guzzardi of Palermo.[28] Nelson himself, it is believed, presented to St Katherine's the trunk of the mainmast of *L'Orient* which is still to be seen in the church.[29]

Nelson also seems to have enjoyed his visit to Captain Foley's elder brother's family at Ridgeway. Mrs Foley had at first been reluctant to receive the Admiral and his companions, unwilling to compromise her reputation and social standing. But she had been persuaded to give way and to allow the avenue to her house to be illuminated with welcoming lanterns. 'The eldest daughter of Mr Foley was a child of about six years old, and when she was brought down to dessert on the evening of Nelson's arrival, was much struck with the gentleman with one eye and one arm, but she got over her astonishment when the Admiral took her on his knee and dropped grapes into her mouth with his *one* hand.'[30]

From Milford, Nelson returned to Monmouth by way of Tenby and Swansea. 'The whole town was at their heels,' wrote a man who saw them at Tenby. 'The Lady is grown immensely fat and equally coarse, while her "companion in arms" has taken the other extreme – thin, shrunk and to my impression in bad health. They were evidently vain of each other . . . Poor Sir William, wretched but not abashed, he followed at a short distance bearing in his arms a cucciolo [puppy] and other emblems of their combined folly.'[31]

At Swansea, Nelson's carriage was drawn to a reception by 'a choice body of exultant tars', and, after being presented with the freedom of the town, he made a patriotic speech which was printed for 'the encouragement of national enthusiasm among the young people of Swansea'.

Before returning to Monmouth, he made time to see the ruins of Chepstow Castle, unusual in being built of stone rather than wood shortly after the Norman Conquest, and, after dinner at Piercefield Park, the noble Cistercian ruin of Tintern Abbey. At Monmouth he took rooms at the Beaufort Arms, to which the Duke of Beaufort, Lord-Lieutenant of the county, had dispatched a haunch or two of venison from Badminton.

The next morning Lord Nelson was taken by coach up the steep path to the top of Kymin Hill where, two years before, a temple had been erected to honour the admirals who had fought against the French and to celebrate the victory of the Nile, a mural of which decorated the stone wall. After breakfast Nelson expressed his pleasure in seeing the building, the only monument of its kind in the whole kingdom.

After dinner at the Beaufort Arms, the admiral made another speech, in which he declared that, should war break out again, he would send every ship and every soldier out of the country and leave England to be protected by 'her sons at home'. He did not doubt that, if the French were to land in England, they might well advance to plunder and destroy a village or two; they might even burn Monmouth, but they would 'never advance as far as Hereford for they would always find Britons ready to receive them . . . It was my good fortune,' he continued,

to have under my command some of the most experienced Officers in the English Navy, whose professional skill was seconded by the undaunted courage of British Sailors; and whatever merit might attach itself to me, I must declare that I had only to show them the Enemy, and Victory crowned the Standard . . . In my own person I have received an overflowing measure of the Nation's gratitude – far more than I ever merited or expected; because the same success would have crowned the efforts of any other British Admiral, who had under his command such distinguished Officers and such gallant Crews. And here let me impress it on the mind of every Officer in the Service, that to whatever quarter of the Globe he may be destined, whether to the East or West Indies, to Africa or America – the eyes of his Country are upon him.[32]

The speech was greeted with loud cheers, which encouraged Lady Hamilton to stand up to sing 'Rule Britannia' with 'such powers of execution as called forth the utmost astonishment', and, as an encore, another song equally patriotic, rendered – so it was recorded by a less than impartial writer – 'with her usual scientific taste and vocal excellence which quite enraptured the whole company'.[33] During a conversation with a fellow guest afterwards, 'the Hero of the Nile' grew quite heated in talking about his '*detestation of the French*' whom he considered 'as a set of damned perfidious rascals'.[34]

The next day in a bookshop, 'with his usual courtesy', Nelson took off his hat to the proprietor who 'was overcome'. 'Monarchs have taken off their hats to your Lordship, permit me to replace yours on your head.' The man then asked to be allowed to print the speeches made the previous night; and the Admiral made 'a curious answer': 'I am an old man [he was forty-three] and may not live long. It is my wish that posterity should know my sentiments. Therefore do it.'[35]

There was another freedom of the city to be presented at Hereford, this time by the slovenly and eccentric eleventh Duke of Norfolk, High Steward of the County, whose wife came from Holme Lacy, south-east of the town.[36]

'The noble party arrived in Hereford about 12 o'clock from Rudhale House near Ross, the hospitable mansion of Thos. Westfaling Esq.,' a local newspaper reported. Mr Westfaling, a descendant of a sixteenth-century Bishop of Hereford, had met Lord Nelson at Naples while he and his wife were on a tour of the Continent, and they made

every preparation to receive his Lordship with the honors due to so distinguished a character. The gardens were thrown open, a band of music attended, and all the principal families of the neighbourhood were invited to join in the fête. An elegant collation with fruit and wines was served on the lawn; and in the evening a grand display of fire-works took place; and an arch, with a star above, formed of variegated lamps made a striking part of the illumination. The following lines were presented to his Lordship with a wreath of laurel:

> Go, laurel, pluck'd from Rudhale's bowers,
> To bind the temples of the brave;
> Crown him amid these festive hours,
> And grace the Hero of the Wave.[37]

The tribute continued for several verses of a similar nature. In 'Hereford', the *Hereford Journal* reported,

the presence of the Hero of Copenhagen and the Nile excited those demonstrations of joy to which his transcendent merit duly entitled him. The populace met him at the entrance to the city, and taking the horses from the carriage, drew it themselves to the Hotel where he proceeded to the Town Hall [where speeches were made and apologies rendered for the absence of the Bishop whose age and infirmity prevented his attendance] ... To this Lord Nelson replied that, as the son of a clergyman, and from having been bred up in 'a sense of the highest veneration for the Church and its able Ministers, while he sincerely lamented the cause of his Lordship's absence, he conceived it a duty, which he would perform with the greatest willingness, to wait upon him at the Palace.' This, upon his return from the Town Hall, he accordingly did ... The noble visitants, before their departure, remained a considerable time in the great room of the Hotel, which afforded the inhabitants a better opportunity of gratifying their wish to see their illustrious guest.[38]

The party then travelled on to Ludlow, where King Henry VIII's brother, Arthur, had died in the Norman castle, and then to Worcester, where they stayed at the Hop Pole Inn outside which huge crowds of people gathered to catch a sight of the hero, who obliged them by making frequent appearances at a window.

The next day, preceded by a band, he went to Chamberlain's china factory, where one of the painters described him as 'a battered looking gentleman. Leaning on his left and only arm was the beautiful Lady Hamilton, evidently pleased at the interest excited by her companion; and then amidst the general company came a very infirm old gentleman. This was Sir William Hamilton.' Having been shown around the factory Nelson declared that although he possessed the finest porcelain that the courts of Dresden and Naples could afford, he had seen none to equal the china shown him here; and he gave an order for numerous pieces, including 'a complete dinner set', an 'elegant vase' decorated with his arms and another 'elegant vase, richly adorned with a miniature of his Lordship supported by a figure of Fame'.[39]

From Worcester, Nelson went on to Birmingham, where he 'kindly gratified a prodigious concourse of people assembled' outside Styles's Hotel 'by repeatedly presenting himself at the window'.

That evening 'his Lordship and friends went to the theatre drawn by the shouting populace; and the house was so crowded that many persons were unable to obtain admission. On their entrance, "Rule Britannia" was played in full orchestra; and the whole audience, respectfully standing up, instantly testified, by their unanimously loud and long continued plaudits, the happiness which they experienced at thus seeing before them the renowned Hero of the Nile.'[40]

Dragged back to Styles's Hotel at midnight by the people 'amidst a blaze of several hundred lighted tourches', the visitors rose early for visits to a succession of factories making swords, buttons, buckles and rings, window sashes, coins and medals. They went to 'the manufactory of Mr Clay, jappaner in ordinary to his Majesty' and 'to Mr Egerton's stained-glass manufactory, where they were received by a party of beautiful young ladies, dressed in white, who liberally strewed the hero with flowers'.

The next day, as church bells rang again, the relentless round of sightseeing continued. 'They proceeded to inspect Mr Radenhurst's whip manufactory, the extensive toy warehouse of Messrs Richards, Mr Phipson's pin manufactory, Mr Bissett's Museum ... They concluded by visiting the famous Blue-Coat Charity School.'[41]

At the theatre the actor playing the part of Falstaff in the *Merry Wives of Windsor* 'set the house in a roar', so it was reported, 'by turning to the stage box as he rolled forth the line, "Before the best Lord in the land, I swear it."' The son of the Irish manager of the theatre, the future actor, William Charles Macready, then a nine-year-old pupil at St Paul's Square School, recalled how the news of Nelson's arrival in Birmingham 'spread like wildfire through the town and when news of his intention of going to the play got abroad, the box-office was literally packed ... At the hour of commencement,' Macready continued,

my father was waiting with candles to conduct the far-famed hero through the lobby ... Being close to my father's side, I not only got a perfect view of the hero's pale and interesting face ... the right arm empty sleeve attached to his breast, the orders upon it ... The melancholy expression of his countenance and the extremely mild and gentle tone of his voice impressed me most sensibly ...

When with Lady Hamilton and Dr Nelson, he entered his box, the uproar of the house was deafening and it seemed as if it would know no end ... Lady Hamilton laughing loud and without stint, clapped with uplifted hands and with all her heart and kicked her heels against the

footboard of the seat, while Nelson placidly and with his mournful look
. . . bowed repeatedly to the oft-repeated cheers.

Next day, my father called at the hotel to thank his Lordship. In the
hall were several sailors waiting to see him, to each of whom the great
Admiral spoke in a most affable manner, inquiringly and kindly, as he
passed through to his carriage, and left them, I believe, some tokens of
remembrance.[42]

A brief tour of Warwick was followed by a visit to Althorp to see
Lord Spencer, who had resigned from the government with Pitt.
The party arrived back at Merton Place after an absence of six
weeks, having intended to be away for three, on Sunday, 5
September.

'We had had a most charming Tour,' Lady Hamilton reported
to Alexander Davison; and to Mrs Matcham she wrote, 'Oh, how
our Hero has been received.' Certainly she had much enjoyed
herself if her husband had not, while Nelson was not left in any
doubt as to the high regard in which the country held him. The
crowds had been immense, the welcome joyous; inns had been
called after him, their signs repainted; children had been christened
with his name; at race meetings, horses called 'Lord Nelson' were
cheered past the post; prize bulls given the title were proudly
paraded round the ring at country-town markets. It was a singular
fact, according to the *Morning Post*, that '*more éclat*' attended Lord
Nelson in his 'provincial rambles' than attended the King. He
himself, feeling as well as he had ever done since his return to
England, was highly gratified. 'Although some of the highest
powers might wish to put [him] down, yet the reward of the
general approbation and gratitude for [his] services' was, he
considered, ample reward for all that he had done. He felt bound
to make a comparison 'not much to the credit of some in the
higher offices of the state'.[43]

28

Surrey

Nelson was deeply concerned on his return to London by the sorry
state of his finances, which had been exacerbated by the cost of the
tour, his half share of which came to almost £250. In a letter to
the Prime Minister he compared his own resources with those of
other admirals, citing in particular the Earl of St Vincent and Lord
Duncan, both of whom had been granted larger pensions than
himself.[1] He set down his own income and expenditure as follows:

LORD NELSON'S INCOME AND PROPERTY

My Exchequer Pension for the Nile	£2,000 0 0
Navy Pension for loss of one arm and one eye	923 0 0
Half-pay as Vice-Admiral	465 0 0
Interest of 1000l.	30 0 0
	£3,418 0 0

OUTGOINGS OF LORD NELSON

To Lady Nelson	£1,800 0 0
Interest of money owing	500 0 0
Pension to my Brother's Widow	200 0 0
To assist in educating my nephews	150 0 0
Expenditure	£2,650 0 0
Income	£3,418 0 0

This left him with a bare £768 per annum, clearly insufficient
for a man whose expenses in a single week following his return
from the West Country amounted to £117 8s 2½d and whose bills for

food and drink at Merton regularly exceeded £50 a week. A considerable part of this sum went to Nelson's wine merchants, who became accustomed to receiving such orders as 'twenty dozen of your best port'. Indeed, Merton's wine cellar was so well stocked that years later, when Lady Hamilton's affairs were wound up, it still held 'very old, rare and curious WINES' valued at £2,000 and later offered for sale by a wine merchant who claimed they had cost him 'a great deal of money', in fact £2,351 10s 11d.[2]

Nelson's dissatisfied mood on his return from his tour found expression in a letter to Alexander Davison. 'London seems absolutely deserted,' he wrote, 'and so hot and stinking that it is truly detestable.' He confessed that he was selfish enough to wish that Davison was himself in London at his house in St James's Square rather than in Northumberland; for at breakfast in Davison's house he could hear all that was going on 'in the great world'. 'It was,' he said, 'a central place where anyone could meet me.' 'I am so very little in the world,' he added, 'that I know little, if anything, beyond Newspaper reports.'[3]

This was scarcely the case. Certainly, very few of 'the great', as he so often referred to them, went to see him at Merton or at the Hamiltons' house in Piccadilly; but Nelson called quite often at 10 Downing Street and at the Admiralty. Also he was quite frequently to be seen in the House of Lords, where he continued to speak from time to time on foreign policy and naval topics, supporting St Vincent's proposal for a commission of inquiry into the dishonesty of prize agents on one occasion and, on another, calling for a renewal of the war against France though, as he insisted, 'no man was more for peace' than he was. He had fought for peace, he told the House, the enjoyment of it constituted the chief part of his happiness; but he 'deprecated having it on dishonourable terms'. 'Don't you think he speaks like an angel in the House of Lords?' Lady Hamilton again asked her sister-in-law, Kate Matcham. 'I love him, adore him; his virtues, his heart, mind, soul, courage, all merit to be adored and everything that concerns his honour, glory and happiness.'*[4]

---

* Kate loved him dearly too, and 'to her dying day would blush hotly at any criticism of her brother's conduct; but even to the most privileged she only said, "He had great excuses" . . . She [Lady Nelson] was so very cold' (Matcham, 183).

He was also to be seen occasionally as a guest of Sir William Hamilton at meetings of the Literary Society; and he went up to London more often than he would have liked to see his lawyers about the protracted case against Lord St Vincent over their disputed prize-money, and to consult Dr Benjamin Moseley – who had been appointed physician at the Royal Hospital, Chelsea, since his return from Jamaica – about the deteriorating sight in his left eye. Moseley had followed up his treatise on tropical diseases with papers on hydrophobia, cow-pox and haemorrhage from the lungs – which he eccentrically believed to be caused by the phases of the moon – but he had no specialist knowledge of ophthalmology. However, Nelson had respect for his opinions and enjoyed his company.

Dinner with Moseley and with their mutual friend from West Indian days, the former sugar planter, Hercules Ross, made some of Nelson's days in London less a duty than a pleasure; but he preferred life at Merton, where Emma did all she could – and sometimes more than he wanted – to make his life there entertaining. On his birthday, for example, there was a jolly party, attended by Dr Nelson's family, Mr and Mrs Goldsmid and their daughters, and James and Anne Perry. After dinner the Goldsmid girls played duets at the piano; Italian opera singers entertained the guests with assorted choruses and arias, and Emma sang one of her patriotic songs in praise of Lord Nelson, 'the hope of our Navy', whose name and glory would be coupled for ever.

At Christmas there were more parties. The William Nelsons were there again; so were various singers; and so were the Boltons, who, with the Matchams, were now on the best of terms with Lady Hamilton. They all stayed on for the New Year when Lady Hamilton gave a children's ball at which the guests stayed up so late that the following day the master of the house came down to find that even at noon there was no one else about.

Not all Nelson's guests and visitors were welcome. One day George Parsons called at the house. Since his days as midshipman in the *Foudroyant* he had qualified as a lieutenant but now that the war was over he was experiencing difficulty in getting his commission signed. He was shown into Nelson's study, where he was alarmed to hear the Admiral's voice raised in angry protest that 'he was pestered to death by young gentlemen, his former shipmates'. Tom Allen, who had known Parsons in their sailing days, hurried off to find Lady Hamilton, who managed to soothe the Admiral's ill temper. His countenance, which, until now, 'had been a thundercloud', brightened. Lady Hamilton dictated a letter to Lord St Vincent which Nelson obediently took down. She handed it to Parsons with instructions to send it to the First Lord at his country house in Essex.[5]

Despite the outburst that greeted Parsons's arrival, the Admiral was rarely appealed to in vain by former shipmates or comrades-in-arms. When the former purser of the *Agamemnon* wrote a begging letter from a debtors' prison, the sum of £25 was soon on its way to him; and when Nelson was served with a subpoena to give evidence for the defence in the trial of a man who had fought beside him in Nicaragua he obeyed the summons without evident reluctance.

This man was the Irishman, Colonel Edward Despard, who, with twelve others, was to face trial for treason on 7 February 1803 at the New Sessions House, Horsemonger Lane, Newington. He had been recalled from his post as administrator in Yucatan about five years before to answer charges which Lord Sydney, Secretary of State in Pitt's administration, had dismissed as frivolous but which Sydney's successor, Lord Grenville, considered worthy of investigation. Accompanied by his black mistress, Despard had arrived in England in 1790, but for two years he had been kept waiting idly in London until the Colonial Office decided that there was no case to answer. Told that, although his post in the Yucatan had been abolished, he would be given another one, he pressed the government to fulfil the offer so relentlessly and forcefully that he was eventually imprisoned. Released, he was soon as much of a nuisance as ever, marching about London airing his grievances, his tall, thin figure a familiar sight in the streets because of the large umbrella he carried with him everywhere. Once more he was arrested and again carried off to prison, where he began to formulate a hare-brained plot which informers revealed to the authorities. He planned, so it was alleged, to instigate a mutiny in the Guards, to seize the Bank of England, the Houses of Parliament and the Tower of London with the help of mutineers, and to assassinate the King by blowing him apart with cannon shot on his way to open Parliament. Having been apprised of this ludicrously impractical conspiracy, armed men from the Bow Street magistrate's office arrested Despard and some forty of his associates, mostly Irishmen, at the Oakley Arms tavern in Lambeth. Despard and twelve of these men were arraigned before a special commission presided over by the Lord Chief Justice, Lord Ellenborough – a judge of violent temper and strong prejudices, a firm believer in the rigours of the criminal code – and it was expected that Despard would be shown little mercy.

The case began equably enough. Lord Nelson, the first witness to be called for the defence, was asked by Serjeant Best, Despard's counsel, how long he had known the accused.

'It is twenty-three years since I saw him,' Nelson replied. 'I became acquainted with him in the year 1779 at Jamaica. He was, at that time, lieutenant in what were called the Liverpool Blues. From his abilities as an engineer, I know he was expected to be appointed . . .'

Lord Ellenborough here intervened: 'I am sorry to interrupt your Lordship, but we cannot hear, what I dare say your Lordship would give with great effect, the history of this gentleman's military life; but you will state what has been his general character.'

'We went on the Spanish main together. We slept many nights together in our clothes upon the ground . . . We slept in the same tent . . . In all that period of time, no man could have shown more zealous attachment to his sovereign and his country than Colonel Despard did. I formed the highest opinion of him as a man and an officer.'

In his cross-examination, the prosecuting counsel, the Attorney-General, wanted the witness to confirm how long it was since he had last seen the accused. Lord Nelson had to say that it was twenty years.

Although the jury recommended mercy, Despard was condemned to a traitor's death In the event, however, he was spared the most disgusting part of this painful punishment. Refusing, as a declared atheist, the prayers of the prison chaplain, Despard was taken to the scaffold outside the gaol at Newington on a hurdle with six of his associates, one of whom remarked, 'I am afraid, Colonel, we have got into a bad situation.' 'There are many better,' Despard replied, 'and some worse.' On the scaffold he made a long speech to a crowd of twenty thousand people. The speech was loudly cheered; the victim then adjusted the rope so that the knot, tightly drawn from behind his left ear, would ensure instant death; the head was then severed from the body and held up to the spectators with the words, 'Behold the head of a traitor.' The remains were then handed over to Despard's mistress, who had them buried in an unmarked grave in St Paul's Churchyard.

While awaiting execution, Despard had written to Nelson, enclosing a petition which he asked the Admiral to pass on to the Prime Minister. Nelson read out the letter to Lord Minto, who described it as 'extremely well written' and 'affecting from any other pen'. Henry Addington – to whom Nelson forwarded it and the accompanying petition without commenting upon either – certainly found it so. He confessed to Nelson that 'he and his family had sat up after supper, weeping over it'.

Although, as Lord Minto said, Nelson had 'merely' sent Despard's letter on to Addington without making any observations upon it, he did recommend a pension for 'Mrs Despard', who, he told Minto, was 'violently in love' with the victim. He did not, however, expect this pension to be granted her because of the Colonel's shocking behaviour in refusing Christian comfort at the end.[6]

Within a few weeks of Despard's execution, Nelson had another death to face. Sir William Hamilton had not been well for some time. He still enjoyed the occasional outing to London and sometimes spent a pleasant day fishing; but he no longer returned contentedly to Merton Place, as he had done one day in October the year before, with over sixty pounds of fish. He remained on good terms with Nelson, but he was finding his wife's extravagant devotion to their friend and her constant entertaining increasingly irksome. Soon after their return from the West Country, he was told that they were to go to the seaside in Kent. Unknown to him it had been decided that his wife's daughter, Horatia – of whose existence he was still, or at least pretended to be, unaware – was in need of a holiday by the sea. She was to be taken on her father's instructions to lodgings in Margate, while the Hamiltons were to go to Ramsgate, a few miles farther south along the coast. Sir William had evidently not wanted to go, and did not like it when he got there, while his wife was anxious and fretful for a reason she could not mention to him: she had lost the address of the lodgings in Margate where Mrs Gibson and her daughter were staying.[7] Husband and wife communicated with each other by notes.

'As I see it is a pain to you to remain here, let me beg of you to fix your time of going,' she wrote to him. 'Weather I dye in Piccadilly or any other spot in England, 'tis the same to me; but I remember the time when you wished for tranquility, but now all visiting and bustle is your liking. However,' she added on a conciliatory note, 'I will do what you please, being ever your affectionate and obedient E.H.'[8]

'I neither love bustle nor great company,' her husband replied on the back of the sheet,

but I like some employment and diversion. I have but a short time to live, and every moment is precious to me. I am in no hurry and am exceedingly glad to give every satisfaction to our best friend, Lord Nelson. The question, then, is what we can best do that all may be perfectly satisfied. Sea-bathing is usefull to your health; I see it is, and wish you to continue it a little longer; but I must confess that I regret, whilst the season is favourable, that I cannot enjoy my favourite pastime of quiet fishing.

He ended, as she had done, on a placatory note: 'I care not a pin for the great world, and am attached to no one as much as to you.'[9]

Sir William later elaborated his dissatisfaction with their way of life in another, longer letter in which he complained that 'the whole of [his] wife's attention' was 'given to Lord N. and his interest at Merton'. Sir William 'well knew the purity' of their friendship and well understood also 'how uncomfortable it would make his Lordship, [their] best friend, if a separation were to take place'. This would be an extremity which would be '*essentially detrimental* to all parties', but would be 'more sensibly felt' by their dear friend than by themselves. He was willing to go on upon the present footing, provided the expenses of housekeeping did not increase 'beyond all measure' – of which he confessed he did 'see some danger'.[10]

'I am arrived at an age when some repose is really necessary,' he went on;

... I was sensible, & said so when I married, that I wou'd be superannuated when my wife wou'd be in her full beauty and vigour of youth. That time is arrived and we must make the most of it for the comfort of both parties.

Unfortunately our tastes as the manner of living are very different. I by no means wish to live in solitary retreat, but to have seldom less than 12 to 14 at table, those varying continually, is coming back to what was so irksome to me in Italy during the latter years of my residence in that Country ... I hope I may be allowed sometimes to be my own master, & pass my time according to my own inclination, either by going to my fishing parties on the Thames or by going to London to attend the Museum, R. Society, the Tuesday Club, & Auctions of Pictures ...

I am fully determined not to have any more of the very silly altercations that happen too often between us and embitter the present moments exceedingly. If really we cannot live together, a *wise well concerted* separation is preferable but I think, considering the probability of my not troubling any party long in this world, the best for us all would be to bear those ills we have rather than flie to those we know not of ... There is no time for nonsense or trifling. I know & admire your talents and many excellent qualities but I am not blind to your defects & confess having many myself; therefore let us bear and forbear for God's sake.[11]

The entertainments in Merton and Piccadilly continued, however. Dances were given for Nelson's nephews and nieces; there were more large dinners; and in February there was a grand musical evening when a hundred guests listened to their hostess singing and playing the pianoforte. Sir William escaped when he could, occasionally accompanied by Lord Nelson, more often on his own. He went to Queen Charlotte's birthday reception at court where Lady Hamilton was not welcome. Lady Nelson might have been present, so Lord Nelson did not go either.

By the end of March it was clear that Sir William did not have long to live. 'He can't in my opinion get over it,' his secretary reported. 'He is going off as an Inch of Candle.'[12] He knew himself to be dying and instructed Greville to ensure that no friend, 'wiser or better' than himself, was permitted to come to see him to disturb his tranquillity by endeavouring to prepare him for death. He died, aged seventy-two, on 6 April 1803, 'without a sigh or a struggle', his wife comforting him in her arms, Nelson sitting by his side, holding his hand. 'Unhappy day for the forlorn Emma,' she wrote by way of an epitaph. 'Ten minutes past ten Dear Blessed Sir William left me.'[13] 'Poor Lady H. is as you may expect desolate,' Nelson told Davison. 'I hope she will be left properly but I doubt it.'[14]

The widow immediately ordered mourning clothes for her household and, for herself, mourning jewellery of a necklace, earrings and bracelet. She then, disregarding Nelson's wish that she should make Merton her permanent home, moved to a house in Clarges Street.

The will contained no surprises. Charles Greville was confirmed as Sir William's heir. Emma was left an annuity of £800 and a capital sum of £800 with £100 for her mother. Her debts were to be paid in addition to £700 which he had already settled on reading a letter from Coutts Bank left out for him to see. The money eventually came to her from Greville who, ignoring that it should be paid 'clear of all deductions', took off an appropriate sum for income tax.[15]

Nelson – whose letters were now written on mourning paper, a practice not yet common – was left two sporting guns and an enamel miniature by Henry Bone of Mme Vigée Le Brun's portrait of Emma as a bacchante. It was 'a small token of the great regard' he had for his lordship, 'the most virtuous, loyal and truly brave character' he had ever met. 'And shame,' Sir William had added, 'fall on those who do not say amen.'*

Mme Vigée-Lebrun, who was then living in London, left a card at Lady Hamilton's house soon after Sir William's death. 'She came round to see me, wearing deep mourning with a dense black veil surrounding her,' Mme Vigée-Lebrun wrote in her memoirs.

She had her splendid hair cut off to follow the new 'Titus' fashion. I found this Andromache enormous, for she had become terribly fat. [She was, as Mme Le Brun noted, drinking huge amounts of porter.] She said that she was very much to be pitied, that in her husband she had lost a friend and father, and that she would never be consoled. I confess that her grief made little impression on me, since it seemed to me that she was playing a part. I was evidently not mistaken, because a few minutes later, having noticed some music lying on my piano, she took up a lively tune and began to sing it.[16]

There were others also who thought that Lady Hamilton's grief was perhaps rather more theatrical than deeply felt. 'A gentleman

---

* Sir William's biographer, Brian Fothergill, suggests that this bequest 'might have been written in irony or bravado': 'Sarcasm was not in Hamilton's line, but there is certainly a hint of ambiguity in the words, which was perhaps what he intended. It was almost superfluous to present a picture (and a copy at that) to the man who already possessed the original. Nelson's own reaction to Sir William's will was expressed in a letter to the Queen of Naples: "The good Sir William did not leave Lady Hamilton in such comfortable circumstances as his fortune would have allowed. He has given it among his relations. But she will do honour to his memory although everyone else of his friends calls loudly against him on that account." The letter was most ungenerous to Sir William's memory. The annual sum he left Emma was ample provision, by the monetary values of the day, for a widow of her rank, and there is no record of anyone except Nelson calling loudly against him on this aspect of his will. He certainly knew better than to give Emma access to capital which she would very rapidly have squandered' (Fothergill, *Sir William Hamilton*, 418–19).

Believing that Lady Hamilton had not been adequately provided for, Nelson wrote to Alexander Davison soon after Sir William's death, 'I beg that you will have the goodness to Pay on my account to Emma Lady Hamilton the Sum of One Hundred Pounds on the first day of every month till further orders' (BL Egerton MSS. 2,240, f. 161, 17 May 1803).

passing along Piccadilly saw a crowd of people at Sir W. Hamilton's door,' recorded the gregarious traveller and archaeologist Sir William Gill.

... Seeing everybody looking up at the window he looked also, and there was to be seen Lady Hamilton in all the *wildness of her grief.* Some said her attitudes were fine; others that they were affected; others that they were natural. At last, as the gentleman was leaving this motley group, some of whom were crying, and others laughing, he heard a child go up to its mamma and say; 'Ma, Mamma, don't cry, pray don't cry, for they say as how it's all Sham.'[17]

Captain Hardy's comment upon Sir William's death was characteristically down to earth: 'Hamilton died on Sunday afternoon. How her Ladyship will manage to Live with the *Hero* of the *Nile* now, I am at a loss to know, at least in an *honourable way.*'[18]

To Lord Minto, 'she talked very freely of her situation with Nelson, and of the construction the world may have put upon it'. She 'protested,' Minto wrote, 'that her attachment was perfectly pure'.[19]

29

The *Victory*

I have every reason to hope that the 6th of June will immortalize your own Nelson your fond Nelson.

The month after Sir William's death England declared war on France. The declaration had been expected for some time, and Nelson had been giving the government the benefit of his advice with the resumption of hostilities in mind. He had advised that the garrison on Malta be maintained, in contradiction of the speech in the House of Lords in which he had belittled the importance of the island. He had also given his views on the payment of prize-money and had suggested that the life of a sailor should be made more secure by opening a register in which the man's name could be recorded and by guaranteeing him an income, whether he were employed or not, after a certain length of service. He proposed two guineas a year after five years' service and four guineas after eight. It might appear 'an enormous sum', he conceded; but when it was borne in mind that the average life of a seaman was 'from old age, finished at forty-five years', it would not prove exorbitant, for the man would not have many years left in which to enjoy the annuity.[1]

As the weeks went by that spring and early summer of 1803 Nelson's visits to the Admiralty became more frequent. He had moved out of 23 Piccadilly immediately after his friend's death, thinking it seemly to do so, even though Sarah Nelson had come up from Norfolk to be with Emma. He had taken his belongings to lodgings at 19 Piccadilly over a saddler's shop, and was often to be seen walking down the Mall towards Whitehall.

He had been told that he was to be appointed to the command in the Mediterranean; and there was much to do before the appointment was officially confirmed. There were tradesmen to interview as suppliers of goods to his new flagship, matters to be settled at Merton, orders to be given to his new secretary, John Scott, the former purser of the *Royal Sovereign*, and arrangements to be made for a proxy to take his place at the installation of Knights of the Bath at Westminster Abbey. His esquires were to have been John Tyson and his nephews, Thomas and Horace. His proxy was now to be Captain William Bolton, the son of a clergyman who was his sister Susannah's brother-in-law. It being necessary that the proxy should also be a knight, Captain Bolton was himself knighted before the ceremony, so that his cousin Kitty, whom he was to marry the day before the ceremony, was Lady Bolton on her wedding day.*

One of Nelson's other duties before leaving for the fleet was to arrange the christening of his daughter, Horatia, now two and a half years old.

This took place in Mrs Gibson's parish of St Marylebone on 13 May 1803. The church, which became the parish chapel after the present church was built in 1813–17 and has since been demolished, was very small, though the parish was one of the largest in London. It was so big, indeed, that on occasions as many as eight coffins were piled up 'in the most indecent manner on the pews' awaiting burial.[2] There was no font, so the infants were baptized with water taken from a bowl placed on the communion table. On the day of Horatia's christening seven other children were baptized. Mrs Gibson was instructed by Lady Hamilton to give both the clergyman and the parish clerk a double fee, and to bring away a copy of the entry in the register which, without recording the name of either parent, gave the name of the child as 'Horatia Nelson Thompson'.[3]

'When you see my elève,' Nelson wrote to Emma soon after his

---

* Nelson had originally proposed that Alexander Davison should be his proxy. To this the King objected strongly: 'The question before the House of Commons on the Ilchester election [see page 348] would make it highly improper that the honour of knighthood should be conferred on Mr Davison. Probably some officer of the Navy may easily be found to represent Lord Nelson on this occasion' (Autograph Letters Addressed to William Marsden, Esquire, William Marsden Papers, 17 May 1803).

arrival in Portsmouth, 'give her a kiss from me, and tell her that I never shall forget either her or her dear good mother, and do you believe me.'

From a room in the George Inn, he addressed another letter to Emma, telling her that he would soon be stepping into a boat to be rowed out to his flagship. 'I can only pray that the great God of heaven may bless and preserve you,' he wrote, 'and that we may meet again in peace and true happiness. I have no fears.'

The streets outside the inn's doors were noisy with the rattle of carts and carriages transporting provisions and officers down to the quay, the shouts of porters carrying baggage on their shoulders and trundling barrows piled with cases and sea chests. Drovers belaboured the hindquarters of cattle with their long poles; sailors sat drinking and smoking their pipes before setting off for their ships.

Nelson's flagship, the *Victory*, lay far out. She was a fine first-rate ship of the line of 104 guns, including thirty thirty-two-pounders capable of penetrating two feet of oak a mile distant. She had been ordered at the Royal Dockyard, Chatham, in 1758, the year of Nelson's birth, and had been launched with her oak timbers fully seasoned in 1765 at a cost of £63,176. The largest ship ever ordered by the Royal Navy, she had twenty-seven miles of standing and running rigging and under all plain sail set four acres of canvas. Fully manned, she carried 850 men, most of whom lived and slept on the lower gun deck, crammed together in the gloom when at sea with the gun ports closed. There were far more than were needed to sail the ship but in battle there was hard work for all hands as well as the gun crews. Their average age was twenty-two. A hundred of them were under twenty; the youngest was ten; four were twelve and six thirteen; less than fifty were over forty years old. One of them was said to be a woman disguised as a man.*

* There was certainly a woman in the *Defiance*. Her name was Jane Townshend. Forty years later she laid claim to the General Service Medal. Queen Victoria thought she should have it, but it was refused her on the grounds of 'dangerous precedent' (Lewis, *Social History of the Royal Navy*, 283).

Below them on the orlop deck were the surgeon's quarters and those of the junior officers. The captain's relatively spacious cabin lay behind the nine-paned upper windows of the stern; below it were the admiral's quarters, his day cabin, dining cabin and sleeping cabin with its cot slung from a pole and enclosed by curtains which were to be embroidered for him by Lady Hamilton. Beside the cot stood a wash-stand with basin and chamber-pot.

The Great Cabin when decorated and furnished to the Admiral's requirements was an attractive and imposing apartment, lit by windows on three sides, its panelling highly polished. The day cabin, where Nelson held informal meetings with his captains, was comfortably furnished with chairs and tables, an armchair and a chest of drawers.

In the dining cabin, beneath J. H. Schmidt's portrait of Lady Hamilton, painted at Dresden in 1800, twenty-four men could sit in comfort on chairs which could be folded quickly and stored away when the ship had to be cleared for action. The long table could be dismantled and stored in twenty-two pieces.[4]

Clean and neat as the Great Cabin looked when prepared for a dinner party, it looked far less inviting when Lord Nelson climbed aboard. His furniture had not yet been unpacked; some of the parcels had not been properly labelled; his wine had not yet passed through the Custom House; his cot had been sent to a frigate far out at sea; the Bibles and prayer-books he had asked the Society for Promoting Christian Knowledge to send for the ship's company had not yet arrived. The Great Cabin still reeked of paint. Indeed, the whole ship was 'in a pretty state of confusion', besides being only half-manned; and her captain, Samuel Sutton, did not think he could get her to sea before Friday morning, to the annoyance of the Admiral, who was anxious to leave 'that horrid place, Portsmouth' as soon as possible.[5]

While he was waiting to sail, his final orders were brought to him: he was to make for Malta and thence, having taken another squadron under command, for Toulon, where he was to keep a close watch on the French fleet in harbour there. On his way he was to offer the *Victory* to Admiral Cornwallis, Commander-in-Chief of the Channel Fleet, and to sail on in another ship if Cornwallis wished to take up the offer. As it happened, he could not find Cornwallis, and, having lost a full day looking for him in vain, he told Captain Sutton to continue the search on his own and to take the *Victory* back to England for further orders if he could not find him after a fortnight's search.

Nelson himself reluctantly went aboard Captain Hardy's frigate, the *Amphion*, and sailed on in her, through rough seas, towards the coast of Portugal. He caught a cold in the unpleasant weather; but, while dreadfully cramped, the *Amphion* was more comfortable than he had expected, and his secretary, John Scott, recorded agreeable dinner parties at which toasts were drunk to Lady Hamilton and Horatia Nelson Thompson, and Nelson expressed hopes of a war just long enough to make him 'independent in pecuniary matters'.

'Your dear picture, and Horatia's are hung up,' he assured Emma. 'It revives me even to look at them. Your health is as regularly drunk as ever.' 'I am thinking of you and her every moment,' he had written earlier. 'My heart is full to bursting . . . I feel a thorough conviction that we shall meet again with Honor, Riches and Health and remain together till a good old age . . . God is good and in His wisdom will unite us . . . Believe me, my dear Emma, your most faithful and affectionate friend till Death, and if possible, longer.'[6]

Such letters poured from his pen:

My dearest beloved to say that I think of you by day night and all day and all night but too faintly expresses my feelings of love and affection towards you . . . I am incapable of wronging you in thought word or deed no not all the wealth of Peru could buy me for one moment it is all yours . . . and certainly from the first moment of our happy dear enchanting blessed meeting the thoughts of such happiness my dearest my beloved makes the blood fly into my head . . . Ever for ever I am yours only yours even beyond this world, Nelson & Bronte for Ever for Ever your own Nelson.[7]

As well as writing letters to Emma, he busied himself with a lengthy paper on Mediterranean strategy which he intended sending to the Prime Minister, to whom he reported his arrival in Sicily and the enthusiastic welcome accorded him there. From Sicily he went on to Naples, where he did not go ashore for fear lest this would be taken as a provocation by the French, who had already landed troops in southern Italy at Brindisi, Otranto and Taranto.

On 8 July the *Amphion* arrived off Toulon, where the *Victory* joined Nelson's fleet, and Captain Hardy took over the flagship from Captain Sutton. Nelson liked Sutton, but no flag-captain suited him better than Hardy. 'How is it,' he once asked him, 'that you and I never disagree, while my other captains never let me do a thing without at first resisting?'

'It is, Sir,' Hardy replied candidly, 'from my being always first lieutenant when you like to be captain, and flag-captain when you have a fancy for being admiral.'[8]

As admiral, Nelson's duty now was to keep the French ships in the port in check and, if they came out, 'to annihilate them'. He had also to protect Gibraltar and Malta from attack and to prevent the French from making further incursions into the Kingdom of the Two Sicilies. He was well aware of the importance of his task, for if the French fleet were allowed to escape from the Mediterranean, and if the French ships in the harbours of Finistère, the Channel and the North Sea ports also escaped the vigilance of Cornwallis and Lord Keith, Bonaparte might well succeed in landing the men of his Grande Armée, now reported to be over 120,000 strong, on the English coast.

It was an irksome and arduous duty. 'Even in summer-time,' Nelson complained, 'we have a hard gale every week and two days' heavy swell.' He wrote this in a letter to Emma, who had proposed going out to the Mediterranean to be with him; and, much as he missed her, he recognized that this would be impossible and strove to put her off: 'It would kill you . . . And I, that have given orders to carry no women to sea in the *Victory*, to be the first to break them!' When the wind dropped and the sun came out the days passed pleasantly enough. The Admiral rose from his cot at five o'clock in the morning and spent two hours walking the deck until breakfast – hot rolls, toast, cold tongue and tea – at seven. There was then much writing and reading to do. So as to rest his eyes, much of his reading was done for him by the chaplain and interpreter, Alexander Scott, whose daily task it was to read aloud to him from letters found in prizes, from French, Spanish and Italian newspapers, as well as from the *Naval Chronicle*, the *European Magazine* and the *Monthly or Critical Review*, all of which were delivered regularly at Merton and sent on to him at sea.[9]

At two o'clock the ship's band struck up and, at a quarter to three, a drum tapped out the rhythm of 'The Roast Beef of Old England', which announced the Admiral's dinner. Eight or so officers, including Captain Hardy and George Murray, whom Nelson had chosen as captain of the fleet, then presented themselves in the Great Cabin. So, too, did the Admiral's secretary, John Scott, Alexander Scott (whom Nelson referred to as 'Dr Scott' to avoid confusion with his namesake) and Dr Gillespie, a Scottish surgeon. Three courses were generally served, Gillespie recorded, 'and a dessert of the choicest fruit, together with three or four of the best wines, champagne and claret not excepted'. All agreed that the fare was excellent, and Nelson took care to ensure that it was so. In a typical letter to Davison he asked his friend to have the goodness to order for him, amongst other items, 'two dozen Yorkshire hams, six Gloster cheeses, twelve pieces of Hamburgh Beef . . . Four kegs of Sour Crout, Twelve Quarts of Chilly or Pepper Vinegar, six boxes of mangoes, six dozen Piccalillies . . . fifty dozen of Browns Stout . . .'[10] 'Coffee and liquers close the dinner about half past four or five o'clock,' Dr Gillespie continued,

after which the company generally walk the deck, where the band of music plays for nearly an hour. At six o'clock, tea is announced, when the company assemble in the Admiral's cabin, where tea is served up before seven o'clock and, as we are inclined, the party continue to converse with his Lordship, who at this time generally unbends himself, though he is at all times free from stiffness and pomp as a regard to proper dignity will admit, and is very communicative. At eight o'clock a rummer of punch with cake or biscuit is served up, soon after which we wish the Admiral a good night.[11]

Nelson himself ate little at dinner, another surgeon on board the

Victory, William Beatty, noticed, often contenting himself with a wing or the liver of a fowl and a small plate of macaroni and vegetables. He never ate salt, which 'he believed to be the sole cause of scurvy', never drank more than four glasses of wine and rarely drank three, and even those were diluted with Bristol or common water. In earlier days, so Beatty said, he had lived for some time even more sparely, denying himself meat and wine and eating only vegetables and drinking milk or water in an attempt to cure himself of gout. There had been a time, however, when Nelson, in Tom Allen's opinion at least, drank more than was good for him, particularly so as he did not have a very strong head. George Parsons recalled an occasion when the Admiral gave a dinner to celebrate the victory of Cape St Vincent. As the youngest guest, Parsons was asked to sit on Nelson's right hand, 'or where the right hand should have been if it had not been forcibly carried off'.

His Lordship, after taking a bumper in honour of the glorious victory of the year ninety-seven, addressed me in a bland tone:
'You entered the service at a very early age to have been in the action off St Vincent?'
'Eleven years, my Lord.'
'Much too young,' muttered his lordship.
At this moment honest Tom Allen pushed in his bullet head with an eager gaze at his master, and after a little consideration, approached the Admiral.
'You will be ill if you take any more wine.'
'You are perfectly right, Tom, and I thank you for the hint. Hardy, do the honours. And, gentlemen, excuse me for retiring, for my battered old hulk is very crazy, – indeed not sea-worthy.'
And the greatest naval hero of the day was led from his own table by his faithful and attached servant, after drinking five glasses of wine.[12]

Although Nelson had the ability to take short catnaps in the day, sitting in one of the black leather armchairs in his cabin with his feet up on the other, Beatty was concerned that his 'wonderful activity of mind' prevented him from 'taking ordinary repose'. He seldom enjoyed two hours of uninterrupted sleep after turning in between half-past eight and nine o'clock. 'On several occasions he did not quit the deck the whole night,' Beatty said.

At these times, he took no pains to protect himself from the wet, or night air, wearing only a thin great coat; and he has frequently, after having his clothes wet through with rain, refused to have them changed, saying that the leather waistcoat which he wore over his flannel one, would secure him from complaint. He seldom wore boots and was consequently very liable to have his feet wet. When this occurred he has often been known to go down to his cabin, throw off his clothes and walk on the carpet in his stockings for the purpose of drying the feet of them. He chose to adopt this uncomfortable expedient rather than give his servants the trouble of assisting him to put on fresh stockings, which, from his having only one hand, he could not himself conveniently effect.[13]

His health suffered from time to time accordingly. 'I really believe that my shatter'd carcase is in the worst plight of the whole fleet,' he was soon to complain.

I have had a sort of rheumatic fever. I am now better of that but have violent pain in my side and night sweats ... the pain in my heart and spasms I have not had for some time now [possibly, he thought, as a result of the camphor and opium his doctor prescribed] ... the constant anxiety I have experienced has shook my weak frame and my rings will hardly keep upon my fingers. What gives me more [concern than anything] is that I can every month perceive a visible (if I may be allowed the expression) loss of sight. A few years must, as I have always predicted, render me blind. I have often heard that blind people are cheerful, but I think I shall take it to heart.'

'My eye-sight fails me most dreadfully,' he wrote in other letters, 'I firmly believe that, in a few years, I shall be stone blind. It is this only of all my maladies, that makes me unhappy, but God's will be done ... I hope to hold out till after the Battle but, as you know, mine is a wretched constitution, and my sight is getting very, very bad.'[14] Beatty agreed that he might well have gone blind 'had he continued at sea';* but in other respects his health was not so bad

* Modern medical opinion does not subscribe to this view. 'Increasing presbyopia [changes that take place naturally in the eye with the advance of age], the inability of the eyes to focus on close objects, coupled with recurrent activity in

as he so often felt and declared it to be. Beatty could confidently assert 'that his Lordship's health was uniformly good, with the exception of some slight attacks of indisposition arising from accidental causes, and which never continued above two or three days ... The only bodily pain which his Lordship felt in consequence of his many wounds, was a sight rheumatic affliction of the stump of his amputated arm on any sudden variation in the state of the weather.'

There were, however, occasions when pain or seasickness made him morose and short-tempered, or, as he put it himself, 'confoundedly out of humour'. Admiral Lord Radstock advised his son, a midshipman in the *Victory*, to beware of this: Lord Nelson was of 'hasty temper'; he was 'a man of strong passions, and his prejudices [were] proportionate'.[15]

Another officer in the *Victory*, Lieutenant Joseph Willcock, recalled how, when pushing against a door that opened on to a ladder leading down to Nelson's cabin, he almost knocked the Admiral over on to the deck. 'Mr Willcock, can't you see what you are doing?' Nelson asked him angrily, as he steadied himself and strode away. He took the trouble, however, to speak kindly to Willcock subsequently. On a later occasion, having had one of

---

the pterygium, is more likely,' the surgeon T. C. Barras thinks, 'to have caused his fear of blindness than the old injury to the right eye.' Barras quotes a *Times* newspaper report of 4 October 1804: 'It is generally understood that the gallant Lord Nelson has lost one eye; and a few days ago a paragraph appeared in one of the papers lamenting that his remaining eye was considerably weaker of late, and expressing an apprehension that he might altogether lose his sight. We beg to inform admirers who are not personally acquainted with him, that Lord Nelson is not blind of either eye ... It is true that he, for a short period lost the sight of one eye but it has happily been restored. He has also had a speck on the other eye; but that he could see with both at no very distant date, we are assured from the very best authority, that of his Lordship's own information, who has declared that "he could see best with (what people called) his worst eye" (T. C. Barras, FRCS, 'I Have a Right to be Blind Sometimes', *Nelson Dispatch*, vol. 2, part 9, January 1987, 163–8). Another surgeon, Timothy G. Williams, has come to conclusions similar to those of Barras, suggesting that Nelson's reduced vision was the result of bilateral medical pterygia (*World Medicine*, 16 October 1982).

his altercations with the quartermaster over the steering of the ship, Nelson went over to Captain Hardy and said lightheartedly, 'Look, Hardy. That man tells me I lie.' He was, indeed, so Willcock said, 'generally mild and calm in his temper', leaving the discipline of the ship to Hardy, who was deemed something of a martinet.[16]

Nelson had more than his fleet and his health to worry about. His thoughts were constantly returning to Merton, to Emma and Horatia. He was concerned that Emma should not 'lay out more than was necessary at Merton', that his daughter, who was there rather more often since Sir William's death, should not come to harm while playing in the grounds, that due care was taken that she did not fall into the canal. Once more he suggested that that some 'strong netting about three feet high' was 'placed round the Nile so that the little thing may not tumble in', adding that he would be 'very anxious' until he knew that this had been done. Soon afterwards he wrote again: 'Only take care that my darling does not fall in and get drowned. I begged you to get the little netting along the edge; and particularly along the bridges . . . Kiss my dearest Horatia for me. I shall hope to see her at Merton on my arrival.' The thought that she was not there nearly as often as she should be preoccupied him. It was not right, he insisted, that she should be left any longer at Little Titchfield Street; the time had come to remove the child from 'a mere nurse and to think of educating her'. She was, after all, 'by no means destitute of a fortune'. Emma's cousin, Miss Connor, should become her 'tutoress' under Emma's eye. He would allow Miss Connor any salary which was thought proper. In letter after letter he expressed his anxiety: 'How is my dear Horatia? I hope you have her under your guardian wing at Merton *fixed*.' He wrote to the solicitor as well as to Emma on the matter; and when Emma gave as an excuse Mrs Gibson's reluctance to part with the child, he wrote a quasi-official letter to 'My dearest Lady Hamilton' in which he informed her of his earnest wishes in the matter, of his desire that Lady Hamilton should take the girl under her guardianship so that she could be 'properly educated and brought up', of his intention to settle a pension of £20 a year upon Mrs Gibson. 'But should Mrs Gibson endeavour, under any pretence, to keep my adopted daughter any longer in her care, then I do not hold myself bound to give her one farthing; and I shall, most probably, take other measures.'[17]

By then Nelson had also been deeply agitated by the news that Emma was pregnant again. She had contrived to conceal the fact from her friends and Nelson's family, taking to her bed with 'soor throat cold cough'. For a month Nelson was in such a state of anxiety that he could scarcely sleep, and when he learnt that the baby had died, 'that "dear little Emma"', as she had been named, 'was no more', he confessed that he was in 'a raging fever all night'. He could only be 'thankful to God' that little Emma's mother and their dear Horatia, who had had smallpox, had both been spared. 'The loss of one – much more of both would have driven [him] mad'.[18]

Despite his worries and preoccupations, Nelson took it upon himself to make sure that the ship, as all other ships in the fleet, was well supplied with vegetables as well as fresh meat. In one characteristic order he told the captain of the *Active* to 'purchase 50 head of good sheep for the use of the sick on board the different ships . . . and 30,000 good oranges for the fleet with onions and any other vegetables that will keep about eight to ten days . . . to remove the taint of scurvy'. In another, addressed to the Agent Victualler at Gibraltar, he asked for cocoa and sugar instead of rice and sugar, rice not being 'much liked by the Ship's companies'.[19] He himself, little as he ate, always took care to ensure that he did not neglect the fruit and vegetables served at his table, being as conscientious in this regard as he was to take the camphor and opium for the spasms and pain in his heart.

He was also conscientious about wearing his hat with its attached green eye-shade, though Mr Beatty, the surgeon, feared that this precaution would not save his sight, since he insisted on spending so much time on deck peering through his telescope in the bright sunlight.

Beatty was equally concerned at the hours he spent at his desk in dealing with the numerous applications which were made to him on behalf of friends and relatives, in writing such official letters as those addressed to the Admiralty asking for more frigates, 'the Eyes of the Fleet', and in composing such letters as that sent to Lady Hamilton's cousin, Charles Connor, who, on receiving his commission, was assured that if he 'deserved well' he could be sure of the Admiral's assistance, and urged to remember that 'you must be a Seaman to be an Officer and that you cannot be a good Officer without being a Gentleman'.[20]

At one point he felt constrained to ask for a few months' sick leave: but then he was beset by worry that there would be so many other officers 'desirous of the Mediterranean Command' that he might not be allowed to return to it and would be 'laid on the shelf'.

The weather did nothing to improve his malaise, exacerbated as it was by his constant fretting about his 'wretched constitution', which was 'most severely shocked',[21] and by his concern for the ships in his fleet, several of which were sadly in need of repair and some of which, from time to time, lost men by desertion when they put in for supplies at Mediterranean ports.

The fear that the French fleet would escape from Toulon was never far from his thoughts. He could have prevented this by blocking the port closely; but he did not want the French to remain in port: his system, he insisted, was the 'very contrary of blockading'. He hoped to entice the enemy admiral into the open sea and thereby destroy his fleet. This admiral was the aristocratic turncoat, the Vicomte Louis de la Touche-Tréville, who had repelled the assault on Boulogne two years before; and Nelson was anxious to avenge the defeat. The Vicomte was cautious, however, occasionally coming out to 'cut a caper' but then going in again and declining for the moment to fight. 'My friend sometimes plays bo-peep in and out of Toulon, like a mouse at the edge of her hole,' Nelson commented; and when a French ship did come out she soon sailed back again, a manoeuvre misreported in the Paris newspapers and repeated in some London ones. 'You will have seen Monsieur La Touche's letter of how he chased me and how I *ran*,' Nelson wrote crossly to his brother William. 'By God, if I take him he shall *Eat* it.'[22]

Soon afterwards, in August, the Vicomte died. He was succeeded in command by a much younger man, Pierre-Charles-Jean-Baptiste-Silvestre de Villeneuve, who had been captain of the *Guillaume Tell*, which Captain Berry had captured after her escape from Abū Qīr Bay; and in January 1805, to Nelson's consternation, Villeneuve succeeded in escaping from Toulon, eluding the British fleet, and sailing God knew whither. 'I am in a fever!' Nelson confessed, at a loss to tell whether his enemy had made for Sardinia or Sicily, Malta, Naples or Alexandria. 'God send I may find them!'[23]

He tried Sardinia at first without success, then Naples, then Malta. But the French were nowhere to be seen. They were not off Alexandria either; and it was not until the third week of February 1805 that Nelson discovered they had been driven by adverse winds back into Toulon. It could only be a matter of time, however, before Villeneuve made another attempt to get out of Toulon and rendezvous with the other French fleets and with the Spaniards, whose government had by now been induced by Bonaparte to declare war on Britain. This was a prospect which the British government was dreading; and in the middle of April it was learned in London that the ministers' fears had been realized: Admiral Villeneuve had escaped not merely from Toulon but through the Strait of Gibraltar and into the Atlantic.

Bonaparte had crowned himself Emperor in Notre-Dame on 2 December the year before, taking the crown from the hands of the Pope and placing it on his own head. Master of the continent of Europe, he now had only the British to subdue. He had planned to do so by ordering his own and his allies' fleets to smash their way through their respective blockades and concentrate in West Indian waters, and then, in a single unassailable armada, to sail back to Europe, overwhelm the outnumbered British navy and clear the Channel for his long-planned invasion.

As soon as he heard that Villeneuve was on his way to the West Indies, Nelson determined to pursue him, though his own fleet was half the strength of the enemy's. Delayed at first by adverse winds, then by one of his ships, the *Superb*, which could not keep up with the others, he buoyed himself up with the hope that a fast passage across the Atlantic might enable him to catch his quarry. Supposing that considerate words would induce the *Superb*'s captain to do his utmost to keep up with the rest of the fleet, he sent over a kindly note to the captain: 'I am fearful that you think the *Superb* does not go as fast as I could wish. However that may be (for if we all went ten knots I should not think it fast enough) yet I would have you assured that I know and feel the *Superb* does all that which is possible for a Ship to accomplish; and I desire that you will not fret on the occasion.'[24]

By the beginning of June he was, so he told Lady Hamilton, 'within Six days of the Enemy'. 'Pray for my success,' he added, 'and my laurels I shall lay with pleasure at your feet and a Sweet Kiss will be ample reward for all your Nelson's hard fag . . . I have every reason to hope that the 6th of June will immortalize your own Nelson your fond Nelson.'[25]

But Villeneuve was not to be found. The British general commanding on the island of St Lucia, Robert Brereton, assured Nelson that the French had sailed south in the direction of Trinidad; and although Nelson himself thought it much more likely that they had gone north to Martinique, he reluctantly accepted the advice, which proved to be misguided. He wrote to Emma to report his bitter disappointment. 'I have ever found,' he told her, 'that if I was left and acted as my poor noddle told me was right, I should seldom err. My genius carried me direct to the spot, and all would have been as well as heart could wish, when comes across the General Brereton's information. . . . I have reason to hate the name of General Brereton as long as I live.'[26] To other correspondents he revealed his anger and chagrin: 'I am as completely miserable as my greatest enemy could wish me; but I neither blame fortune nor my own judgement. Oh, General Brereton! General Brereton! . . . Nelson would have been, living or dead, the greatest man in his profession that England ever saw.'[27]

He continued his fruitless search, sailing from island to island, greeted by reports of French arrivals and departures but encountering nothing more substantial than three planks which he thought must have come from the French fleet. Feeling 'very miserable', he set sail for Europe. Villeneuve, disobeying Napoleon's orders, had already departed; and, although Sir Robert Calder captured two of his ships, he managed to get the rest into Ferrol, north of Corunna.

Arriving off Gibraltar on 20 July 1805, Nelson went ashore for the first time since June 1803. He had been, as he said, aboard the *Victory* for 'two years wanting ten days'. It had been a most frustrating time. As he told Lady Hamilton, it had been 'mortifying, not being able to get at the enemy' in all those months; and now John Bull was probably angry, 'though he never had an officer who [had] served him more faithfully'.[28]

30

Return to Merton

All I beg in this World is that you will be kind and affectionate to my dear Daughter Horatia.

When he stepped ashore in England, however, Nelson found that he was still as much a hero with John Bull as ever. Blaming the false information he had been given in the West Indies for his inability to catch Villeneuve there, he told the seventy-nine-year-old Lord Barham – who had just succeeded his near relation Lord Melville as First Lord of the Admiralty – that his failure had almost broken his heart. But others did not consider he had failed. Indeed, Lord Minto's brother, Hugh Elliot, the British ambassador at Naples, wrote to congratulate him on his success. 'To have kept your ships afloat, your rigging standing and your crews in health and spirits . . . for two long years,' Elliot told him, 'is an effort such as never was realised in former times nor, I doubt, will ever again be repeated by any other admiral.' Moreover, had he not saved Jamaica, while a much older admiral, Sir Robert Calder, had failed – where Nelson would surely have succeeded – in preventing the French fleet escaping into Ferrol?[1]

From his first appearance in England Nelson was acclaimed wherever he went. On Portsmouth Point he was cheered as he stepped ashore, immediately recognized by everyone on the quayside with his right sleeve pinned to his chest, his glittering stars, the green shade protecting his eye. In London – where, careful to observe the conventions, he chose to take rooms at Gordon's Hotel in Albemarle Street rather than to stay with Lady Hamilton in Clarges Street – he could not appear, so an American visitor to London, the geologist and chemist, Benjamin Silliman, observed, 'without immediately collecting a retinue':

When he enters a shop the door is thronged, till he comes out, when the air rings with huzzaz and the dark cloud of the populace again moves on and hangs upon his skirts. He is a great favourite with all descriptions of people . . . My view of him was in profile. His features are sharp and his skin is now very much burnt from his having been long at sea; he has the balancing gait of a sailor; his person is spare and of about the middle height.[2]

Lord Minto thought that it was 'really quite affecting to see the wonder and admiration and love and respect of the whole world and the genuine expression of all these sentiments' the moment he was seen. It was 'beyond anything represented in a play or a poem of fame'. Minto came across him surrounded by 'a mob in Piccadilly'. He 'got hold of his arm so that he was mobbed too'.[3]

'Wherever he appears he electrifies the cold English character,' Lady Elizabeth Foster confirmed, 'and rapture and applause follow all his steps. Sometimes a poor woman asks to touch his coat. The very children learn to bless him as he passes, and doors and windows are crowded.'[4] Another witness of Nelson's fame and popularity in London was John Theophilus Lee who had gone to sea as a boy, had been in Hallowell's *Swiftsure* at the Battle of the Nile when still only twelve years old, and was afterwards to make a fortune in civilian life.

Having been to see Lee, Nelson asked him to walk with him down the Strand to the shop of John Salter, the sword cutler and jeweller. Most unusually for him, Nelson was not wearing uniform, but he still presented a remarkable sight in 'a pair of drab green breeches, high black gaiters, a yellow waistcoat, and a plain blue coat, with a cocked hat, quite square, a large green shade over the eye'. He was carrying a gold-headed stick in his hand.

The crowd ran down the Strand before him, giving him 'repeated and hearty cheers'. Indeed, he and Lee could scarcely 'get to Salter's shop, so dense was the crowd'. Nelson said, 'Does this not remind you of former days at Naples, when the crowd thus pressed on me?' 'On arriving at Salter's shop, the door was closed, and his Lordship inspected all his swords which had been presented at different times, the diamond aigrette, numerous snuffboxes etc.'[5]

The print shops near by were full of the hero's likenesses; and he was always ready to supply them with more. Busy as he was on this short leave, he found time to sit for new portraits, patiently posing at the same time for a modeller of wax medallions, Catherine Andras, and a miniaturist, to whom he observed complacently as they sat on opposite sides of him that he was not used to being attacked from port and starboard at the same time.[6]

The windows of Hannah Humphrey's shop in St James's Street, of William Fores's in Piccadilly and William Holland's in Oxford Street, of Laurie and Whittle's in Fleet Street and Ackerman's in the Strand were all crowded with caricatures in which Lord Nelson appeared prominently. The days had long since gone when he was lampooned. He was now the 'Defender of England's Shores', the 'Hero of the Nile', 'Noble Nelson, the Lord of the Main'. In one print, published within a short time of his return to England, he is shown with sabre in hand, crying 'Old England, *Death* or *Victory!*' and leading a party of outnumbered British sailors against a rabble of Spanish 'Dons and French monkeys'.[7]

Nelson arrived home at 'dear, dear Merton' at six o'clock in the morning on 22 August; and, as Emma said, how happy he was to see them all there. She had invited as many of his relatives as could be fitted into the house's fifteen bedrooms. 'We have Room for all of you,' she wrote blithely, 'so Come as soon as you can. We shall be happy, most happy.' Already there, or soon to arrive, were Sir Peter Parker, Mrs Cadogan and Dr Nelson and his family, Maurice Nelson's 'poor Blindy' and assorted Boltons and Matchams, including young George Matcham, who was required to share a bedroom with Tom Nelson, a cousin he scarcely knew.[8] Also there was Horatia, now four and a half years old and brought back hurriedly from Mrs Gibson's for her father's homecoming, for, despite his repeated injunctions, she had not been settled permanently at Merton in his absence.

The little girl seemed contented enough. She had had occasional outings while living at Mrs Gibson's: for instance, her mother took her with Charlotte Nelson to Eton on the Fourth of June when, in

Charlotte's words, they saw her brother Horace 'in a beautiful Gold and White dress' being rowed by 'Gallie Slaves' in a boat rigged out as a Roman galley.[9] Charlotte's uncle wrote to tell her how pleased he was that she was fond of Horatia.

I am truly sensible of your kind regard for that dear little orphan Horatia. Although her parents are lost yet she is not without a fortune and I shall *curse* them who *curse* her and heaven bless them who bless her. Dear Innocent she can have injured no one. I am glad to hear that she is attached to you and if she takes after her parents so she will to those who are kind to her. I am ever dear Charlotte your affectionate uncle Nelson & Bronte.[10]

Horatia had received regular letters from her 'dear god-papa', and one inscribed 'your most affectionate Father'. They enjoined her 'to be obedient and attentive' to 'her Guardian' so that should he himself not live to see her 'virtuously brought up', she would 'prove to be an ornament to [her] sex'.

He sent her 'twelve books of Spanish dresses'. Later he gave her a child's set of knife, fork and spoon engraved with her name, and a silver-gilt goblet inscribed, 'To my much loved Horatia'.

He promised to send her a watch in a characteristic letter:

My Dear Horatia
I feel very much pleased by your kind letter and for your present of a lock of your beautiful hair. I am very glad to hear that you are so good and mind everything which your governess Miss Connor and dear Lady Hamilton tell you, I send you a lock of my hair and a pound note to buy a locket to put it in and I give you leave to wear it when you are dressed and behave well, and I send you another to buy some little thing for Mary and your governess.

As I am sure that for the world you would not tell a story, it must have slipt my memory that I promised you a Watch therefore I have sent to Naples to get one and I will send it home as soon as it arrives – the Dog I never could have promised as we have no Dogs on board ship, Only I beg my dear Horatia be obedient and you will ever be sure of the affection of NELSON & BRONTE.[11]

When the watch arrived it came with a short letter: 'I send you a Watch which I give you permission to wear on Sundays and on very particular days when you are dressed and have behaved exceedingly Well and Obedient. I have kissed it and send it with the Affectionate BLESSING of YOUR Nelson & Bronte.'[12]

Worried about the child's health and future, Nelson had written – too late – to Emma about his concern that she had not yet been 'innoculated with the cow-pox', and about his wish – to be incorporated in a codicil to his will and not be communicated 'to any person breathing' – that his 'adopted daughter', as well as receiving £4,000, should marry his nephew, Horatio, and thus bear his name, if the boy should prove worthy of such a treasure as he was sure she would prove to be.[13] Concerned also about her money, he told Emma that as soon as he got home he intended putting it out of her power 'to spend Horatia's money'. He was going to 'settle it in trustees' hands and leave nothing to chance'.[14] 'All I beg in this World,' he wrote in another letter, 'is that you will be kind and affectionate to my *dear Daughter Horatia*.'[15] It was not to be wondered at if Emma felt rather put out by these persistent instructions and admonitions and if she felt perhaps a little jealous of the child.

She had certainly endeavoured to arouse jealousy in him, telling him of the proposals of marriage she had received in his absence, one from the son of a viscount, another from an earl. But Nelson was not to be provoked, as he had been in the past by stories of the attentions of the Prince of Wales: he cared 'nothing for her titled offers'. He hoped one day she would be Duchess of Bronte and 'then a fig for them all!'[16]

It was clear that Lady Hamilton did not want Horatia to interfere with her own busy and restless life during Nelson's absences. She had been much in demand, dining at Lady Cawdor's, dancing at Lady Cholmondeley's, performing her 'Attitudes' at Lady Abercorn's, and still doing them beautifully, according to Lady Bessborough, 'notwithstanding her enormous size'. At Clarges Street she had been a generous and assiduous hostess, entertaining opera singers and that disreputable wreck, the Duke of Queensberry, as well as such grand ladies as the Duchess of Devonshire and the Countess of Macclesfield. Often she had left

London, darting about the country from Southend to Norfolk, from Ramsgate – where her 'fat shoulders and breast' reminded Joseph Farrington of Rubens's bacchantes – to Canterbury, where Dr Nelson's fellow clergy and their wives were shocked by her exuberant behaviour and her remarkable consumption of champagne.

Everywhere she went she spent money. Despite persistent applications both by Lord Nelson and on her own behalf, she had so far failed in her efforts to get a pension as a reward for all the work she claimed to have done in Naples and all the expenses that Sir William had incurred there; and she had been obliged in emergencies to turn to Nelson's friends for loans, even asking his former secretary, John Tyson, to lend her £150, though she had recently, with carefree generosity, lent Mr Bolton £200 and given Mrs Bolton a most expensive tippet as a Christmas present.[17]

Nelson allowed her £100 a month for housekeeping at Merton, yet she spent far more than this and owed money not only to the village tradespeople but even to the head gardener, Thomas Cribb, who – reported Mrs Cadogan in her capacity as housekeeper when her daughter was in London – was 'quite distrest for money'. 'He would be glad if you could bring him the £13 he paid to the mowers,' Mrs Cadogan wrote. 'My dear Emma, I have got the baker's and butcher's bills cast up; they come to 1 hundred pounds, seventeen shillings.'[18]

Emma had also by now expended huge sums of money on improvements and alterations to the house and grounds and would have spent even more had not Alexander Davison checked her. The downstairs rooms had been redecorated – as indeed had the house in Clarges Street – and new kitchens had been built. Water-closets and dressing-rooms had been installed upstairs; outside in the enlarged grounds no fewer than twenty men and boys had been put to work under Thomas Cribb. The tunnel beneath the road had been completed; and a new walk, known as 'The Poop', had been laid out leading to a Palladian summer-house. Nelson was forced to conclude with sad resignation that he hardly knew how to find the money to pay for all this but it was now 'too late to say a word'. He had already told Emma that, although he would bring home 'a most faithful and honourable heart', he would not return with 'any riches – [those] the Administration took care to give to others'. He told Davison he really would have to make economies somehow, yet Lady Hamilton must continue to have her own way so far as his money allowed: 'I will admit no display of taste at Merton but hers ... I hope [she] will continue to improve and beautify it to the day at least of my death.'[19]

He seemed delighted to be back at Merton. His little Horatia struck him as a most appealing child. She trotted happily round the garden, followed by the black girl, Fatima; she rode her rocking-horse on the terraces, 'equipped with riding-crop and top hat – a very enterprising little Amazon'.[20] She was 'uncommonly quick' and, so Emma told the child's father, had begun to learn Italian as well as French and had started piano lessons. 'I love my dear god-papa,' she once told her mother, so Emma said, 'but Mrs Gibson told me he killed all the peoples, and I was afraid.'[21] Emma herself, now forty years old and stouter than ever, was as vivacious and as attractive to him as she had always been. As Lord Minto observed when he came to dinner that summer, the passion was 'as hot as ever'.[22]

Lord Minto sat down to his meal surrounded by the family of whom Nelson was so clearly fond. Lady Hamilton sat at the head of the table, 'Mother Cadogan at the bottom'. Nelson 'looked remarkably well and full of spirits': his conversation was 'cordial in these low times'. The Worcester china on the table was decorated with the Viscount's coat of arms; the plate, £500 worth of which had been presented to him by the Committee of Lloyd's, was incised with his monogram; on the walls hung pictures celebrating his achievements. But the talk was easy and informal; and, as George Matcham said, his uncle was 'so far from being the hero of his own tale' that he never, in Matcham's presence, alluded 'voluntarily to any of the great actions of his life. He delighted in quiet conversation, through which occasionally ran an undercurrent of pleasantry not unmixed with caustic wit. At his table he was the least heard among the company ... He was remarkable for a demeanour, quiet, sedate and unobtrusive, anxious to give pleasure to everyone about him, distinguishing each in turn by some act of kindness, and chiefly those who seemed to require it the most.'[23]

The Danish historian, J. A. Andersen, who drove to Merton with a copy of his account of the bombardment of Copenhagen on the very day of Nelson's own arrival, also wrote of his quiet, unostentatious bearing. Andersen was 'ushered into a magnificent apartment where Lady Hamilton sat at a window'. He at first 'scarcely observed his Lordship, he having placed himself immediately at the entrance'. He was wearing a 'uniform emblazoned with the different Orders of Knighthood ... He received me with the utmost condescension,' Andersen continued.

Chairs being provided, he sat down between Lady Hamilton and myself, and having laid my account of the Battle of Copenhagen on his knee a conversation ensued ... The penetration of his eye threw a kind of light upon his countenance, which tempered its severity, and rendered his harsh features in some measure agreeable ... Lord Nelson had not the least pride of rank; he combined with that degree of dignity which a man of quality should have, the most engaging address.[24]

Although wearing his uniform and decorations on this occasion he was more often to be seen at Merton in civilian clothes, his colourful mixture of green breeches, black gaiters, yellow waistcoat and blue coat in the daytime, a black coat in the evenings. According to Benjamin Goldsmid's son, Lionel, 'that funny-looking fellow Lord Nelson' was not at all careful in his dress when at home or visiting friends. At Roehampton one day Lionel saw him walking up and down the large drawing-room with his mother. 'He was dressed in a naval coat, white naval breeches, silk stockings, hanging on as if not pulled up, too large, and shoes rather high in the quarters large with buckles.'[25]

Old friends were welcome but still not 'the great', except the Duke of Clarence, who came over once from Bushy Park – but then the Duke, who did not like to stand upon ceremony, was more like an old salt than a member of the royal family. In the past several of his naval friends had been to stay, including Foley, Fremantle, Hallowell and Ball, though all without their wives; and Hardy – disapproving as he was of Nelson's relationship with Lady

Hamilton – called more than once.*[26] Yet for the most part the dinner guests at Merton were members of Nelson's family with whom he felt comfortably at ease and he liked to keep it so.

His awkwardness with strangers which led him to outbursts of bombastic absurdity was observed at this time by the Duke of Wellington, then Major-General the Hon. Sir Arthur Wellesley, who, having recently returned from distinguished service in India, came across him in a room of the Colonial Office where they were both waiting to see Lord Castlereagh. Years later the Duke recalled this meeting with 'a gentleman, whom from his likeness to his pictures and the loss of an arm, I immediately recognized as Lord Nelson. He could not know who I was,' Wellington told John Wilson Croker,

but he entered at once into conversation with me, if I can call it conversation, for it was almost all on his side and all about himself and, in reality, a style so vain and so silly as to surprise and almost disgust me.

I suppose something that I happened to say may have made him guess that I was *somebody* and he went out of the room for a moment, I have no doubt to ask the office-keeper who I was, for when he came back he was altogether a different man, both in manner and matter.

His 'charlatan style' had quite vanished and 'he talked of the state of the country and of the aspect and probabilities of affairs on

---

* The quarrel with Troubridge had never been made up. When Troubridge had been ill and unable to write, Nelson had sent him 'a fractious note accusing him of ingratitude. The effect was catastrophic. "It has really so unhinged me that I am quite unmanned and crying. I would sooner forfeit my life, my everything, than be deemed ungrateful to an officer and a friend, I feel it so much. Pray, pray, acquit me for I really do not merit it. There is not a man I love, honour and esteem more than your Lordship." A friendly letter from Nelson brought some comfort, but it could not alter Troubridge's general state of mind. From now on his letters become one long catalogue of complaints, criticism and abuse' (Kennedy, *Nelson's Band of Brothers*, 194–5). Distressed by Troubridge's refusal to go to Merton, Nelson wrote to Captain Murray, 'I thank you for driving seven miles to make me a visit; for could you believe it there are those who I thought were my firm friends, some of near thirty years standing, who have never taken the trouble.' James Saumarez did not visit Merton either, but he and Nelson were not close (ibid., 273).

the Continent with a good sense and a knowledge of subjects both at home and abroad. The Secretary of State kept us long waiting,' Wellington continued,

and certainly for the last half or three-quarters of an hour, I don't know that I ever had a conversation that interested me more. Now, if the Secretary of State had been punctual ... I should have had the same impression of a light and trivial character that other people have had, but luckily I saw enough to be satisfied that he was really a very superior man; but certainly a more sudden or complete metamorphosis I never saw.[27]

Nelson's call upon Castlereagh was one of several he paid that summer upon various government ministers, including the Prime Minister himself, to give his advice on naval matters. Encouraged by Emma to believe that he could become as great a statesman as he was a sailor, his thoughts occasionally turned again to the possibility of a political life for himself when the war was over. He strongly disliked party politics, however, and regretted having followed Alexander Davison's advice and given his proxy vote in the House of Lords to Lord Moira.

Davison had scarcely been the wisest choice as counsellor in such a matter. A disappointed politician himself, he had tried to enter Parliament as Member for Ilchester and had served a term of imprisonment in the Marshalsea following charges of wholesale bribery of the electorate. He was subsequently to go to prison again, having been found guilty, as a government contractor, of receiving 'by means of false vouchers and receipts a commission on the amount of goods which he himself had supplied as a merchant from his own warehouse'.[28]

Lord Moira, who spoke in his friend Davison's defence, was also a surprising choice as proxy. One of 'the great' whom Nelson distrusted, he was a son of the first Earl of Moira and a grandson of the ninth Earl of Huntingdon. He had proved himself a severe martinet as well as a brave and skilful soldier in the American war. An intimate friend and confidant of the Prince of Wales, he had almost bankrupted himself by lending him money, and was later to have to answer charges of having clandestinely attempted to procure evidence of adultery against the Princess of Wales. Stately and courtly, inconsistent and extravagant, he was not the kind of man to whom Nelson was likely to warm; and, regretting having accepted Davison's advice to trust him with his vote – while acknowledging that he was a 'distinguished officer' – he withdrew the proxy and soon afterwards decided he would withdraw from active politics altogether.

He explained his point of view to Pitt, with whom Moira had quarrelled, telling the Prime Minister that, since he 'had not been bred in courts' and 'could not pretend to a nice discrimination between the use and abuse of Parties', he could not be expected to range himself 'under the political banners of any man in place or out of place'. England's welfare was 'the sole object of [his] pursuit' and he would always vote with that object in view, irrespective of party. When he was unsure of the rights or wrongs of any particular case he would not vote at all.

'Mr Pitt listened with patience and good humor,' Nelson told his solicitor, William Haslewood, 'indeed paid me some compliments, and observed that he wished every officer in the service would entertain similar sentiments.'[29]

Lady Hamilton was not so pleased. She had hoped that, when he had won his next great victory over the French, she would see him appointed to some high office, to have him made First Lord of the Admiralty at least. For his part, having declared his intention of abandoning his ideas of a political career, Nelson felt his 'mind at ease', and could return to thinking about what he understood best, naval strategy and tactics.[30]

31

Portsmouth

I had their huzzas before. I have their hearts now.

At Merton one day Nelson elaborated his ideas to Captain Richard Keats, who listened enthralled, if a little puzzled by the Admiral's proposed methods, which ran counter to what he called 'the old system of Fighting Instructions'. They owed something to the writings of John Clerk, a Scottish amateur strategist, which Captain Hardy once saw Nelson reading with attention and which advocated breaking the enemy's line, overwhelming part and compelling the rest to close action or flight. But they were essentially Nelson's own, based on long experience and deep study of his predecessors' methods.[1]

'Well, what do you think of it?' Nelson asked Keats, having formulated his intended plan of attack, which entailed the risk of bringing down a potentially devastating fire upon his leading ships.

Keats was silent.

'I'll tell you what I think of it,' Nelson continued. 'I think it will surprise and confound the enemy. They won't know what I am about. It will bring forward a pell-mell battle, and that is what I want.'*[2]

The arrival of a post-chaise at Merton at five o'clock on the

---

* In commenting on Nelson's tactics, Admiral Collingwood, in a letter to his favourite aunt's uncle, Dr Alexander Carlyle, wrote, 'Lord Nelson is an incomparable man ... Without much previous preparation or planning he has the faculty of discovering advantages as they arise, and the good judgement to turn them to his use. An enemy that commits a false step is in his view ruined and [he] comes at him with an impetuosity that allows no time to recover' (Collingwood, *The Private Correspondence*, ed. Hughes, 130).

morning of 2 September 1805 brought Nelson the news that this battle was now imminent. Out of the carriage stepped Captain Henry Blackwood, whose ship, the *Euryalus*, was serving with the fleet watching the movements of Admiral Villeneuve. He was taking dispatches to the Admiralty from Admiral Collingwood, commander of the British ships in the Gulf of Cadiz, and had stopped on his way to warn Lord Nelson that the combined French and Spanish fleets of over thirty ships of the line were now in Cadiz harbour. Nelson, already up and dressed and ready to make his customary inspection of his property, did not wait to be told what had brought Blackwood to Merton. 'I am sure,' he said, 'that you bring me news of the enemy fleets and that I shall have to beat them yet.'[3]

Before midday he was in London, conferring with government ministers about the steps to be taken to ensure that Villeneuve did not escape a second time. Nelson, told that he was to be given a wide-ranging command, including the Atlantic approaches to the Strait of Gibraltar, urged that a blockade of Cadiz would not be enough; nor would mere naval victory. What was needed was the annihilation of the enemy fleets, and for this every available ship would be required. The government seemed inclined to agree, to give their 'best hope a *carte blanche*'. After agreeing upon the number of ships to be sent, so George Matcham was told by Nelson, the Prime Minister asked the Admiral, 'Now who is to take command?'

'You cannot have a better man than the present one, Collingwood.'

'No, that won't do, you must take the command.'

'Sir, I wish it not,' Nelson claimed improbably to have replied, 'I have had enough of it, and I feel disposed to remain quiet the rest of my life.'

Mr Pitt, 'having overruled his objections, told him he must be ready to sail in three days. "I am ready now," replied Lord Nelson.'[4]

At the Admiralty, Lord Barham handed him a Royal Navy List and asked him to make a choice of his own officers. 'Choose yourself, my Lord,' Nelson had replied, 'the same spirit actuates the whole profession. You cannot choose wrong.' But the First Lord insisted that he pick out the names himself. 'This is my secretary,' Barham said. 'Give your orders to him.'[5]

Spurred to a new burst of activity, Nelson settled all his outstanding accounts, paying the builders for recent work at Merton: £646 to the carpenter, £578 to the bricklayer, £319 to the plumber and lesser though considerable sums to the mason, slater and smith, and instructing Davison to pay for future work already ordered by Lady Hamilton which would 'cost three times as much as if it had been done at first'.[6]

He went over all the grounds with Cribb, arranging about the next year's planting; and, hearing that Mrs Cribb was soon to have her first child, he gave her husband money for a christening gown with the words, 'If it's a boy call him Horatio, if a girl Emma.'[7] He attended meeting after meeting, dinner party after dinner party. He dined at the Ship, Greenwich, with various 'rich and fashionable' people; he called again on Lord Castlereagh and on the Foreign Secretary, Lord Mulgrave; he went to see Lord Sidmouth, as Henry Addington had by now become; he saw Lord Barham once more at the Admiralty; and he called again upon Mr Pitt, who pleased him much by escorting him to the door and out of the room to his carriage, an act of courtesy which he thought the Prime Minister 'would not have shown even to a Prince of the Blood'.[8] He obeyed a summons from the Prince of Wales's devious and bustling little red-faced factotum, Colonel McMahon, to attend at Carlton House, at any hour he named, as early as he liked, to bid farewell to the Prince who had come back to London from Weymouth especially for the purpose.[9] He was a guest at the house of the immensely rich James Crawford where Lady Bessborough, the Duke of Devonshire and Lady Elizabeth Foster were also of the company, and Harriet Bessborough observed he was 'far from appearing vain and full of himself, as one had always heard. He was perfectly unassuming and natural.' When Lady Hamilton asked him to give an account of how he was cheered in the London streets whenever he appeared, he interrupted her. 'Why,' she protested, 'you like to be applauded – you cannot deny it.' He agreed that he did but commented that no man ought to be elated by it; it might be his turn one day to feel the tide set as strongly against him as it ever had been for others.[10] Nor did Nelson forget his old friends. He visited Abraham Goldsmid at Morden Hall and Benjamin Goldsmid at Roehampton where one of the Goldsmids' sons found him 'kind in the extreme' and said that 'we all loved him'.* He made time to visit the school, Eagle House, which Thomas Lancaster, the vicar of Merton, ran. He listened to the boys recite and asked the master to give a day's holiday to the school, thereafter known as Nelson House.[11] He invited Lord Minto to Merton as well as William Beckford, the latter an unattractive guest in the opinion of the young George Matcham, who noted in his diary, 'Talkative. Praised his own composition. Play'd extempore on the Harpsichord. Sung. I thought it a very horrible noise.'[12]

Lord Minto found Lady Hamilton's grief at her lover's departure tiresomely theatrical, as large tears fell on to the table beside him during the meal. 'She could not eat, and hardly drink,' Minto recorded; and was 'near swooning, and all at table'. 'It is a strange picture,' he concluded, not for the first time. 'He is in many points a great man, in others a baby ... She tells me nothing can be more pure and ardent than this flame.'[13]

In the face of all appearances, Nelson himself continued to strive to persuade the world and his own conscience that their relationship was as pure as it was ardent. Considering that he was married to Emma in the sight of God, he arranged for them to take the sacrament together and to exchange gold rings; and after the ceremony, and in the presence of the parson, he said to her solemnly, 'Emma, I have taken the Sacrament with you this day to prove to the world that our friendship is most pure and innocent and of this I call God to witness.'

Countess Spencer, who was a witness of the ceremony, hurried

---

* Nelson was fond of children and good with them. The poet, Samuel Rogers, once told an American visitor, 'I have seen him spin a teetotum with his one hand a whole evening for the amusement of some children' (Alison Lockwood, *Passionate Pilgrims: The American Traveller in Great Britain, 1800–1914*, 107).

back to London to tell her daughter-in-law, Lavinia, what had been done. 'Lavinia,' she said, 'I think you will now agree that you have been to blame in your opinion of Lady Hamilton.'[14]

Lady Hamilton grew more tearful as the time for departure came. She was 'broken-hearted' she said; and when Nelson asked her, in the event of his death, to sing a dirge which he had heard in Naples and had written down and placed in the coffin that Captain Hallowell had made for him, she protested, 'But how could that be? For unless I sung it in madness, if I lost [you] I should be unable to sing.'

'Yes,' Nelson said, 'yes, I suppose you would.'[15]

She knew, though, that she must not try to dissuade him from rejoining the fleet. 'Brave Emma!' he comforted her gratefully, so she told James Harrison. 'Good Emma! If there were more Emmas, there would be more Nelsons.'[16]

Just before he left Merton, he went upstairs to the room where Horatia lay sleeping in her cot. In Lady Hamilton's presence he knelt down to pray; and returned to the room four times before going downstairs for the last time and out to the post-chaise.

His brother-in-law, George Matcham, who had joined him and Lady Hamilton for their last dinner together, went with him, too overcome by emotion to speak. Nelson said how sorry he was that he had not so far been able to repay the £4,000 which Matcham had generously lent him in order to buy some land to extend the Merton Place estate. 'My dear Lord,' said Matcham, once again in command of himself as they shook hands, 'I have no other wish than to see you return home in safety. As to myself, I am not in want of anything.'[17]

'Be a good boy till I come back again,' Nelson said to the stable lad who was holding the door open for him. Then, at half-past ten, the door shut and he drove from 'dear, dear Merton, where [he left] all that [he] held dear in this world, to go to serve [his] King and Country'.[18]

In the darkness of the rattling coach, he composed a prayer which he wrote down in his diary when the horses were being changed at a coaching inn in Liphook:

May the great God whom I adore, enable me to fulfil the expectations of my country; and if it is His good pleasure that I should return, my thanks will never cease being offered up to the Throne of His mercy. If it is His good Providence to cut short my days upon Earth, I bow with the greatest submission, relying that He will Protect those so dear to me, that I must leave behind – His will be done: Amen, Amen, Amen.[19]

Next morning, not long after dawn, the coach drew up at the George in Portsmouth. Waiting here was Thomas Lancaster, who had come down with his fourteen-year-old son, whom Nelson had agreed to take to sea with him as a first-class volunteer in the *Victory*. The Admiral promised to report upon the boy's progress as soon as he could, a promise shortly fulfilled.[20] The boy's father was returning to Merton immediately, so Nelson took the opportunity of writing a brief note to Emma, dated 'six o'clock George Inn' and addressed to 'my dearest and most beloved of Women, Nelson's Emma'. 'If possible I shall be at sea this day,' he told her. 'God protect you and My Dear Horatia prays ever your most faithful Nelson and Bronte.'[21]

So dense were the crowds in the High Street and along Portsmouth Point that the Admiral's barge was ordered to come to fetch him on the beach at Southsea. But here, too, hundreds of people had gathered on the common and on the shingle around the bathing machines to watch the hero depart. The American, Benjamin Silliman, who was one of them, described the excited crowds 'passing all around and pushing to get a little before him to obtain a sight of his face'. 'I stood on one of the batteries near which he passed and had a full view of his person,' Silliman wrote. 'He was elegantly dressed and his blue coat splendidly illuminated with stars and ribbons.'[22]

Some of the people pushed their way forward to try to shake his hand; others knelt down to pray for victory and for his survival; 'many were in tears'.[23] 'As the barge in which he embarked pushed away from the shore, the people gave him three cheers, which his Lordship returned by waving his hat.' As he sat down he said proudly to Thomas Hardy, 'I had their huzzas before. I have their hearts now.'[24]

Aboard the *Victory* the Great Cabin was being prepared for a dinner party. George Canning, 'a very clever deep headed man', in Nelson's opinion,[25] one day to be Prime Minister, at that time the Treasurer of the Navy, was coming; so was George Rose, Vice-President of the Board of Trade, whom Nelson had known for years and to whom he had spoken more than once in the recent past about a government pension for Lady Hamilton. He brought up the subject again now, asking Rose also to try to do something for his brother-in-law, Thomas Bolton, and for his impecunious chaplain, Mr Scott, should he not survive the immediate battle. Now and in the next few days, such intimations of mortality frequently came to mind. He spoke of a wish to be buried in St Paul's Cathedral rather than Westminster Abbey, since he had heard that the abbey was in danger of sinking into the marshy ground on which it had been built. He recalled a fortune-teller in the West Indies who had foreseen his future up to the year 1805 but confessed she could see no further. 'Ah, Katty! Katty!' he had said to his sister, 'That gypsy!'[26] To Davison, he wrote of the forthcoming battle. 'Let the battle be when it may, it will never have been surpassed. My shattered frame, if I can survive that day, will require rest and that is all I can ask for. If I fall on such a glorious occasion, it shall be my pride to take care that my friends shall not blush for me: these things are in the hands of a wise and just Providence and His will be done.'[27]

In writing to Emma he struck a more cheerful note: 'I love and adore you to the very excess of the passion, but with Gods blessing we shall soon meet again. Kiss dear Horatia a thousand times for me ... I entreat, my dear Emma, that you will cheer up; and we will look forward to many, many happy years, and be surrounded by our children's children ... God Almighty can, when he pleases, remove the impediment. My heart and soul is with you and Horatia.'[28]

Emma replied to say that Horatia had been sent back to Mrs Gibson's. 'My heart is broke away from her,' she wrote. 'You will be ever fonder of her when you return ... Dearest angel that she is! Oh Nelson, how I love her but how do I idolize you – the dearest husband of my heart, you are all in this world to your

Emma ... May God send you victory and home to your *Emma, Horatia* and *paradise Merton*, for when you are there it will be paradise.'[29]

32

The Atlantic Approaches

I hope in God that I shall live to finish my letter after the Battle.

Setting sail on 15 September, the *Victory* arrived off Cadiz on the 27th, having been in danger of being blown into Weymouth where Nelson might have had to endure another embarrassing interview with the King who was on holiday there. It was, he told Emma, 'the place of all others I should wish to avoid. If it continues modte [moderate], I hope to escape without anchoring, but if I should be forced I shall act as a man and your Nelson, neither courting nor ashamed to hold up my head before the greatest Monarch in the *World*.'[1]

He had ordered that no welcoming salutes be fired so that the enemy should not be alerted to his arrival; but there could be no doubt that the officers and men of the fleet were delighted by it. They had not been happy under the command of Admiral Collingwood, a stern and silent disciplinarian who showed little of the kindliness and none of the quiet humour for which his friends and family warmed to him in his private life. Collingwood was not a believer in flogging. Instead, offenders would usually be put on short rations, have their grog watered, be forced to perform extremely arduous or unpleasant duties, or given those severe lectures which midshipmen dreaded. He had forbidden all visiting between ships except for important duties; and had refused permission for provisions to be bought from the boats that came out laden with tempting goods from the North African coast. At his table conversation was stilted and frivolity not encouraged. As William Hoste commented, 'Old Collingwood likes *quiet people.*' Indeed, he seemed to prefer the company of his beloved dog, Bounce – his friend for many years until, nearly twenty years old, he fell overboard – to that of his fellow officers. Most of these officers were bored beyond measure. Thomas Fremantle of the *Neptune* told Betsey that ennui was making him extremely ill-tempered; his first lieutenant, who had been in the ship far longer than himself, was extremely bossy and touchy; one of his servants was a drunkard, another violent; the ship's only goat had fallen down a hatch in a storm so he had to do without milk in his tea. It would not have been so bad if he had had a band, but negotiations to bring aboard the band of a militia regiment whose numbers were being reduced had fallen through at the last minute.

Edward Codrington was homesick as well as bored, longing for the company of his pretty young wife and their two babies. Nelson's arrival was a godsend. 'A sort of general joy has been the consequence,' Codrington said. Two days later, to celebrate his forty-seventh birthday, the Admiral invited fifteen of his captains to one of his enjoyable dinner parties; the rest receiving invitations for the day before or the one after. 'What our late chief will think of this I don't know,' Codrington commented, 'but I well know what the fleet think of the difference.'[2]

His guests found their host full of enthusiasm and vigour, one of them, Captain Fremantle, commenting, 'He looks better than ever I saw him and is grown fatter.' For his own part, Nelson was perfectly content with his officers. 'The Secretary Scott is a treasure,' he told Emma; 'and I am very well mounted: Hardy is everything I could wish or desire.'[3]

He said that his reception 'on joining the fleet caused the sweetest sensation in [his] life'. 'The officers who came on board to welcome my return forgot my rank as Commander-in-Chief in the enthusiasm with which they greeted me,' he wrote. 'As soon as these emotions were past, I laid before them the plan I had previously arranged for attacking the enemy.' In its essentials this plan was quite simple, as he had already explained to Captain Keats. Something like it, sudden and impromptu, had proved successful before in the victory won by Rodney and Hood in the Battle of the Saints in 1782 and again off Cape St Vincent in 1797. Nelson meant to attack the ships in the centre and rear of the enemy line, intending to destroy them before the leading ships could turn to their help. The efficiency and bravery of his well-trained gun crews, who could fire twice as fast as the French and Spanish, would compensate for any advantage in numbers which the enemy might have. As for the handling of the ships when the smoke of the guns obscured all signals, no captain could go wrong if he placed his ship alongside that of an enemy.

'When I came to explain to them the "*Nelson touch*" it was like an electric shock,' Nelson congratulated himself in a letter to Emma. 'Some shed tears, all approved – "It was new – it was singular – it was simple!" and, from the admirals downwards, it was repeated – "It must succeed, if ever they will allow us to get at them! You are, my Lord, surrounded by friends whom you inspire with confidence." Some may be Judas's, but the majority are certainly much pleased with my commanding them.'[4]

Before and after dinner, while his sailors painted their ships with yellow stripes and their gun ports black, Nelson was kept busy writing his official and personal correspondence, one day sitting for seven hours at his desk, and suffering the consequences early the next morning by being woken up at four o'clock with one of his 'dreadful spasms', which he thought was a heart attack. The ship's surgeon, Mr Beatty, diagnosed indigestion.

Admiral Collingwood had been to dinner the night before. Nelson had hoped to soften the blow of taking over his command by sending Collingwood a friendly letter before leaving London: 'My dear Coll: I shall be with you in a very few days, and I hope you will remain as Second-in-Command. You will change the *Dreadnought* for the *Royal Sovereign*, which I hope you will like.'[5]

But Collingwood did not much like the *Royal Sovereign*; nor did he much care for her captain, Edward Rotherham, a Northumberland doctor's son, who was said to have gone to sea in a collier; and he did not care at all for being replaced in the command of the fleet by a man eight years younger than himself with no claim to greater experience. Collingwood was not a man to show resentment, however; and, with regard to Rotherham, soon showed himself prepared to accept Nelson's injunction to remember that 'in the presence of the enemy, all Englishmen should be brothers' and that there should be 'no little jealousies'.[6]

Nelson was also successful in soothing ruffled feathers in his dealings with the elderly Sir Robert Calder, Collingwood's former second-in-command, who was ordered home to face a court martial for his failure to intercept Villeneuve on his return from the West Indies. Calder, a touchy and obstinate man, was so convinced that no blame could be attached to him that he had independently demanded an inquiry into his conduct. Indeed, he considered himself entitled to praise for having taken two of Villeneuve's ships rather than to censure, so much so that he had written to Lord Barham asking him to bear his nephew in mind when the honours due to him were being considered. He now insisted upon sailing home, with two captains prepared to speak in his defence, in his own ship, the ninety-gun *Prince of Wales*, which Nelson could ill afford to spare. Nelson, who sympathized with Calder, and said that he might not have done better with his small force himself, endeavoured to persuade him to take a smaller ship; but Calder insisted upon the *Prince of Wales*; so, when another three-decker arrived from England, Nelson gave way, excusing himself with the hope that, although he might be 'thought wrong as an officer', he would be 'considered to have done right as a man and to a brother officer in affliction. My heart could not stand it and so the thing must rest.'[7]

The departure of the *Prince of Wales* reduced Nelson's fleet to twenty-seven ships of the line, most of them, like most of the enemy ships, mounting seventy-four guns. From time to time a ship would leave the fleet for Gibraltar to take on water or provisions and occasionally a ship would arrive from England, as 'the dear *Agamemnon*' did under the command of his brave, impulsive friend, Sir Edward Berry. 'Here comes that damned fool Berry!' Nelson announced with satisfaction. '*Now* we shall have a battle.'[8]

He wished that the *Agamemnon* had been accompanied by frigates, the lack of which had caused him so much disquiet in the past; he had once told Lord Spencer that, when he died, 'Want of Frigates' would be stamped on his heart.[9] 'I am most exceedingly anxious for more *eyes*,' he now wrote, 'and hope the Admiralty are hastening them to me. The last fleet was lost to me for want of frigates. God forbid this should.'[10]

He knew that the enemy had thirty-three ships of the line in Cadiz, eighteen of them French, fifteen Spanish. But while unconcerned that he was thus outnumbered, he was worried that he would not receive adequate notice of Villeneuve's movements and probable intentions.

Villeneuve had, in fact, been superseded by a senior admiral, Rosily, on the orders of Napoleon, who had come to regard Villeneuve with contempt. In the summer the Emperor had hoped that Villeneuve would break out of Ferrol, join the French fleet from Brest and enter the Channel, so that his long-planned invasion of England could take place. But now it was too late for that. Austria and Russia had entered the war on England's side; and the Grande Armée had had to be moved from the French coast to Germany. The Franco-Spanish fleet at Cadiz had consequently been ordered to sail into the Mediterranean, land troops at Naples, then make for Toulon; and, since Villeneuve was considered incapable of carrying out this mission properly, the duty had been entrusted to Admiral Rosily. But Rosily had been delayed in Spain by a carriage accident; and Villeneuve had decided to get his fleet on the move before his successor arrived to take over, profoundly relieved that he was not now expected to get into the Channel and that he might escape into the Mediterranean and thus avoid a battle he felt sure he could not win with crews no match for those of the enemy, deprived as he was of many officers whom the Revolution had killed or driven to seek refuge overseas. 'I should be sorry to meet twenty [English ships],' Villeneuve told the Minister of Marine. 'Our naval tactics are antiquated. We know nothing but how to place ourselves in line, and that is just what the enemy wants.'[11]

'My dearest beloved Emma, the dear friend of my bosom,' Nelson wrote as soon as he learned that the French were preparing to move,

the Signal has been made that the Enemy's Combined fleet are coming out of port. We have very little Wind, so that I have no hopes of seeing them before tomorrow. May the God of Battles crown my endeavours with success. At all events I will take care that my name shall ever be dear to you and Horatia, both of whom I love as much as my own life; and, as my last writing before the Battle will be to you, so I hope in God that I shall live to finish my letter after the Battle. May heaven bless you, prays your Nelson and Bronte. . . . May God Almighty give us success over these fellows and enable us to get a peace.[12]

He also wrote to Horatia: 'Love dear Lady Hamilton, who most dearly loves you. Give her a kiss for me.' Horatia was his 'dearest Angel'. He signed himself 'your Father'.[13]

In the frigate *Euryalus*, Henry Blackwood was keeping a sharp eye on the movements of the enemy fleet and signalled to the *Victory* whenever he had new information to impart. He counted nineteen ships sailing out of Cadiz, then twenty-five and finally all thirty-three. They appeared 'determined to push to the westward'. 'That,' Nelson wrote in his diary, 'they shall not do, if in the power of Nelson and Bronte to prevent them.'

On the *Victory*'s poop, Nelson remarked to a group of midshipmen, 'This day 20 October or tomorrow, will be a fortunate one for you young gentlemen.' Later he said more than once, 'The 21st will be our day,' adding that it was the anniversary of some festival in the Nelson family.*[14]

In the *Royal Sovereign*, Admiral Collingwood began the day as calmly as he did any other. While he was shaving he asked a servant if he had noticed the enemy yet. The servant pushed his head out of the dimly lit cabin and reported that he could see 'a crowd of great ships' through the mist. They would soon 'see a great deal more of them', Collingwood laconically observed as he went on shaving. When his first lieutenant came into the cabin, Collingwood advised him to change his boots and wear shoes and silk stockings as he was himself. They were, he said, 'so much more manageable for the surgeon'. Collingwood's flag-captain, Edward Rotherham, who was fortunately not to need the attentions of the

---

* Nelson's uncle, Captain Maurice Suckling, commanding the *Dreadnought*, had helped to defeat a French squadron on 21 October 1757 in the Seven Years' War. The 21st was also the day of Burnham Thorpe's autumn fair.

surgeon that day, seemed however to invite them. He appeared on deck in full dress uniform, complete with his large cocked hat. He had always fought so attired, he said, and always would.[15]

Lord Nelson's dress was causing concern on the quarterdeck of the *Victory*. It was noticed that, unusually, he was wearing no sword. This had been removed from its rack in his cabin and put out for him; but he had left it behind on a table. It was also noticed that he was not wearing his full dress coat, but a rather worn undress coat, the skirts of which were lined with a woollen material rather than silk.* On his left breast, however, the surgeon Beatty noticed the familiar 'four stars of different Orders'. These would surely mark him out as a target for the sharpshooters perched in the rigging of the enemy ships. Beatty suggested that someone ought to speak to him about this. Both the Admiral's secretary and his chaplain appeared unwilling to do so; and when Beatty undertook to bring up the subject himself, John Scott warned him, 'Take care, doctor, what you are about. I would not be the man to mention such a matter to him.' Even so, Beatty decided that he would do so if an opportunity presented itself when he was making his sick report for the day.

The night before, the *Victory* had been sailing on a course parallel with that of the French fleet, keeping some twenty miles distant, so as not to alarm Villeneuve by posing a threat that might drive him back into port. On 21 October, however, at four o'clock in the morning, Nelson had ordered a sudden change of direction so as to confront him; and, as the sky lightened and signals could be seen, the ships' captains were ordered to take up battle stations. Then, in two columns, one led by the *Victory*, the other by Collingwood's *Royal Sovereign*, the British fleet sailed slowly into action.

There was time yet for personal business; so Nelson asked Hardy and Blackwood, who had come aboard from the *Euryalus*, to go

---

* Nelson had always scorned the prevailing fashions. The year before, when asking Davison to order 'two or three pair of shoes' for him, he had emphatically specified 'no *square* toes or new fashion' (BL Egerton MSS., 2,240, f. 204, 19 March 1804).

down to his cabin with him. Here he produced a document which he asked them both to witness:

October the twenty-first, one thousand eight hundred and five, then in sight of the Combined Fleets of France and Spain, distant about ten miles.

Whereas the Eminent Services . . . performed in Naples and hereinafter enumbered . . . of Emma Hamilton, widow of the Right Honourable Sir William Hamilton, have been of the very greatest service to our King and Country, to my knowledge, without her receiving any reward from either our King or Country . . . Could I have rewarded these services, I would not now call upon my Country; but as that has not been in my power, I leave Emma Lady Hamilton, therefore, a Legacy to my King and Country, that they will allow her an ample provision to maintain her rank in life. I also leave to the beneficence of my Country my adopted daughter, Horatia Nelson Thompson; and I desire She Will Use in future the name of Nelson only.

These are the only favours I ask of my King and Country at this moment when I am going to fight their Battle. May God bless my King and Country, and all those who I hold dear My relations it is needless to mention they will of course be amply provided for.[16]

Having signed this document, Hardy and Blackwood returned with Nelson to the quarterdeck and accompanied him on his rounds of the ship. He seemed 'in excellent spirits' as he walked about, exchanging pleasantries with the sailors, speaking often of victory, as cheerful as he had been the night before when he had spoken airily of the possibility of losing a leg in the forthcoming battle and had suggested that, were he to be killed, such glory would reflect on the naval profession that there would be a general desire to follow his example. He asked Blackwood how many prizes he thought they would take. He himself would not be satisfied with less than twenty. Blackwood thought that even fourteen would be 'a glorious result'.

As the fleet closed towards the enemy, sails spread to catch the light breeze, bands played stirring tunes. All loose furniture had been lashed down or packed away; the men clearing the Admiral's cabin were told to be particularly careful with Lady Hamilton's portrait. 'Take care of my guardian angel,' he said to them.

Later, on his rounds, he came across a sailor carving a notch on a gun carriage next to a row of other marks. The man said that the existing marks denoted previous British victories; he was cutting out another now in case he was dead when the battle was over. 'You'll make notches enough in the enemy's ships,' the Admiral told him.[17]

His tour over, Nelson went down to his cabin for the last time. On the bare boards, cleared of the tables and chairs which had been taken down to the hold, he knelt down to write out another prayer he had composed earlier that morning:

May the Great God, whom I worship, grant to my Country and for the benefit of Europe in general, a great and glorious victory; and may no misconduct in anyone tarnish it; and may humanity after Victory be the dominant feature in the British Fleet. For myself, individually, I commit my life to Him who made me, and may His blessings light upon my endeavours for serving my Country faithfully. To him I resign myself and the just cause which is entrusted to me to defend. Amen. Amen. Amen.[18]

When the signals lieutenant, John Pasco, came down to the Admiral's cabin to approach him on a personal matter, he found Nelson still on his knees. 'I of course remained stationary and quiet until he rose,' Pasco recorded, 'and I became mute not wishing to distract his devotions.' Then, deciding he 'could not disturb his mind with any grievances' of his own, Pasco returned to the poop where the Admiral soon joined him.[19] In the meantime, Nelson had had a few words with Henry Blackwood, to whom he had said, 'I will now amuse the fleet with a signal. Do you think there is one yet wanting?' Blackwood doubted that there was; by now all his captains surely knew what they had to do.

'Mr Pasco,' he said, 'I wish to say to the fleet "England confides that every man will do his duty." You must be quick,' he added, 'for I have one more signal to make, which is for close action.'

Pasco, having regard to the fact that the word 'confides' was not in the Signal Book and would have to be hoisted letter by letter, asked if he might substitute 'expects' which could be signalled by a single flag. 'That will do,' Nelson told him. 'Make it directly.'[20] According to one report the signal was greeted 'with three cheers in every ship'; Captain Blackwood averred that its reception was 'truly sublime'. Collingwood's response was down to earth. 'What is Nelson signalling about?' he demanded with grumpy irritation. 'We all know what we have to do.'[21]

Between decks in the *Victory*, the response to the signal apparently echoed Collingwood's. 'There were murmurs from some,' a lieutenant of Marines reported, 'whilst others in an audible whisper murmured, "Do your duty! Of course we'll do our duty. I've always done mine, haven't you?" Still, they cheered – more, I believe, from love and admiration for their Admiral than from an appreciation of this well known signal.'

The men, Americans, Germans, Dutch and Swiss, even Spaniards and Frenchmen among the British, were mostly stripped to the waist, handkerchiefs round their heads to stop the sweat getting into their eyes, their ears covered also to deaden the noise of the guns. Some of them were sharpening cutlasses; a few, so the marine lieutenant noticed with surprise, were dancing a hornpipe.[22]

33
Trafalgar

Doctor, I have not been a great sinner.

Less than three miles of deep blue water now separated the two fleets; and Nelson's exposure on the *Victory*'s poop and quarterdeck became of increasing concern to his officers. Beatty had still not spoken to him about his glittering stars when all officers whose duties did not require their presence on the quarterdeck were ordered to their proper stations. After Beatty had gone below, Hardy took it upon himself to suggest that the decorations would identify the Admiral too clearly to sharpshooters when the French and Spanish ships came within musket range. It was too late now, Nelson said, 'to be shifting a coat'. Besides they were 'military orders and he did not fear to show them to the enemy'.[1]

Captain Blackwood was no more successful when he suggested that the Admiral should come aboard the frigate, where he would not only be less exposed but would have a clearer view of the battle; nor would Nelson listen to Captain Hardy when he proposed letting the ninety-eight-gun *Téméraire*, which was lying astern of the *Victory*, take the lead in their division. Indeed, when the *Téméraire* seemed to be getting too close to the *Victory*, as though her captain, Eliab Harvey, intended overtaking her, Nelson, 'speaking as he always did, with a slight nasal intonation', protested sharply. 'I'll thank you, Captain Harvey, to keep in your proper station, which is astern of the *Victory*.' If this were to be his last battle, he was determined to direct it himself and, as in his other battles, he wanted to be seen directing it himself. It would 'add to my grief,' he had told Emma, 'if any other man was to give them the Nelson touch'.[2]

East of the *Victory*, the *Royal Sovereign*, sailing at the head of her division, was the first to come under fire. She sailed on, as if despising the shot. 'See how that noble fellow Collingwood carries his ship into action,' Nelson said. Aboard the *Royal Sovereign*, Collingwood remarked to one of his officers, 'What would Nelson give to be here!'[3]

Keeping his glass trained on the van of Collingwood's division as it began to be obscured by smoke, Lieutenant Pasco announced, 'There is a top-gallant yard gone!'

'Is it the *Royal Sovereign?*' Nelson asked.

'No, my Lord, an enemy's.'

'Collingwood is doing well.'

Shortly afterwards the *Victory* also came under fire. The first two shots fell harmlessly into the water; the third flew past the sails. Nelson told Blackwood and the captain of another frigate to return to their ships and take orders to all the captains of ships of the line to get into action straight away: they could do so in whatever way they 'thought best, provided it led them quickly and closely alongside an enemy ship'.

Before hurrying off, Blackwood shook the Admiral's hand. 'I trust, my Lord,' he said, 'that on my return to the *Victory* . . . I shall find your Lordship well and in possession of twenty prizes.'

'God bless you, Blackwood,' said Nelson, adding words which shocked the captain and left him 'with a heart very sad': 'I shall never speak to you again.'[4]

The shots were flying more thickly now, as seven or eight enemy ships directed their broadsides against the British flagship. Shots tore into the *Victory*'s sails, ripping bits of canvas away, and hurtled across the quarterdeck. One struck John Scott, the Admiral's secretary and cut him almost in two. 'Is that poor Scott?' Nelson asked as the torn corpse was bundled overboard on the orders of an officer of Marines, eight of whose own men were killed by a ball that came tearing along the bulwarks. Nelson told the officer to disperse the survivors around the ship.

Scott's duties were taken over by Hardy's clerk, but he, too, was killed before he had taken down a single word. Another shot hit the *Victory*'s wheel, smashing it to pieces so that the ship had to be steered by forty seamen labouring with all their strength to turn the immense tiller on the lower gun deck. On the deck above them a splinter dented the buckle of Captain Hardy's left shoe. Nelson glanced at him and commented wryly, 'This is too warm work to last long.'[5] He had never, he said, seen his sailors fight so bravely and with such determination. Enveloped in smoke from their own guns firing with their muzzles inside the ports, deafened by the concussion, ignoring the hot blast of the enemy's muzzle flashes, they fought on even when wounded. One young man lost three fingers and later congratulated himself in a letter to his 'honoured Fathre' that it wasn't his head; another, told by an officer to go below to get a shattered toe attended to, said he needn't leave his post for a scratch and cut the toe off; a third sang 'Rule Britannia' all the way through while a surgeon amputated his arm.[6]

The time had now come for the *Victory*, which had been sailing as though to attack the leading ships in Villeneuve's line, to turn against the ships in the centre. Which of the three nearest should he engage first, Hardy asked the Admiral: there was not enough space between them to break the line; he would have to go on board one of them. 'It does not signify,' Nelson said, 'Take your pick.'[7]

Hardy chose the eighty-gun *Bucentaure*, which happened to be the French Admiral's flagship; and as the *Victory* passed across her stern, Hardy's gun crews fired a devastating broadside through her cabin windows, raking the length of her gun decks. Shots and splinters hurtled through the smoke as the ships on both sides exchanged a ferocious fire across the narrow stretch of intervening water. The French ships were now so near to each other – 'closed like a forest' in Hardy's words – that the *Victory* crashed into a French ship lying astern of the *Bucentaure*, the seventy-four-gun *Redoutable*. The *Victory* rocked away at the first rebound; but her yard-arm became entangled in the *Redoutable*'s rigging as her gun crews, supported by those of the *Téméraire*, still worked their cannon, firing on the starboard side into the *Redoutable* – which was so close that they could clearly hear the French sailors' shouts above the roar of the battle – and on the port side into the immense Spanish ship, the 140-gun *Santísima Trinidad*, which some of them had encountered off Cape St Vincent eight years before.

Over their heads sharpshooters on platforms above the main

yards of the *Redoutable* took aim at the figures on the *Victory*'s quarter-deck, which they could briefly glimpse through the swirling smoke.

Some time after one o'clock, Hardy, still pacing the *Victory*'s quarterdeck and stopping to give the occasional order, as grenades exploded around him, suddenly became aware that the Admiral was no longer by his side. He turned to see him on his knees, supporting himself with the fingertips of his hand on the deck, slippery with blood, near to the spot were John Scott had been killed that morning. Hardy saw Nelson's arm give way as he fell on his side. 'Hardy,' he said, smiling as though in apology, 'I do believe they have done it at last.'

'I hope not.'

'Yes, my backbone is shot through.'*

* 'Lord Nelson was covered with decorations on the day of the battle of Trafalgar, and thus became an object for a humble sharp-shooter to mark out,' wrote Colonel Drinkwater Bethune, who had known Nelson when they were sailing together in the *Minerva* in 1797. 'Relating not long ago, the above anecdote to an acquaintance, he told me that his family, whilst residing in the neighbourhood of Paris, after the general peace of 1815, employed a French artificer who was on board the French ship, the *Redoutable*, in the battle of Trafalgar. This man professed himself to be an intimate of the man who, from that ship, killed Lord Nelson, and who was living then in Paris. According to his account, the attention of his shipmate had been attracted, during the battle, to an officer in the *Victory*, whom, from the decorations he wore, he suspected to be the British Admiral. Under this impression, the man obtained four ball-cartridges, with which, and his rifle, he went aloft, saying to his companions – "*Si je ne le tue pas de ces trois, je me brûle la cervelle avec la quatrième.*" If this man's story is to be believed, the report of some officer on board the *Victory* having killed the man who shot Nelson, must be unfounded' (Bethune, 89).

   The ball which killed Nelson was extracted from the wound by the surgeon, William Beatty, when he performed the autopsy and, on the orders of Captain Hardy, was placed in a locket contained in a silver case. The relic was presented to Beatty and, after Beatty's death, came into the possession of his nephew, the Rev. F. W. Baker, rector of Beaulieu, Hampshire. In 1852 it was given to Queen Victoria and remains in the Royal Collection. It is on display in the Grand Vestibule at Windsor Castle. The course of the bullet as described in Beatty's report indicated that it could have been fired only from the mizzen top of the *Redoutable* (*Nelson Dispatch*, vol. 2, part 11, July 1987).

A sergeant-major of Marines and two seamen carried him down towards the surgeon's quarters. On the way he asked the men to wait a moment so that he could give some advice to a midshipman who was not handling the tiller properly. He then took a handkerchief from his pocket and placed it over his face, for fear lest the sight of the Admiral being carried past the light of the lanterns below the water-line should cause alarm among the crew.

The darkness of these nether regions of the ship was deepened by the dark red in which they were painted – a colour decreed, so it was said, by Robert Blake, commander of the British fleet in the seventeenth century – in order that the squeamish might grow accustomed to the colour of blood. Here on the orlop deck – where the candles flickered and dimmed as the air was sucked out of their horn lamps by the concussion of broadsides from the gun decks – the scene seemed to the chaplain, Alexander Scott, 'like a butcher's shambles'. The groans and screams of wounded men, laid out in rows on strips of sailcloth, rose above the roar of gunfire and the crashing of timber. William Beatty, two other surgeons and their assistants, their sleeves rolled up over blood-smeared forearms, were at work with saws and knives and all the various instruments of their craft, as more wounded men were carried down from the gun decks and dosed with rum as a crude anaesthetic. The sights and smells had proved too much for the chaplain, who had rushed to the foot of a ladder for air after seeing a dying young officer tearing off his bandages in apparent delirium. When the Admiral's body was carried down, however, Scott recovered himself and went to his side, where he was to remain throughout the long afternoon.

'Ah, Mr Beatty,' Nelson said, as the surgeon came forward to attend to him. 'You can do nothing for me. I have but a short time to live. My back is shot through.'

Beatty removed the Admiral's coat and shirt, revealing around his neck a locket containing a miniature of Lady Hamilton as a bacchante. The coat, already covered with blood, was 'rolled up and put as a substitute for a pillow under the head of a midshipman, George Westphal, whose wounded head was 'bleeding very much'. 'When the Battle was over, and an attempt made to remove the Coat,' Westphal recalled years later, 'several of the bullions of the epaulette were found to be so firmly glued into my hair by the coagulated blood from my wound, that the bullions, four or five of them, were cut off and left in my hair.'[8]

Having looked at the Admiral's wound, Beatty said he would not put him to the additional pain of examining it. Was he already in much pain, Beatty asked him. He had felt the shot break his back, Nelson replied, yet now had no feeling at all in the lower part of his body. He found it difficult to breathe, though, and he was conscious of a 'gush of blood every minute' inside his chest. He complained of feeling hot and thirsty, so a fan was made to waft air over his face and cups of lemonade and watered wine were brought to his lips. 'Fan, fan,' he kept muttering, 'drink, drink.'

Occasionally he roused himself to ask a question: why were the men cheering on the gun decks? Lieutenant Pasco, also wounded, suggested that they must have seen through their gun ports an enemy ship strike her colours in surrender. Where was Hardy? Would no one bring Hardy to him? Had he been killed? A midshipman, cut about the face, reported formally – after the admiral's request to see his flag-captain had been taken up to the quarterdeck several times – 'Circumstances respecting the fleet require Captain Hardy's presence on deck. He will avail himself of the first favourable moment to visit his Lordship.'

Who had brought that message, Nelson asked; and, on being told it was Mr Bulkeley, the son of an army officer he had met years ago in Nicaragua, he said that he recognized the voice. To Bulkeley himself he said, 'Remember me to your father.' On hearing another young voice he recognized, that of a midshipman whose leg had been taken off by a cannon shot, he called out, 'Mind that youngster is not forgot.'

To the chaplain he spoke anxiously of his concern for those he would leave behind: 'Doctor, I told you. Doctor, I am gone . . . Remember me to Lady Hamilton. Remember me to Horatia. Remember me to all my friends. Doctor, remember me to Mr Rose. Tell him I have left a will and left Lady Hamilton and Horatia to my country.' To Walter Burke, the purser, who was helping Scott prop up the pillows against which his head was resting, Nelson also spoke of his imminent and inevitable death; and when Burke attempted to comfort him with the idea that he would return in triumph to England, he said, 'It is nonsense, Mr Burke, to suppose I can live. My sufferings are great but they will soon be over.'

At last, at about half-past two, an hour or so after the Admiral had first been hit, the bulky figure of Captain Hardy appeared on the steps leading down to the orlop deck. He approached the group of figures under the lantern where Nelson lay and took the Admiral's hand. Beatty recorded his replies to Nelson's questions:

'Well Hardy, how goes the battle? How goes the day with us?'

'Very well, my Lord. We have twelve or fourteen of the enemy's ships in our possession, but five of their van have tacked, and show an intention of bearing down upon the *Victory*. I have, therefore, called two or three of our fresh ships round us, and have no doubt of giving them a drubbing.'

'I hope none of *our* ships have struck, Hardy?'

'No, my Lord. There is no fear of that.'

'I am a dead man, Hardy. I am going fast; it will be all over with me soon. Come nearer to me.'

Hearing these words, Burke was embarrassed, supposing that a confidence was about to be imparted and that he ought not to hear it. He made as if to move his arm, but was asked not to do so, and heard Nelson's voice, scarcely above a whisper, give Hardy the message. 'Pray let dear Lady Hamilton have my hair, and all other things belonging to me.'

'Is your pain great?'

'Yes, but I shall last half an hour longer yet.'

Captain Hardy, like Mr Burke, would not allow that all hope was past; and, when Beatty returned, having performed yet another amputation, Hardy suggested that there was surely a good prospect of recovery. 'Oh, no,' said Nelson, answering for the surgeon. 'It is impossible. My back is shot through. Beatty will tell you. Ah, Mr Beatty, all power and motion and feeling below my breast are gone.'

Beatty was then told to go away to attend to the other wounded, although, as he said, his assistants and the other two surgeons were quite capable of doing all that was necessary. A few minutes later he was called back. 'Ah! Mr Beatty,' Nelson said, 'I have sent for you to say, what I forgot to tell you before – that all power of motion and feeling below my breast are gone.'

'My Lord, you told me so before,' replied Beatty who, in the belief that the dying man might be reassured by it, set about a hopeless examination of the lower part of his body until stopped by the words, 'Scott and Burke have tried that already . . . You know I can live but a short time. Ah, Beatty, I am certain of it. You *know* I am gone.'

Beatty felt constrained to admit that there was little doubt of it. 'My Lord,' he said, before turning away to hide his emotion, 'unhappily for our country, nothing can be done for you.'

'I know,' Nelson murmured. 'I feel something rising in my breast which tells me that I am gone . . . God be praised, I have done my duty.' Then, in reply to a question about the pain he was suffering, he said that it was so severe he wished he were dead, adding pathetically, 'Yet, one would like to live a little longer . . . How dear is life to all men . . . What would become of poor Lady Hamilton if she knew my situation?'

The roar and thudding of another broadside from the guns above brought forth the quiet protest, 'Oh, *Victory*! *Victory*! How you distract my poor brain!'

As the noise of gunfire subsided, Captain Hardy reappeared and, hat in hand, again approached the group of men around the dying Admiral. He found Scott and Burke still propping up the pillows, Scott gently rubbing Nelson's chest with his spare hand, an attention which seemed to afford some relief. Also kneeling by the crumpled sheet which covered the lower part of his body were Nelson's steward, Chevalier, and William Beatty. Standing close by were the Admiral's Neapolitan valet and Admiral Collingwood's young kinsman, Midshipman Francis Collingwood. Captain Hardy, bending his bald head to take Nelson's hand, reported 'a brilliant victory'. He did not know exactly how many enemy ships had been taken, fourteen or fifteen for sure.

'That is well,' Nelson commented, 'but I bargained for twenty.' Then, convinced as he had been for some time that a gale was blowing up, he added, '*Anchor*, Hardy, *anchor!*'

'I suppose, my Lord, Admiral Collingwood will now take upon himself the direction of affairs.'

'Not while I live, I hope, Hardy,' Nelson protested in a sudden access of energy, raising himself from the pillows. 'No, do *you* anchor, Hardy.'

'Shall we make the signal, sir?'

'Yes, for if I live I'll anchor.'

After a brief silence, Nelson said, 'Don't throw me overboard, Hardy.'

'Oh, no, certainly not.'

'Then you know what to do. And take care of my dear Lady Hamilton, Hardy. Take care of poor Lady Hamilton. Kiss me, Hardy.'

'The captain now knelt down,' Beatty recorded, 'and kissed his cheek, when his Lordship said: "Now I am satisfied. Thank God I have done my duty."' Hardy 'stood a minute or two in silent contemplation'. Then, as though he thought Nelson might think he had kissed him only because he had been asked to do so, he knelt down again and kissed his forehead.

'His Lordship said, "Who is that?"'

'The Captain answered: "It is Hardy," to which his Lordship replied, "God bless you, Hardy."'

The gunfire had ceased altogether now. Nelson's murmured instructions to Burke and Scott, 'Fan, fan . . . rub, rub . . . drink, drink . . .' could be heard quite distinctly. He asked his valet to turn him on to his right side; but this gave him scant comfort, merely allowing the blood to leak from one lung into the other.

'I wish I had not left the deck,' he murmured, 'for I shall soon be gone.'

His voice was very weak now, and was fainter still when he said to Scott, 'Doctor, I have not been a *great* sinner . . . Remember, that I leave Lady Hamilton and my Daughter, Horatia, as a legacy to my Country . . . Never forget Horatia.'

Beatty, having left his side for a moment, returned to hear him murmur yet again, 'Thank God I have done my duty.' When the surgeon came back the next time, the voice had faded away and the pulse could scarcely be felt. Nelson looked up as Beatty took his wrist and then closed his eyes again. At half-past four, after three hours' suffering, Nelson died. The chaplain continued to rub his chest, until a hand was placed on his shoulder.

'Partial firing continued until 4.30 p.m.,' Hardy entered in the ship's log, 'when, a victory having been reported to the Right Hon. Lord Nelson, K.B., Commander-in-Chief, he died of his wounds.'

It was a brilliant victory. Eighteen ships of the enemy fleet had been destroyed or captured, the British fleet having lost not one. The Royal Navy was in undisputed control of the seas around England's shores.

Yet the cost had been heavy. In a fierce battle in which the ships had blasted each other with cannon shot at point-blank range, almost 6,000 of the enemy had been killed and wounded and a further 20,000 had been taken prisoner, including Admiral Ville-neuve, who had surrendered his flagship to Captain Israel Pellew of the *Conqueror*, younger brother of Admiral Lord Exmouth. In the British ships there had been 1,700 casualties.

The crippled *Victory*, her masts and hull cut and splintered by shell in numerous places, was a scene of mourning; and, in other ships also, seamen wept openly at the death of their Admiral. 'I never set eyes on him,' one of them wrote home from the *Royal Sovereign*, 'for which I am both sorry and glad; for to be sure I should like to have seen him, but then, all the men in our ship who have seen him are such soft toads, they have done nothing but Blast their Eyes and cry ever since he was killed. God bless you! Chaps that fought like the Devil, sit down and cry like a wench!'[9]

34

Mourning

He died the death he wished.

The body of the man the sailors mourned, clothed only in a shirt, the hair cut off in accordance with his instructions,* was placed in a cask of brandy, mixed with camphor and myrrh, which was lashed to the *Victory*'s damaged mainmast and guarded by a sentry night and day. Towed for much of the way through heavy seas, the ship arrived a week later at Gibraltar where the wounded were put ashore and Nelson's corpse was transferred to a lead-lined coffin filled with spirits of wine, after sailors had sampled the brandy which had previously preserved it.[1] An autopsy revealed that the internal organs of the dead man – who in his lifetime had suffered at various times from malaria, mercurial poisoning, possibly yellow fever, probably neuralgia, certainly scurvy, severe influenza, night sweats, violent coughs and all manner of other complaints – were without exception in remarkable condition, 'more like those of a youth than a man who had attained his forty-seventh year'.[2]

Sailing home to England ahead of the *Victory*, the schooner *Pickle*, her ensign at half-mast, carried Collingwood's dispatch with news of the country's loss and the fleet's victory. Soon after the dispatch reached London, a messenger arrived at Merton to break the sad news from Trafalgar to Lady Hamilton before the details

---

* In January 1807, Lady Hamilton sent a lock of this 'Dear Hair', set in an oval frame, to Captain Jonas Rose, then in command of the *Agamemnon*. The present was accompanied by a letter from Rose's 'affectionate and grateful *but unhappy* Emma Hamilton'. The hair was sold, with the letter, on 18 February 1988 by Lawrence Fine Art in Crewkerne, Somerset (Lot 296) for £5,500.

were published in the newspapers.

Lady Hamilton was in bed when the messenger, Captain Whitby, arrived carrying a letter from Sir Andrew Snape Hamond, Comptroller of the Navy. 'I sent to enquire who was arrived,' she recorded.

They brought me word, Mr Whitby from the Admiralty. 'Show him in directly,' I said. He came in, and with a pale countenance and faint voice said, 'We have gained a great Victory.' – 'Never mind your Victory,' I said. 'My letters – give me my letters' – Captain Whitby was unable to speak – tears in his eyes and a deathly paleness over his face made me comprehend him. I believe I gave a scream and fell back, and for ten hours I could neither speak nor shed a tear.[3]

A week later Lady Elizabeth Foster called upon Lady Hamilton at Clarges Street. She 'found her in bed':

She had the appearance of a person stunned and scarcely as yet able to comprehend the certainty of her loss. What shall I do? and How can I exist? were her first words. She then showed me some of the letters which were lying on her bed – they were from Lord Nelson . . . I asked her how she had heard the dreadful news. 'I had come to Merton,' she said, 'my house not being ready, and feeling rather unwell I said I would stay in bed, on account of a rash. Mrs Bolton was sitting by my bedside when all of a sudden I said, 'I think I hear the Tower guns. Some victory perhaps in Germany' . . . 'Perhaps,' said Mrs Bolton. 'It may be news from my brother.' 'Impossible, surely. There is not time.'[4]

Lady Hamilton was still in bed when the Goldsmids called to see her. Lionel Goldsmid, then eight years old, remembered in later years how he was allowed to 'accompany my mother and those of the family who made up the party from our House':

I was a great favourite of Lady Hamilton's and bathed in tears at times as she talked over [Lord Nelson's] virtues and exhibited the various gifts he had made her on different occasions. I was on the bed to aid in passing the rings, shawls, bracelets, etc shewn to the company of about 15 persons seated in a semi-circle at the foot of the bed. I came in for numerous kisses and her usual remark – thank you my funny boy – or child – you must come every day. The very coat in which the dear old Admiral was dressed in the fatal battle and received his death wound was on the outside of the bed – the hole where the bullet passed through stiffened with congealed blood. There was most certainly a very serio-comic performance throughout the visit.*⁵

To some observers, Lady Elizabeth Foster's grief, 'her sobs, her grunts, her groans, her black cockades, the name of Nelson embroidered on every drapery she wore', appeared quite as extravagant as Lady Hamilton's. 'She is all day displaying franks to Captains and Admirals and heaven knows what,' wrote the exasperated Lady Harriet Cavendish, 'and whilst she is regretting that she could not have "died in his defence," her peevish hearers almost wish she had.'⁶

Lieutenant John Richards Lapenotière of the *Pickle* schooner had arrived at the Admiralty at one o'clock on the foggy morning of 5

---

* Captain Hardy – who as Captain Blackwood said, 'had spoken his mind on former occasions more freely than [Lady Hamilton] would have wished' (Morrison, ii. 272), and who thought Lady Nelson 'one of the best women in the world' – had returned home with these relics and in a letter to Lady Hamilton had assured her, 'It shall be my constant study to meet your wishes, as it was our dear Lord's last request to be kind to you, which, I trust, I shall never forget . . . I have his hair, lockets, rings, breast-pin, and all your Ladyship's pictures in a box by themselves, and they shall be delivered to none but yourself' (Stuart, 128). The coat was subsequently claimed by Nelson's brother William, whose wife wrote to Lady Hamilton: 'In point of *right* there can be no doubt to whom this precious relic belongs, and it certainly is my Lord's most ardent wish as well as my son's who spoke very feelingly on the subject . . . to have it retain'd in his possession to be kept as a memorial . . . but notwithstanding all these feelings My Lord is willing, tho' done with a bleeding heart, to part with it provided, my dear friend, you will give us assurance it shall at some future time be restored to the heir to the title' (BL Add. MSS. 34, 992, 13 February 1806). Desperate for money at a later time, Lady Hamilton sold the coat to Alderman Joshua Smith, who had befriended her. In June 1845 Sir Nicholas Harris Nicolas, the editor of Nelson's dispatches and letters, approached the alderman's widow, who agreed to sell the coat for £150. The Prince Consort, on hearing of this, offered the money himself and presented the coat to the Greenwich Hospital (Nicolas, vii, 350–51).

15. Nelson being received by Admiral Jervis after the Battle of St Vincent, 14 February 1797, a painting by A. D. McCormack

16. Richard Westall's painting of Nelson's encounter with the Spanish gunboat off Cadiz on 3 July 1797

17. A pastel of Emma Hamilton by Johann Heinrich Schmidt, painted in Dresden in 1800. She is wearing the enamelled Maltese Cross awarded her by the Grand Master of the Order of St John. This was the portrait that was displayed in the dining cabin of Nelson's flagships until his death

18. Horatia, daughter of Nelson and Emma Hamilton, standing beside her rocking horse in the garden at Merton Place

19. Merton Place, the house in Surrey which Nelson bought for £9,000 in 1801

Four portraits of Emma Hamilton by George Romney:

20. One of Romney's earliest portraits of her, painted in 1782, depicts her as *Circe*, the mythical sorceress

21. A *bacchante*, a priestess of Bacchus, god of wine

22. 'The divine lady', as Romney called her, portrayed as *Ariadne*

23. As *Cassandra*, whose beauty induced Apollo to bestow upon her the gift of prophecy

24. Sir William Beechey's portrait, painted in London in 1800

25. Lemuel Francis Abbot's portrait shows the Admiral wearing his foreign decorations, with the *chelengk* given him by the Sultan of Turkey in his hat

26. A full-length study by John Hoppner. Nelson was bitterly disappointed that, to the medals for the Battles of St Vincent and the Nile, he could not add one for the Battle of Copenhagen, which the Admiralty did not consider should be commemorated in the same way

27. A portrait painted in the Hôtel de Pologne Dresden, by Johann Heinrich Schmidt, when Nelson was forty-nine

28. William Sadler's painting of the Battle of Copenhagen, 2 April 1801

29. The *Gallant heroes who commanded at Trafalgar on the 21st October 1805*, by W. L. Craig. Nelson explains his proposed plan of attack

32. Captain Hardy stands over the dying Nelson in the painting by Arthur Devis, who spent three weeks in the *Victory* making sketches and talking to survivors of the battle

30. (*opposite above*) The Battle of Trafalgar by J. M. W. Turner, who went to Sheerness to inspect the *Victory* when she was brought back to England after the battle

31. (*opposite*) Denis Dighton's impression of the scene aboard the *Victory* at the moment Nelson was shot by a French sharp-shooter

33. Benjamin West's picture of the apotheosis of Nelson, portraying the hero being carried heavenwards in the arms of the winged figure of Victory

34. The life-sized wax effigy of Nelson commissioned after his death from Catherine Andras by the Dean and Chapter of Westminster Abbey. It was so like him that Lady Hamilton would have kissed its lips had she not been warned that the colour was not yet dry

35. *Britannia Bringing Her Dead Hero to Britannia's Shore*, a painting on glass, one of hundreds of ornaments, pictures and mementoes in various forms commemorating Nelson's achievements

November, and was taken immediately to William Marsden, Evan Nepean's successor as First Secretary, who was on his way from the Board Room to his private apartments.

In accosting me [Marsden recorded] the officer used these impressive words, 'Sir, we have gained a great victory; but we have lost Lord Nelson!' . . . The First Lord [Barham] had retired to rest as had his domestics, and it was not till after some research that I could discover the room in which he slept. Drawing aside his curtain with a candle in my hand, I awoke the old peer from a sound slumber; and to the credit of his nerves be it mentioned, that he showed no symptom of alarm but calmly asked, 'What news, Mr M.?'[7]

Marsden later told his wife that Barham 'received the account of this important victory with all the coolness and undisturbed tranquility of an octogenarian'.[8] He got up immediately, however, to read Collingwood's dispatch, which announced the 'ever-to-be-lamented death of Vice-Admiral Lord Viscount Nelson' before describing the victory which his fleet had won. Barham then went to his desk where he was still at work at five o'clock that morning. Marsden also 'sat up the remainder of the night, with such of the clerks as [he] could collect, in order to make the necessary communications at an early hour to the King, the Prince of Wales, and other members of the Cabinet, and to the Lord Mayor, who communicates the intelligence to the shipping interest at Lloyd's Coffee-house'.[9]

On receiving Marsden's letter, the King, so James Harrison improbably alleged, exclaimed, 'with tears rolling from the royal eyes', 'We have lost more than we have gained.'[10] Marsden, however, heard that the King, while deeply affected, 'remained silent for nearly 5 mins'.[11] His private secretary's reply to the Admiralty's communication briefly expressed his Majesty's sorrow at the death of Lord Nelson whose loss the King could 'never sufficiently regret'; but the letter went on to bestow the most contrastingly fulsome praise upon Lord Collingwood, 'an officer of such consummate valour, judgement and skill . . . every part of whose conduct [was] deserving of [his Majesty's] entire approbation and admiration. The feeling manner in which he has described the events of that great day ... and the modesty with which he speaks of himself, whilst he does justice in terms so elegant and so ample to the meritorious exertions of the gallant officers and men under his command, have also proved extremely gratifying to the King.'[12]

The Prince of Wales, at odds as usual with his father and claiming a far more intimate friendship with the fallen hero than he had ever actually enjoyed, mourned Nelson as 'the greatest character England could ever boast of'; and – much to the annoyance of his father, who reminded him that it was against all custom for the heir to the throne to attend the funeral of any of the King's subjects other than those of the royal family – announced his intention of attending the hero's funeral as chief mourner.[13]

At 10 Downing Street, the Prime Minister, close to death himself, could not get back to sleep after being given the news of Trafalgar and of Lord Nelson's death. He told Lord Malmesbury the next day that, although he had often been aroused with urgent messages in the past, he had never allowed them to disturb his night's rest. On this occasion, however, he had felt so agitated that he had dressed and gone downstairs at three o'clock in the morning.[14]

When a *Gazette Extraordinary* announced the news, and the newspapers carried more detailed reports, there were muted celebrations in London. That evening lamps were lit outside several houses; theatre audiences sang 'Rule Britannia'; guns fired salutes at the Tower and in the royal parks. But, as the *Naval Chronicle* reported, 'there was a damp upon the public spirit, which it was impossible to overcome. Even many of the devices and transparencies indicated that the loss of Lord Nelson was more lamented than the victory was rejoiced at.' *The Times* remarked upon the nation's 'deep and universal affliction': 'We do not know whether we should mourn or rejoice. The country has gained the most splendid and decisive Victory that has ever graced the naval annals of England; but it has been dearly purchased. *The great and gallant* NELSON *is no more.*' The *Morning Post*, while mourning 'the fate of Britain's darling', was consoled by the thought that he had 'closed his career in a war which [would] place his name so high in the Tablets of immortality'. The *Morning Chronicle* thought it 'impossible to conceive a human being of more pure benevolence and of more active virtue than Lord Nelson'.[15]

Elegiac verses, popular ballads and hymns were composed in his memory; the print shops were filled with engravings of his various portraits; his features appeared on commemorative plates and mugs, on the lids of snuffboxes and jamjars, on pipe bowls and tea trays, in children's picture books, on tea canisters and carefully embroidered samplers. Sermons were preached in praise of his Christian qualities; prayers were said for him at services of thanksgiving; posters were stuck upon walls calling upon passers-by to emulate the brave and good hero: 'Fear God, Fear Sin and then Fear Nothing.' Tableaux verged on the blasphemous in their portrayal of Nelson as the second Christ and his 'Band of Brothers' as his disciples; all over the country plans were discussed for memorials to him and statues of him; ships were named after him, streets, squares and taverns, even towns.* 'In one place we see him as a gooseberry,' a journalist wrote in the *Morning Post*, 'in another as a carnation – sometimes as a race-horse, sometimes as a prize ram.'

Artists were busy at work on representations of scenes from his life and depictions of his last hours, just as he would have wished. Some years before he had been sitting at dinner next to Benjamin West, Sir Joshua Reynolds's successor as President of the Royal Academy. He had remarked that he regretted not having acquired

---

* There are still nearly fifty Nelson Streets, Roads, Places, Rows, Walks, Passages, Squares or Terraces in the Greater London area alone. Trafalgar Square was planned and laid out in the 1830s and 1840s. The 145 ft high, fluted Corinthian Nelson Column was erected in 1839–42. Designed by William Railton, its cost was met by subscriptions raised by the Nelson Memorial Commitee. The 17 ft Craigleith stone statue of Nelson by E. H. Baily was placed on top of the column in 1843. The bronze bas-reliefs at the base of the column, cast from cannon captured in Nelson's battles, were completed in 1849. They represent the Battle of Cape St Vincent (sculptor M. L. Watson), the Battle of the Nile (W. F. Woodington), the bombardment of Copenhagen (J. Ternout) and the death of Nelson (J. E. Carew). (*The London Encyclopaedia*, ed. Weinref and Hibbert (new edition, London, 1993), 553–4.)

a taste for art in his youth and having so little discrimination in artistic matters. But there was one picture, he had added, which always had impressed him and which he always stopped to look at when he saw a reproduction of it in a print-shop window, and that was West's *Death of Wolfe*. He asked West why he had done no more like it. 'Because, my Lord,' West had replied, 'there are no more subjects.'

'Damn it,' said Nelson, 'I didn't think of that.'

'My Lord, I fear your intrepidity may yet furnish me with another such scene, and if it should, I shall certainly avail myself of it.'

'*Will* you, Mr West?' Nelson had said eagerly, pouring out more champagne. 'Then I hope I shall die in the next battle.'[16]

He had made a similar comment to John Flaxman, when introduced to the sculptor by Sir William Hamilton. 'Pray, stop a little, my Lord,' Hamilton had said when Nelson was about to leave the room. 'I desire you to shake hands with Mr Flaxman, for he is a man as extraordinary in his way as you are in yours. Believe me, he is the sculptor who ought to make your monument.'

'Is he?' Nelson had replied, seizing Flaxman's hand with what William Hayley, who was also present, described as 'great alacrity and spirit', 'then I heartily wish he may.'*[17]

The modeller Catherine Andras was commissioned by the Dean

---

* Both West and Flaxman responded to the call. Flaxman's statue stands in the transept nave of St Paul's Cathedral, where, as Sir Nikolaus Pevsner remarked, it is 'so convincingly a portrait that it makes most of the others around look dummies'. West's 'Death of Nelson' is now in the Walker Art Gallery, Liverpool, as is Daniel Maclise's painting of the same subject. An imaginative rather than historically accurate study, West's painting depicts a series of disparate incidents as though they all took place at the same time. A more faithful portrayal of the death of Nelson is the picture by Arthur William Devis, now in the National Maritime Museum, Greenwich. Devis, the son of the distinguished portrait painter, sponsored by Alexander Davison, went aboard the *Victory* as soon as she arrived home and spent three weeks in the ship, making sketches, talking to survivors of the battle, and persuading those who were with Nelson when he died to pose for him. In his picture he heightened the cockpit so that Hardy could be shown standing almost upright and added characters who were not, in fact, present at the time of the Admiral's death; but the picture, allowing for such licence, is accurate in detail (*Nelson Dispatch*, vol. 2, part 9, January 1987).

and Chapter of Westminster Abbey to make a life-sized wax effigy of Nelson as an attraction for fee-paying visitors; and this was so like him that tears streamed down Lady Hamilton's cheeks when she saw it and she would have kissed its lips had she not been warned that the colour was not yet dry.

In taverns and coaching inns sailors who claimed to have known him or served under him told stories of his courage, his easy, pleasant manner, his humanity. 'His glory is certainly at its summit,' Lord Minto commented, 'but he might have lived to enjoy it.' Minto himself was 'extremely shocked and hurt' when he heard of his death, he confessed. It kept him 'low and melancholy all day'. He had a sense of 'irreparable loss'.[18]

The hero's faults were forgotten in grief at his death. The shadows of his ill behaviour at Naples were driven out of sight by his glorious apotheosis at Trafalgar; his self-centred vanity, which had on occasions seemed absurd or downright objectionable in the past, was dismissed as a rather disarming quirk; his occasional weakness and petulant childishness appeared as nothing when weighed in the scale against his humanity and generosity; his rejection of an unwanted wife was seen as the natural consequence of an overwhelming love for another, irresistible woman. Indeed, it could not in the end be doubted that, for all his faults, he was recognized as having been a great man, the first truly national hero to be accepted as such in his own day, that as a sea officer he had merited the admiration and devotion that he had inspired, and that it was not only his victories that entitled him to be regarded as his country's greatest admiral, but also the standards of behaviour he had set among the men who had helped him win them.

These men had grown not only to respect and admire him but to regard him with the kind of affection that had induced the crew of the *Lowestoffe* to present him with an ivory model of their frigate, filled with dominoes, which he afterwards displayed in his cabin. They knew that he would go out of his way to see that they were as well fed and clothed as could be arranged, that he would do his best, as Colonel Stewart had noticed in the Baltic, to find occupations for them in the long and boring hours of life at sea, that he would strive to see that good behaviour was rewarded and that, when they were unjustly treated, he would do all he could to right the wrong, as he had done in the case of Captain William Layman, who had been punished for losing a sloop through negligence not his own. They accepted that discipline aboard ship could be maintained only by harsh punishments, since so many of them were serving reluctantly and so many were accustomed to living by crime or on the verge of criminal life ashore. But they knew that Lord Nelson would not tolerate unjust or unnecessarily savage punishments. He, and officers like him, gave them pride in being seamen in the finest navy in the world.

With his midshipmen, 'his children' as he called them, Nelson was particularly solicitous. 'The timid he never rebuked,' Lady Hughes had noticed when sailing to the West Indies in the *Boreas* years before,

but always wished to show them he desired nothing of them that he would not instantly do himself: and I have known him say. 'Well, Sir, I am going a race to the mast-head, and I beg I may meet you there.' No denial could be given to such a wish, and the poor fellow instantly began his march. His Lordship never took the least notice with what alacrity it was done, but when he met him in the top, instantly began speaking in the most cheerful manner, and saying that such a person was to be pitied that could fancy there was any danger, or even anything disagreable in the attempt . . . In like manner, he everyday went into the School Room, and saw them do their nautical business.[19]

He was solicitous also for the welfare of the powder monkeys. One of these was fond of relating in his old age how, when making his usual inspection of the gun decks before going into battle at Trafalgar, Nelson called to him as he was running about on some errand. The Admiral tapped him on the shoulder and, indicating the shirt which might have been struck by a spark in the forthcoming fighting, he said to him kindly, 'Take off that, my boy, or you'll be in trouble later in the day.'[20].

Nelson watched the subsequent careers of his 'children' with the closest attention, using his influence to advance them whenever it was in his power to do so, not always wisely, as in the cases of his young relations like Josiah Nisbet and the charming, wayward

William Bolton, more profitably in the cases of the young Peter Parker and William Hoste.

For Hoste, Nelson was simply the 'best friend' he had ever had. Thomas Fremantle had never known a man who 'seemed to gain such complete possession of another's heart'.[21] The Duke of Clarence said, 'I did not think it possible, but for one of my dearest relations, to have felt what I have done, and what I still do, for poor Nelson.'[22] Even Collingwood, rarely given to emotional confidences, said that he could not reflect upon the moment he learned of Nelson's mortal wound 'without suffering again the anguish of that moment'. The name of his 'dear friend would ever be dear to the British Navy'. His heart was 'rent with the most poignant grief'. Captain Blackwood told his wife that, 'on such terms', Trafalgar was a victory he never wished to have witnessed; while Hardy wrote, 'It has cost the country a life that no money can replace, and one whose death I shall forever mourn.'[23]

Alexander Scott told a friend that he grieved for the loss of the 'most fascinating companion [he] ever conversed with – the greatest and most simple of men – one of the nicest and most innocent'. Scott 'had not shed a tear for years before the 21st of October', but 'since, whenever alone,' he confessed, he was 'quite like a child'. 'Setting aside his heroism,' Scott added, 'when I think what an affectionate, fascinating little fellow he was, how kind and condescending his manners, I become stupid with grief for what I have lost.'[24]

'When Nelson died,' wrote Samuel Taylor Coleridge, who was in Naples at the time on his way home from his duties as Ball's secretary on Malta, 'it seemed as if no man was a stranger to another: for all were made acquaintances in the rights of a common anguish. Never can I forget the sorrow and consternation that lay on every countenance . . . Numbers stopped and shook hands with me, because they had seen tears on my cheek, and conjectured I was an Englishman; and some, as they held my hand, burst themselves into tears.'[25] Their Queen, Maria Carolina, thought that she would regret him all her life; 'nothing could console for his loss.'[26]

Lady Elizabeth Foster thought that 'no, no words, no expressions [could] give any idea of the effect of this beloved hero's death. This day will be ever memorable for the greatest victory and the greatest loss this country ever knew. Nelson, dear, dear Nelson is no more. Great, gallant and generous Nelson . . .'[27]

Children were deeply affected, as well as their parents. Lady Brownlow, who was fourteen years old at the time, related how someone 'rushed in and said that there had been a great Naval victory – that the French and Spanish fleets were annihilated but that Nelson was killed. On hearing this, to the utter astonishment of my governess and the others in the room, I fell down as if I had been shot. On after reflection I felt no less astonished myself, for I had never seen Nelson.'[28]

The poet, Robert Southey, thirty-one at the time and to publish a biography of the Admiral eight years later, recalled that the death of Nelson was felt in England as something more than a national calamity. 'Men started at the intelligence and turned pale, as if they had heard of the loss of a dear friend. An object of our admiration and affection, of our pride and our hopes, was suddenly taken from us and it seemed as if we had never, till then, known how deeply we loved and reverenced him.'*[29]

The Prince of Wales continued to be 'affected most extremely' by Nelson's death, Mrs Fitzherbert reported.[30] He had 'loved him as a friend', the Prince reported himself. And Lady Hamilton with blatant mendacity informed Alexander Davison – in a letter which she hoped would be passed on to his Royal Highness – that the love was reciprocated: Nelson 'adored' the Prince. For the moment the Prince still insisted upon being chief mourner at the funeral, 'a distinguished honour' which Dr William Nelson, by then the second

---

* One voice not to be heard in this almost universal paean was that of Lord St Vincent, who gave orders that his own funeral be conducted in the most modest manner and did not attend Nelson's. 'Lord Nelson's sole merit was animal courage,' he wrote; 'his private character most disgraceful in every sense of the word.' As for Lady Hamilton she was a 'diabolical bitch' (Berchman, 239, 240; Emilio J. Moriconi, 'Jervis and Nelson', *Nelson Dispatch*, vol. 4, part 5, January 1992).

Baron Nelson, naturally relished, writing to Colonel McMahon to say 'how deeply the family of [his] lamented brother [were] impressed with a sense of his Royal Highness's condescension & how highly they [estimated the honour which would] be conferred on Lord Nelson's remains by such a proof of his Royal Highness's consideration & regard'.[31]

Two days after this letter was written, William Nelson was created Earl Nelson in consideration of his brother's services. He came post-haste to London to act his appropriate part, taking rooms in Fitzroy Square before renting a house in Charles Street, Berkeley Square.

'I suppose all the public reward of money will go to the parson, who of all the dull stupid fellows you ever saw, perhaps he is the most so,' Collingwood wrote in a characteristic comment. 'Nothing in him like a gentleman. Nature never intended him for anything superior to a village curate and here has Fortune, in one of her frisks, raised him, without his body and mind having anything to do with it, to the highest dignity.'[32]

The public reward of money did, indeed, go to the parson, who declined to give up his prebendal stall at Canterbury to Dr Scott as his brother had hoped he would when William came into his inheritance. It was decreed by Act of Parliament that 'a Sum not exceeding Ninety thousand Pounds of lawful Money of Great Britain' should be granted to him for the purchase of a suitable estate and that, in addition to this huge sum, an annuity of £5,000 should be bestowed upon him and his successors in the title of Earl Nelson of Trafalgar and Merton.*[33] Lady Hamilton commented sardonically in a letter to George Rose that the new Earl must have 'great courage' to accept the honour of calling himself by '*that name*'.†[34]

---

* This annuity, granted to 'Earl Nelson and the Heirs Male of the Body of the said Earl Nelson, and to such other persons to whom the said Title, Honour and Dignity of Earl Nelson shall descend, was abrogated by the Labour government after the Second World War.
† Ridiculed for his pretensions and his eagerness to live in a style appropriate to the great wealth he had suddenly acquired – and known to have his eye on

In addition to the honour and riches bestowed upon their brother, the government agreed to allow his sisters £10,000 each, later increased to £15,000 each. The Dowager Lady Nelson, to whom Lord Barham wrote a letter of condolence upon the death of her 'illustrious partner', was granted a pension of £2,000 a year.

Plead as she did, and importunate as her mother and friends were on her behalf, Lady Hamilton waited in vain for similar recognition, making the improbable claim, to George Rose and others, that it was she who had persuaded her 'glorious and dear departed Nelson' to go forth upon the enterprise which had cost him his life and won the nation so great a victory.[35] George Rose approached Pitt, but the Prime Minister was too ill to consider the

---

Houghton Hall, much to the annoyance of its owner, the Earl of Cholmondeley – Earl Nelson was reported to have observed that the day of Trafalgar was a great day for him because of the honour it had brought him. It was not until 1814 that he bought Stanlynch Park, near Downton, Wiltshire, thereafter known as Trafalgar House. This was designed by John James of Greenwich, one of Sir Christopher Wren's assistants, with two wings by John Wood the Younger. It remained in the Nelson family until the death of the 4th Earl Nelson in 1947. In 1990 the house, by then separated from its original estate, was bought by the Swedish entrepreneur, Gunnar Bengtsson, long an admirer of Nelson and owner of the Lady Hamilton, Lord Nelson and Victory Hotels in Stockholm. At the time of writing the house was again on the market and was expected to fetch £1.5 million.

Earl Nelson's wife died in 1828 and in the next year, by then 'exceedingly and impatiently deaf', according to Sir William Hotham, he married Hilaire, widow of his cousin, George Ulric Barlow, and third daughter of Admiral Sir Robert Barlow. Two years after the Earl's death, his widow, Hilaire, married George Thomas Knight, a nephew of Jane Austen. The Earl's son, Horace, died aged nineteen in 1808. His daughter, Lady Charlotte, married Baron Bridport in 1810 and, on her father's death, succeeded to his Sicilian title as Duchess of Bronte. (See family tree on page xii.) Cuthbert Collingwood was treated less generously than Nelson's family. He was created Baron Collingwood of Caldburne and Hethpoole and was granted a pension of £2,000 for life with, after his death, £1,000 to his widow, and £500 to each of his two daughters. He was anxious that the title should pass to the elder of these daughters, whose husband changed his name to Collingwood; but this was not permitted. Captain Hardy was created a baronet but, having daughters and no sons, his baronetcy, like Collingwood's title, became extinct upon his death.

matter; Pitt's successor, the 'cold-hearted' Lord Grenville, as Emma described him, was not sympathetic; while Earl Nelson did nothing to support the claims of a woman he was before long to drop altogether. Others to whom she applied made unfulfilled promises. Alexander Davison took it upon himself to write personally and confidentially to the Prince of Wales, enclosing a copy of Lord Nelson's 'last request to his King and country in favour of Lady Hamilton, whose sufferings, poor woman are beyond description'. The Prince acknowledged the letter, giving his assurances that were it to depend upon him, 'there would not be a wish or desire of our ever to be lamented and much loved friend, as well as adored Hero', which he would not consider as 'a solemn obligation upon his friends and Country to fulfill'. It was a duty they owed to 'his memory and his matchless and unrivalled excellence'.[36] The letter was passed on to the King's ministers who, considering that Lady Hamilton had been amply provided for by her late husband and that Nelson had been misinformed about her alleged services in Italy, chose to ignore it. The 'poor woman' was not even to attend her lover's funeral. The King himself remained totally unsympathetic to the claims of the adulteress. When the new Earl Nelson went to restore his brother's insignia of the Order of the Bath to his Majesty, the King looked at it, fumbled with it a little, and was walking away without a word when the Earl expressed his gratitude for the honours heaped on him and his family owing to his 'loved and honoured brother'. The Earl then proceeded to speak of his brother's religion – 'the true religion that teaches us to sacrifice one's life for one's King and country' – to which the King merely replied, 'He died the death he wished.'[37]

35
St Paul's

I hope he is in Heaven.

In the first week in December the *Victory*, with Nelson's coffin aboard, was towed past the ships of the Channel Fleet whose upper decks were crowded with sailors. For a week the *Victory* remained anchored at Spithead before continuing her journey along the Sussex and Kent coasts to the Nore, and then on to Greenwich, where Nelson's coffin was placed inside another lead coffin, which was itself encased in yet another coffin of wood. It was to lie in state for three days beneath the ceiling of the Great Hall, painted by Sir James Thornhill a hundred years before. Admiral Lord Hood, Governor of the Royal Hospital at Greenwich, was extremely anxious about the immense crowds which gathered outside the Hospital and thought it as well to write to the Home Secretary:

The Mob assembled here is so very numerous & tumultuous that it is absolutely necessary that your Lordship should apply for a very *strong* party of Cavalry to line the street on each side from Deptford Bridge to the entrance of the Hospital & to attend the other Gates early on Wednesday morning or it will not be possible for the procession to move from here – The mob consisted yesterday of upwards of 30,000 & equally so today and more outrageous – Townsend & the other peace officers from Bow Street say they never saw anything like it before.[1]

From Greenwich the coffin was taken up river in the Admiral's barge. It was accompanied by Lord Hood and Admiral of the Fleet Sir Peter Parker, who was chief mourner, the Prince of Wales having obeyed his father's orders not to break with family tradition but to attend the funeral with his brothers in a private capacity.

Escorted by black-draped boats and watched by thousands of

people crowded on the river bank, the barge, pulled by sailors from the *Victory*, moved slowly upstream in a strong wind as the minute-guns boomed from the Tower. At Whitehall Stairs the coffin was carried from the barge and, attended by Alexander Scott, taken to a room at the Admiralty where it remained that cold night.

Early the next morning, 9 January 1806, as the drummers of the volunteer corps beat to arms, crowds began to assemble along the long route between Whitehall and St Paul's. Ticket holders took up their seats; windows filled with faces. The great bell in the cathedral's south-west tower began to toll as the sun came out.

George Matcham, who had arrived a few days before at the Gloucester Coffee House on the corner of Piccadilly and Berkeley Street, had been to see his uncle, the Earl, who 'talked much about his precedence at the Funeral and was very angry at not being presented with tickets'. Having picked up the Boltons, Matcham returned, early on the morning of the funeral, to the Earl's, 'where breakfast was laid out'.

'Saw the two sons of Lord Walpole, gentlemanly looking,' he recorded in his journal. 'Were not received at all by the Earl, nor introduced to anybody ... About half past eight the Mourning Coaches came ... Went into St James Park.' There he found a gaggle of admirals and captains in full-dress uniforms with black waistcoats 'much confused, not being able to find their carriages'.[2] There were thirty-two admirals altogether in attendance and over a hundred captains. There were numerous soldiers too, among them the King's second son, Field Marshal the Duke of York, Commander-in-Chief, and the old Scottish general, Sir David Dundas, who had been recalled from his retirement to command the military escort of some ten thousand troops, comprising for the most part soldiers who had served in Egypt after the Battle of the Nile.

The Scots Greys led the procession, which was so long that they reached the door of the cathedral before the mourners bringing up the rear had left the Admiralty. Muffled drums and pipes played the dead march; minute-guns continued to boom in the distance; but the spectators were so quiet as the coffin passed by on a funeral car – fashioned in the shape of the *Victory* with a winged figure of Fame bearing a laurel wreath on the prow – that a witness observed the only general sound to be heard was one resembling a murmuring sea as men respectfully removed their hats. Ahead of the coffin marched sailors from the *Victory* carrying their ship's white ensign, which from time to time they displayed to the crowds on either side, showing the shot-holes in the fabric.

At the cathedral door, the sailors removed the coffin from the funeral car. It was escorted inside the building by six admirals carrying a canopy.

The service lasted four hours. The choir sang anthems; lessons were read; all the stages of a state funeral as laid down by the College of Arms were meticulously observed, not all of them satisfactorily in George Matcham's opinion: the Bishop of Chichester, John Buckner, who read the first lesson did so in a voice heavy and monotonous. And, as the coffin was being moved from the choir to the space beneath the dome where it was to be buried, the Duke of Clarence, in a characteristically tactless act, ambled across to Nelson's brother, the Earl, to shake his hand and to say in an assumed whisper loud enough for all to hear, 'I am come to pay my last duties here, and I hope you and I shall never meet on such a like occasion.'[3]

Beneath the dome, where a chandelier with 130 lamps cast a brilliant light within the surrounding gloom, Garter King at Arms intoned Lord Nelson's styles and titles, and then accepted the white staves which were handed to him by three of the Admiral's friends, acting as officers of his household, Alexander Davison as treasurer, William Haslewood as comptroller and William Marsh, the navy agent, as steward. Garter King at Arms threw the broken staves upon the coffin, which was lowered into the crypt.*[4]

All this was as the College of Arms decreed; but what was certainly not provided for was the action of the sailors carrying the

---

* Nelson's tomb is immediately below the dome. The graceful black marble sarcophagus was designed originally for Cardinal Wolsey by the Florentine, Benedetto da Rovezzano, but was confiscated by Henry VIII and lay neglected at Windsor Castle for nearly three centuries until used for Nelson's interment.

ensign who, instead of reverently furling it and placing it upon the coffin, tore a large piece out of it and ripped this into smaller fragments which they stuffed inside their jackets. 'That was *Nelson*,' Captain Codrington's wife commented; 'the rest was so much the Herald's Office.'[5]

In contrast to this defiance of ordained and seemly conduct, the obituaries rolled from the presses, respectful, pious, adulatory not to say idolatrous. Nelson would have relished them; yet he would have delighted even more in the more heartfelt tributes of his sailors, in the story of the *Victory*'s boatswain, who, learning of his death, had been unable to pipe the hands to quarters because of his tears, sobbing, 'Hang me, I can't do it?.'[6] He would also surely have delighted in Charles Williams's caricature, 'Jack and Poll at Portsmouth', depicting a seaman in squashed hat, striped trousers and buckled shoes helping himself to a pinch of snuff on Portsmouth Point.

'Welcome! Welcome home! my dear Jack,' says his girlfriend, leaning on his shoulder. 'Ah! But you have not brought the brave Lord Nelson home with you. Well, I hope he is in Heaven.'

'In Heaven,' says the sailor, looking grimly down into his tobacco pouch. 'Aye to be sure he is, Poll. What in Hell should prevent him?[7]

The Fate of Characters Whose End
is not Recorded in the Text

JOHN ACTON. Fled to Sicily with the royal family when the French attacked Naples again in 1806. He died at Palermo on 12 August 1811. His second son, Charles Januarius Edward, was proclaimed a cardinal in 1842.

HENRY ADDINGTON, FIRST VISCOUNT SIDMOUTH. Invited to join the coalition government in 1806, he became Lord Privy Seal, then President of the Council, before becoming a stern Home Secretary in 1812. He retired from that office in 1821 and from the Cabinet in 1824, dying in 1844 at the age of eighty-six.

TOM ALLEN. Bitterly disappointed by not having been aboard the *Victory* at Trafalgar, having duties to undertake ashore, Allen maintained that his master would have survived had he been able to look after him. He returned to Norfolk after Nelson's death, but, having soon spent his modest prize-money, he fell on hard times until taken into the service of Captain Sir William Bolton, husband of Nelson's niece, Kitty. On Sir William's death at the age of fifty-three in 1830, Allen again became destitute until a Norwich surgeon, whose sympathy he had enlisted, used his influence to gain him a place as a pensioner at Greenwich Hospital. When Captain Hardy became Governor of the Hospital, Allen was appointed pewterer, which entitled him to a salary of £65 a year and a set of apartments where he lived with his wife and granddaughter until his death in 1834 aged seventy-four. Captain Hardy paid for a headstone to be erected to his memory in the Hospital's cemetery; and, since his salary came to an end with him, arrangements were made for a pension to be paid to his widow.

ALEXANDER BALL. Remained Governor of Malta, where he was extremely popular, for the rest of his life. He was created a baronet and promoted rear-admiral. He died on the island in 1809 and was buried there.

CHARLES MIDDLETON, FIRST BARON BARHAM. Was succeeded as First Lord of the Admiralty by Charles Grey in 1806. He died in 1813, having taken no further part in public life.

WILLIAM BEATTY. Published his *Authentic Narrative of the Death of Lord Nelson* in 1807. He obtained the degree of MD at St Andrews University in 1817 and was knighted in 1831. He died in London in 1842, having resigned two years earlier as physician at Greenwich Hospital.

WILLIAM BECKFORD. For over twenty years after entertaining Nelson and the Hamiltons at Fonthill, Beckford remained there in that 'cathedral turned into a toyshop', as Hazlitt was to describe it, in virtual seclusion. The high tower collapsed because of its hurried construction by workmen labouring by night as well as by day; its successor later also fell down. In 1822, his great fortune largely dissipated, Beckford sold Fonthill and moved to Bath, where he built a less extravagant folly. An inveterate collector to the end, he died in Bath in 1844.

EDWARD BERRY. Captain of the *Agamemnon* at Trafalgar and in the action off San Domingo in 1806, Berry transferred to the *Sceptre* in 1811 and the *Barfleur* the next year. In 1813 he was given command of one of the royal yachts, and promoted rear-admiral in 1821. After a long illness, he died in 1831. The baronetcy conferred upon him in 1806 became extinct.

BETHUNE, *see* DRINKWATER.

HENRY BLACKWOOD. Acted as train-bearer to Admiral Parker,

chief mourner at Nelson's funeral. While in command of the eighty-gun *Ajax* in 1806, his ship was inadvertently set alight by a drunken steward, and Blackwood was almost drowned. Transferred to the *Warspite*, he was created a baronet in 1814 and appointed Commander-in-Chief in the West Indies in 1819. After a short spell as Commander-in-Chief at the Nore, he died, a vice-admiral, in 1832.

WILLIAM BLIGH. Appointed Governor of New South Wales in 1805, he was forcibly deposed by an army major after a harsh rule of some three years. The major was cashiered and Bligh was promoted rear-admiral after his return to England, where he died in 1817.

SUSANNAH BOLTON. Lived contentedly at Cranwich after her brother's death, welcoming Lady Hamilton and Horatia there from time to time. Following the family's removal to Bradenham Hall, Lady Hamilton was only once again a guest of the Boltons. In 1811 she was a witness at the marriage of Susannah's daughter, Elizabeth, to her cousin, the Rev. Henry Girdlestone. Mrs Bolton died in 1813 and was buried, at her request, in her father's old churchyard at Burnham Thorpe.

MARY CADOGAN (LYON). 'Mrs Cadogging', as Horatia referred to her, remained a good, protective and efficient mother to Lady Hamilton for the rest of her life, helping to manage her affairs as best she could. She died on 14 January 1810 and was buried in the graveyard of the recently built church of St Mary on Paddington Green, where Sarah Siddons was to be buried in 1831 and Wilkie Collins's father, the painter William Collins, in 1847.

ROBERT CALDER. The court martial for which he was sent home before the Battle of Trafalgar sentenced Calder to be severely reprimanded. Even so, he became an admiral by seniority in 1810 and was created KCB in 1815. He died in 1818.

THOMAS CAPEL. Commanded the *Phoebe* at Trafalgar and was

afterwards appointed to the *Endymion*. Having served on the North American station during the war with the United States, he was appointed to the command of the royal yacht in 1821 and to the West Indian command in 1834. Promoted admiral in 1847, he died in 1853.

CAREW, *see* BENJAMIN HALLOWELL

EMMA CAREW. Went to live abroad before settling in a convent in the East End of London.

CUTHBERT COLLINGWOOD, BARON COLLINGWOOD OF CALD-BURNE AND HETHPOOLE. After Trafalgar, Collingwood spent four uneventful years in the Mediterranean. Suffering from what he called 'a very severe complaint' in his stomach, no doubt cancer, he died at sea in March 1810 aged fifty-nine, less than seven months after his beloved dog Bounce. The barony became extinct.

ALEXANDER DAVISON. After his release from prison, Davison lived quietly. A catalogue of his collection of paintings by British artists 'of subjects selected from the History of England as arranged in St James's Square' was printed in 1806. He died at the age of seventy-nine in Brighton in 1829.

JOHN DRINKWATER. Held the office of Comptroller of Army Accounts for twenty-five years until 1835. His *Narrative of the Battle of St Vincent* was republished with new anecdotes of Nelson in 1840. He assumed the name of Bethune upon his wife's inheritance of property in Scotland from her brother. He died in 1844.

JOHN THOMAS DUCKWORTH. Promoted vice-admiral in 1804, he defeated a French squadron off San Domingo in 1806 and forced the passage of the Dardanelles in 1807, destroying a squadron of Turkish frigates. From 1810 to 1813, when he was created a baronet, he was Governor of Newfoundland, and in 1817, for a short time until his death, Commander-in-Chief at Plymouth.

GILBERT ELLIOT, FIRST EARL OF MINTO. Appointed Governor-General of India in 1806. Superseded by the Prince Regent's friend, Lord Moira, he returned to England in May 1814, having been created Viscount Melgund and Earl of Minto for his distinguished services. He died the following month. His eldest son, the second earl, was successively ambassador to Berlin, First Lord of the Admiralty and Lord Privy Seal. His second son became an admiral; his daughter married Lord John Russell; and his great-grandson, the fourth earl, became Viceroy of India in 1905.

HUGH ELLIOT. Transferred in 1782 from Berlin to Copenhagen, where he remained for nine years. After conducting a secret mission in Paris, he was sent to Dresden and then to Naples. In 1809 he was appointed Governor of the Leeward Islands and in 1814 Governor of Madras. Returning to England in 1820, he died ten years later.

FATIMA (Fatima Emma Charlotte Nelson Hamilton). When Lady Hamilton could no longer keep her, Fatima was placed in Bear Lane Workhouse, where ten shillings a week was paid for her. She was later removed by Thomas Cribb, the Merton Place gardener, to St Luke's madhouse, where she died.

FERDINAND IV. After Napoleon's defeat, Ferdinand returned as King of the Two Sicilies to Naples, where he died suddenly in 1825.

THOMAS FOLEY. Too ill to accept Nelson's offer of the command of the fleet off Cadiz in 1805, Foley had little further opportunity to distinguish himself. Appointed commander-in-chief in the Downs in 1811 and commander-in-chief at Portsmouth in 1830, he died in 1833, an admiral and a KCB. His widow, who survived into her eightieth year, was the youngest daughter of the Duke of Leinster.

LADY ELIZABETH FOSTER. After the death of her friend Georgiana, Duchess of Devonshire, Lady Elizabeth married the Duke, whose mistress she had been. She died in 1824.

THOMAS FREMANTLE. After commanding the *Neptune* at Trafalgar, Fremantle served in the Mediterranean and the Adriatic. Created KCB in 1818, he was appointed to be Commander-in-Chief in the Mediterranean that year but died at Naples in December 1819. His eldest son, granted a baronetcy on the strength of his father's achievements, was raised to the peerage as Lord Cottesloe in 1874; a younger son became Admiral Sir Charles Howe Fremantle. His widow, Betsey, the diarist, died in 1857 in her eightieth year.

ABRAHAM GOLDSMID. Embroiled in financial difficulties, Goldsmid, who had been very kind and generous to Lady Hamilton in her own difficulties, shot himself in the grounds of Morden Park in September 1810. His elder brother Ascher, who bought Merton Place for £12,930, and paid £1,801 for the furniture and effects, never lived there, and seems to have employed Lady Hamilton's housekeeper, Dame Francis, as caretaker. The house was demolished in 1846, houses in the present Nelson, Trafalgar, Victory, Hardy and Hamilton Roads being built on the site.

SAMUEL GRANSTON GOODALL. After serving as Governor of Toulon, Goodall was promoted vice-admiral in 1794 and was second-in-command to Admiral Hotham. Disappointed by not being appointed to the command, he asked for leave to strike his flag. He was promoted admiral in 1799 and died two years later.

PRYSE LOCKHART GORDON. Remained in Italy with Lord Montgomerie until 1801 and, having married 'an amiable young widow', which greatly improved his financial position, he once more went on his travels, again with Montgomerie, in 1811. In 1814 he went to live in Brussels, where he died in the late 1830s. His *Companion to Italy* was published in 1823 and his *Personal Memoirs* in 1830.

CHARLES GREVILLE. Having made many economies in his way of life, in the unfounded belief that his financial circumstances made them necessary, Greville died at his house in Paddington Green aged fifty in 1809. His estates in Wales, inherited from Sir William

Hamilton, together with the responsibility for paying Lady Hamilton's quarterly allowance of £200, passed to his brother Robert Fulke Greville (1751–1824), husband of Louisa, Countess of Mansfield in her own right. During her exile in France, Lady Hamilton asked Robert Fulke Greville to send her allowance to Calais. He replied that he could not do so, since he had received applications from people who said she had pledged money to them. Instead he sent her various demands from her creditors. This Greville's elder daughter married Lieutenant-General the Hon. Sir George Cathcart, one of Wellington's aides-de-camp at Waterloo, who was killed at Inkerman during the Crimean War.

BENJAMIN HALLOWELL. Detached to Gibraltar with the *Tigre*, Hallowell was not present at Trafalgar. Appointed commander-in-chief at the Nore in 1821, he was promoted admiral in 1830 and died in 1834. He took the name Carew in accordance with the will of a cousin whose estates he inherited.

EMMA HAMILTON. Despite increasing financial difficulties, Lady Hamilton continued to live as extravagantly and behave as generously as ever. Friends and relations were entertained at Merton and at Clarges Street as though money were not a problem for her. Hard as she tried, however, and numerous as were the people whom she approached for help – including the Prince of Wales and successive prime ministers – sending them copies of Nelson's 'last and most interesting Codical', she was disappointed in her hopes of obtaining a pension and felt obliged to turn to friends and relations for loans. The sale of Merton to Ascher Goldsmid gave her temporary respite, as did her move from Clarges Street to more modest accommodation in Bond Street, where she had to share a sitting-room with the owner of the house. The Duke of Queensberry gave her the use of a house, Heron Court (now largely demolished), next to the Castle Inn near Richmond Bridge. From here she moved back to London in 1810, living first at 76 Piccadilly, then in Dover Street, then in Bond Street. From Bond Street, she moved to Elizabeth Billington's house in Fulham. Her debts continually mounting, she borrowed money where she could and eventually mortgaged her annuities. Disappointed by not receiving regular rental from the Bronte estate, which John Graefer managed so incompetently, she also failed to obtain a promised bequest from the Duke of Queensberry, whose will, contested by a tradesman, was the subject of a lengthy suit in Chancery.

By then, aged forty-six, she had become 'an old woman, divested of all her charm', according to Pryse Lockhart Gordon, who met her one day in Greenwich Park. 'Age and circumstances had made sad ravages in her former splendid countenance . . . The lovely hair which was wont to hang over her polished forehead was now tucked away under a huge cap, or perhaps it had become grey – be that as it may, it no longer served as an ornament.' It had to be conceded, though, that her eyes, while less brilliant, were still beautiful and 'that fascinating mouth from which sculptors had modelled yet retained its expression'.

In 1813 she was arrested for debt and forced to live within the rules of the King's Bench Prison, where she wrote to complain to the Prince of Wales, now Prince Regent: 'The slender provision left by Lord Nelson for the bringing up of his daughter comes short of which I deem necessary for the education of one of her descent, the only Living Blood of that glorious man who Loved and adored your Royal Highness.'

The next year, taking Horatia with her, she fled to Calais, having extracted £250 owing to her from Earl Nelson. She had been suffering from jaundice, exacerbated by heavy drinking, and had grown fatter than ever. At Calais, she and her daughter took rooms at Dessin's in the Rue Royale, the hotel where Laurence Sterne had stayed and which, so another guest, the Russian historian Nikolai Karamzin, said, was always 'full of Englishmen'. From here they moved to a house just outside the town, where Emma began to recover her health. She employed a French maid, and sent for her former housekeeper at Merton to come to look after her modest household. While living at Dessin's, Horatia had attended a school run by an Englishwoman in Calais; after moving to the house in the country Emma took over the child's education herself.

Beset by ever-growing insolvency, they moved back to Calais in

1814 to dismal lodgings in a house near Dessin's. Here Emma died on 15 January 1815, having 'for a very long time before her death', so Horatia said, taken 'little interest in anything but the indulgence of her unfortunate habit'. Her large bills for wines and spirits were paid by Henry Cadogan, agent in Calais for Lloyd's of London. She was buried in the graveyard of the church of St Pierre, where she and Horatia had worshipped regularly. She never told Horatia that she was her mother; and Horatia would not accept that she was so. 'With all her faults – and she had many,' Horatia said of her years later, 'she had many fine qualities, which, had she been placed earlier in better hands, would have made her a very superior woman ... It is but justice to say that through all her difficulties she invariably till the last few months expended on my education etc., the whole of the interest of the sum left me by Lord Nelson and which was left entirely in her control.'

THOMAS MASTERMAN HARDY. Created a baronet in 1806, Hardy was soon afterwards given command of the *Triumph* on the North American station. He returned to England in June 1815; and in 1819 was appointed to the command in South America which he held until 1824. Promoted rear-admiral the next year, he became First Sea Lord in 1830 and in 1834 was appointed Governor of Greenwich Hospital. He died in 1839, having married a rather flighty and much younger woman, who, having found a new husband, outlived Hardy by thirty-seven years. The baronetcy became extinct.

HASTINGS, *see* MOIRA

ALEXANDER HOOD. Appointed second-in-command of the Channel Fleet under Lord Howe in 1793. The following year he was created Baron Bridport and took part in the action known as the Glorious First of June. He became a viscount in 1801 and died in 1814.

SAMUEL HOOD, VISCOUNT HOOD. Held the post of Governor of

Greenwich Hospital until his death at the age of ninety-one in 1816. He was buried in the Hospital's cemetery.

WILLIAM HOSTE. Having been sent by Nelson on a mission to the Bey of Tunis, and thus having missed the Battle of Trafalgar – 'enough to make one mad', as he told his father – Hoste remained in command of the thirty-six-gun *Amphion*, which destroyed over two hundred enemy ships over a period of eighteen months. This looked well on paper, Hoste commented, but did not put much cash in his pocket, 'owing to the difficulty attending their being sent to port'. In March 1811 he was badly wounded in a hard fought action off Lissa, where he encouraged the men under his command by hoisting the signal 'Remember Nelson'. After this action, the *Amphion* was ordered home for repairs; and, a year later, Hoste was appointed to the command of a frigate, the *Bacchante*, in which he distinguished himself in several engagements, including the reduction of the enemy stronghold of Cattaro. His health broken, he returned to England where he was granted a baronetcy in 1814 and appointed KCB the following year. In 1817 he married Lady Harriet Walpole, daughter of Horatio, second Earl of Orford. He died in London in December 1828 at the age of forty-eight.

HENRY HOTHAM. Became Captain of the Fleet on the North American and West Indian station in 1813. He was knighted in 1815 and promoted vice-admiral in 1825. A Lord of the Admiralty in 1818–22 and 1828–30, he died on Malta as Commander-in-Chief in the Mediterranean in 1833.

WILLIAM HOTHAM. On his return to England in 1795, having been relieved by Sir John Jervis, Hotham saw no further service. He was created Baron Hotham in 1797 and died in 1813.

RICHARD HOWE, EARL HOWE. Became First Lord of the Admiralty in 1783 and was created an earl in 1788. He took command of the Channel Fleet in 1793 and gained the victory of the 'Glorious First of June' the next year. He died in 1799.

RICHARD HUGHES. Appointed Commander-in-Chief at Halifax in 1789, he was promoted admiral in 1794. He died in 1812.

JOHN JERVIS, *see* ST VINCENT

RICHARD KEATS. Promoted rear-admiral in 1807 and vice-admiral in 1811, he resigned his command because of ill health in 1812 after long and arduous duties at sea. In 1813 he was appointed Governor of Newfoundland, and, in 1821, Governor of Greenwich Hospital. He died in 1834.

GEORGE KEITH ELPHINSTONE, VISCOUNT KEITH. Remained Commander-in-Chief in the North Sea until 1807. The next year he married Mrs Thrale's daughter, Hester Maria. Appointed Commander-in-Chief of the Channel Fleet in 1812, he was created Viscount Keith in 1814. He died in 1823. His daughter by his first wife married Napoleon's aide-de-camp, the Comte de Flahault.

ELLIS CORNELIA KNIGHT. Returned to England with the reputation of being Nelson's poet laureate. Chosen to be companion to Queen Charlotte, she relinquished the appointment in 1813 for a more lively one with Princess Charlotte, only daughter of the Prince Regent, who dismissed Miss Knight and his daughter's other attendants a year later. In 1816 she went abroad again and died in Paris in 1837. Nelson's niece's husband, the Rev. Henry Girdlestone, entertained the bizarre notion that Miss Knight ('high-spirited and romantic') was Horatia's mother.

WILLIAM LAYMAN. Nelson's efforts on behalf of 'poor Captain Layman' were unavailing. Having been severely reprimanded and placed at the bottom of the list, he spent much of the rest of his life writing pamphlets on naval subjects. He committed suicide in 1826.

THOMAS LOUIS. Having been sent to fetch fresh water and provisions from Gibraltar and Tangier, Louis was not present at Trafalgar. In November he took his ship, the *Canopus*, to the West

Indies and fought in the battle of San Domingo in February 1806. He was rewarded with a baronetcy. He died in the *Canopus* the next year.

MARIA CAROLINA, QUEEN OF NAPLES. Having again involved Naples in war with France, she and her husband were forced to flee to Sicily in January 1806, thus ending any hopes that Lady Hamilton might have entertained of going back to Naples after Nelson's death. The Queen quarrelled with the British ambassador, Lord George Bentinck, who induced King Ferdinand to have her exiled from the island. She returned to Austria, her birthplace, where she died in September 1814.

CATHERINE MATCHAM. Like her sister, Susannah Bolton, Mrs Matcham was kind to Lady Hamilton after Nelson's death and had her to stay, with Horatia, at Ashfold. When Lady Hamilton was arrested for debt, she offered to look after Horatia, but the child's mother was reluctant to part with the girl who constituted her claim upon respectable society. Horatia seems to have deeply resented having had to share Lady Hamilton's degradation; and, so Haslewood later told the Matchams, 'I believe, when warm with wine and anger, Lady Hamilton sometimes bestowed upon Miss Nelson epithets less kind and flattering than that of Lord Nelson's child.' When Horatia did eventually go to live at Ashfold after her mother's death, Mrs Matcham did all she could to make her life happy there. After Horatia left to live with the Boltons, Mrs Matcham kept closely in touch with her and became godmother to her first child. Widowed in 1833, Catherine Matcham died in 1842.

GEORGE MATCHAM, the elder. Restless as ever, Matcham moved from Norfolk to Ashfold, near Horsham in Sussex, in 1806. Thereafter, he and his wife travelled widely on the Continent, spending time in Lisbon, renting a large house outside Paris, visiting Italy and, in the words of their son, wandering so much that they 'completely lost the English habits of society'. They returned to England in 1828, renting a house in Kensington. Matcham remained an occasional author, his *Parental Chitchat* following his *Anecdotes of a Croat*. He died aged eighty in 1833.

GEORGE MATCHAM, the younger. After reading law at Cambridge, Matcham was admitted to Doctors' Commons in 1820. Appointed chairman of Wiltshire Quarter Sessions in 1836, he was also, like his father, an occasional writer, mostly upon topographical subjects. His *Notes on the Character of Lord Nelson*, originally contributed to *The Times*, was reprinted in 1861. Matcham married Harriet Eyre in 1817 and was presented by his father with a small estate near the parental home in Ashfold. He died in 1877.

MIDDLETON, *see* BARHAM

RALPH WILLET MILLER. Did not long survive the Battle of the Nile, being killed off Acre in May 1799 when some shells exploded accidentally aboard his ship.

MINTO, *see* ELLIOT

FRANCIS RAWDON-HASTINGS, SECOND EARL OF MOIRA. Appointed Governor-General of India in 1813. He resigned in 1821 after unproved charges of corruption had been made against him. From 1824 until his death in 1826 he was Governor of Malta.

BENJAMIN MOSELEY. Held the post of physician at the Royal Hospital, Chelsea, until his death in 1819.

GEORGE MURRAY. Detained in England by legal disputes over his father-in-law's will, Murray did not accompany Nelson on his last voyage. Sent to South America in 1807, he was promoted vice-admiral in 1809 and knighted in 1815. He died suddenly in 1819.

CHARLOTTE NELSON. By her husband, the Hon. Samuel Hood, who became Baron Bridport in 1814, Lady Charlotte had seven children. She died in 1873. She inherited the title of Duchess of Bronte. Her elder son, Alexander Nelson Hood, who became

Viscount Bridport in 1868, succeeded her as Duke of Bronte. The title is now held by the fourth viscount.

FRANCES HERBERT NELSON, VISCOUNTESS NELSON. Lady Hamilton's scorn and dislike of Lady Nelson, 'Tom Tit', continued to the end. 'What a sad thing it is to think such a man as him should be entrapped with such an infamous woman as that apothecary's widow,' she wrote to Alexander Davison the year before Nelson's death. 'Whilst I am free – with talents he likes, adoring him, that never a woman adored a man as I do my Nelson, loving him beyond the world, and yet we are both miserable . . . Patience.' It seemed in 1805 when Lady Nelson fell ill that her patience would be rewarded, but Lady Hamilton's hopes were dashed when the woman recovered. Lady Nelson remained in indifferent health, however. For a time she lived in Paris with her son's family. Her eldest grandchild, also Fanny, remarked on her good nature and her continued devotion to her husband's memory. She was in the habit of taking up a miniature of him, looking at it fondly and kissing it. 'When you are older, little Fan,' she once said to the girl, 'you may know what it is to have a broken heart.' Returning to England she settled in Exmouth. She died in Harley Street on 4 May 1831 and was buried by the side of Josiah in the churchyard of St Margaret and St Andrew, Littleham.

HORATIA NELSON. After Lady Hamilton's death, Horatia, then fourteen years old, was brought back to England by the Lloyd's agent, Henry Cadogan, who handed her over to the kindly care of the Matchams. She stayed with them until 1817, when she went to live with the Thomas Boltons, who were equally kind to her. When she was sixteen she became engaged to a curate. The engagement was soon broken off, however; and in 1822 she married another clergyman, the Rev. Philip Ward. She bore him nine children and died in her eighty-first year at Pinner, on 6 March 1881. To the end she had shut her mind to the belief that Lady Hamilton could be her mother, while proud to acknowledge that she was Lord Nelson's daughter. An obituary in *The Times*, which referred to her as Lady Hamilton's daughter, was contradicted on behalf of her family in a letter which declared that 'the name of the mother was known to Mr Haslewood ... long the confidential friend and professional adviser of Lord Nelson ... but he was prevented by a sense of honour from disclosing it. Against the presumption that Lady Hamilton was the child's mother, it has also to be considered that at the probable date of its birth, Lady Hamilton was living with her husband at his house in Piccadilly surrounded by an establishment of servants.'

WILLIAM NELSON, FIRST EARL NELSON OF TRAFALGAR AND MERTON. His wife, Sarah, having died in 1828, he married again soon afterwards at the age of seventy-one in the declared hope of bringing 'the title back into the authentic line' and producing an heir to replace his son, Horace, who had died in 1808 of typhoid fever. The earl himself died in London aged seventy-seven on 28 February 1835. His second wife having failed to bear him another heir, he was succeeded in the earldom by Thomas Bolton, only son of his sister, Susannah, who changed his surname to Nelson (see family tree on page xii).

EVAN NEPEAN. After many industrious years at the Admiralty as Secretary and later one of the Lords Commissioners, he was appointed Governor of Bombay in 1812. He died in 1822, his son, Molyneux Hyde, succeeding to the baronetcy which he had been granted in 1802.

JOSIAH NISBET. Sullen and quarrelsome as he had been in the Navy, after leaving it Nisbet became a highly successful businessman in France. In 1819 he married Frances Herbert Evans, by whom he had seven children, four of whom died young. Having returned to England he settled at Exmouth and spent much of his time on his yacht. He died in his house on the Champs-Elysées while on a business visit to Paris in July 1830 and was buried in the churchyard of St Margaret and St Andrew, Littleham.

ARTHUR PAGET. Was transferred from Naples to Vienna in 1801 and to Constantinople in 1807. He retired in 1809, having been knighted in 1804.

HYDE PARKER. Saw no further service after his recall following the Battle of Copenhagen. He died in 1807.

PETER PARKER. Eighty-five years old when he acted as chief mourner at Nelson's funeral, Parker died in 1811 at the age of ninety.

JOHN PASCO. Badly wounded in the right arm at Trafalgar, Pasco was granted a pension after the battle. He was appointed to the command of the *Victory* at Portsmouth in 1846 and died in 1853.

JAMES PERRY. The *Morning Chronicle* continued to prosper, but from 1817 Perry was in increasingly indifferent health and died at his house in Brighton in 1821.

GEORGE BRYDGES RODNEY, FIRST BARON RODNEY. After his return from the West Indies in 1782, Rodney lived in retirement until his death ten years later.

GEORGE ROSE. Having resigned as Vice-President of the Board of Trade upon Pitt's death, Rose returned to that office in 1807, resigning again in 1812. He remained in office, however, as Treasurer of the Navy and died, a rich man, in 1818.

FABRIZIO RUFFO. Having fallen out with King Ferdinand, Ruffo lived in retirement in Naples when the French occupied the city, first under Joseph Bonaparte and then under Joachim Murat. On King Ferdinand's return, he was once again received at court and for a time was a government minister. He died in 1827.

JOHN JERVIS, EARL OF ST VINCENT. The year after Trafalgar, St Vincent resumed the Channel Command, although by then over seventy years old. His request to be relieved on the grounds of ill health was granted in April 1807. At the coronation of King George IV he was promoted Admiral of the Fleet, a rank which could officially be held by only one officer at a time and was already held by the Duke of Clarence. He died in March 1823 aged eighty-eight. His wife had borne no children and the earldom became extinct. The viscountcy devolved upon his only surviving nephew, Edward Jervis Ricketts.

JAMES SAUMAREZ. In command of the Guernsey station between 1803 and 1807, Saumarez thereafter served in the Baltic. Commander-in-Chief at Plymouth between 1824 and 1827, in 1831 he was raised to the peerage as Baron de Saumarez of Saumarez in Guernsey. He was buried on the island in 1836.

ISAAC SCHOMBERG. Having been sent home to England, Schomberg was put on half pay. Soon afterwards, however, he was appointed first lieutenant of the *Barfleur*. In 1794 he was given command of the *Culloden*, in which he fought on the 'Glorious First of June'. Thereafter he had no further active service. From 1808 until 1813, the year of his death, he was Deputy Comptroller of the Navy.

ALEXANDER JOHN SCOTT. Although Nelson called him Dr Scott, he did not receive the degree of Doctor of Divinity until after the Admiral's death. In 1816 he was appointed chaplain to the Prince Regent and presented to the crown living of Catterick in Yorkshire, where he died in 1840.

SIDNEY SMITH. Continued his varied and erratic career in the Mediterranean, off Constantinople and in South America until his return to England in 1814. He accompanied Wellington's army to Paris, where he mostly lived thereafter and where he died, aged seventy-five, in 1840. He was promoted admiral in 1821.

GEORGE JOHN SPENCER, SECOND EARL SPENCER. Became Home Secretary in 1806, retiring from government, never to return to office, in the following year. He died at Althorp in 1834, his wife having predeceased him in 1831.

WILLIAM STEWART. Distinguished himself in the war in the Peninsula, where he was known as 'Auld Grog Willie' because of the extra rum which he issued to his men and which Wellington made him pay for. He was promoted lieutenant-general in 1813 and, wounded six times in seventeen campaigns, he died in 1827. His first son was christened Horatio at Nelson's request.

FREDERICK THESIGER. Promoted to the rank of post-captain after the Battle of Copenhagen, he saw no further service. He died in 1805.

HORATIA NELSON THOMPSON, see HORATIA NELSON.

THOMAS THOMPSON. Created a baronet in 1806, he was Comptroller of the Navy until 1816 when he was appointed Treasurer of Greenwich Hospital. He was promoted vice-admiral in 1814 and died in 1828. He married a daughter of Robert Raikes, the promoter of Sunday schools.

THOMAS TROUBRIDGE. Promoted rear-admiral in 1804, he was appointed Commander-in-Chief in the East Indies the next year, then sent to command at the Cape of Good Hope. He was drowned when his ship foundered off the coast of Madagascar. He was succeeded in the baronetcy by his son, Edward Thomas, who had served aboard the *Victory* and was promoted rear-admiral in 1841.

PIERRE-CHARLES-JEAN-BAPTISTE-SILVESTRE DE VILLENEUVE. Taken prisoner to England after Trafalgar, he was soon released. On returning to France he was found stabbed to death in an inn at Rennes in April 1806. He probably committed suicide, but there were persistent rumours that he had been assassinated.

HORATIA NELSON WARD, see HORATIA NELSON.

Chronology

1758 *29 September* Horatio Nelson born at Burnham Thorpe, Norfolk.

1767 *26 December* His mother, Catherine Nelson, dies.

1770 War threatens between Britain and Spain over the Falkland Islands.
27 November Entered as midshipman in the *Raisonnable*.

1771 *March* Joins the *Raisonnable*.
15 May Transferred to the *Triumph*.
August Sails to the Caribbean on a West Indian merchant ship.

1772 *July* Returns to England and rejoins the *Triumph*.

1773 *4 June to 19 September* Serves in an expedition to the Arctic.
November Sails to the East Indies as a midshipman in the *Seahorse*.

1775 *April* American War of Independence begins.

1777 *9 April* Passes examination for lieutenant.
10 April Appointed to the *Lowestoffe*.
19 July Returns to the West Indies.

1778 *February* Alliance between France and the United States of America.
14 July Captain Maurice Suckling dies.
5 September Transferred to the *Bristol* and promoted to first lieutenant.

8 December Given command of the *Badger*.

1779   *11 June* Promoted to post-captain in command of the *Hinchinbrooke*.

            16 June Spain declares war on Britain.

1780   *January to April* Commands naval force in San Juan expedition.

            April Appointed to command the *Janus*, but unable to take it up because of bad health.

            1 December Arrives as invalid in England.

1781   *23 August* Takes command of the *Albemarle*.

            October to December On convoy duty in Baltic and North Sea.

            18 October Cornwallis surrenders to Washington at Yorktown.

1782   *April* Sails across the Atlantic to Quebec.

            November On convoy duty off New York and in the West Indies.

1783   *8 March* Fails to retake Turks Islands from the French.

            3 September Treaty of Versailles ends American War of Independence.

            October Sails to France.

1784   *18 March* Appointed to command the *Boreas* in the West Indies.

            July Meets Mary Moutray at Antigua.

1785   *2 May* Meets Mrs Frances Nisbet at Nevis.

1786   *2 December* Meets Prince William Henry.

1787   *11 March* Marries Frances Nisbet.

            July Arrives in England.

            November On half pay after the *Boreas* is paid off.

            17 December Trial of James Carse for murder in London.

1788   Unemployed in Norfolk.

1789   *14 July* Storming of the Bastille in Paris.

1793   *6 January* Re-engaged by the Admiralty.
21 January Execution of King Louis XVI of France.
30 January Appointed to command the *Agamemnon*.
1 February France declares war on Britain.
7 February Joins the *Agamemnon*.
July and August Blockades Toulon.
27 August British capture Toulon.
September Goes on mission to Naples and meets the Hamiltons.
22 October Engaged with French frigates off Sardinia.
19 December French recapture Toulon.

1794   *January to August* Campaign in Corsica.
12 July Wounded in right eye at Calvi.
10 August Calvi surrenders.
19 September Lord Hood succeeded by Vice-Admiral Hotham as Commander-in-Chief in the Mediterranean.
17 December Lord Spencer appointed First Lord of the Admiralty.

1795   *14 March* Action with *Ça Ira* off Genoa.
1 November Admiral Hotham succeeded by Vice-Admiral Sir Hyde Parker.
21 December Vice-Admiral Parker succeeded by Vice-Admiral Sir John Jervis.

1796   *1 March* Promoted commodore.
11 June Transferred to the *Captain*.
5 October Spain declares war on Britain.
10 December Transferred to *La Minerve*.

1797   *14 February* Battle of Cape St Vincent.
20 February Promoted rear-admiral of the Blue.
April Mutiny at Spithead.
May Mutiny at the Nore.
17 May Created a Knight of the Bath.
27 May Joins the *Theseus*.

24 July Loses right arm at Santa Cruz.

September Returns to England in the *Seahorse*.

1798   *14 March* Hoists his flag in the *Vanguard*.

24 April Arrives in the Mediterranean.

May to July Searches for the French Fleet.

1 August Battle of the Nile at Abū Qīr.

September Returns to Naples.

6 November Created Baron Nelson of the Nile.

28 November Occupies Leghorn.

December Evacuates the royal family and the Hamiltons from Naples after defeat of King Ferdinand and Marshal Mack by French.

1799   *14 January* Promoted rear-admiral of the Red.

23 January French occupy Naples.

22 April French evacuate Naples.

16 June Lord Keith succeeds Lord St Vincent as Commander-in-Chief in the Mediterranean.

24 June Returns to Naples and cancels the truce with the rebels.

29 June Execution of Admiral Caracciolo.

June Disobeys orders to sail to Minorca.

July Commands in the Mediterranean during Keith's absence.

August Created Duke of Bronte.

December Bonaparte becomes First Consul.

1800   *23 January* Accompanies Keith to Malta.

18 February Captures *Le Généreux*.

July to November Returns to England with the Hamiltons.

20 November Takes his seat in the House of Lords.

December Christmas at Fonthill with the Hamiltons.

1801   *1 January* Promoted vice-admiral of the Blue.

January Parts from his wife.

January Hoists his flag in the *San José*.

29 January Horatia born.

12 February Transferred to the *St George*.

6 March Joins Admiral Parker at Yarmouth.

12 March Sails to the Baltic.

14 March Lord Spencer leaves Admiralty.

25 March Transferred to the *Elephant*.

2 April Battle of Copenhagen.

9 April Signs armistice with Denmark.

6 May Succeeds Parker as Commander-in-Chief.

22 May Created Viscount Nelson of the Nile and Burnham Thorpe.

1 July Returns to England.

24 July Appointed to command of the naval forces in the English Channel.

1 and 15 August Unsuccessful attacks on Boulogne.

18 September Buys Merton Place.

1 October Armistice signed between Britain and France.

1802   *27 March* Treaty of Amiens establishes peace between Britain and France.

26 April His father dies.

July Tours West Country.

1803   *6 April* Sir William Hamilton dies.

14 May Appointed Commander-in-Chief in the Mediterranean.

16 May Britain declares war on France.

18 May Hoists his flag in the *Victory*.

6 July Joins the fleet blockading Toulon.

1804   *14 December* Spain declares war on Britain.

1805   *17 January* Villeneuve leaves Toulon.

20 February Villeneuve driven back to Toulon.

30 March Villeneuve puts to sea again.

14 May Villeneuve reaches Martinique in the West Indies.

May to July Nelson follows Villeneuve to the West Indies and then back across the Atlantic.

22 July Admiral Calder engages French off Finisterre.

1 August Villeneuve puts into Ferrol.

10 August Arrives in England and goes to Merton.
20 August French and Spanish fleets reach Cadiz.
14 September Re-embarks in the *Victory*.
28 September Rejoins the British fleet off Cadiz.
18 October Villeneuve puts to sea.
21 October Battle of Trafalgar.

1806   *9 January* State funeral in St Paul's Cathedral.

1815   *15 January* Death of Lady Hamilton.

References

Abbreviations:

BBC	The Ben Burgess Nelson Memorabilia Collection, Norwich
BL	British Library
Llangattock Papers	The Lady Llangattock Collection, Nelson Museum, Monmouth
NMM	National Maritime Museum, Greenwich
PRO	Public Record Office
RA	Royal Archives
RNM	Royal Naval Museum, Portsmouth
WM	William Marsden Papers, Chelmorton

For full titles see the bibliography on pages 444 ff.

Chapter 1 (pp. 1–8)

1. Matcham, 8
2. ibid., 25
3. Moorhouse, *Nelson in England*, 58
4. Matcham, 87–8
5. *London Encyclopaedia*, 428
6. Matcham, 57
7. ibid., 37
8. Quoted in Oman, 37; Edmund Nelson, 'A Family Historicall Register' (1781); Fiske, *Notices of Nelson*, 5–6
9. Nicholas, i, 88
10. Matcham, 107
11. *Walpoliana*, i, 62
12. Gronow, i, 28; Harries, 185–6; Forder, 150
13. Clarke and M'Arthur, i, 7; Southey, *Life*, 3; Matcham, 22

14. Clarke and M'Arthur, i, 8
15. ibid.; Matcham, 22; Moorhouse, *Nelson in England*, 10–12
16. Southey, *Life*, 1
17. Clarke and M'Arthur, i, 7; Pettigrew, i, 2

Chapter 2 (pp. 9–23)

1. Harrison, i, 12
2. Rodger, *Wooden World*, 40–41, 261
3. *The Interesting Narrative of the Life of Equiano* (1789), i, 118
4. Bernard Coleridge, quoted in Howarth, *Trafalgar*, 20
5. Rodger, *Wooden World*, 83–6, 91–2
6. Nicolas, i, 2
7. Clarke and M'Arthur, i, 10–11
8. ibid., 12; Phipps, *passim*; Savours, *passim*; 'Nelson's Arctic Voyage', *Nelson Dispatch*, vol. 2, pt 5, 90–91
9. Kennedy, *Band of Brothers*, 79
10. Clarke and M'Arthur, i, 14
11. BBC, File 7
12. Pettigrew, i, 6
13. Nicolas, i, 22
14. Clarke and M'Arthur, ii, 150
15. Nelson's 'Sketch of My Life' in Clarke and M'Arthur, i, 5, 16–17; Pettigrew, i, 6
16. Nicolas, i, 23; Clarke and M'Arthur, i, 16
17. Clarke and M'Arthur, i, 5; Mahan, i, 15
18. Quoted in Pocock, *Nelson*, 27
19. Nicolas, vi, 450–51
20. Clarke and M'Arthur, i, 30
21. Quoted in Pocock, *Nelson*, 36
22. ibid., 34

Chapter 3 (pp. 24–29)

1. Pocock, *Young Nelson*, 82; *London Gazette*, 18 July 1780
2. Pocock, *Young Nelson*, 87–9
3. Dancer, quoted in ibid., 104
4. Nicolas, 1, 34; Moseley, *passim*
5. Nicolas, i, 34
6. Quoted in Pocock, *Young Nelson*, 158
7. Nelson's 'Sketch of My Life' in Clarke and M'Arthur, 1, 22–3
8. Christie's New York catalogue, December 1986, lot number 197

Chapter 4 (pp. 30–37)

1. Quoted in Pocock, *Young Nelson*, 163

2. Clarke and M'Arthur, i, 43
3. Roger Manvell, *Sarah Siddons: Portrait of an Actress* (London, 1970), 58
4. Nicolas, i, 90
5. Bl Add. MSS. 34,988, f. 22, 18 December 1781
6. Nicolas, i, 101, 105, 134
7. ibid., 167
8. Clarke and M'Arthur, i, 52; Pocock, *Young Nelson*, 180
9. Clarke and M'Arthur, i, 52
10. ibid., 53
11. Llangattock Papers, E.478
12. Nicolas, i, 205, 214
13. Clarke and M'Arthur, i, 55; Ziegler, 43; Pocock, *Sailor King*, 42
14. Robert Huish, *The History of the Life and Reign of William IV* (London, 1837), 126

Chapter 5 (*pp. 38–50*)

1. Nicolas, i, 80–81
2. ibid., iv, 100
3. Arthur Young, *Travels in France in 1787–1789* (London, 1889), 124
4. Tobias Smollett, *Travels through France and Italy* (London, 1766), 224
5. Nicolas, i, 86
6. ibid., 83; Clarke and M'Arthur, i, 61
7. Nicolas, i, 86
8. Quoted in Oman, 51
9. Nicolas, i, 91
10. ibid., 93–4
11. Pettigrew, i, 424
12. ibid., 425
13. BL Add. MSS. 34,988, f. 37, 20 January 1783
14. Harrison, i, 102
15. Nicolas, i, 98
16. Warner, *Portrait*, 14
17. Nicolas, i, 100
18. ibid., 104
19. ibid., 110, 112, 132, 156
20. Pettigrew, ii, 568; Southey, *Life*, 26
21. Nicolas, i, 122
22. Clarke and M'Arthur, i, 68
23. Quoted in Oman, 61
24. Clarke and M'Arthur, i, 70
25. Quoted in Pocock, *Horatio Nelson*, 72
26. Nicolas, i, 113
27. ibid., 129–31
28. ibid., 134–6
29. ibid., 115

30. Clarke and M'Arthur, i, 71
31. ibid., ii, 468
32. ibid., i, 83; Pettigrew, i, 26
33. Clarke and M'Arthur, i, 77
34. Nicolas, i, 114
35. ibid., 112
36. ibid., 110

Chapter 6 (*pp. 51–60*)

1. Pettigrew, i, 32; Pocock, *Horatio Nelson*, 69
2. Nicolas, i, 124, 126
3. ibid., 131; Pocock, 'Captain Nelson and Mrs Moutray', in *Nelson Dispatch*, vol. 1, pt 4, October 1982, and 'My Dear Sweet Friend', in *Country Life*, 22 September 1983
4. Quoted in Oman, 64
5. Clarke and M'Arthur, i, 77; Pettigrew, i, 32–3
6. Clarke and M'Arthur, i, 78
7. Quoted in Oman, 66; Pocock, *Horatio Nelson*, 74, 75, 78
8. Llangattock Papers, E.413, 14 November 1785
9. Naish, letter no. 1, 19 August 1785
10. Nicolas, i, 162
11. Llangattock Papers, E.413, 14 November 1785
12. ibid.; Nicolas, i, 144–5
13. ibid., 140, 154, 188
14. Pettigrew, i, 34–5; Mahan, i, 70; Clarke and M'Arthur, i, 79, 84
15. Quoted in Pocock, *Horatio Nelson*, 78
16. Nicolas, i, 206
17. Pocock, *Sailor King*, 93; Aspinall, i, 276, 282–3, 311
18. Nicolas, i, 210–11
19. ibid., 215–16
20. ibid., 250
21. Pocock, *Sailor King*, 101
22. ibid., 98
23. ibid., 105; Ziegler, 61–2
24. Clarke and M'Arthur, i, 93; Nicolas, i, 218, 203
25. Rupert Willoughby, 'Nelson and the Dents', *Nelson Dispatch*
26. Warner, *Portrait*, 64
27. Quoted in Oman, 79
28. Clarke and M'Arthur, i, 94

Chapter 7 (*pp. 61–73*)

1. Oman, 81
2. Pocock, *Nelson*, 81
3. Oman, 79

4. Clarke and M'Arthur, i, 100; Nicolas, i, 251–2
5. Pocock, *Nelson*, 81
6. Nicolas, i, 252
7. ibid., 268
8. H. L. Cryer, 'Horatio Nelson and the Murderous Cooper', *The Mariner's Mirror*
9. Nicolas, i, 274
10. ibid., i, 274
11. ibid., i, 275–6
12. Quoted in Keate, 55
13. Oman, 87; Pocock, *Nelson*, 86–7
14. Carmarthenshire Record Office, MUS 460, letter to Captain Foley, 16 February 1804
15. Quoted in Pocock, *Nelson*, 89
16. Nicolas, i, 287; Clarke and M'Arthur, i, 110
17. Nicolas, i, 99
18. Clarke and M'Arthur, i, 109
19. Matcham, 81
20. ibid., 69
21. Nicolas, i, 290
22. Quoted in Pocock, *Nelson*, 91
23. Southey, *Life*, 41
24. Pocock, *Nelson*, 95
25. Clarke and M'Arthur, i, 119–20
26. ibid., 109; Nicolas, i, 277
27. Clarke and M'Arthur, i, 109
28. Nicolas, i, 294
29. Quoted in Pocock, *Nelson*, 92
30. Quoted in Oman, 88
31. Nicolas, i, 277–97
32. Quoted in Pocock, *Nelson*, 94
33. Coke Papers; Stirling; Clarke and M'Arthur, i, 121; Moorhouse, 62
34. Clarke and M'Arthur, i, 121; Nicolas, i, 294

Chapter 8 (*pp. 74–81*)

1. Clarke and M'Arthur, i, 123
2. Pocock, *Remember Nelson*, 17
3. Nicolas, ii, 90; Pettigrew, ii, 150; Oman, 150
4. Parsons, 79
5. Moorhouse, *Nelson in England*, 76
6. Pocock, *Nelson*, 102
7. Nicolas, i, 299
8. Hoste, i, 87
9. P.-J. Grosley, *Observations on Italy and the Italians* (1770), *passim*
10. Piozzi, 227

11. Wraxall, i, 272
12. Flora Fraser, 94; Acton, 92; Fothergill, *Hamilton*, 53–5
13. Knight (ed. Fulford), 41
14. Gunn, 152–3
15. 'Thomas Finlayson Henderson' in *Dictionary of National Biography*, i, 68
16. Harrison, i, 108–9

Chapter 9 (*pp. 82–92*)

1. Quoted in Flora Fraser, 34
2. W. C. Sydney, *England and the English in the Eighteenth Century* (London, 1892), i, 317–23
3. Morrison, i, 78
4. BL Add. MSS. 42,071, ff. 3–6; Flora Fraser, 65–6
5. Morrison, i, 103–4; Flora Fraser, 67; Sichel, 4, 14
6. Morrison, i, 110
7. Flora Fraser, 85; Sichel, 89
8. Morrison, i, 114–19
9. ibid., 118
10. Goethe, 315
11. Gordon, 11, 385–6
12. Morrison, i, 119; Flora Fraser, 95; Sichel, 92
13. Flora Fraser, 139
14. Morrison, i, 130–31
15. ibid., 151
16. Stuart, 59
17. Quoted in Connell, 248
18. NMM MSS 76/015, 25 November 1796
19. Flora Fraser, 171–3
20. Morrison, i, 176, 208–9
21. Nicolas, i, 326
22. Clarke and M'Arthur, i, 134
23. Nicolas, i, 328–30

Chapter 10 (*pp. 93–104*)

1. Nicolas, ii, 1
2. Quoted in Oman, 116
3. Oman, 118
4. Nicolas, ii, 46
5. Clarke and M'Arthur, i, 154; Nicolas, i, 361–9
6. Clarke and M'Arthur, i, 155; Nicolas, i, 367–8
7. Clarke and M'Arthur, i, 181
8. BL Add. MSS. 4,490, f. 24; Nicolas, i, 436–7, 442, 484–5
9. Nicolas, ii, 3
10. Mahan, i, 153

11. Nicolas, i, 326, 161, 405
12. ibid., ii, 64, 133, 188
13. Mahan, i, 256
14. Naish, 182–3
15. Clarke and M'Arthur, i, 210
16. Nicolas, ii, 6; Harrison, i, 27
17. Nicolas, i, 419, ii, 2
18. ibid., i, 491, 488
19. Clarke and M'Arthur, i, 191
20. Chevalier, ii, 174
21. Quoted in Pocock, *Nelson*, 122
22. Pocock, *Nelson*, 123
23. Naish, 201-5
24. Nicolas, ii, 60, 26
25. Quoted in Pocock, *Nelson*, 125
26. Quoted in Oman, 156
27. Tucker, i, 370–80
28. ibid., 328
29. Nicolas, ii, 402
30. Dann, 192
31. ibid., 209

Chapter 11 (*pp. 105–112*)

1. Quoted in Oman, 158
2. Llangattock Papers
3. NMM E431, 1 November 1796
4. Mahan, i, 267
5. Bethune, 21; Oman, 176
6. Oman, 177; Pocock, *Nelson*, 129
7. Quoted in Howarth, *Nelson*, 161
8. Palmer, 31–46; Nicolas, ii, 370; Warner, *Portrait*, 96; Collingwood, *Private Correspondence*, 79–81
9. Nicolas, ii, 356; Pettigrew, i, 91
10. Drinkwater, 45
11. Nicolas, ii, 346; Clarke and M'Arthur, 350–51; Harrison, 165
12. Quoted in Oman, 184
13. Collingwood, *Private Correspondence*, i, 55
14. Bethune, 87–8
15. Nicolas, ii, 350
16. Bethune, xi
17. Mahan, i, 277
18. ibid., 280

Chapter 12 (*pp. 113–126*)

1. Quoted in Warner, *Portrait*, 97

2. Nicolas, ii, 369; Clarke and M'Arthur, ii, 6
3. Mahan, i, 285
4. Nicolas, ii, 400; Clarke and M'Arthur, ii, 21
5. Llangattock Papers, I.152; Naish, 327; Nicolas, ii, 399–400; Fiske, 'Nelson and Associated Heraldry', 17–18
6. Quoted in Pocock, *Nelson*, 134
7. Llangattock Papers, E.608
8. Phillips's catalogue, 11 June 1981
9. Mahan, i, 256
10. Nicolas, ii, 359
11. Llangattock Papers, E.631
12. Nicolas, ii, 18
13. Naish, 304 and *passim*
14. Harrison, ii, 124
15. Christie's catalogue, 21 June 1989, lot 214
16. Quoted in Hardwick, 49; Warner, *Portrait*, 74; Pocock, *Nelson*, 125
17. Nicolas, ii, 388
18. ibid., ii, 405
19. Clarke and M'Arthur, i, 11; ii, 2
20. Nicolas, ii, 412
21. Mahan, i, 297
22. *Fremantle*, ii, 162–3
23. ibid., 185
24. Quoted in Pocock, *Nelson*, 144
25. Clarke and M'Arthur, ii, 35; Nicolas, ii, 420–21; Naish, 574
26. Nicolas, ii, 421; Clarke and M'Arthur, ii, 33
27. Nicolas, ii, 422; Clarke and M'Arthur, ii, 35
28. Clarke and M'Arthur, ii, 35, 51–9
29. Hoste, i, 73
30. Naish, 375
31. Quoted in Pocock, *Nelson*, 142
32. Quoted in Oman, 213
33. Nicolas, ii, 423
34. Clarke and M'Arthur, ii, 41; Nicolas, ii, 434–5; Pettigrew, i, 110
35. Quoted in Pocock, *Nelson*, 145
36. Quoted in Oman, 216–17
37. Fremantle, ii, 188
38. ibid., 188–90
39. ibid., 189

Chapter 13 (pp. 127–136)

1. Nicolas, ii, 436–7
2. ibid., 441
3. Minto, iii, 2
4. Clarke and M'Arthur, ii, 46–7

5. Quoted in Pocock, *Nelson*, 147
6. ibid., 148
7. BL Add. MSS. 30,170, f. 23; Naish, 379
8. Moorhouse, *Nelson in England*, 111
9. NMM BRP/6, 5 November 1797
10. Edgecumbe, ii, 37
11. ibid., 39; Moorhouse, *Nelson in England*, 108–9, 114–15
12. Naish, 424–5
13. Quoted in Oman, 238
14. Quoted in Pocock, *Nelson*, 152
15. Llangattock Papers, E.50; Nicolas, iii, 17–18; Clarke and M'Arthur, ii, 58
16. Kennedy, *Band of Brothers*, 116
17. Quoted in Pocock, *Nelson*, 154
18. Nicolas, iii, 31–45

Chapter 14 (*pp. 137–148*)

1. Quoted in Oman, 245
2. Quoted in Pocock, *Nelson*, 157
3. Quoted in Oman, 252
4. [Edward Berry], *Authentic Narrative of the Proceedings of his Majesty's Squadron . . . from the Minutes of an Officer of Rank in the Squadron* (London 1798); 29
5. Clarke and M'Arthur, ii, 77; Nicolas, iii, 55
6. Berry, op. cit., 32
7. Quoted in Warner, *Portrait*, 129
8. Quoted in Oman, 256
9. Nicolas, iii, 55; Pettigrew, i, 133
10. Berry, op. cit., 81
11. Quoted in Pocock, *Nelson*, 166
12. ibid., 167
13. Quoted in Oman, 263
14. Berry, op. cit., 97
15. Pettigrew, i, 140
16. Quoted in Harrison, i, 292–3
17. Clarke and M'Arthur, ii, 90, 100; Pettigrew, i, 147–8
18. Naish, 438–58, 348, 530; Morrison, ii, 81

Chapter 15 (*pp. 149–155*]

1. Nicolas, iii, 100
2. Knight, *Autobiography* (1861), i, 113–15
3. Minto, ii, 364–6
4. Nelson, *Lord Nelson's Letters to Lady Hamilton*, 27
5. ibid., 28
6. Pettigrew, i, 150

7. BL Add. MSS. 34,989, f. 4
8. Nicolas, iii, 71
9. Jeaffreson, *Queen of Naples*, ii, 7; Pettigrew, i, 140–41
10. Acton, 304; Clarke and M'Arthur, ii, 99
11. Clarke and M'Arthur, ii, 101
12. Knight (ed. Fulford), 64
13. Acton, 303
14. Harrison, i, 326; Pettigrew, i, 150
15. Quoted in Pocock, *Nelson*, 176
16. Llangattock Papers, E.413
17. Keate, 146–7; Harrison, i, 328; Sichel, 231
18. Rawson, *Nelson's Letters*, 207; Nicolas, iii, 144–5
19. Llangattock Papers, E.415

Chapter 16 (pp. 156–171)

1. Edgcumbe, 172; Moorhouse, *Nelson in England*, 123
2. Nicolas, iii, 74
3. Warner, *Portrait*, 131
4. Quoted in Pocock, *Nelson*, 182
5. George, *British Museum Catalogue*, vol. vii, 9250, 9251
6. James Woodforde, *The Diary of a Country Parson, 1788–1802*, entry for Thursday, 29 November 1798
7. Llangattock Papers, E.662, 26 October 1798
8. Matcham, 164
9. Naish, 443, 459
10. Pettigrew i, 144–5; *Naval Chronicle*, iv, 472; Harrison, i, 237
11. Nicolas, iii, 75; Mahan, i, 361
12. Nicolas, iii, 80; Harrison, i, 334
13. Harrison, i, 373
14. Naish, 462; Sichel, 227
15. BL Add. MSS., 34,989, f. 16, 26 October 1798
16. BL. Add. MSS. 34,989 f. 18, 27 October 1798
17. Morrison, ii, 34
18. Nicolas, iii, 145
19. ibid 138; Rawson, *Nelson's Letters*, 206
20. Nicolas, iii, 141; Pettigrew, i, 168
21. Llangattock Papers, E.52; Giglioli, 79
22. Nicolas, iii, 148; Pocock, *Nelson*, 180
23. Clarke and M'Arthur, ii, 116
24. Giglioli, 78; Harrison, i, 346; Pettigrew, i, 171; Hoste, i, 113; Nicolas, iii, 147
25. NMM 76/015, 6 November 1798
26. Quoted in Fothergill, *Sir William Hamilton*, 322
27. Quoted in Pocock, *Nelson*, 186
28. Acton, 312

29. Nicolas, iii, 195
30. Quoted in Pocock, *Nelson*, 188
31. Knight, *Autobiography* (1861), i, 124; Giglioli, 96
32. Morrison, ii, 35; Flora Fraser, 230; Sichel, 247–56
33. Knight, *Autobiography* (1861), i, 28
34. ibid.
35. Nicolas, iii, 202
36. ibid., 227
37. Acton, 319
38. Oman, 293
39. Acton, 320
40. Flora Fraser, 232
41. Acton, 328; Giglioli, 282
42. Knight, *Autobiography* (1861), i, 42

Chapter *17* (*pp. 172–183*)

1. Nicolas, ii, 272
2. ibid., iii, 248
3. ibid., 246
4. Gordon, i, 208–25
5. ibid., 210
6. Sermoneta, 164
7. Quoted in Pocock, *Nelson*, 193; Richard Faber, ed., *The Faber Book of Letters*, 1992; *Nelson Dispatch*, vol. 3, pt. 7, 1989, 134
8. Quoted in Oman, 303
9. Gutteridge, 36
10. Harrison, ii, 136
11. Quoted in Pocock, *Nelson*, 195
12. ibid.
13. Pettigrew, i, 214; Nicolas, iii, 333
14. Quoted in Warner, *Portrait*, 153
15. Sichel, 278; Giglioli, 217; Palumbo, 63
16. Gutteridge, 74
17. Llangattock Papers, E.71
18. Giglioli, 267–8
19. ibid., 270–71
20. Harrison, ii, 138
21. Gamlin, i, 103
22. Nicolas, iii, 386–8
23. Gutteridge, 217; Pettigrew, i, 243
24. Nicolas, iii, 387
25. Gutteridge, 205–32; Morrison, 405–11; Nicolas, iii, 385; Fothergill, *Sir William Hamilton*, 353–9; Pettigrew, i, 243–9

Chapter *18* (*pp. 184–195*)

1. Pettigrew, i, 233–5
2. Gutteridge, 268–9
3. ibid., 271–2
4. Quoted in Oman, 315
5. Parsons, 6; Pettigrew, i, 253
6. Gutteridge, 278–9
7. Parsons, 4; Giglioli, 327; Sacchinelli, 265
8. BL Add. MSS. 34,012, f. 134
9. Nicolas, iii, 398; ; Gutteridge, 279–80
10. Flora Fraser, 243; Sichel, 306–7
11. Giglioli, 95
12. Parsons, 7
13. Acton, 400
14. Gutteridge, 288
15. Parsons, 9
16. Pettigrew, i, 260–76
17. ibid., 277; Sichel, 303–4
18. Llangattock Papers, E.448, 17 July 1799
19. Giglioli, 352
20. Quoted in Pocock, *Nelson*, 204
21. Fraser, 245; Jack Russell, 107–8; Oman, 321; Morrison, ii, 52–3
22. Nicolas, iii, 401–2; Pettigrew, ii, 572
23. Parsons, 19
24. ibid.
25. Giglioli, 341; Colletta, ii, 160
26. Parsons, 20
27. Giglioli, 341
28. Clarke and M'Arthur, ii, 189
29. Parsons, 21
30. Nicolas, iii, 434
31. Oman, 321; Morrison, ii, 54; Colletta, i, 392
32. Nicolas, iii, 409; Pettigrew, i, 283
33. Nicolas, iii, 438–9
34. Llangattock Papers, E.601, 15 August 1799
35. Harrison, ii, 242–3
36. Naish, 493

Chapter *19* (*pp. 196–205*)

1. Flora Fraser, 247
2. Parsons, 16; Harrison, ii, 162–4
3. Quoted in Oman, 328
4. Parsons, 27
5. Grant, 17
6. Quoted in Flora Fraser, 251

7. Grant, 21
8. ibid., 22–4
9. ibid., 23
10. Quoted in Warner, *Portrait*, 168; Pocock, *Nelson*, 208–9
11. Sichel, 318; Keate, 157
12. Quoted in Oman, 333
13. PRO, 70–12, 7 September 1799
14. Quoted in Oman, 331
15. BL Eg. MSS. 2,240, f. 11
16. BL Eg. MSS. 2,240, ff. 29–32
17. Oman, 331; Warner, *Portrait*, 169–71
18. Knight (ed. Fulford), 67
19. Sichel, 323
20. Quoted in Warner, *Portrait*, 107
21. Parsons, 29
22. Kennedy, *Band of Brothers*, 167
23. Nicolas, iv, 205
24. Mahan, ii, 33
25. Minto, iii, 127

Chapter 20 (*pp. 206–224*)

1. Quoted in Warner, *Portrait*, 173
2. Flora Fraser, 255
3. Knight, ed. Fulford, 70
4. Pocock, *Nelson*, 212
5. Sermoneta, 179–80
6. Quoted in Flora Fraser, 261
7. Pettigrew, i, 378–9
8. Flora Fraser, 262; Oman, 341; Knight, *Autobiography* (1861), i, 155
9. Oman, 342; Flora Fraser, 263; Pocock, *Nelson*, 210
10. Quoted in Oman, 342
11. Minto, iii, 139–40
12. Knight, ed. Fulford, 120–21
13. ibid.
14. Pocock, *Nelson*, 213–14
15. Knight, ed. Fulford, 124
16. Minto, iii, 147
17. ibid., 114
18. Sichel, 332–3; Malmesbury, ii, 24
19. Quoted in Flora Fraser, 267
20. Quoted in Warner, *Portrait*, 179; Pocock, *Nelson*, 214
21. Quoted in Flora Fraser, 265
22. Quoted in Warner, *Portrait*, 180
23. Trench, 105–12
24. ibid.

25. Quoted in Flora Fraser, 273
26. Warner, *Portrait*, 181
27. Harrison, ii, 258–9
28. ibid., 262–6
29. *Morning Chronicle*, 11 September 1800; *Morning Post*, 29 April, 15 September 1800; Russell, 165–6
30. NMM MSS. WAL/10 J703
31. Knight, *Autobiography* (1861), i, 139
32. Naish, 516–18 and *passim*; Pettigrew, i, 221, 368, ii, 643
33. Harrison, ii, 266–8

Chapter 21 (pp. 225–235)

1. Warner, *Portrait*, 182; Oman, 354; Pocock, *Nelson*, 217
2. Quoted in Oman, 355
3. Quoted in Moorhouse, *Nelson in England*, 139
4. Knight, *Autobiography* (1861), i, 158
5. NMM CRK 19/249, 15 October 1801
6. Quoted in Luttrell, 129
7. Nicolas, iv, 278; Collingwood, *Private Correspondence*, i, 110
8. *The Diary of Sir John Moore* (ed. J. F. Maurice, London, 1904), i, 367
9. Edgcumbe, i, 78–9; Keate, 197; Moorhouse, *Nelson in England*, 144
10. Flora Fraser, 276
11. Knight, *Autobiography* (1861), i, 162
12. Flora Fraser, 277; Pocock, *Nelson*, 219–20
13. Harrison, ii, 278
14. Paget, ii, 17
15. Diary of Sir William Hotham, quoted in Mahan, ii, 50
16. *Naval Miscellany* (ed. Sir J. Knox Laughton, Navy Records Society, 1912), ii, 329–30
17. Stuart, 90
18. Flora Fraser, 276
19. Morrison, ii, 118–19
20. Oliver, 240
21. Fothergill, *Beckford*, 262
22. Quoted in Pocock, *Nelson*, 221
23. NMM MSS. 76/015
24. Redding, ii, 127
25. Britton, *Illustrations of Fonthill Abbey*, 28–31, quoted in Fothergill, *Beckford*
26. NMM MSS. 76/015
27. Redding, ii, 326–7
28. Britton, 28–31; Fothergill, *Beckford*, 393–6; Flora Fraser, 278–80; *Gentleman's Magazine*, April 1801, 298; Hardwick, 73–5
29. Quoted in Sichel, 339
30. Nicolas, vii, 392; Pettigrew, ii, 642

31. BL Add. MSS. 28,333, f. 5; Oman, 366

Chapter 22 (*pp. 236–249*)

1. Quoted in Oman, 364
2. Sherrard, *St Vincent*, 199; Morrison, ii, 128
3. *Naval Miscellany*, ii, 330; quoted in Moorhouse, 153
4. Sherrard, *St Vincent*, 200
5. Quoted in Howarth, *Nelson*, 259
6. Quoted in Moorhouse, *Nelson in England*, 142
7. Naish, 618–19
8. RA Add. 16/11, 17 Feb. 1801, 22 Feb. 1801; Aspinall, v, 283; Morrison, ii, 113–20, 128, 543–4; Sichel, 360–61; Christie's catalogue, 18 July 1991, lot 440
9. Morrison, ii, 123; Flora Fraser, 287; Pocock, *Nelson*, 224
10. George, *Catalogue*, 9573, 9550, 9752
11. Quoted in Howarth, *Nelson*, 239–40
12. Morrison, ii, 109
13. ibid., 111–12, 116–18; Rawson, *Nelson's Letters*, 302
14. Quoted in Flora Fraser, 286
15. Naish, 578; Gérin, 3
16. ibid., 5, 19
17. Sichel, 355
18. Morrison, ii, 108–10
19. ibid., 114
20. ibid., 112–25, 121; Rawson, *Nelson's Letters*, 307–8; Pettigrew, ii, 652; Nelson, *Lord Nelson's Letters to Lady Hamilton*, 20, 23, 90
21. *Exeter Flying Post*, 22 January 1801; Gamlin, i, 64; Sichel, 350; Moorhouse, *Nelson in England*, 154
22. Nicolas, iv, 279
23. Quoted in Pocock, *Nelson*, 226
24. Warner, *Portrait*, 58, 112, 191
25. Quoted in Pocock, *Nelson*, 226
26. ibid, 227; BL Add. MSS. 34,274, f. 61, 24 May 1801
27. Nicolas, vii, 374; Pettigrew, ii, 139; Gérin, 23
28. Sichel, 366
29. Naish, 619–20
30. ibid., 579
31. ibid., 580; Morrison, ii, 125; Pettigrew, ii, 643; Sichel, 366
32. BL Add. MSS. 28,333, ff. 3–4
33. ibid.

Chapter 23 (*pp. 250–259*)

1. BL Add. MSS. 34,918, f. 315, quoted in Pope, *Great Gamble*, 181
2. Sherrard, *Life of Lord St. Vincent*, 175; Howarth, *Nelson*, 243–4; Kennedy, *Nelson's Band of Brothers*, 223

3. Morrison, ii, 127–8
4. Stewart's 'Narrative of Events' in BL Add. MSS 34,918; Pope, *Great Gamble*, 185
5. Quoted in Pocock, *Nelson*, 231
6. Quoted in Mahan, ii, 67
7. 'Lieutenant William Layman's Account', *Naval Chronicle*, vol. 37, 446
8. Quoted in Oman, 380; Pocock, *Nelson*, 232
9. Layman, op. cit.
10. Quoted in Mahan, ii, 69
11. Quoted in Pope, 281; Pettigrew, ii, 3–5; Mahan, ii, 75–7
12. Mahan, ii, 79; Morrison, ii, 132
13. Quoted in Mahan, ii, 78
14. Nicolas, iv, 499–500
15. Midshipman W. S. Millard, 'The Battle of Copenhagen', *Macmillan's Magazine*, June 1895
16. ibid.
17. Pope, *Great Gamble*, 324; Nicolas, iv, 304
18. Quoted in Oman, 387
19. Millard, op. cit.

Chapter 24 (*pp. 260–272*)

1. Cumloden Papers, quoted in Pope, *Great Gamble*, 409; Llangattock Papers, E.264; Clarke and M'Arthur, ii, 270
2. Pope, *Great Gamble*, 409–14; Nicolas, iv, 309; Clarke and M'Arthur, ii, 270
3. Quoted in Pope, *Great Gamble*, 418; Nicolas, iv, 315; Clarke and M'Arthur, ii, 272
4. Pope, *Great Gamble*, 419; Clarke and M'Arthur, ii, 405
5. Nicolas, iv, 316
6. Southey, *Life*, 198
7. Quoted in Oman, 394
8. Quoted in Pope, *Great Gamble*, 436
9. Nicolas, iv, 321–2
10. Pettigrew, ii, 18–19
11. Nicolas, iv, 339; quoted in Warner, *Portrait*, 214
12. Nicolas, iv, 326–7; Clarke and M'Arthur, ii, 275
13. Nicolas, iv, 326–7; Clarke and M'Arthur, ii, 276
14. Harrison, ii, 301; Southey, *Life*, 201
15. Nicolas, iv, 339–41; Pope, *Great Gamble*, 469–73; Pettigrew, ii, 28
16. Warner, *Portrait*, 218; Mahan, ii, 105; Southey, *Life*, 208
17. Quoted in Pocock, *Nelson*, 241
18. Dyfed County Record Office, MUS. 473
19. Pettigrew, ii, 44
20. Pettigrew, ii, 10
21. BL Add. MSS, 34,274, f. 61
22. BL Eg. MSS. 2,240, ff. 83–99
23. Morrison, 567; Pettigrew, ii, 42

24. Morrison, 561
25. Pettigrew, ii, 35
26. Mahan, ii, 102
27. Nicolas, i, 14; Clarke and M'Arthur, ii, 4
28. Pettigrew, ii, 33

Chapter 25 (*pp. 273–284*)

1. Moorhouse, *Nelson in England*, 160
2. Naish, 586
3. BL Eg. MSS. 2,240, f. 39
4. Harrison, ii, 137
5. BL Eg. MSS. 2,240, f. 73
6. Naish, 585–6
7. ibid., 596–7
8. Morrison, ii, 248
9. Quoted in Howarth, *Nelson*, 272
10. BL Eg. MSS. 2,240, ff. 85–6
11. Morrison, ii, 156; Pettigrew, ii, 108
12. Morrison, ii, 150, 165; Sotheby's catalogue, 20 July 1989, lot 335
13. Nicolas, iv, 228
14. Matcham, 25
15. NMM Girdleston Collection, 9590/2, 9 May 1805
16. Stuart, 123
17. ibid.
18. Wraxall, 164–5
19. Pettigrew, ii, 121; Harrison, ii, 348
20. Naish, 591
21. Llangattock Papers E.95, 29 July 1801
22. Nicolas, iv, 465
23. Quoted in Pocock, *Nelson*, 249
24. Moorhouse, *Nelson in England*, 176
25. Pettigrew, ii, 158; Nicolas, iv, 496–7; Warner, *Portrait*, 231
26. Pettigrew, ii, 190–94; Llangattock Papers, E.108
27. Pettigrew, ii, 195, 212; Nelson, *Lord Nelson's Letters to Lady Hamilton*, 38
28. Moorhouse, *Nelson in England*, 169
29. Pettigrew, ii, 220–21

Chapter 26 (*pp. 285–295*)

1. Harrison, ii, 372–3; *Victoria History of the County of Surrey* (ed. H. E. Malden, London, 1912), iv, 65; Surrey Record Office, MSS. 3185/9/1
2. BL Eg. MSS. 2,240, f. 99, f. 106; Llangattock Papers, E.96, 27 August 1801
3. BL Eg. MSS. 2,240, f. 99
4. BL Eg. MSS. 2,240, f. 106

5. Nelson, *Lord Nelson's Letters to Lady Hamilton*, 42
6. Southey, *Life*, 221
7. Morrison, ii, 8
8. Pettigrew, ii, 222; Sichel, 345; Nelson, 46, 57
9. Sotheby's catalogue, 20 July 1989, lot 331
10. Pettigrew, ii, 217
11. Llangattock Papers, E.112, 13 October 1801
12. RNM McCarthy Collection, 30 September 1801; Morrison, ii, 168, 170, 172
13. Pettigrew, ii, 208
14. Llangattock Papers, E.107, 23 September 1801
15. Naish, 591; Pettigrew, ii, 231; Sichel, 387; Nelson, 35, 62
16. Morrison, ii, 175–6
17. Pettigrew, ii, 230; Nelson, 59
18. Quoted in Pocock, *Nelson*, 260
19. Harrison, ii, 374
20. Bonsor Papers, quoted in Pocock, *Nelson*, 262
21. Moorhouse, *Nelson in England*, 182; Nelson, 45
22. Quoted in Sichel, 506
23. Matcham, 23
24. Minto, ii, 242–3
25. Bonsor Papers, quoted in Pocock, *Nelson*, 270
26. NMM BRP/4
27. Minto, ii, 252
28. Morrison, ii, 182
29. Quoted in Flora Fraser, 296

Chapter 27 (pp. 296–311)

1. BL Add. MSS. 34,989, f. 21
2. Pettigrew, ii, 124
3. ibid., ii, 144
4. *Parliamentary History of England*, vol. 36, 28, 185; Harrison, ii, 376; Pettigrew, ii, 232
5. Sotheby's catalogue, 20 July 1989, lot 331; Warner, *Portrait*, 236
6. Matcham, 205
7. BL Add. MSS. 34,989, ff. 24, 29
8. BL Add. MSS. 34,989, f. 36
9. Naish, 579
10. Llangattock Papers, E.650, 13 October 1801
11. Naish, 593–5; Morrison, ii, 173
12. Christie's catalogue, 8 May 1985
13. NMM BRP/4, 8 April 1801
14. ibid.; BL Add. MSS. 34,989, ff. 36–51
15. Pettigrew, ii, 211
16. Naish, 596

17. Matcham, 193
18. Harrison, ii, 516–19; Christie's catalogue, 8 May 1985
19. Matcham, 194
20. Naish, 599
21. NMM MSS. 76/015; Moorhouse, *Nelson in England*, 194
22. BL Eg. MSS. 2,240, f. 127
23. Harrison, ii, 380
24. ibid., 382
25. *Gloucester Journal*, 26 July 1802
26. Llangattock Papers, E.178; Nicolas, v, 24–8
27. Information supplied by Dyfed County Record Office, HDX/114/14; E. C. Freeman and Edward Gill, *Nelson and the Hamiltons in Wales and Monmouthshire, 1802* (Newport, 1962), *passim*
28. Pettigrew, ii, 260
29. Information supplied by Dyfed County Record Office
30. Moorhouse, *Nelson in England*, 210
31. Quoted in Kenneth McKay, 'Then and Now, No. 528', *Western Telegraph*, 10 July 1991
32. Nicolas, v, 24
33. Harrison, ii, 393
34. Horatia Durant, 'Lord Nelson's Visit to Monmouth', *Memorials of Monmouth*, No. 4 (Monmouth Antiquarian Society, n.d.)
35. Charles Heath, *The Excursion down the Wye from Ross to Monmouth* (1805)
36. ibid.
37. *Hereford Journal*, 25 August 1801
38. ibid.
39. Hereford and Worcester Record Office, MSS. b. 899:31, BA 3762/8; Gill, 74
40. Harrison, ii, 400
41. ibid., 401–2
42. Pollock, 33–4
43. BL Eg. MSS. 2,240, f. 149

Chapter 28 (*pp. 312–322*)

1. Nicolas, v, 49, 60
2. BL Eg. MSS. 34,988, ff. 387, 404; Pettigrew, ii, 294; Nicolas, v, 32, 47, 59; Naish, 600; Sichel, 386; *Nelson Dispatch*, vol. 1, pt 2, April 1982, 20–21; Peter Walson, 'A Blind Eye to Nelson's Marriage à Trois', *Observer*, 10 June 1990, an article based on the Edwin Wolf II Papers; John Wilson catalogue, no. 70, 1991; Christie's catalogue, 3 December 1986
3. BL Eg. MSS. 2,240, f. 149
4. BL Add. MSS. 34,989, f. 25
5. Parsons, 11; Moorhouse, *Nelson in England*, 96–7
6. *The Whole Proceedings on the Trial of Colonel Despard . . . at the New Sessions House, 7 and 9 February 1803*; Gurney, *passim*.

7. NMM NWD/9594/9
8. Morrison, ii, 195; Sichel, 396
9. Morrison, ii, 196
10. ibid., 197
11. ibid.; Sichel, 388
12. Matcham, 206
13. Pettigrew, ii, 295
14. BL Eg. MSS. 2,240, f. 157
15. Flora Fraser, 300–301; Morrison, ii, 203
16. *The Memoirs of Mme Vigée Le Brun*, translated by Lionel Strachey, quoted in Gérin, 61
17. Bury, iv, 130–31
18. Sotheby's catalogue, 20 July 1989, lot 331; Moorhouse, 220
19. Minto, ii, 283; Sichel, 399

Chapter 29 (pp. 323–338)

1. Nicolas, v, 44–5, 53
2. *Gentleman's Magazine*, July 1807, quoted in Gérin, 62
3. Gérin, 62
4. L. M. Jay, *H.M.S. Victory* (ed. Jane Wilton Smith), 2–3, 12–18; Howarth, *Trafalgar*, 22–6; B. W. Smith, *passim*; Fenwick, *passim*
5. Morrison, ii, 210
6. Pettigrew, ii, 302; NMM CRK 19/258, 22 May 1803; Morrison, ii, 211
7. NMM CRK/19, 26 August 1803
8. Quoted in Kennedy, *Nelsons Band of Brothers*, 167; Warner, *Portrait*, 172, 199
9. Gatty; Mahan, ii, 235; Christie's catalogue, 3 December 1786; Pocock, *Nelson*, 274
10. BL Eg. MSS. 2,240, f. 190
11. *The Times*, 26 August 1803; Pocock, *Nelson*, 296–7
12. Parsons, 247–8
13. Beatty, 34
14. Nicholas, v, 311, 462
15. Mahan, ii, 237
16. Pocock, *Nelson*, 298–9
17. NMM TRA/14/9421; Morrison, ii, 239; Nelson, *Lord Nelson's Letters to Lady Hamilton*, 138; Gérin, 83–6; Pettigrew, ii, 319, 393; Nicolas, v, 440, vii, 384, 444
18. NMM BRP 9292/4, CRK 19/270; Morrison, ii, 239; Gérin, 71–2; Nelson, *Lord Nelson's Letters to Lady Hamilton*, 107
19. Nicolas, v, 309; WM
20. Nicolas, v, 311
21. WM
22. Quoted in Mahan, ii, 219
23. Quoted in Pocock, *Nelson*, 302
24. Quoted in Oman, 496
25. Llangattock Papers, E.167, 4 June 1805

26. Llangattock Papers, E.416, 16 June 1805; Pettigrew, ii, 480, 482
27. ibid., 483
28. ibid., 470, 471

Chapter 30 (pp. 339–349)

1. Quoted in Pocock, *Nelson*, 305
2. Silliman, 189
3. Minto, iii, 363
4. Stuart, 249
5. Warner, *Portrait*, 287–8
6. Pocock, *Nelson*, 311
7. George, *Catalogue*, 10039, 10065, 10119, 10123, 10276, 10422
8. Matcham, 226, 230
9. NMM BRP 9292/1
10. NMM CRK/15 J894, 19 June 1804
11. NMM NWD/17 J717; NMM NWD/9494/16, Gérin, 68–9, 70
12. Llangattock Papers, E.161, 20 January 1804
13. Nicolas, vii, 380
14. Pettigrew, ii, 421; Morrison, ii, 239; Gérin, 67–8, 85
15. Llangattock Papers, E.169, 4 May 1805
16. Quoted in Oman, 472
17. Flora Fraser, 308, 315
18. Morrison, ii, 259; Sichel 421
19. BL Eg. MSS. 2,240, f. 188
20. Gérin, 91
21. NMM NWD/9594
22. Minto, ii, 363
23. *The Times*, 6 November 1861; Gérin, 96; Moorhouse, *Nelson in England*, 201
24. Quoted in Pocock, *Nelson*, 307
25. Emden
26. Kennedy, *Band of Brothers*, 272–3
27. Croker, 233–4
28. 'Henry Manners Chichester', in *Dictionary of National Biography*, v, 624
29. Llangattock Papers, E.244; Pettigrew, ii, 425, 499; Morrison, ii, 240–41
30. Llangattock Papers, E.249

Chapter 31 (pp. 350–357)

1. John Clerk, *Essay on Naval Tactics* (London, 1790, 1797, 1804); Colin White, 'Nelson – Man or Icon', *Nelson Dispatch*, vol. 1, pt 2, April 1982
2. Nicolas, vii, 241n.
3. Clarke and M'Arthur, ii, 422
4. Matcham, 234
5. Clarke and M'Arthur, ii, 422

6. BBC, File 4, 10 September 1805
7. Jagger; Gérin, 98
8. Matcham, 253
9. Pettigrew, ii, 495–6; Morrison, ii, 265
10. Quoted in Flora Fraser, 319–20
11. J. K. Laughton, *Nelson's House at Merton* (n.d.); Gérin, 92
12. Matcham, 231
13. Minto, iii, 370
14. Edgcumbe, i, 79; Flora Fraser, 320–21
15. Quoted in Flora Fraser, 322
16. Harrison, ii, 456; Sichel, 509
17. Quoted in Oman, 524
18. Pettigrew, ii, 496
19. Nicolas, vii, 33–5
20. ibid., 40; Nelson, *Lord Nelson's Letters to lady Hamilton*, 149
21. Llangattock Papers, E.180; Nicolas, vii, 40; Pettigrew, ii, 497
22. Silliman, 193
23. Southey, *Life*, 246
24. Pettigrew, ii, 498; Clarke and M'Arthur, ii, 423
25. Phillips's catalogue, 7 October 1982
26. Mahan, ii, 335–6, quoting information supplied to him by the 3rd Earl Nelson
27. BL Eg. MSS 2,240, f. 240
28. Nicolas, vii, 40; Nelson, *Lord Nelson's Letters to Lady Hamilton*, 148
29. NMM NWD/9594

Chapter 32 (*pp. 358–367*)

1. Llangattock Papers, E.429, 16 September 1805
2. Quoted in Howarth, *Nelson*, 312, 323, 315
3. Nelson, 95
4. Nicolas, vii, 60; Nelson, *Lord Nelson's Letters to Lady Hamilton*, 150–51
5. Nicolas, vii, 32
6. Pettigrew, ii, 513
7. Nicolas, vii, 56–7; Southey, *Life*, 245
8. Quoted in Pocock, *Nelson*, 319
9. Nicolas, iii, 98
10. Quoted in Pocock, *Nelson*, 319
11. Quoted in Howarth, *Nelson*, 326
12. Morrison, ii, 269
13. Pettigrew, ii, 515–16; Nelson, 151–2
14. Nicolas, vii, 138; Beatty, 12
15. Murray, 174, 180; Clarke and M'Arthur, ii, 447
16. Nicolas, vii, 140–41
17. Beatty, 14
18. Nicolas, vii, 139

19. ibid., 140; Llangattock Papers, E.256
20. Nicolas, vii, 149–50; Llangattock Papers, E.256
21. Murray, 275
22. Warner, *Portrait*, 305; Warner, *Trafalgar*, 80–83; Howarth, *Trafalgar*, 140–41; Pocock, *Nelson*, 323–5; Oman, 538–40

Chapter 33 (*pp. 368–377*)

1. Francis Edwards' catalogue 706, William Davies to Sir Thomas Graves, 8 November 1805
2. Llangattock Papers, E.183
3. Clarke and M'Arthur, ii, 447
4. ibid., 447
5. ibid., 449; Warner, *Portrait*, 306
6. Howarth, *Nelson*, 343
7. Clarke and M'Arthur, ii, 448
8. Nicolas, vii, 350
9. Beatty, *passim*; Clarke and M'Arthur, ii, 450–54; Pocock, *Nelson*, 330–32; Howarth, *Trafalgar*, 214–16; Warner, *Trafalgar*, 125–34; Warner, *Portrait*, 310–11; Kennedy, *Nelson's Band of Brothers*, 321–6; Howarth, *Nelson*, 345–51; Oman, 550–57

Chapter 34 (*pp. 378–391*)

1. Thompson family records (personal information)
2. Beatty, 57
3. Quoted in Flora Fraser, 326
4. Stuart, 127–8
5. *Transactions of the Jewish Historical Society*, xiv, 225–45, quoted in Gérin, 111
6. Stuart, 128
7. Marsden, 116
8. WM, Elizabeth Marsden's manuscript marginalia in Marsden, *Brief Memoir*
9. Marsden, 117
10. Harrison, ii, 508
11. Marsden, 118
12. *Notes and Queries*, 2nd series, vol. iii, no. 59; *Annual Register*, xlviii, 360; WM, Elizabeth Marsden's marginalia in Marsden's *Brief Memoir*, 116
13. Christopher Hibbert, *George IV: Prince of Wales* (London, 1972), 250–51; Aspinall, v, 276
14. Nicolas, vii, 302
15. *The Times*, *Morning Post* and *Morning Chronicle*, issues of 7 November 1805
16. Quoted in Warner, *Portrait*
17. Sotheby's catalogue, 17 May 1985
18. Minto, ii, 238
19. Nicolas, i, 124

20. *Nelson Dispatch*, vol. 1, pt 6, April 1983, 94–5
21. Phillips's catalogue, 17 March 1983, lot 408
22. Fitzgerald, i, 120
23. Phillips's catalogue, 17 March 1983, lot 408
24. Quoted in Pocock, *Nelson*, 332
25. Samuel Taylor Coleridge, *The Friend*, essay 6; Warner, *Portrait*, 314
26. Acton, 516
27. Stuart, 127
28. WM, Elizabeth Marsden's marginalia in Marsden's *Brief Memoir*
29. Southey, *Life*, 267
30. Creevey, i, 173
31. Aspinall, v, 276, 283
32. Quoted in Warner, *Trafalgar*, 168
33. 46° Georgii III Cap. 146 [22 July 1806]
34. Rose, i, 245
35. ibid.
36. Nicolas, vii, 310
37. Stuart, 129

Chapter 35 (pp. 392–395)

1. Llangattock Papers, 6 January 1806
2. Matcham, 245
3. ibid., 247
4. Clarke and M'Arthur, ii, 463–5; *A Complete Account of . . . the Funeral of Lord Nelson* (Exeter, 1806)
5. Quoted in Howarth, *Nelson*, 360
6. Quoted in Pocock, *Nelson*, 333
7. George, *British Museum Catalogue*, viii, 10515, 1 January 1806

Bibliography

COLLECTIONS OF MANUSCRIPTS

Autograph Letters Addressed to William Marsden, Esquire, First Secretary
to the Admiralty, Chelmorton
Ben Burgess Nelson Memorabilia Collection, Norwich
British Library, London
    BL Add. MSS. 28,333 (Documents relating to Lady Nelson)
    BL Add. MSS. 34,274 (Nelson's letters to Lady Hamilton)
    BL Add. MSS. 34,902–92 (the Nelson Papers)
    BL Add. MSS. 35,191 (the Bridport Papers)
    BL Egerton MSS. 2,240 (Nelson's letters to Alexander Davison)
Coke Papers, Holkham
National Maritime Museum, Greenwich
    Berry Papers; Bridport Papers; Cornwallis Papers; Elliot Papers;
    Girdlestone Papers; Hoste Papers; Jervis Papers; Keith Papers;
    Nelson-Ward Papers; Phillips Papers; Trafalgar House Papers;
    Walter Papers
Nelson Museum, Monmouth
    Llangattock Papers
Public Record Office, Kew
    Sir William Hamilton's reports in the Foreign Office files, 70–11, 70–12
Royal Naval Museum, Portsmouth
    McCarthy Papers

JOURNALS AND PERIODICALS

The Gentleman's Magazine
The Mariner's Mirror: The Journal of the Society for Nautical Research
The Naval Chronicle (40 vols., 1799–1819)
The Nelson Dispatch, the Journal of the Nelson Society
The Trafalgar Chronicle: The Year Book of the 1805 Club

NEWSPAPERS

Bath Advertiser; Bath and Bristol Chronicle; Bath Journal; Bell's Weekly Messenger; Berrow's Worcester Journal; Birmingham Gazette; Bury and Norwich Post; Examiner; Exeter Flying Post; General Evening Post; Gloucester Journal; Hampshire Chronicle; Hampshire Telegraph and Naval Chronicle; Hereford Journal; Ipswich Journal; Jackson's Oxford Journal; Morning Chronicle; Morning Herald; Morning Post; Norfolk Chronicle; Norfolk News; Norwich and Yarmouth Courier; Pope's Bath Chronicle and Weekly Gazette; Portsmouth Chronicle; Portsmouth Gazette and Weekly Telegraph; Portsmouth Telegraph; Salisbury and Winchester Journal; Salmon's Mercury; Sussex Weekly Advertiser; The Times

BOOKS AND ARTICLES

Acton, Harold, *The Bourbons of Naples* (London, 1957)

Allardyce, Alexander, *Admiral Lord Keith* (London, 1882)

Allen, Joseph, *The Life of Viscount Nelson* (London, 1853)

Andersen, J. A., *A Dane's Excursions in Britain* (London, 1807)

Anson, W. V., *The Life of John Jervis, Admiral Lord St Vincent* (London, 1913)

Anspach, Margravine of, *Memoirs*, vol. 1 (London, 1826)

Argyll, Duke of, ed., *Intimate Society Letters of the Eighteenth Century* (2 vols., London, 1910)

Aspinall, A., ed., *The Correspondence of George Prince of Wales, 1770–1812* (8 vols., London, 1963–71)

Badham, F. P., *Nelson and Ruffo* (London, 1905)

——*Nelson at Naples: A Journal for June 10–30 1799* (London, 1900)

Baily, J. T. Herbert, *Emma, Lady Hamilton: A Biographical Essay with a Catalogue of her Published Portraits* (London, 1905)

Barham, Charles, Lord, *see* Laughton

Barker, M. H., *The Life of Nelson* (London, 1836)

Barrow, John, *The Life and Correspondence of Admiral Sir William Sidney Smith* (2 vols., London, 1848)

Baynham, H., *From the Lower Deck* (London, 1969)

Beatty, Sir William, *The Authentic Narrative of the Death of Lord Nelson* (London, 1807)

Bellamy, R. R., ed., *Ramblin' Jack, the Journal of Captain Jack Cremer, 1700–1774* (London, 1936)

Bennett, Geoffrey, *The Battle of Trafalgar* (London, 1977)

——*Nelson the Commander* (London, 1972)

Berchman, Evelyn, *Nelson's Dear Lord: A Portrait of St Vincent* (London, 1962)

Beresford, Lord Charles, and Wilson, H. W., *Nelson and His Times* (12 parts, London, 1897–8)

Bethune, *see* Drinkwater

Bonner-Smith, David, ed., *The Letters of Admiral of the Fleet the Earl of St Vincent* (vols. LV and LXI, London, Navy Records Society, 1922 and 1926)

Bourchier, Jane Barbara, Lady, *A Memoir of the Life of Admiral Sir Edward Codrington* (2 vols., London, 1873)

Bowen, Marjorie, *Patriotic Lady: A Study of Emma, Lady Hamilton and the Neapolitan Revolution of 1799* (London, 1935)

Bradford, Ernle, *Nelson: The Essential Hero* (London, 1977)

Brenton, Edward Pelham, *Life and Correspondence of John, Earl of St Vincent* (2 vols., London, 1838)

Britton, John, *Graphical and Literary Illustrations of Fonthill Abbey* (London, 1823)

Broadley, A. M., *Three Dorset Captains at Trafalgar* (London, 1906)

Broadley, A. M., and Bartelot, R. G., *Nelson's Hardy: His Life, Letters and Friends* (London, 1909)

Brockman, H. A. N., *The Caliph of Fonthill* (London, 1956)

Browne, G. Lathom, *Nelson, the Public and Private Life of Horatio, Viscount Nelson as Told by Himself, His Comrades and His Friends* (London, 1891)

Bryant, Arthur, *Nelson* (London, 1970)

——*The Years of Endurance, 1793–1802* (London, 1942)

——*The Years of Victory, 1802–1812* (London, 1944)

Bugler, Arthur, *H.M.S. Victory: Building, Restoration and Repair* (2 vols., London, 1966)

Bullock, J. G., ed., *The Tomlinson Papers* (London, 1935)

Bury, Lady Charlotte, *Diary Illustrative of the Times of George the Fourth* (ed. John Galt, 4 vols., London, 1839)

Callender, Sir Geoffrey, *The Story of H.M.S. Victory* (London, 1914)

Capes, Ranalt, *Poseidon: A Personal Study of Admiral Lord Nelson* (London, 1947)

Chamberlain, W. H., *Reminiscences of Old Merton* (London, 1923)

Chapman, Guy, *Beckford* (London, 1937)

Charnock, John, *Biographical Memoirs of Lord Viscount Nelson* (London, 1806)

——*Biographia Navalis* (6 vols., London, 1794–8)

Chevalier, E., *Histoire de la Marine Française sous le Consulat et l'Empire* (Paris, 1886)

Childe-Pemberton, W. S., *The Earl Bishop* (2 vols., London, 1925)

Clarke, James Stanier, and M'Arthur, John, *The Life of Admiral Lord Nelson K. B. from his Lordship's Manuscripts* (2 vols., London, 1809)

Clarke, Richard, *The Life of Horatio, Lord Viscount Nelson* (London, 1813)

Coco, Vincenzo, *Saggio storico sulla rivoluzione di Napoli* (3 vols., Naples, 1800)

Coke, Lady Mary, *Letters and Journals*, vols. III and IV (Edinburgh, 1892–6)

Colletta, Pietro, *History of the Kingdom of Naples 1734–1825* (trans. S. Horner, Edinburgh, 1858)

Collingwood, Cuthbert, Lord, *The Private Correspondence of Admiral Lord Collingwood*, ed. Edward Hughes, vol. XCVIII, London, Navy Records Society, 1957)

——*A Selection from the Public and Private Correspondence of Vice-Admiral Lord Collingwood* (ed. G. L. Newnham, London, 1828)

Collison-Morley, Lacy, *Naples through the Centuries* (London, 1925)

Connell, Brian, *Portrait of a Whig Peer* (London, 1957)

Corbett, Julian S., *The Campaign of Trafalgar* (London, 1910)

——*Fighting Instructions: Nelson's Tactical Memoranda* (London, 1905)

——*The Private Papers of George, Second Earl Spencer, First Lord of the Admiralty, 1794–1801* (vols. XLVI and XLVII, London, Navy Records Society, 1913, 1914)

Cornwallis-West, G., *The Life and Letters of Admiral Cornwallis* (London, 1927)

Cowie, Leonard W., *Lord Nelson 1758–1805: A Bibliography* (Westport, 1990)

Craig, Hardin, 'Lord and Lady Nelson: Some Unpublished Letters' (*Huntington Library Quarterly*, vol. XI, November 1947)

Creevey, T., *The Creevey Papers: A Selection from the Correspondence and Diaries* (ed. H. Maxwell, 3rd edn, London, 1905)

Cremer, Jack, *see* Bellamy

Croce, Benedetto, *La rivoluzione napoletana del 1799* (Bari, 1912)

Croker, John Wilson, *Correspondence and Diaries of J. W. Croker* (ed. Louis J. Jennings, vol. 2, 2nd edn, 1885)

Cumloden Papers (privately printed, Edinburgh, 1871)

Dancer, Dr Thomas, *A Brief History of the Late Expedition against San Juan* (London, 1781)

Dann, John C., ed., *The Nagle Journal: A Diary of the Life of Jacob Nagle, Sailor, from the Year 1775 to 1841* (New York, 1988)

D'Auvergne, Edmund B., *Dear Emma: The Story of Emma, Lady Hamilton, Her Husband and Her Lovers* (London, 1936)

Dawson, Warren R., ed., *The Nelson Collection at Lloyd's* (London, 1932)

De Nicola, Carlo, *Diario napoletano, 1798–1825* (Naples, 1906)

Desbrière, Édouard, *The Naval Campaign of 1805* (Paris, 1907; trans. Constance Eastwick, 2 vols., Oxford, 1933)

Drinkwater, Col. John, *A Narrative of the Battle of Cape St Vincent* (London, 1840)

Edgcumbe, Richard, ed., *Diary of Frances, Lady Shelley* (2 vols., London, 1912)

Edinger, George, and Neep, E. J. C., *Horatio Nelson* (London, 1930)

Emden, Paul H., 'The Brothers Goldsmid and the Financing of the Napoleonic Wars' (*Transactions of the Jewish Historical Society*, XIV, London, 1939)

Farington, Joseph, *The Farington Diary* (ed. James Grieg, London, 1922)

Fenwick, Kenneth, *H. M. S. Victory* (London, 1959)

Fiske, R. C., *Notices of Nelson Extracted from 'Norfolk and Norwich Notes and Queries'* (Nelson Society, 1989)

Fitchett, W. H., *Nelson and His Captains: Sketches of Famous Seamen* (London, 1902)

Fitzgerald, Percy, *The Life and Times of William IV* (2 vols., London, 1884)

Foote, Captain E. J., *Vindications of His Conduct when Captain of His Majestey's Ship Seahorse . . . in . . . 1799* (London, 1810)

Forder, Charles, *A History of the Paston School* (North Walsham, 1975)

Fothergill, Brian, *Beckford of Fonthill* (London, 1979)

——*Sir William Hamilton: Envoy Extraordinary* (London, 1969)

Fraser, Edward, *The Sailors Whom Nelson Led: Their Doings Described by Themselves* (London, 1913)

Fraser, Flora, *Beloved Emma: The Life of Emma, Lady Hamilton* (London 1986)
Fremantle, Anne, ed., *The Wynne Diaries 1789–1820* (3 vols., Oxford, 1935–40)
Gamlin, Hilda, *Nelson's Friendships* (2 vols., London, 1899)
Gatty, Mrs and Dr, *Recollections of the Life of the Rev. A. J. Scott* (London, 1899)
George, Prince of Wales, *see* Aspinall
George, Mary Dorothy, *Catalogue of Political and Personal Satires* (British Museum, vols. V to VIII, 1938–47)
Gérin, Winifred, *Horatia Nelson* (London, 1970)
Giglioli, Constance H. D., *Naples in 1799: An Account of the Revolution of 1799 and of the Rise and Fall of the Parthenopean Republic* (London, 1903)
Gill, Edward, *Nelson and the Hamiltons on Tour* (Gloucester, 1987)
Goethe, Johann Wolfgang, *Travels in Italy* (trans. A. J. W. Morrison and C. Nisbet, London, 1892)
Gordon, Pryse Lockhart, *Personal Memoirs* (2 vols., London, 1830)
Gore, John, *Nelson's Hardy and His Wife* (London, 1935)
Grant, N. H., *The Letters of Mary Nisbet of Dirleton, Countess of Elgin* (London, 1926)
Granville, Castilia, Countess, *Lord Granville Leveson-Gower: Private Correspondence 1781–1821* (2 vols., London, 1916)
Gronow, R. H., *The Reminiscences and Recollections of Captain Gronow* (3 vols., London, 1889)
Gunn, Peter, *Naples, A Palimpsest* (London, 1961)
Gurney, Joseph and William, *The Trial of Edward Marcus Despard for High Treason* (Dublin, 1803)
Gutteridge, H. C., ed., *Nelson and the Neapolitan Jacobins: Documents Relating to the Suppression of the Jacobin Revolution at Naples* (vol. XXV, London, Navy Records Society, 1903)
Hardwick, Mollie, *Emma Lady Hamilton: A Study* (London, 1969)
Harland, John, *Seamanship in the Age of Sail* (London, 1984)
Harries, Richard, with Cattermole, Paul, and Mackintosh, Peter, *A History of Norwich School* (Norwich, 1991)
Harris, Nathaniel, *The Nelsons: The Family of Horatio Nelson* (London, 1977)
Harrison, [James], *The Life of the Right Honourable Horatio, Lord Viscount Nelson* (2 vols., London, 1806)
Hattersley, Roy, *Nelson* (London, 1974)
Helm, W. H., *Vigée Le Brun* (London, 1915)
Herbert, J. B., *The Life and Services of Admiral Sir Thomas Foley* (London, 1884)
Hewitt, James, ed., *Eyewitnesses to Nelson's Battles* (Reading, 1972)
Hodgkin, Louis, *Nelson and Bath* (The Nelson Society, Corsham, 1991)
Hood, Dorothy, *The Admirals Hood* (London, 1941)
Hoste, Lady Harriet, *Memoirs and Letters of Capt. Sir William Hoste* (2 vols., London, 1833)
Hough, Richard, *Nelson* (London, 1980)
Howarth, David, *Trafalgar: The Nelson Touch* (London, 1969)

Howarth, David and Stephen, *Nelson: The Immortal Memory* (London, 1988)
Hutchinson, J. R., *The Press Gang Afloat and Ashore* (London, 1913)
Ilchester, Earl of, ed., *The Journals of Elizabeth, Lady Holland* (2 vols., London, 1908)
Isaacson, Cecil J., *Nelson's 'Five Years on the Beach' and the Other Horatio Nelson of Burnham Thorpe* (Fakenham, 1991)
Jagger, Rev. J. E., *Lord Nelson's Love and Life at Merton* (Surrey Record Office, 3185/9/1, n.d.)
James, Admiral Sir William, *The Durable Monument: Horatio Nelson* (London, 1948)
——*The Naval History of Great Britain*, vols. 1–4 (London, 1886)
——*Old Oak, the Life of John Jervis, Earl of St Vincent* (London, 1950)
Jeaffreson, John Cordy, *Lady Hamilton and Lord Nelson* (2 vols., London, 1897)
——*The Queen of Naples and Lord Nelson* (2 vols., London, 1889)
Jowett, Evelyn M., *An Illustrated History of Merton and Morden* (London, 1951)
Keate, E. M., *Nelson's Wife* (London, 1939)
Keigwin, K. P., 'Lord Nelson's Journey through Germany' (*Mariner's Mirror*, vol. XXI, no. 2)
Keith, Lord, *see* Lloyd; Perrin
Kemp, Peter, ed., *The British Sailor: A Social History of the Lower Deck* (London, 1970)
——*The Oxford Companion to Ships and the Sea* (Oxford, 1976)
Kennedy, Ludovic, *Nelson's Band of Brothers* (London, 1951)
——*Nelson and His Captains* (a revised edition of the above, London, 1975)
Kerr, Admiral Mark, *The Sailor's Nelson* (London, 1932)
Kircheisen, Friedrich M., *Nelson: The Establishment of British World Dominion* (London, 1931)
Knight, Cornelia, *Autobiography* (vol. 1, London, 1861)
——*The Autobiography of Miss Knight* (ed. Roger Fulford, London, 1960)
Laughton, Sir John Knox, *The Nelson Memorial: Nelson and His Companions in Arms* (London, 1896)
Laughton, Sir John Knox, ed., *Letters and Papers of Charles, Lord Barham 1758–1813* (London, 1907)
—*Letters and Dispatches of Horatio, Viscount Nelson* (London, 1886)
——*The Naval Miscellany*, vols. 1 and 2 (vols. XX and XL, London, Navy Records Society)
Lavery, Brian, *Nelson's Navy: The Ships, Men and Organisation 1793–1815* (London, 1989)
Layard, G. S., ed., *The Letters of Lord Nelson to Lady Hamilton with a Supplement* (2 vols., London, 1814)
Legg, Stuart, ed., *Trafalgar: An Eye-witness Account of a Great Battle* (London, 1966)
Leveson-Gower, Iris, *The Face without a Frown: Georgiana, Duchess of Devonshire* (London, 1944)
Lewis, Michael, *England's Sea-officers* (London, 1948)
—*The History of the British Navy* (Harmondsworth, 1962)
—*A Social History of the Royal Navy, 1793–1815* (London, 1960)

Liverpool, Lord Russell of, *Knight of the Sword: The Life and Letters of Admiral Sir William Sidney Smith* (London, 1964)

Lloyd, Christopher, *The British Seaman* (London, 1968)

— 'Nelson's Prize Money' (*Mariner's Mirror*, vol. 66, 1980)

— *The Nile Campaign* (London, 1973)

— *St Vincent and Camperdown* (London, 1963)

Lloyd, Christopher, ed., *The Keith Papers* (vols. XC and XCVI, London, Navy Records Society, 1950, 1955)

— *The Naval Miscellany* (vol. XCII, London, Navy Records Society, 1952)

Long, W. H., *Memoirs of Emma, Lady Hamilton with Anecdotes of Her Friends and Contemporaries* (London, 1815)

Luttrell, Barbara, *The Prim Romantic: A Biography of Ellis Cornelia Knight* (London, 1965)

Macready, *see* Pollock

Mahan, Captain A. T., *Life of Nelson: The Embodiment of the Sea Power of Great Britain* (2 vols., London, 1897)

Malmesbury, 3rd Earl, ed., *Diaries and Correspondence of James Harris, First Earl of Malmesbury* (4 vols., London, 1844)

Marie-Amélie, *see* Vendôme

Mark, William, *At Sea with Nelson, being the Life of William Mark, a Purser who Served under Admiral Lord Nelson* (London, 1929)

Marsden, William, *A Brief Memoir of the Life and Writings of William Marsden* (privately printed, London, 1838)

Marshall, John, *Royal Navy Biography* (8 vols., London, 1823–35)

Masefield, John, *Sea Life in Nelson's Time* (London, 1905)

Matcham, M. Eyre, *The Nelsons of Burnham Thorpe* (London, 1911)

Meade-Featherstonhaugh, and Warner, Oliver, *Uppark and Its People* (London, 1964)

Melville, Lewis, *The Life and Letters of William Beckford of Fonthill* (London, 1910)

'Memoir of Captain d'Auvergne' (*Naval Chronicle*, XIII)

Memoir of the Life of Lord Nelson (Norwich, 1802)

Memoirs of Lady Hamilton (London, 1815)

Memoirs of the Life and Achievements of Lord Nelson by a Captain of the British Navy (London, 1805)

Memoirs of the Life and Services of John Theophilus Lee (privately printed, 1805)

Memoirs of the Professional Life of Horatio Viscount Nelson (London, 1806)

Miles, J. M., *Vindication of Lord Nelson's Proceedings in the Bay of Naples* (London, 1843)

Miller, Lady Anne, *Letters from Italy in the Years 1770 and 1771* (3 vols., London, 1776)

Minto, Countess of, ed., *The Life and Letters of Sir Gilbert Elliot, First Earl of Minto from 1751 to 1806* (3 vols., London, 1874)

Moorhouse, E. Hallam, *Nelson in England: A Domestic Chronicle* (London, 1913)

—— *Nelson's Lady Hamilton* (London, 1907)

Morrison, Alfred, ed., *The Collection of Autograph Letters and Personal Documents*

Formed by Alfred Morrison: The Hamilton and Nelson Papers (privately printed, 2 vols., 1893–4)

Moseley, Benjamin, *Treatise on Tropical Diseases* (London, 1795)

Murray, Geoffrey, *The Life of Admiral Collingwood* (London, 1936)

Nagle, *see* Dann

Naish, G. P. B., ed., *Nelson's Letters to His Wife and Other Documents, 1785–1831* (London, 1958)

Nash, Michael, ed., *The Nelson Masks* (Hoylake, 1993)

Nelson, Horatio, *Lord Nelson's Letters to Lady Hamilton* (ed. Douglas Sladen, London, 1905)

See also Clarke, J. S.; Craig; Laughton; Layard; Naish; Nicolas; Rawson

Newbolt, Sir Henry, *The Year of Trafalgar* (London, 1910)

Nicol, John, *The Life and Adventures of John Nicol, Mariner* (London, 1822)

Nicolas, Sir Harris, ed., *Dispatches and Letters of Vice-Admiral Lord Viscount Nelson* (7 vols., London, 1844–6)

Nisbet, Mary, *see* Grant

Oman, Carola, *Nelson* (London, 1947)

Oliver, J. W., *The Life of William Beckford* (London, 1932)

Padfield, Peter, *Nelson's War* (London, 1976)

Paget, Rt Hon. Sir Augustus, ed., *The Paget Papers* (2 vols., London, 1896)

Palmer, M. A. J., 'Sir John's Victory: The Battle of Cape St Vincent Reconsidered' (*Mariner's Mirror*, vol. 77, Feb. 1991, pp. 31–46)

Palumbo, Raffaele, ed., *Maria Carolina, Regina delle Due Sicile, suo carteggio con Lady Hamilton* (Naples, 1877)

Parry, Ann, *The Admirals Fremantle* (London, 1971)

Parsons, George Samuel, *Nelsonian Reminiscences, Leaves from Memory's Log* (London, 1843)

Perrin, W. G., ed., *Letters and Papers of Admiral Viscount Keith* (vol. LXII, London, Navy Records Society, 1926)

Pettigrew, Thomas, *Memoirs of the Life of Vice-Admiral Lord Viscount Nelson* (2 vols., London, 1849)

Phillimore, Augustus, *The Last of Nelson's Captains* (London, 1906)

Phipps, Constantine, *A Voyage towards the North Pole* (London, 1774)

Piozzi, Mrs Hester Lynch, *Observations and Reflections Made in the Journey through France, Italy and Germany* (London, 1789)

Plunkett, Capt. the Hon. E., *Sketches of the Last Naval War* (London, 1848)

Pocock, Tom, *Horatio Nelson* (London, 1987)

—— 'My Dear Sweet Friend: Mrs Moutray and Captain Nelson' (*Country Life*, 22 Sept. 1983, 778–80)

—— *Nelson and His World* (London, 1968)

—— 'Nelson's Norfolk' (*Country Life*, vol. 165, no. 4, 266, 12 April 1979)

—— *Remember Nelson: The Life of Captain Sir William Hoste* (London, 1977)

—— *Sailor King: The Life of King William IV* (London, 1991)

—— *The Young Nelson in the Americas* (London, 1980)

Pollock, Sir Frederick, ed., *Macready's Reminiscences and Selections from His Diaries* (London, 1875)

Pope, Dudley, *England Expects* (London, 1960)

Pope, Dudley, *The Great Gamble* (London, 1972)
—— *Life in Nelson's Navy* (London, 1981)
Popham, Sir Home, *Telegraphic Vocabulary* (London, 1803)
Pugh, P. D. Gordon, *Nelson and His Surgeons* (London, 1968)
Rathbone, Philip, *Paradise Merton: The Story of Nelson and the Hamiltons at Merton Place* (Windlesham, 1973)
Rawson, Geoffrey, ed., *Nelson's Letters* (London, 1960)
—— *Nelson's Letters from the Leeward Islands* (London, 1953)
Redding, Cyrus, *Memoirs of William Beckford* (2 vols., London, 1859)
Richmond, H. W., *The Private Papers of George, Second Earl Spencer* (vols. LVIII and LIX, London, Navy Records Society, 1923–4)
Rodger, N. A. M., *The Insatiable Earl: A Life of John Montagu, 4th Earl of Sandwich* (London, 1993)
—— *The Wooden World: An Anatomy of the Georgian Navy* (London, 1986)
Rose, Rt Hon. George, *The Diaries and Correspondence of the Rt Hon. George Rose* (ed. Leveson Vernon Harcourt, 2 vols., London, 1860)
Russell, Jack, *Nelson and the Hamiltons* (London, 1969)
Russell, W. C., *Life of Admiral Lord Collingwood* (London, 1891)
Sacchinelli, Domenico, *Memorie storiche sulla vita del Cardinale Fabrizio Ruffo* (Naples, 1836)
Saint Vincent, Earl of, *see* Bonner-Smith; Brenton
Savours, Ann, '"A Very Interesting Point in Geography": The 1773 Phipps Expedition to the North Pole' (*Arctic*, vol. 37, no. 4, December 1984, pp. 402–81)
Schom, Alan, *Trafalgar: Countdown to Battle, 1803–1805* (London, 1990)
Sermoneta, Vittoria Caetani, Duchess of, *The Locks of Norbury* (London, 1940)
Shelley, Frances, Lady, *see* Edgcumbe
Sherrard, O. A., *A Life of Emma Hamilton* (London, 1927)
—— *A Life of Lord St Vincent* (London, 1933)
Sichel, Walter, *Emma, Lady Hamilton from New and Original Sources and Documents* (London, 1905)
Silliman, Benjamin, *A Journal of Travels in England, Holland, Scotland, and of Two Passages over the Atlantic in the Years 1805–1806* (2 vols., New York, 1810)
Smith, B. Webster, *H. M. S. Victory, Nelson's Flagship at Trafalgar* (London, 1939)
Smith, E., *The Life of Sir Joseph Banks* (London, 1911)
Smith, Sir William Sidney, *see* Barrow; Liverpool
Solmi, Angelo, *Lady Hamilton* (Milan, 1982)
Southey, Robert, *The Life of Horatio Lord Nelson* (2 vols., London, 1813)
—— *Southey's Life of Nelson* (ed. Sir Geoffrey Callender, London, 1922)
Spencer, George, 2nd Earl, *see* Corbett; Richmond
Spinney, J. D., 'Nelson at Santa Cruz' (*Mariner's Mirror*, vol. 45, pp. 207–23)
Stewart, The Hon. Sir William, *Journal of the Baltic Expedition and Battle of Copenhagen* (London, 1801)
Stirling, A. M. W., *Coke of Norfolk and His Friends* (London, 1908)

Stuart, Dorothy M., *Dearest Bess: The Life and Times of Lady Elizabeth Foster* (London, 1955)

Swinburne, Henry, *The Courts of Europe at the Close of the Last Century* (2 vols., London, 1895)

Taylor, Gordon, *The Sea Chaplains* (Oxford, 1978)

Terraine, John, *Trafalgar* (London, 1976)

Tours, Hugh, *The Life and Letters of Emma Hamilton* (London, 1963)

Trench, Richard Chevenix, ed., *Remains of the late Mrs Richard Trench* (London, 1862)

Tucker, Jedediah, *Memoir of Admiral The Rt Hon. the Earl of St Vincent* (2 vols., London, 1844)

Vendôme, la Duchesse de, *La Jeunesse de Marie-Amélie, Reine des Français, d'après son Journal* (2 vols., Paris, 1935)

Vigée-Lebrun, M. L., *Souvenirs* (2 vols., Paris, 1867)

Walder, David, *Nelson* (London, 1978)

Walker, Richard, 'Foreign Impression of a British Hero' (*Country Life*, 25 September 1986, pp. 986–8)

—— 'Puppet on a Provincial Stage: the Guzzardi Portraits of Nelson' (*Country Life*, 18 July 1985, pp. 186–8)

Walpole, Horace, *Letters*, (ed. P. Cunningham, vols. III–IX, London, 1857–9)

Warner, Oliver, *The Battle of the Nile* (London, 1960)

—— 'Collingwood and Nelson' (*History Today*, vol. 16, 1966, pp. 811–17)

—— *Emma Hamilton and Sir William* (London, 1960)

—— *The Life and Letters of Vice-Admiral Lord Collingwood* (London, 1968)

—— *Lord Nelson: A Guide to Reading with a Note on Contemporary Portraits* (London, 1955)

—— *Nelson's Battles* (London, 1965)

—— *Nelson's Last Diary and the Prayer before Trafalgar: a Facsimile* (London, 1971)

—— *A Portrait of Lord Nelson* (London, 1958)

—— *Trafalgar* (London, 1959)

White, Arnold, and Moorhouse, E. Hallam, *Nelson and the Twentieth Century* (London, 1905)

Wilkinson, Clennell, *Life of Nelson* (London, 1931)

Willyams, Rev. Cooper, *A Voyage in the Mediterranean in H. M. S. Swiftsure* (London, 1802)

Winter, Leslie, *Nelson and the Norfolk He Knew* (privately printed, 1975)

Wraxall, Sir Nathaniel, *Historical Memoirs of My Own Time* (2 vols., London, 1815)

Wynne Diaries, see Fremantle

Ziegler, Philip, *King William IV* (London, 1971)

Index

Nelson's name is abbreviated to N, Frances Nelson's to F, and Lady Hamilton's to E.

90 Horseneck Road
Montville, N.J. 07045